Praise for *For All the People*

John Curl has been around the block when it comes to knowing workers' cooperatives. He has been a worker owner. He has argued theory and practice, inside the firms where his labor counts for something more than token control and within the determined, but still small universe where labor rents capital, using it as it sees fit and profitable.

So his book, *For All the People: The Hidden History of Cooperation, Cooperative Movements, and Communalism in America*, reached expectant hands, and an open mind when it arrived in Asheville, NC. Am I disappointed? No, not in the least.

Curl blends the three strands of his historical narrative with aplomb, he has, after all, been researching, writing, revising, and editing the text for a spell. Further, I am certain he has been responding to editors and publishers asking this or that. He may have tired, but he did not give up, much inspired, I am certain, by the determination of the women and men he brings to life.

Each of his subtitles could have been a book, and has been written about by authors with as many points of ideological view as their titles. Curl sticks pretty close to the narrative line written by worker owners, no matter if they came to work every day with a socialist, laborist, anti-Marxist grudge or not. Often in the past, as with today's worker owners, their firm fails, a dream to manage capital kaput. Yet today, as yesterday, the democratic ideals of hundreds of worker owners support vibrantly profitable businesses. Does capitalism offer any assurances?

For historians, Curl's book is a must. For young women and men considering the idea of starting a business they own and manage, he recounts just about as many ways your counterparts in the past fail as you can imagine. And for the philosophers among us, Curl does not ignore the theoretical threads.

>   —Frank T. Adams, co-author with Dr. Gary B. Hansen of *Putting Democracy to Work*.

D0911345

FOR ALL
THE PEOPLE

FOR ALL
THE PEOPLE

Uncovering the Hidden History of Cooperation, Cooperative Movements, and Communalism in America

John Curl

PM Press

2009

For All The People: Uncovering the Hidden History of Cooperation, Cooperative Movements, and Communalism in America

John Curl

ISBN: 978-1-60486-072-6
Library of Congress Control Number: 2009901373

PM Press
PO Box 23912
Oakland, CA 94623
www.pmpress.org

Cover Design by John Yates/Stealworks.com
Layout by Josh MacPhee/Justseeds.org

Printed in the USA on recycled paper with soy ink.

The earth for all the people. That is the demand. The machinery of production and distribution for all the people. That is the demand. The collective ownership and control of industry and its democratic management in the interests of all the people. That is the demand. The elimination of rent, interest, profit, and the production of wealth to satisfy the wants of all the people. That is the demand. Cooperative industry in which all shall work together in harmony as a basis of a new social order, a higher civilization, a real republic. That is the demand.[1]

—Eugene V. Debs, 1902

Contents

ous small collectives running not-for-profit activities, and other small cooperatives fly below the statistical radar. *Communities Directory* lists over 900 intentional cooperative communities. But in 2008, there were only approximately 300 worker cooperative businesses in the United States.[3]

Given that there are so many cooperatives of different types in America, why are so few of those worker cooperatives? Is that important? What is a worker cooperative? This historical survey will attempt to shed some light on those questions.

THE BOSS SYSTEM

The vast majority of working Americans today are employees, and most spend their entire occupational lives as one. Yet, only 200 years ago, just a tiny percentage of the workforce were employees, and the vast majority of free working people were self-employed farmers, artisans, and merchants.[4] In 1784, Benjamin Franklin wrote:

> The great business of the continent is agriculture. For one artisan, or merchant, I suppose we have at least one hundred farmers, by far the greatest part cultivators of their own fertile lands, from whence many of them draw not only food necessary for their subsistence, but the materials of their clothing, so as to need very few foreign supplies; while they have a surplus of productions to dispose of, whereby wealth is gradually accumulated.[5]

Being an employee was considered a form of bondage, only a step above indentured servitude. One submitted to it due to economic hardship for as short a time as possible, then became free once more, independent, one's own boss. As the country industrialized during the 19th century, the transformation from a nation of self-employed "free" people to a nation of employees took place relentlessly, and continued through the 20th century. In 1800, there were few wage earners in America; in 1870, shortly after the Civil War, over half the workforce consisted of employees; in 1940, about 80 percent; in 2007, 92 percent of the American workforce was employees and the number of self-employed was under 9 percent.[6]

The working population did not accept that transformation docilely. While the economic system was in its formative years, generation after generation of American working people challenged it by organizing visionary social movements aimed at liberating themselves from what they experienced as the abuses of the system, and

Introduction

What must we do? I answer, study the best means of... embarking in a system of co-operation, which will eventually make every man his own master, — every man his own employer; a system which will give the laborer a fair proportion of the products of his toil. It is to co-operation, then, as the lever of labor's emancipation, that the eyes of the workingmen and women of the world are directed, upon co-operation their hopes are centered, and to do it I now direct your attention... There is no good reason why labor can not, through co-operation, own and operate mines, factories, and railroads. By co-operation alone can a system of colonization be established in which men may band together for the purpose of securing the greatest good for the greatest number, and place the man who is willing to toil upon his own homestead.
—Terence V. Powderly, Knights of Labor, 1880[2]

COOPERATIVES IN AMERICA

In 2008, more than 120 million people in the United States are members of 48,000 cooperatives, about 40 percent of the population. Some 3,400 farmer-owned cooperatives market about 30 percent of all American farm products today. More than 6,400 housing cooperatives provide homes for more than 1 million households. Two million homes get service from two hundred and seventy telephone cooperatives. Nearly 1,000 rural electric cooperatives provide power to 36 million people. Over 50,000 independent small businesses belong to 250 purchasing cooperatives for group buying and shared services. Over 10.5 million people belong to ESOPSs (Employee Stock Ownership Plans) in 9,650 plans, with over $675 billion in assets. Eighty-four million Americans belong to credit unions. Numer-

abolishing what they called *wage slavery*. The Random House online dictionary defines *wage slave* as "a person who works for a wage... with total and immediate dependency on the income derived from such labor." The assertion that wage work coerced by social conditions is actually a form of slavery has been traced back to a group of women millworkers striking in Lowell in 1836.[7] From that era onward, early American workers planned to accomplish their liberation from wage slavery by substituting for it a system based on cooperative work and by constructing parallel institutions that would supercede the institutions of the wage system.

This book documents that struggle and its repercussions throughout American history.

BENEFITS OF COOPERATIVES

Historically, worker cooperatives offered a way for people to get out of the boss system entirely, and to reorganize their lives on a different basis. They still offer that today. They proffer group self-employment to people without the resources to start a business alone. They empower their members through internal democracy and increased job security in place of the typical hierarchical command structure and job insecurity of the capitalist form of business. Cooperatives provide innumerable goods and services at cost. Beyond the benefits to the lives of the individual members, worker cooperatives—and all cooperatives—offer numerous other benefits to community and society.

Cooperatives exist in almost every human activity. A cooperative can have as few as three members, or can be a multi-million dollar business. Around the world cooperatives provide jobs for more than 100 million people and have more than 800 million members.[8] Cooperatives are often categorized as industrial, service, agricultural, fisheries, consumer, financial services, housing, health, insurance, utilities, retailers, community, and social. There are cooperatives for homes, childcare, funerals, transportation, medicine, social care, music, art, schools, sports, taxis, buses, car-sharing, water, electricity, gas, tourism, credit, banking, and almost every other type of work and play, fulfilling every human need.[9]

A BRIEF HISTORY OF THE MOVEMENT

The history of cooperatives and cooperative movements in America chronicles the struggles of our working population. The history documents how cooperatives were an integral part of numerous American communities in many time periods, and how the working people of this country turned time and again to cooperation for both personal liberation and as a strategy for achieving larger social goals. By following this saga over a long period of time, a bigger picture emerges of forces playing themselves out over generations. Recognizing those larger patterns can help us understand that in our short human lifetimes, we personally see only a small part of the picture.

From the earliest period, opposition movements among wage earners to the imposition of the wage system took the form of protective and mutual-aid organizations. These can be categorized as unions, cooperatives, and parties. Many were all three at the same time. They strove not only to better their members' income and working conditions, but also to raise their members out of wage slavery entirely. The greatest labor associations of most of the 19th century promoted and organized worker cooperatives as a way to cross the class boundary between employee and self-employed.

The first impetus of worker cooperatives as a serious social movement came from the National Trades' Union in the 1830s, with at least eighteen production cooperatives. Many of these lasted only a few years, a pattern repeated in subsequent waves.[10] The Associationist movement produced some twenty-two industrial cooperatives in the 1840s. The movement greatly expanded after the Civil War. With the National Labor Union's leadership, over ninety-five production cooperatives were organized in the late 1860s. Another ninety were started in the 1870s. The movement peaked in the 1880s, with one study listing 334 worker cooperatives organized in that decade.[11] At the core of that group was a chain of approximately 200 industrial cooperatives organized by the Knights of Labor, mostly between 1886-88. Almost a million members strong, the Knights were the largest labor organization in the world. The Knights planned that these cooperatives would grow and spread in every industry across America, eventually exerting democratic control over the entire economic system, until they transformed the country into what they came to call a Cooperative Commonwealth. Wage slavery would be abolished and the American promises of equality, freedom, and democracy made a living reality.

Workers and their unions were not alone in this struggle, but were closely allied with organizations of farmers. In the years following the Civil War, many small farmers effectively became financial captives to the railroads, middlemen and bankers, with most of their land in mortgage. To fight back, the greatest farmer associations of the 19th century — the National Grange in the 1870s and the Farmers' Alliance in the late 1880s   also organized extensive cooperative networks that today would be considered counter-institutional. In 1887, while the Knights' cooperatives were struggling but still strong, the Farmers' Alliance, with over three million members, opened the first of an extensive network of cooperatives that they planned as the agricultural backbone of a newly structured cooperative economic system.[12] Historian Michael Schwartz has called the Farmers' Alliance Exchanges "the most ambitious counterinstitutions ever undertaken by an American protest movement."[13]

When employers used the powers of government to attack the worker cooperatives, and bankers and railways did the same against the farmer cooperatives, the Grange and the Farmers' Alliance forged successive coalitions with the Knights of Labor and organized new political parties to try to take political power themselves, and change the economic system so their cooperatives could prosper. These were the most important "third" parties of the 19th century: the Greenback-Labor Party, and the Populist Party.[14]

Almost all of the Knights' worker cooperatives were destroyed in the wake of the "Great Uprising," the monumental confrontation between labor and capital that had been building for the entire century, and that resulted in the collapse of the Knights by the end of the 1880s and the consolidation of corporate rule in America. The Farmers' Alliance Exchanges met a similar destiny.[15]

Worker cooperation changed but did not die with the Knights, and continued in new guises to play an important role in shaping the 20th century and beyond. As capitalism restructured itself in response to the challenges of the 20th century, the cooperative movement changed with it. In the 1930s, cooperatives offered a powerful response to the Great Depression, played an important role in key union struggles, and were a vital ingredient in the programs of the New Deal. That world was swept away by World War II, and most American cooperatives went with it. McCarthyism attacked the few cooperatives that survived the war, and most were purged of any connection to a social movement.

Running parallel to these labor and farmer movements, a recurring consumer cooperative movement likewise set out to abolish the abuses of the economic system, which it attempted to do by democratizing the distribution system. The consumer cooperative movement began in the 1830s with the New England Association (NEAFMOW). It was followed by the Protective Unions (1845-60), the Union Cooperative Association (1862-66) movement during the Civil War, and the Sovereigns of Industry (1874-79). Both the Knights of Labor and the Grange organized many cooperative stores, as did various unions affiliated with the American Federation of Labor.[16] The modern consumer cooperative movement can be said to have begun with the Cooperative League in 1916.[17]

Finally, the long American communalist tradition was intimately tied to all of these recurring cooperative movements. Communalism as a social movement attempted to transform society through cooperative colonies. These were formed mostly on the Westward-moving frontier, where land was cheaply available and urban people might go to escape socially oppressive conditions. Only when this early communalist strategy failed to reform society, did reformers look to cooperatives to achieve similar results. Communalist social movements started with Owenite Socialism (1825-28), involving at least ten communities; the Associationists (1841-46) organized at least twenty-eight colonies; before the Civil War there were several Abolitionist colonies (1830-65); the "Modern" Socialist movement (1886-1919) involved at least twenty communities, most of them large.[18] (I am including only secular and democratic intentional communities in these figures.) Many other communities were organized apart from these surges. Spiritual and "perfectionist" communities were also numerous. Because the history of communalism diverges in important respects from the history of other cooperatives, I will trace it in a separate section.

In the 1960s and 1970s, a new generation rediscovered cooperation, collectivity, and communalism, creating its own structures and definitions, inspired by a new political movement and in turn shaping that movement. In a unique way, the 60s gave new life to a vision of America that, unknown to most to the visionaries themselves, closely reflected the older cooperators' dreams. Like their forebears, the new co-ops and collectives struggled between their dual identities as "pure and simple" cooperatives and a radical social movement.

WHY THIS HISTORY IS IMPORTANT

It has been often said that the winners write history. Cooperatives have been widespread and important in many periods of American history, and more people are members of cooperatives today than ever before. Yet it might almost seem as if they don't exist and never existed in the US, because cooperatives are almost universally absent from history classes and almost never appear in the American media. An unbalanced emphasis has been placed on the self-reliant, individualistic frontiersman as typical of the Westward movement of American history, while this has only been one element in a much more complex situation.

Worker cooperatives played a key role as the main opposition force to corporate domination at a key turning point in American history. If the Knights of Labor, the Farmers' Alliance, and the Populist Party had succeeded, worker cooperatives might have become a basic sector of the American system. What the old cooperators called "economic freedom" might have been recognized as a basic American right. Today, involuntary bondage is supposed to have been abolished in America, yet how many would remain employees if they felt they had any choice?

Worker cooperatives are increasingly recognized throughout the world as a necessary element in any sustainable economic system of the future. The United Nations documents included in the appendix of this book demonstrate a wide acceptance that global peace and stability require solving the problems of poverty and unemployment, and that cooperatives can help accomplish this. In 2002, the UN General Assembly recognized that cooperatives "are becoming a major factor of economic and social development," and urged governments to promote their growth by

> utilizing and developing fully the potential and contribution of cooperatives for the attainment of social development goals, in particular the eradication of poverty, the generation of full and productive employment and the enhancement of social integration; encouraging and facilitating the establishment and development of cooperatives, including taking measures aimed at enabling people living in poverty or belonging to vulnerable groups to engage on a voluntary basis in the creation and development of cooperatives; taking appropriate measures aimed at creating a supportive and enabling environment for the development of cooperatives

by, inter alia, developing an effective partnership between Governments and the cooperative movement.[19]

Although the international movement will not be examined in detail in this book, it is vital to understand the importance of cooperatives in the world today. The US is of course inextricably interconnected with the rest of the planet, so to examine its history outside of the international context distorts the picture. Every country has had its own cooperative movement, and many have been extraordinary. It is far beyond the scope of any book to look at them all. However, several countries have had cooperative movements so unusual and important that they must be pointed out to anyone interested in deeper study. Even the shortest list would include the cooperatives of Basque Spain's Mondragon, Italy's Emilia-Romagna region, Venezuela, and the former Yugoslavia.

WHAT IS A COOPERATIVE?

For the purposes of this history, a group will be called a *cooperative* when the work is organized democratically among equals and its fruits are divided fairly among the workers. The International Cooperative Alliance defines a cooperative today as "an autonomous association of persons united voluntarily to meet their common economic, social and cultural needs, and aspirations through a jointly owned and democratically controlled enterprise," and considers the minimum number of members to be three.[20]

A *collective* is a small work group of equals, based on direct democracy. A cooperative can involve much larger numbers than a collective. The term *collective* sometimes indicates that the work is done by and for the group as a whole, and not necessarily divided up at all. The term *commune* indicates that the group shares a common household or is a very close-knit community.[21] All three terms— *cooperative, collective,* and *commune*—imply free, voluntary, democratic equalitarian situations. For example, if a group were digging a ditch cooperatively, they might decide that each would spend two hours at it or that each was responsible for finishing six feet. If they were digging the ditch collectively (or communally, if they lived together), they would not worry if one did more than another as long as it felt generally fair.

The modern worker (or producer) cooperative is owned and operated only by its worker-owners. Only the workers can own memberships or shares; there are no outside owners, such as customers in a consumer cooperative, or nonprofits as in some social enterprises. One worker-member equals one vote, and only one share may be issued to each worker-member in most cases.[22] Worker cooperatives commonly operate in industrial and artisanal production, construction, services, transport, intellectual and creative activities, health and social care. Worker cooperatives often exist in areas of the economy considered marginal, in which a combination of hands and minds can compensate for minimal capital. The form of the modern worker cooperative was developed as a specific type of corporation or joint-stock company. Small informal cooperatives are often unincorporated associations.[23]

Historically, cooperatives have been organized differently at different times for different purposes. For most of these periods, no adequate legal structures for cooperatives existed, and none are totally adequate today. Cooperative movements have struggled for most of American history to convince state and federal legislators to provide these structures, but with only limited success, probably due to the concern of the dominant corporate culture that they are a challenge to the status quo.[24]

Cooperatives can be profit-making or nonprofit organizations, depending on a number of factors. As profit-making organizations, many worker cooperatives in the 19th century took the structure of joint-stock companies, but with one vote per stockholder regardless of the number of shares owned. There were many variations. State laws were often at odds with the cooperative structure, and often sabotaged it. Most cooperatives stipulated that only worker-members could own stock. Others permitted outsiders to own stock but not vote. Some permitted only members to work for the cooperative, while others hired non-members as help or in other capacities. Many different formulas were used for distributing profits or surplus income. Most worker cooperatives distributed annual dividends to members according to their amount of worktime, as well as to shareholders for their investments as in any corporation.[25]

Historically, many worker cooperatives have also been nonprofit. This has always been typical of artisan cooperatives in which each member has a separate business, and the nonprofit cooperative exists to furnish workspace, machinery, supplies, or marketing. The most widespread 19th-century worker cooperatives were in industries such as shoemaking or barrelmaking that still used artisanal methods of production. Even when the umbrella artisanal cooperative was a joint-stock company, most of the members did piece work, and the extent of the cooperative was often to buy materials in bulk and to provide marketing. Farmer cooperatives took similar forms, each member having a separate business and the nonprofit cooperative providing joint marketing and purchasing of supplies. Consumer cooperatives, providing an extensive variety of services and goods to their member-owners, have also always typically been nonprofit.[26]

WHERE THIS BOOK COMES FROM

When I began this study of the history of cooperatives back in the 1970s, I set out to answer several questions for myself. As a member of a number of cooperatives and collectives in my community, I considered them superior to the dominant economic system. Yet we were just a small corner of cooperation in a world dominated by institutionalized competition. I wondered why cooperatives were so marginalized and I set out to try to discover if there was any way to make them a more integral sector of the larger society. As a young adult, I first got involved in worker cooperatives because I hated being an employee. Even when I liked my boss, I hated the authoritarian structure. I didn't want to escape the employee's fate by becoming a boss myself. I wanted to empower myself, but not at the price of becoming what I hated.

As a kid, I first learned the rough principles of cooperation from the spontaneous groups we formed to play games. When not deformed by bullies, they usually had an egalitarian structure. This was in contradiction to the authoritarian structure in my school. The only alternative to being an employee or a boss I saw in the world around me was self-employment, and I didn't see a lot of it. Almost every adult I knew was an employee. In school, I was taught that this was freedom, the best possible system in the world, which produced the greatest good for the greatest number, the envy of the planet. A few other malcontents and I didn't buy it. My personal search for an alternative way of living led me to cooperatives and collectives, and I have remained involved ever since. I have been a member of Heartwood Cooperative Woodshop for over thirty years, and belonged to many other cooperatives and collectives along the way, so I've seen how they work, good and bad, from the inside. In the course of this study, I will discuss some of the groups to which I have belonged, including the rural commune Drop City in the

1960s, the urban work collective Bay Warehouse in the 1970s, and the old Berkeley Co-op in the 70s and 80s.

I brought out an early draft of this book in 1980 under the title *History of Work Cooperation in America*, which was distributed through the then-widespread "underground" media. Now, almost three decades later, I am pleased to offer this completely rethought, rewritten, updated, and greatly expanded version of that earlier work. The intervening decades, and my research and experience since, have served to confirm and—I hope—deepen my understandings and conclusions.

This book is written for the general reader, for anyone who's ever been a member of a cooperative, and for anyone who's ever been an employee. There is a bibliography at the end, which directs the interested reader to the sources of this history. There is a large body of writing about particular groups, eras, and leaders from which you can discover much more.

As I write this, the book is in its final phases of editing in the midst of the economic collapse of October 2008. The crisis is unfolding daily all around me. So this book does not cover the effects and repercussions of the crisis, but ends on a snapshot of the situation at that dramatic moment.

ACKNOWLEDGMENTS

I want to particularly thank several people for their help with this volume: Bernard Marszalek for the impetus and persistence that inspired me to undertake this revised edition; Melissa Hoover for her many suggestions, ideas, and critical abilities; Andrea Gibbons for her numerous insights, broad vision, and hard work; Romy Ruukel for her thoroughness and knowledge; Ramsey Kanaan for his faith and insistence.

1

COOPERATIVES & COOPERATIVE MOVEMENTS

1.
Early Cooperation in America

NATIVE AMERICAN COOPERATION

The first North Americans to practice collectivity, cooperation, and communalism were, of course, Indigenous. The hundreds of tribes and nations north of Mexico each had its own distinct culture, language, traditions, and history, yet almost every account stresses community over individualism as their overriding core value, even among comparatively individualistic peoples. Cultural patterns of economic cooperation were clearly engrained in the fabric of every tribe. While this is a vast and complex area of study, some very general observations can help put what follows into perspective.[1]

The typical unit of an Indian society was the extended family, with a number of related adults in the same household who shared a common store of provisions and tools, and worked for the common benefit. Groups of extended families were organized into larger cooperative units, clans and bands. The collection of these family groups, clans, and bands made up the tribe. The concept of individual private property in land or natural resources was unknown. Tools were commonly shared within the communal group. It was unthinkable, for example, for one Inuit in a band to have two harpoons while another had none.[2]

Hunting and gathering peoples followed their food sources around with the seasons; food availability and the methods of gathering determined the size of the living group. At certain times of year, usually scattered groups would join into larger units for cooperative production, using methods not possible in smaller units.[3]

Shoshone families wandering west of the Wyoming Rockies would gather periodically with other families in their bands for cooperative rabbit hunts with nets. A successful hunt was not possible without a large enough number of coordinated people. They would form the nets into a semi-circle hundreds of feet long, then beat the brush and chase the startled rabbits into the trap. The Shoshone traditionally divided the catch equally among the families until common survival needs were met. Any family without nets—the means of production—usually got a slightly smaller share. They considered this fair because there was much work involved in tying, repairing and hauling the nets around, and because they made nets from readily available materials, accessible to any family who chose to put in the labor. These mutual-aid gatherings were not only for work, but were also social celebrations, and formed an integral part of Shoshone societal structure.[4]

The introduction of horses made hunter cooperation on a larger scale possible for the Lakota and many other tribes. Horses spread to the Western Native nations several generations before contact with whites, and a culture arose based on them, resulting in those celebrated epic buffalo hunts across the Great Plains involving hundreds of hunters. These were similar to the rabbit hunts but on a larger scale. They were mutual-aid gatherings of usually scattered bands, combining work and social connection. "The buffalo hunt was under the supervision of chosen and responsible leaders... It was understood that the herd was the prey of the entire community and that the chase was to be a united, group activity."[5] Hunters could win a larger share of the kill by their prowess, but no one went without. Preparing the great feasts that followed were cooperative and collective endeavors.[6]

Cooperation and collectivity also formed the backbone of the way of life of agriculture-oriented peoples. Since ancient times, the Southwest Pueblos have practiced collective and cooperative farming (and later herding). The Rio Grande valley Pueblos used cooperative irrigation and, in the high desert further west, the Hopi practiced cooperative dry farming.[7]

The Northwest coast tribes such as the Hupa, Yurok, Tillamook, and Chinook were based upon collective fishing. The tribe channeled the entire catch to an elder whose only power was to assure an equitable distribution according to need.[8]

Some form of collective democracy formed part of almost every Native social system north of Mexico. The Iroquois confederacy developed inter-tribal democracy on a large scale. Their Council of Sachems consisted of male elders from the various tribes appointed by female elders, and made decisions by unanimous collective consensus. Variations of the council-consensus system are the most typical form of Native political organization.[9]

Even today, sheep herding is largely pooled in a traditional Navajo extended family, although the animals are individually owned. The Navajo extended family members work collectively in many of their economic and domestic chores, such as harvesting planted fields. The group lives in a cluster of hogans (and today, houses) centered on an older woman, and includes her husband, unmarried children, married daughters with their husbands and children, and possibly other relatives. If they move to another location due to weather, foliage for the animals, or to seasonal camps for harvesting piñon nuts, they move as a group. A married man often visits his mother's or sisters' extended families and joins in their work.[10]

Despite the ravages of European invasion, collectivity, communalism, and cooperation remain the dominant texture of Indian life today, particularly of those tribes able to hold onto their land. Many tribes have tribal enterprises and production cooperatives, organized on partly traditional, partly "modern" lines. Collectivity and communalism are as integral to Native American culture and religion as are the tribe and the land.[11]

Today's powwows are inter-tribal in essence, based on traditions combined from many tribes, yet with an infinite number of ever-changing variations. "Every summer there are powwows on every reservation and in urban communities where there is more than one Indian. We eat and dance and we have a good time. But there is more to it than that. We are sharing. We share the food, the dances, and the good times."[12]

THE EARLY COLONIAL TRADITIONS

Close community survival cooperation permeated the entire way of life in Colonial America. This was true of all the waves of settlers: British, French, and Spanish. Settlers raised houses and barns, plowed fields, and built fences cooperatively and collectively. Mutual aid events like corn-husking bees, log-rolling bees (to clear land), sewing and quilting bees, apple paring bees, grain rings (threshing), bull rings (slaughtering), and ship launchings also served as social structures and gatherings that welded together the fabric of the working community of settlers in the same way that similar gatherings did among the Native peoples.[13] As one historian has commented, "This power of the newly arrived pioneers to join together for a common end without the intervention of governmental institutions was one of their marked characteristics."[14]

Barter and labor exchanges were widely practiced. Money was scarce and in many areas used only sporadically, making early country stores mostly barter centers. The incessant waves of displaced humanity found warmth and shelter on these troubled shores through cooperation, mutual aid, and sharing. As another historian noted, settlers banded together "because they needed each other. Westward-moving pioneers everywhere found group travel and group living normal."[15] Cooperation, not competition, resounded as the dominant chord across the continent among the working population.

THE SPANISH COLONIES

The Spanish settled the territories that are now the American Southwest through land grants made by the King of Spain to groups of emigrant families, usually twenty or more, beginning in the late 1600s.[16] The Spanish Crown initiated this system to entice Mexican colonists to frontier areas with an offer of free land, which appealed to landless groups.[17]

"Community land grants," issued to groups of ten or more married settlers, contained large sections of common lands called ejidos set aside for the use of the entire community. "Individual land grants," made to particular people and families, also usually designated ejidos for general communal use, and common areas for pasture, watering, wood gathering, or hunting. Grants were also often made to newly founded towns, providing adjacent common lands for use by all residents. In addition, land grants were made to Indian pueblos, often simply confirming ancient rights to these territories, in exchange for their recognition of the Spanish Crown. These land grant policies governed settlement in all the colonies of Spanish America, and were modeled on similar customs in medieval Spain.[18] The ejido system also had roots in indigenous Mexico. The basic unit of Aztec social organization was a group of interrelated families who farmed cooperatively called a *calpulli*.[19] Mexican Indians usually accompanied colonist groups traveling north. After independence in 1821, the Mexican government continued these policies of land distribution. Spain and Mexico made a total of 295 land grants in the territory that eventually became the American Southwest, of which 154 were community land grants, including 23 grants of communal lands to the indigenous Indian pueblos.[20] In 1848, most of the territory was still sparsely populated, with only a few large towns, and most of the approximately 60,000 settlers lived in these subsistence agricultural communities.[21]

Community land grants typically kept about 90 percent of their land in common, including pastures and forests, for collective use. The common ejido land could not be sold. Beyond that, each family owned a house and a farmable plot. The ejidos were self-governing and all males had a vote in biennial elections. Much work was done cooperatively and, on occasions, the whole village joined in projects for the common good, such as annual repairs of irrigation systems and roads. Tools were often collectively owned and used. The system was geared for group self-sufficiency under harsh conditions.[22]

Under the Treaty of Guadalupe Hidalgo, which formally ended the US-Mexican war in 1848, Mexico ceded a vast area to the US, including California, Nevada, Arizona, New Mexico, Utah, and parts of Colorado, Wyoming, Oklahoma, and Texas. The US in turn agreed to recognize all existing property ownership in the territories. But in practice, the US often did not protect the property of Mexican-Americans and their descendants, and in particular the common lands of community land grants. These have been in dispute ever since.[23]

In Mexico below the Rio Grande, ejidos were also under attack by land grabbers, and their restoration became one of the central goals of the Zapatistas in the Mexican Revolution of 1910.[24] According to a celebrated account about the almost-mythic Emiliano Zapata, a full-blooded Indian, "In early 1914 some emissaries from a Michoacán rebel came to his camp at Pozo Colorado, to see if he was sincere. What was he really fighting for? How could he prove it? He had Robles [his aide] bring the Anenecuilco [his home village] documents, and he showed them to his visitors. '*Por esto peleo*,' he said. '*For this I am fighting*.'"[25] The documents that had been entrusted to him were the almost-sacred land grants of his village, written in the Nahuatl language and representative of the collective rights of the people to the land. New Mexico land grantees felt similarly about their ejidos, and many of their descendants, displaced from their ancestral lands, continue to do so today.[26]

THE ENGLISH COLONIES

During their first three years in America, from 1620 to 1623, the Pilgrims of Plymouth farmed and worked communally, depositing all the products of their work into a common warehouse and taking their needs from a common store.[27] The first New England colony began as a commune, and later reorganized into a cooperative community. As an early historian stated, "Any attempt to treat of the cooperative efforts in Massachusetts without commencing with a reference to the Pilgrim Church, the township, and the fisheries, would be like a record of the Revolution with Samuel Adams, Lexington and Concord left out."[28]

The Pilgrim Separatists financed their voyage from England to America through the backing of a group of capitalists, the Merchant Adventurers.[29] The colony was to be a base for fur trading with the Indians, cutting timber, and for fishing on the Grand Banks. The Pilgrims would send these products back to England to pay off the debt and for supplies that the investors would continue to send. The settlers would each put in seven years labor and receive a share of the profits, which would not be divided until the end. At that time "the capital and profits, viz. the houses, lands, goods, and chattels," would be equally divided between the investors and settlers and the contract would be dissolved.[30] In the original agreement, every family was to have a plot of land to garden for its own needs, and the right to work "two days a week for their own private employment, for the more comfort of themselves and their families," and four days a week working for the corporation.[31] At the last minute, however, the investors insisted on changes to the agreement, because they were afraid that the colonists would work their own plots to the detriment of the enterprise's profits. They threatened to withdraw their financing unless the settlers agreed to work entirely for the corporation with no separate plots. The colonists, most of them tenant farmers in the open fields of an old manorial hunting park in Nottinghamshire, considered that the investors' demand essentially reduced them to serfdom. The settlers were asking for no more than was normal under England's manorial system in effect since the Middle Ages. Peasants worked in the lord's fields but also had time to work individual plots for their household needs. The serf, in a stricter form of bondage than the peasant, had no time to himself and no right to an individual plot.[32]

At an impasse and with the entire project at risk, one of the Pilgrim leaders signed the restrictive agreement without authorization from the group. This set up a conflict that would play itself out in the first years of the colony.[33]

The original core of thirty-five gathered sixty-seven others into the group shortly before leaving. Most of these newcomers were indentured servants, required to work in bondage for a fixed time period with the master receiving a share of the enterprise's profits from the servant's labor. More than half of the 102 people aboard the *Mayflower* were indentured servants. But the day before landing, the servants staged an insurrection and declared they were seizing their freedom. The bulk of the Pilgrims—"free" workers—sided with the servants. The masters had no choice but to agree to the demands. All adult males signed the Mayflower Compact, affirming that all were now free, and establishing a government in which all males had equal voice and vote. Thus, revolutionary servants set up the most democratic political system of its time in colonial America, although it still excluded women.[34]

Relations between the Pilgrim settlers and the investors quickly deteriorated. The colonists struggled through many hardships, expecting that the investors would send them regular supplies of food, clothes, and tools. Instead, subsequent ships came laden only with new colonists, and the settlers were left to fend for themselves for survival while sending the returning ships back laden with furs, lumber, and salt fish to be sold by the investors.[35]

After three years, in 1623, the conflict between the colonists and the corporation reached the breaking point. The Pilgrim governor unilaterally broke the contract and assigned individual plots. These varied in size depending on the size of each family; the families were given use of the land, but no inheritance rights. Two years later, relations with the corporation had deteriorated even further. At that point, a group of Pilgrims terminated the agreement after buying out the investors, and Plymouth achieved self-government.[36]

The reorganized cooperative economic system became the basis for future towns that spun off from Plymouth, and for the settlement of most of the Puritan Commonwealth organized soon after by the Massachusetts Bay Colony. Though founded after Plymouth, the Massachusetts Bay Colony quickly grew much larger, and eventually assimilated the other. Ruling the colony from England soon proved as impossible for the Massachusetts Bay Company as it had for the Plymouth investors, and corporate government gradually gave way to local self-rule.[37]

Contradictory forces were pulling in opposite directions at the same time. The democracy of the Mayflower Compact had served only to elect a governor with extensive powers that today we would consider dictatorial. Masters imported new shiploads of servants, who would not be declared free. A theocratic oligarchy took control of Plymouth, limiting the number of people eligible to vote, requiring property qualifications for voting, and institutionalizing the right to hold slaves.[38] Land was plentiful only at the price of the genocide of the Indians.[39]

Meanwhile, as Plymouth became increasingly less democratic, the system of New England town meeting democracy was hatched in the spin-off towns. Under the Massachusetts system, each village or town had a large commons like a medieval estate. This land belonged to the community as a whole, which assigned it to landless individuals and families to use. The early Puritan system saw it as society's duty to assure that no one was alienated from this most basic means of survival. Much of Puritan Massachusetts was thus community property.[40]

Technically, Plymouth and the Massachusetts Bay Company were granted the land by the king, and they in turn granted land mostly to groups of settlers as towns. In the beginning, the group held the land in common and determined the method of individual allocation along with the locations of residences, planted fields, grazing meadows, and woods. These allocations varied from town to town, in part reflecting differing customs in the settlers' origin in various regions of England. Allocations were usually based on the principle of the individual family's ability to work the land. In many areas, they minimized individual holdings and used the open-field system, regulating who could gather wood or graze on the common land.[41]

However, unrestrained market forces were working to destroy this system. Some townships quickly divided almost all their land. Transferable deeds permitted land to become a commodity. A real estate market sprang up, and land speculation became rampant. Land speculators who were powerful in the General Court—as they called the colonial government—introduced the practice of selling or granting large sections of frontier land to wealthy citizens, who subdivided and sold it to the highest bidder. Several generations of this process destroyed the early Puritan common-land system.[42] Still, mutual aid and cooperation remained a basic substance of their way of life. The first major independent industry in Plymouth was a fishing cooperative.[43]

From the beginning, worker cooperation in America had two faces, economic and political. Workers came together in labor not only to survive, but also to defend themselves against the ruling moneyed classes. Small farmers commonly organized squatters' associations to fight off the land speculators who were wreaking havoc in their rural communities.[44]

In New England it became a tradition for the discontented in a community to band together and "hive" like bees into a new spot deeper in the wilderness. New settlements tended to be collective or communal at first, like Plymouth. While each family staked a separate plot, they still retained their cooperative way of life. Most of these people were former servants who had worked off their indentures.[45]

Most of the fertile flatlands were quickly claimed by the wealthy for their large farms and plantations. In both North and South, poorer families were pushed to the harsher lands in the mountains, where they created a culture based on community cooperation. Most mountain people were fierce defenders of liberty and freedom; their descendants in the South eventually formed many of the tracks of the Underground Railroad that secreted escaped slaves from the lowland plantations to the North; there were very few slaves anywhere in the mountains.[46]

The British monarchy chartered the Southern colonies as plantations under the dictatorial rule of corporations and aristocrats untempered by any religious sect. The Virginia Company of London received its royal charter in 1606. The next year, the corporation founded Jamestown, the first permanent English settlement in North America. The charter of the province of Carolina was granted to eight Lord Proprietors in 1663. The corporations and aristocrats planned at first to exploit the wealth of America with the labor of Indian slaves and British indentured servants. Servants made up between one-half and two-thirds of the workforce in British America throughout the 17th century. Many thousands signed themselves into servitude in exchange for passage, in ultimate hope of a better life. Many other thousands, including many children, were kidnapped into it by labor contractors called *soul drivers*, or sentenced to it for "crimes" such as unemployment or debt.[47] Only when it became clear that the Indians could not be made into profitable slaves on their ancestral soil did the corporations switch over to a policy of genocide and began replacing them with blacks displaced far from their homelands. Traders dragged the first black slaves in British America to the corporate military plantation of Virginia in 1619, a year before the *Mayflower* landed. The first slaves at Plymouth were Indians, captives of war; there were also many Indian servants at the colony. The "unfree" at Plymouth made up at least a quarter of the population.[48] Slaves from Africa were first brought to Massachusetts in 1624, and the institution of slavery received its first legal recognition in British America in Plymouth in 1641.[49] There were probably about 4,000 blacks in the North around 1710, mostly in urban areas. The first US census in 1790 counted 2,805 slaves in New England (primarily in Connecticut), and 13,975 free blacks; 36,323 slaves and 13,059 free blacks in the Mid-Atlantic colonies; and 655,079 slaves and 32,162 free blacks in the South.[50]

Mutual aid and survival cooperation were universal in African-American communities in both the South and the "free" North. Cooperative networks among slaves, invisible to the masters, became used as channels for organized resistance. People attended to each other's survival at mutual-aid gatherings known as "hush-hush meetings" at night in swamps or forests. Elected ministers often preached a religion of liberation at these meetings, and were often leaders in the many revolts and escapes planned there. Over 250 slave insurgencies are recorded, many of the early ones involving white indentured servants.[51] Escaped slaves set up "maroon" communal settlements in forests and swamps. These outlaw communes, many with both black and Indian members, appeared wherever slavery spread, and many were used as bases for guerrilla raids on the slavers. At least fifty maroon colonies are documented to have existed in the South.[52] The Underground Railroad itself is one of the best-known examples of a mutual aid organization.[53] Benefit societies—formed for mutual-aid—were widespread not only among Southern blacks fighting for freedom, but were increasingly formed by nearly every ethnic, religious, trade, professional, and social group throughout the colonies and in the new independent nation.[54]

In 1731, Benjamin Franklin organized fifty of his neighbors and friends to form the first subscription library in America, the Library Company of Philadelphia. Each paid forty shillings to start the collection.[55]

Another of the earliest recorded cooperatives in America was a firefighting company organized in 1736 by Franklin and four of his friends, the Union Fire Company, for mutual aid in case of fire. In their written agreement, each agreed to have at ready "six leather buckets" for water and "two stout linen bags" to carry rescued property.[56] That cooperative became the prototype of the volunteer fire-fighting company, which spread to almost every locale in America. In 1750, the Union Fire Company began "a fund for an Insurance Office to make up the Damage that may Arise by Fire among this Company."[57] Thus, the Union Fire Company also became the prototype of the mutual insurance company. Mutual insurance is an agreement among a number of persons to insure each other against loss, as by fire, death, or accident. In a mutual insurance company, the policyholders as a group own the company, which is operated for their benefit. Other local firefighting companies wanted to join Franklin's cooperative insurance pool, so in 1752 they set up the Philadelphia Contributionship for the Insurance of Houses from Loss by Fire.[58] Others emulated the Contributionship, and by 1800 there were ten mutual insurance cooperatives in America, all of them urban.[59] The idea spread rapidly among farmers in the 1820s. Mutual fire insurance organizations became a school of cooperation for early American farmers, leading to many other forms of farmer cooperatives. The Contributionship continues to this day.[60]

Mutual-aid in free black communities was closely connected to churches and benefit societies. Also called benevolent associations or friendly societies, these groups had roots in tribal initiation associations of West Africa, and often involved secret rituals. The Preseverance Benefit and Mutual Aid Association, the first recorded benevolent association among free blacks, was founded in New Orleans in 1783.[61] The Free African Society (FAS), a non-denominational benefit society funded by membership dues, was formed in 1787 in Philadelphia by clergymen Richard Allen (who later founded the African Methodist Episcopal Church), Absalom Jones, and others, to provide mutual aid among freed blacks.[62] FAS was particularly noted for its work with victims of yellow fever in the epidemic of 1793. Black benevolent associations were numerous, both before and after emancipation. In New Orleans, most societies began to include a band in funeral processions; on the way back from the cemetery, the music became upbeat, the mourners now celebrating the deceased's life. These "jazz funerals" became the fountainhead of the new American music. Black benefit societies also became the organizational base for the Carnival Mardi Gras Indian "krewes."[63]

Rural cooperative traditions moved west with the frontier and continued strongly in those areas well beyond the colonial period. A traveler to the Midwest and upper Mississippi valley in 1809-11 described a typical house-raising he witnessed:

> On the morning of the appointed day they assemble, and divide themselves into parties, to each of which is assigned its respective duty; one party cuts down trees, another lops and cuts them to proper lengths, a third is furnished with horses and oxen, and drags them to the spot designated for the site of the house; another party is employed in making shingles to cover the roof, and at night all materials are ready on the spot; and on the night of the next day, he and his family sleep in their new habitation. No remuneration is expected nor would it be received... [This] is not confined to the newcomer only, it occurs frequently in the course of a year amongst the old settlers, with whom it is a continued bond of amity and social intercourse.[64]

Alexis de Tocqueville saw mutual-aid associations as omnipresent in his nine-month tour of the US in 1831. "In no country in the world has the principle of association been more successfully used or applied to a greater multitude of objects than in America," he wrote in *Democracy in America*.[65]

> The political associations that exist in the United States are only a single feature in the midst of the immense assemblage of associations in that country. Americans of all ages, all conditions, and all dispositions constantly form associations. They have not only commercial and manufacturing companies, in which all take part, but associations of a thousand other kinds... I have often admired the extreme skill with which the inhabitants of the United States succeed in proposing a common object for exertions of a great many men and in inducing them voluntarily to pursue it...[66]

Residents in the coastal cities organized guild-like mutual-aid benefit societies in almost every trade. In different industries, the societies had various functions, sometimes even regulating industry work standards. At first specializing in sickness, accident, and death benefits, they essentially served as mutual-aid groups with some aspects of brotherhoods, founded on the basic agreement to help each other, particularly in hard times.[67] The ubiquitous Franklin helped to organize the journeymen printers of Philadelphia into a benefit society in the early 1790s, which reorganized in 1802 as a trade union with benefit features.[68] These early societies in the trades had roots in guilds that dated back to before the European Middle Ages. In the earliest societies, journeymen and masters were in the same organizations. Masters generally dominated these early associations. Journeymen eventually broke away over the issues of wages and working conditions, and formed their own mutual-aid societies: the trade unions.[69]

2.
The Revolutionary Movements Begin 1800–40

At the time of the American Revolution in 1776, independent self-employed workers formed the backbone of the "free" American population. The vast majority of these were small and subsistence farmers, and the rest were artisans, "mechanics" (skilled workers), or laborers. But of course not all Americans were "free." Slaves formed a fourth of the workforce. Most by this time were African—or African-American—but Indian slavery could still be found in some areas. White indentured servants, slaves with a time limit on their bondage (usually four to seven years), had been the main form of labor through most of the colonial period and still made up a large portion of the newer immigrants. Employees were only a tiny sector of the population. Most wage-workers were former indentured servants. This growing class of employees embodied some conditions of both freedom and bondage.[1]

As long as hand tool production predominated and land was readily available, independence was within the grasp of almost all "free" workers. Wave after wave of immigrant indentured servants worked off their bondage, winding up penniless; the vast majority then took jobs as wage earners for a few years, just long enough to raise a stake or learn a trade, then either disappeared into the wilderness to become small farmers or remained in more settled areas to become self-employed in some productive way.[2]

While tools were simple and good land was plentiful (at the price of genocide of the Native peoples), individual ownership of those means of production meant real freedom for the "free" American working people. That was the greatest attraction of America to European workers.[3] But the social system was ruled by and favored the rich. Even where "free" people had won some degree of local self-government, as in New England, the vast majority of working people was still excluded from voting and holding office due to property and gender qualifications.

The decade before the Revolution was increasingly one of hard times for all American workers. As England suffered in the throes of the first economic depression of its emerging capitalist system, the British rulers tried to place as much of the burden on the colonies as possible. The local colonial rulers in turn passed the burden down onto the backs of the workers.[4] In both cities and frontier communities, working people were increasingly pressed.

The spirit of revolt grew strong among small and subsistence farmers, artisans, mechanics, laborers, wage earners, servants and slaves, men and women. The general uprising that culminated in the American Revolutionary War was not only against British domination, but against domination by the local landed and merchant-capitalist ruling cliques which were everywhere in control. Large numbers of these ruling cliques wound up fleeing to Canada. The rank-and-file laborers, artisans, mechanics, small farmers and traders, members of the Sons of Liberty and other groups, formed the main support of the revolutionary movement and insisted on the more radical demands. Their constant demonstrations, boycotts, riots, and sabotage led to the eventual break.[5]

The League of the Iroquois inspired the concept of a federation of colonies. Canassatego, an Onondaga Iroquois chief, was the first person to propose at an Indian-British conference in Pennsylvania in 1744 that the colonies unify as the Iroquois had done and speak with one voice. A decade later, Benjamin Franklin, Indian commissioner of Pennsylvania, proposed at the colonial Albany Congress of 1754 that the colony delegates unite into a federation like the League of the Iroquois.[6] Thomas Paine, journeyman printer, who called for a democratic republic in his pamphlet *Common Sense* (1776) and rallied the working people to the revolutionary cause, experienced Native democracy firsthand as secretary in negotiations between the rebels and the Iroquois near Philadelphia in 1777.[7] Inspired by the Native political system, Paine studied the Iroquoian language, and thereafter used Indian society as an exemplary model in his writings. He condemned England for abusing the Indians, was the first person in the colonies to demand the abolition of slavery, and proposed the name, "United States of America."[8]

But the revolutionary victory brought the working people few immediate advantages. Merchant-capitalists, land speculators, and plantation owners remained the ruling elite, and the property-less were still disenfranchised. Indentured servitude was still widespread among the immigrant population, then mostly Irish and German. Democratic gains soldiers thought they had won in battle were whittled away.[9] Alarmed at the situation, the Boston Committee of Correspondence, a force in the Revolution, became active again and flooded the area with leaflets urging citizens to form committees guarding against further encroachments on their liberties.[10] Strikes and civil disturbances began to flare again.

At that point, Thomas Paine published another pamphlet, *Agrarian Justice* (1797), in which he called for an end to poverty and proposed a remedy for social injustice. Since the earth is the rightful common inheritance of all, Paine reasoned that the introduction of the system of private property in land had thus deprived many of their rightful inheritance for which they needed to be compensated. To remedy this, he proposed to limit the accumulation of wealth through a 10 percent inheritance tax on land; the tax would finance a national fund to provide a compensatory grant to each person at age twenty-one, and social insurance for the aged and disabled.[11]

In 1786, small farmers in Western Massachusetts rose to halt foreclosures and oppression of debtors; with the leadership of Daniel Shays, they staged an armed insurrection, seizing the centers of merchant power in the Eastern seaboard for a short time.[12] These revolts finally won the Bill of Rights. Nonetheless, the constitutional convention wrote slavery into the Constitution and allowed it to spread to the Southwest Territory. Speculators and slavers were permitted to seize almost all the Western lands. Property qualifications still restricted voting.[13]

In the following years, refugees from the French Revolution and the United Irishmen revolt poured onto American shores. They formed communities in the seaboard cities, where they immediately set up cooperative mutual-aid structures among themselves to assist in gaining a toehold. All subsequent waves of immigrants followed this pattern.[14]

"Democratic societies" modeled after the Sons of Liberty began forming in all the major centers. These came together in an uprising of small farmers and urban workers to put Jefferson in the presidency.[15] But the aristocratic Federalists met them by staging America's first "red scare." They charged that the democratic societies were part of a vast secret international conspiracy called "the

Illuminati," financed by "Paris gold" with the aim of "subverting the government and wiping out religion."[16] Nevertheless, Jefferson's Democratic-Republican (later just Democratic) Party swept into power in 1800. During his presidency, democracy was extended,[17] the African slave trade outlawed, and the Louisiana territory partly opened to homesteaders.[18]

Jefferson's social vision was to create a general equality in land through free homesteads. He advocated society adopting whatever "devices for subdividing property"[19] were necessary to "prevent the accumulation and perpetuation of wealth in select families."[20] He believed that "whenever there are in a country uncultivated lands and unemployed poor, it is clear that the laws of property have been so far extended as to violate the natural right. The earth is given as a common stock for man to labor and live on."[21] "I sincerely believe, with you," he wrote to a friend, "that banking establishments are more dangerous than standing armies."[22] He advocated a constitutional convention every twenty years when each new generation could agree to a new social contract.[23]

INDUSTRIALIZATION AND CLASS DIVISIONS

The beginnings of industrialization under the capitalist system in the early 19th century forced an ever-growing number of workers to become permanent wage earners. Hand tool production soon became obsolete; the new machines and processes were both prohibitively expensive and could be operated only by ever-larger numbers of coordinated workers.[24] While the vast productive power unleashed by technological advances promised freedom and plenty for all, numerous artisanal workers were left unable to make a living using the old tools, so had no choice but to find bosses and submit to becoming employees. Meanwhile, land costs skyrocketed: the road to independence as a small farmer was quickly being closed.[25] Vast new areas were continually annexed to the fledgling United States, but that enormous wealth went mostly for the further enrichment of a small number of land speculators, ultimately the same financiers who were behind the factories in the North and the plantations in the South.[26]

As hand tools gave way to machinery and accessible farmable land was fenced off, alienation from those means of production resulted in virtual bondage for ever-greater numbers. Control of all means of survival was becoming concentrated in increasingly fewer hands while the population was expanding many times over. America was being transformed from a land where almost all "free" workers had control of their basic means of survival to one where the great majority were alienated from and denied those means and exploited and controlled by those who had them. Meanwhile, the financial powers in control of the government proceeded to transform the wealth of the American continent into private profits, permitting only a bare minimum to flow back into the pockets of the workers who were indispensable in creating it. The emerging capitalist system needed a labor pool, a sufficient number of people scarcely surviving and therefore willing to "voluntarily" submit to becoming employees. Those stuck in that position for years became "wage slaves," forced to work long hours under oppressive conditions for little pay.[27]

To be "free" meant that one was not physically forced by police action to work for someone else, like a chattel slave. "Free" workers could choose their bosses and quit their jobs. However, when one was forced by economic necessity to sell labor, it amounted to voluntary submission to work bondage. The bondage was voluntary in a technical sense, and was only between specified hours and for agreed-upon pay.[28]

During the colonial period, journeymen and apprentices in the skilled trades worked for and with masters, not "bosses." The master was a worker, too. As long as tools were simple, it was within almost any worker's grasp to become a master. The "boss system" became prevalent in the early 19th century. Masters took the step to become "bosses," "employers," no longer workers but businessmen exploiting labor.[29]

In response to the economic vicissitudes of the late colonial period and the early republic, the two classes of wage earners and independent workers both formed cooperatives. One class was struggling to raise itself out of wage-bondage, the other to keep from falling down into it. These two classes met in the cooperatives and became one. Worker cooperatives were bridges across a class boundary, elevating workers from dependence to independence, from work bondage to real freedom.[30]

EARLY STRIKERS' COOPERATIVES

In 1768, twenty journeymen tailors in New York City walked out because of a reduction in pay. This was the first recorded wage earners' strike against a boss in America.[31] They had no strike fund. Their impromptu organization served as their only union. The first ongoing union in America had not yet been organized. To help support themselves during the strike, the tailors set up their own cooperative "house of call" in opposition to their masters. Finding themselves locked out and their jobs filled by scabs, they tried to make a go of their cooperative. History does not record their degree of success.[32]

The sun-to-sun workday system prevailed at that time, meaning a seventy-five hour work-week in the summer.[33] In 1791, shortly after the US Constitution was ratified, a group of journeymen carpenters in Philadelphia demanded that their workday be limited to ten hours. When their employer refused, they walked out of their jobsite, declaring a strike. To help support themselves during their strike, they formed a cooperative and tried to undercut their boss by charging 25 percent less, announcing that they were eliminating his profit. They gave themselves the ten-hour day they were striking for. But the cooperative was planned to last only as long as the strike, and with the end of the strike, the cooperative was disbanded.[34]

In 1792, the Philadelphia shoemakers organized the first full-fledged trade union in America, with a constitution, regular meetings, and dues.[35] Shoemaking was typical of the level of industrial organization of the period, before the advent of complex machines and the assembly line. Early manufactories were large shops where a group of journeymen artisans would each work on a whole piece.[36]

In 1794, shoemakers in Baltimore formed the United Journeymen Cordwainers and demanded that the standard piece-work rate be raised to six shillings. When they were unable to negotiate a settlement, the Cordwainers went out on strike, taking with them over half the workers in the city.[37] In the midst of it, they organized the first cooperative manufactory in the United States. Located on the main commercial street, it was a large workshop open to all journeymen boycotting the masters' shops. The union appointed two shop foremen to oversee the work. Several masters soon began paying the higher rates, and the union approved workers returning to these shops.[38]

In 1806, a group of Philadelphia shoemakers under the leadership of Peter Polin and Undriel Backes unionized and struck for higher wages. Their boss had them arrested for conspiracy. The judge instructed the jury to find them guilty, which they proceeded to do. Beaten but unbowed, the shoemakers refused to slink back to a boss and organized a cooperative boot and shoe manufactory instead. The degree of success of this early venture is not recorded.[39]

Workers repeated the actions of these early strikers time and again in the following century. Striking workers forming cooperatives became a common pattern in the early labor movement as a logical reaction to oppressive working conditions. Soon, workers no longer waited until striking to form cooperatives, but began to organize them in preparation for strikes and ultimately with an eye to never having to strike again.[40]

The wage earners' cooperative, in its rejection of work-bondage, stemmed from the same thrust toward freedom that impelled so many colonists to separate from Europe and create cooperative communities throughout America. As the 19th century progressed, independence through self-employment was ever more thoroughly blocked by the economic system and increasing numbers of American workers turned to social revolution. The strike-to-cooperative transformation of the New York journeymen tailors and Philadelphia carpenters was expanded in later decades into the strategy of a national general strike to transform the entire economic system.

Wage earners had few rights in colonial times, and this continued unchanged in the early years of the Republic. Most workers could not vote in local elections, because they did not meet the property qualifications for voting.[41] Under English common law, which extended to the colonies, unions were considered conspiracies in constraint of trade. This forced them underground as secret societies, even though these laws were apparently less enforced in the colonies than in Britain. The early unions were protective organizations, incorporating features such as sickness, accident, and death benefits.[42] Written records of American unions legally prosecuted as conspiracies in constraint of trade begin after American independence. Union members were brought to court by their employers on those charges at least six times between 1806 and 1815. The Cordwainers Conspiracy Cases, as these trials are called, declared that any group action of workers to raise their salaries could be illegal.[43]

COOPERATIVE WAREHOUSES

Cooperatives were becoming more widespread, and striking wage earners were not the only ones forming them in the early period. Individual self-employed artisans and handcraft manufacturers were caught between the banks and the merchants, and were being squeezed dry. Artisans could not get raw materials at prices they could pay, and the banks refused them credit. On the other end, wholesalers and store owners took the biggest bites of the selling prices.[44]

These individual producers, facing impoverishment, organized cooperative "warehouses" to get raw materials at reasonable cost, often on credit, and to distribute their products without middlemen. In the early 19th century, when productive work was still done almost entirely with hand tools, cooperating artisanal workers ordinarily collectivized resources (including credit to obtain raw materials) and distribution facilities. It was not until the 1840s, when the factory system and expensive machinery made hand tool production almost universally obsolete, that cooperative workers collectivized their major tools.[45] The earliest cooperative warehouses were primarily focused on the wholesale trade, but most catered equally to retail by 1830. Some of these were assisted by philanthropic societies, others were solely organized by unions.[46] There was a thriving cooperative warehouse in Baltimore as early as 1809.[47] The Pittsburgh and Vicinity Manufacturing Association opened a cooperative warehouse in 1818, doing much barter as well as sales of industrial products for farm produce.[48] The New England Society for the Promotion of Manufactures and the Mechanic Arts organized several cooperative warehouses in Massachusetts beginning in 1825.[49] These artisan supply purchasing and distribution cooperatives differed from later worker cooperatives in that they maintained individual construction processes. Small farmers were organizing cooperatives that were functionally identical to these artisan cooperatives during this same time period.[50]

Almost all of the cooperative warehouses met with great success for a number of years. The Baltimore Society's sales for 1809 were $17,000 (a sizable sum at the time), $32,000 for the next thirteen months, and $51,000 for 1811. The Pittsburgh Association's annual gross sales "for many years after 1823" were $60,000. The New England Society, which held biannual auctions, grossed almost two million dollars in its first five sales.[51]

STRATEGIES FOR SOCIAL REFORM: WORKER COOPERATIVES OR COOPERATIVE COMMUNITIES?

The seven years following the War of 1812 saw general economic expansion and boom,[52] but the panic of 1819 brought the era to an abrupt halt. The economy collapsed, with numerous bank failures and foreclosures, followed by widespread unemployment and a long decline in agriculture and manufacturing. The depression of 1819-22 was the first major economic crisis of the US, setting the pattern of boom-and-bust that followed.[53]

The intense suffering of working people in those hard times sparked America's first communalist movement. The idea was first articulated by Cornelius Blatchly in his *Essay on Common Wealth* (1822),[54] in which he advocated the transformation of society through cooperative communities to achieve social justice. In the same essay he introduced the ideas of Robert Owen, a Welshman, who coined the term Socialism to describe the goal of the communalist movement. Blatchly invited Owen to America. Owen came and in 1825 founded New Harmony, Indiana, as the prototype of the movement. At least nine other communities were also formed. New Harmony and the others enjoyed a brief success, but all soon collapsed[55]

In 1826, Langdon Byllesby, a Philadelphia printer, criticized Blatchly and Owens' communalist plan as impracticable in *Observations on the Sources and Effects of Unequal Wealth*,[56] and proposed that worker cooperatives were a more practical means of transforming society. This ideological debate over whether worker cooperatives or cooperative communities were the most effective means to transform society would be repeated over and over in successive waves in the following decades. Both plans saw the cooperative system proving itself superior to the existing capitalist economic system, and transforming society by its infinite replication.[57]

Byllesby advocated that wage earners withdraw their labor from the capitalist system and join into cooperatives in every industry and trade. These cooperatives could then federate and grow large enough to draw in the entire working population, thus creating a new economic system in America free of poverty and inequality. Byllesby considered himself a Jeffersonian, and believed that this plan would fulfill the promise of equality in America. Byllesby's ideas laid the base for the National Trades' Union's cooperative movement of the mid-1830s.[58]

COOPERATIVE STORES

Early country stores were traditionally focuses of barter and exchange, centers for the informal mutual aid that continued to pervade most rural communities. In the early 19th century, customers often still paid their bills by trading produce, livestock, or artisanal products for merchandise. But the separation of producers and consumers by ever-larger distances resulted in domination by middlemen. Some working families began turning to buying cooperatives to eliminate middleman profits as much as possible, and thus reduce their cost of living. The first co-op stores were connected with these same social justice reform movements.[59]

Robert Owen's store in 1825 at New Harmony was the earliest prototypical cooperative store. New Harmony's economy revolved around this store, which did business based on labor notes redeemable in the store. It was nonprofit; community members received supplies, clothing, and groceries on credit, which they redeemed with time credits for work performed. Owen based this system of exchange on his theory of labor value, as he explained in *Report to the County of Lanark* (1821): "the natural standard of value is, in principle, human labour" because "manual labor, properly directed, is the source of all wealth."[60] When New Harmony split into several separate communities, the store continued, and the labor notes were used at the store for trading between the communities.[61]

Josiah Warren lived in New Harmony for two and a half years and conducted the orchestra there.[62] After leaving the community in 1827, he organized the Cincinnati Labor for Labor Store, better known as the "Time Store." Warren took the store idea from inside a cooperative community out into the world. The Time Store facilitated exchange primarily among small self-employed producers, who individually had no capital for marketing their products or services. It attempted to undercut the market and money systems by basing the value of a store-bartered product on the labor-time contained in it. Members received time credit for each product deposited, which they could use towards the barter of other products. The store added the time it took the store clerk to make the transaction to the bill. An hour's work was considered worth an hour's work; no adjustment was made to account for the different hourly values of every different type of work on the capitalist market. Instead of gold, Warren considered corn the standard, with one hour of labor "in carpenter work" worth twelve pounds of corn. People could also offer their services in their areas of skill on the same barter basis. The Time Store was not a cooperative proper; Warren was the sole proprietor, and never took on help. He nonetheless based it on cooperative principles of exchange.[63] The Time Store was so successful that a neighboring store also converted to barter. In spite of its success, Warren closed the Time Store after three years, and went on to found several mutualist communities with connected time stores. He is generally recognized as America's earliest and foremost exponent of mutual aid, or mutualism.[64]

The Time Store inspired a group of small producers in Philadelphia to organize a similar barter store they called the Producers' Exchange Association (PEA) in 1828.[65] PEA began as a labor exchange: money transactions were forbidden and exchanges were only through barter. But PEA soon revised its system to permit cash sales as well, and opened the store to customers from the community, becoming functionally indistinguishable from the artisan cooperative marketing warehouses organized a decade earlier in Massachusetts and Pittsburgh.[66] PEA was run democratically, with pricing based on production time plus cost of materials. Producer-members paid twenty-five cents per month for overhead. A committee concluded that since "great numbers of that class of the community for whose special benefit the system of Exchange of Labor was originally designed, are, owing to their depressed condition in society, unable to avail themselves of its benefits," they recommended that the back room remain reserved for barter while the store front should sell artisanal products on commission for cash, with prices set by members.[67] Customers were entitled to make cash purchases in the store by similarly paying twenty-five cents per month. Customer-members could not vote, so it was never actually a consumer cooperative proper. PEA was so successful that they expanded into two other stores in Philadelphia. Following its lead, that city became a center of cooperative activism in the early 1830s, when the trade unions began organizing industrial and artisanal cooperative warehouses in a number of trades. PEA's later history is not known, but it probably met the fate of the other Philadelphia cooperatives in the depression of 1837.[68]

According to historian Frances E. Parker, another store doing "distributive cooperation" was opened in New York City in 1829, "one of the organizers being the former secretary of an association in Brighton, England."[69] Brighton was an Owenite cooperative center in this period, and the organizer was surely William Bryan, who immigrated to America at that time.[70] The New York store (whose name the historian does not provide) had a membership that "never exceeded 40 and gradually 'faded out.'" No further information about this cooperative is available.[71]

NEW ENGLAND ASSOCIATION

The early 1830s saw the first great rise of unions in the United States. Labor organizations were transforming themselves from benefit societies into trade unions. Runaway paper-money inflation caused workers' wages to lag behind prices and cost of living, and employers hit them with wage cuts and layoffs. They formed trade unions to fight back; many struck and lost, then turned to worker cooperatives.[72]

American wage earners' experience had long taught them that small strikes were not getting them the larger things they wanted, even when they won. Offensive strikes, waged when the bosses needed workers (often when the economy was on an upswing), sometimes did win small concessions on wages or working conditions. But their gains were usually soon whittled away by inflation and employers' strategies such as speedup. As soon as recession hit, employers shoved layoffs and wage cuts down workers' throats.[73] Defensive strikes in response to these aggressions almost invariably lost.[74] The bosses simply didn't need the strikers any more; unemployment created a large labor pool so workers had to compete furiously to survive and bosses could call all the shots. It was during and after these defensive strikes that wage earners first formed cooperatives. Many soon realized that this was a bit late and unions later formed cooperatives in expectation of hard times.[75] The cooperatives took in unemployed union members. Less unemployment meant less competition in the labor market and therefore could mean higher wages. Thus the formation of cooperatives became part of a larger labor strategy—both a tactic and a vision.[76]

Two successive organizations led the movement in this period, the New England Association of Farmers, Mechanics and Other Workingmen (NEAFMOW), followed by the National Trades' Union (NTU).[77] Some of the same leaders played important roles in both organizations. NEAFMOW was active between 1831 and 1834, holding annual conventions, attended by delegates from five New England states to set their agenda for each year's work. NEAFMOW was a broad organization, and carried out both economic actions and electoral campaigns.[78] The National Trades' Union rose as NEAFMOW faded, and organized conventions in the following years. Unlike NEAFMOW, the NTU was limited to trade unionists, and stayed out of electoral politics.[79]

NEAFMOW arose from the struggle for a shorter work-week.[80] The ten-hour day was becoming the central issue for workers up and down the coast, and the Working Men's Party was also involved in this campaign.[81] Skilled workers in Boston went on strike for it in both 1825 and 1830 without success, and the mechanics and machinists in Providence, Rhode Island, resolved to work only ten hours in 1831.[82] Shortly after that, a group of delegates from different parts of New England met in Providence, and founded NEAF-MOW to agitate on a larger scale for the shorter work week and improved working conditions.[83] Historian John R. Commons called NEAFMOW "the most important New England Labour movement of this period... a new type of labour organization, in part economic and in part political."[84] NEAFMOW took as its mission to organize all working people into one big union, thus foreshadowing the Knights of Labor. The membership included farmers, mechanics (skilled workers), urban workers, master workmen, and factory workers. Its constitution pledged, "Each and every person that shall sign this constitution, except practical farmers, shall... stand pledged on his honor, to labor no more than ten hours for one day, unless on the condition of receiving extra compensation."[85] NEAFMOW members resolved to lobby the state governments to legislate the ten-hour day at the same time, as work hours had never been legislated. They set up a fund to give financial help to members who lost their jobs after refusing to work more than ten hours. The conference also discussed "cooperative trading," and "some 40 cooperatives were reported to have been started as a result of the interest thus stimulated."[86] These were surely cooperative warehouses and stores marketing artisanal products, and probably included agricultural produce. John Kaulback, a NEAFMOW member in Boston, went on to organize America's first widespread cooperative store movement, the Protective Unions.

NEAFMOW was the first worker organization to actively organize factory workers, but with limited success. Industrialists had been setting up factories and mills in towns outside the main urban centers, and these were quickly taking over New England's economy. Factory workers were drawn primarily from the rural population, and often included women and children. Carpenter Seth Luther was America's first anti–child labor crusader, and traveled throughout the region for NEAFMOW, delivering an address that called for action to rectify the many social evils of the system.[87] The first strikes of factory workers in America took place in 1828 in textile mills in Paterson, New Jersey, and in Dover, New Hampshire.[88] In Paterson, the workers were mostly children, and the state militia was called out to put them down. In Dover, they were mostly women and girls, and 400 of them paraded in protest through the town.[89]

NEAFMOW's ten-hour movement hit a wall in the Boston shipyards in the summer of 1832, when journeymen ship carpenters and caulkers were met with a lockout by the merchant shippers and shipowners. After a bitter struggle in the midst of a heat wave and a cholera epidemic, the strike was broken.[90]

After this defeat, NEAFMOW backed off from the pledge of members to work no more than ten hours, and turned to political lobbying and electoral politics. Among its demands were legislation to regulate factory abuses (particularly child and women's labor), to dismantle bank monopolies, and to establish free public education.[91]

Many leaders of the organization were also union leaders in various trades. At the time that NEAFMOW was most active, unions in most of the Eastern cities were organizing themselves into citywide federations. The first trades' union federations were organized in New York, Philadelphia, and Baltimore. Boston followed suit, with NEAFMOW activists in the leadership, and founded the Boston Trades' Union in March, 1834.[92] Charles Douglas, former president of NEAFMOW, called the meeting to order. Seth Luther was elected secretary. One of the first acts of the new Boston organization was choosing delegates to send to the founding convention of the National Trades' Union, which was to be held in August of that year.[93]

NEAFMOW scheduled its annual convention for that September. It was coordinated with the nominating convention of the Massachusetts Working Men's Party for the 1834 election, in which many of them were also active. The NEAFMOW convention transformed itself into the state chapter of the political party, nominated candidates for state offices, and conducted a third-party election campaign. However in the election most of the working population voted for Andrew Jackson's Democrats. That turned out to be the last NEAFMOW convention. Unable to improve the conditions of the working population through this form of a regional umbrella organization, the leadership split off into other directions.[94]

NATIONAL TRADES' UNION

Before 1830, most trade organizations were benefit societies, primarily organized to insure members against times of sickness and death. In the 1830s, most of these organizations became trade unions. Typical of this transformation was the Philadelphia Typographical Association. Organized in 1802 as a benevolent society, it became a union in 1833 with the "primary and paramount intention... [of] the determination and support of adequate wages for journeymen printers."[95]

In the early 1830s, unions first began coming together into citywide federations or "trades' unions," the first organizations of American wage earners to cut across trade lines and look to the interests of wage earners as a class.[96] In 1834, the General Trades' Union of New York invited all the trades' unions to send representatives to a convention, where they joined into America's first national labor organization, the National Trades' Union (NTU). The first convention, chaired by Ely Moore, president of the New York Union, had representatives from Philadelphia, Boston, Brooklyn, Poughkeepsie, and Newark. Later conventions included Baltimore, Pittsburg, Reading, Washington, Cincinnati, and Albany.[97]

The NTU looked beyond simple trade union concerns. It aimed at raising its members from wage slavery entirely, and abolishing that form of bondage in a new cooperative economic system.[98]

In 1834, the Pennsylvania Society of Journeymen Cabinet Makers opened a cooperative warehouse in Philadelphia; it was one of the largest furniture stores in the city by 1836.[99] Much of the Philadelphia trade union movement soon swung to cooperation: the hand loom weavers opened five cooperative shops in 1836, followed by the tailors, hatters and saddlers. The shoemakers of that city opened a cooperative store early that same year, and after five months had to move to larger quarters. In 1836 shoemakers' unions opened cooperatives in New Brunswick, Cincinnati, St. Louis, and Louisville; in the last three cities, tailors' unions followed suit. Painters' unions in New York City and Brooklyn lost strikes in 1837 and formed cooperatives in response.[100]

The third annual convention of the NTU in Philadelphia in 1836, with Alexander Jackson of Baltimore as president, set up a committee to enquire "into the sources of the great system of speculation (through which) they who produce nothing receive nearly all the products of the labour of those that produce, while they who produce all receive but a mite of their own labour." The committee concluded that the heart of the problem lay in "a fluctuating currency," in which speculation is encouraged by "the division of... employers and journeymen," and proposed that a system of cooperation could restore to each worker "the disposal of his own products."[101] They set up a special committee on cooperation, which recommended that all unions investigate setting up cooperatives, because "until a system of Cooperation is adopted by which the producers of wealth may also be its possessors... the great burden of the evils of which we so justly complain, will never be removed."[102]

Later in 1836, the Philadelphia Trades' Union adopted a resolution "to place in the Constitution a clause allowing the funds of the Union to be loaned to the Societies [individual unions] for the purpose of Cooperation."[103] Its official newspaper urged each local union to start a fund through regular member contributions to raise capital to begin a cooperative of its members. At the same time, it asked each local to contribute ten cents monthly to the Trades' Union fund to help start cooperatives.[104] A conference of nearly 200 union delegates in 1837 resolved that each union work out an estimate for setting up a cooperative to support ten members. But in the middle of this conference, the capitalist financiers panicked, beginning a new depression that temporarily wiped out not only the cooperatives but almost the entire union movement. The boom of 1834-37 had been initiated when President Jackson moved all government deposits from the United States Bank to eighty-eight state banks. These banks issued large volumes of paper money, setting off aggressive economic growth, unbridled speculation and rampant inflation. The bubble burst in late 1836 when Jackson ordered land agents selling former Indian territories (spoils of his "Indian removal") to accept cash only. An instant devaluation of paper money followed, touching off a run on the banks for hard money that they didn't possess. The depressed state that followed in the East continued, with a slight relief from the gold rush following California's seizure from Mexico, until 1862 when the Civil War was well under way.[105]

The experience of 1837 shows that while hardening times can cause a cooperative movement to blossom, the hardest of times can destroy it, at least in its more visible forms. In the depths of the depression, cooperatives could no longer pay their rent to landlords and were forced to close shop. It did not mean the end of the cooperative movement, however. Hardship merely forced it to flower on a different level, going underground during the hardest years as happened time and again in the years to follow. Then as now, neighbor cooperation, barter, labor exchange, and mutual survival aid of every sort grew in every community. When times became ripe again, the movement resurfaced.

WORKERS' PARTIES

Cooperatives played an important role in the periodic emergence of "third" parties in America throughout the 19th century. Worker and farmer cooperators became intermittently politically active over issues affecting their ability to solve their economic problems through their cooperative movements. When the dominant political parties proved unwilling to support legislation promoting economic cooperation among the working population, workers turned to new and independent parties. When farmer organizations and unions found their cooperatives wrecked by economic machinations, time and again their response was to transform their cooperative organizations into bases for political uprisings. They formed independent "third" parties pledged to reform the economic system so that it would promote cooperation and social justice rather than advance individual and corporate accumulation.

Wage earners first organized their own independent parties in cities and towns in the East during the intense depression years between 1828-30.[106] These parties came out of the ten-hour movement, and met with some electoral success. They were municipal and county organizations, and had programs centered on overturning legislation that facilitated economic inequities, particularly those arising from the introduction of machinery. They looked to the interests of a coalition of artisans, mechanics, laborers, farmers, and factory operatives. These local parties were common in seven states from New York to Ohio, and from Vermont to Delaware.[107]

The first Working Men's Party was organized in Philadelphia in 1928 by a convention called by the city Mechanics Union, a central mutual aid organization of trade societies. In its first election, twenty-one of the candidates endorsed by the party (all also on the Jackson ticket) won local offices. Inspired by this success, a series of meetings of New York City "mechanics and others" in 1829 resulted in the creation of the New York Working Men's Party. The next year their first candidate, a carpenter, was elected assemblyman.[108]

At least fourteen municipalities in upstate New York also organized parties, and their local tickets swept the elections in Albany, Syracuse, Troy, and Canandaigua in the spring of 1830. Later that year, the New York parties held a statewide convention and nominated candidates for the fall gubernatorial election. A Working Men's slate won the 1830 election in Newark, New Jersey. In New London, Connecticut, a "mechanics and workingmen" slate elected three state legislators in 1830, and their candidates swept the local offices the next year. Members of NEAFMOW formed the Boston Working Men's Party; another followed in Plymouth, and in most Massachusetts counties. Parties were formed in Burlington, Middlebury, and Woodstock, Vermont. Eight Pennsylvania towns had workers' parties, including Pittsburgh, Harrisburg, and Erie. In Wilmington, Delaware, the workingmen's slate won thirteen offices. Parties ran slates in Canton and Zanesville, Ohio.[109]

Josiah Warren, the mutualist organizer of the Time Store, was active in the Philadelphia party. The New York party was deeply influenced by George Henry Evans and Thomas Skidmore, both advocating political action to solve working people's problems. Evans published the *Working Man's Advocate*, a New York newspaper, in which he advocated the abolition of wage and chattel slavery, equal rights for women, and free homesteads.[110] Skidmore, a machinist, called for a new constitutional convention[111] in his *The Rights of Man to Property!* (1829) to consider a decree that all property belonged to the nation, and to both abolish inheritance and cancel all debts. The state would assign each citizen a fair and equal share of property upon maturity.[112] The New York party split between supporters of Skidmore's equalitarianism, and Evans' free land and Abolitionism.[113] Frances Wright and Robert Dale Owen (Robert Owen's son), both former communalists, were among the leaders of the Evans group, and raised the first call for free public education which did not exist at that time. On this, they pinned their hopes for social change.[114]

Each municipal party had its own variation of program and demands. In general, they called for a system of free public education; a mechanics lien law; an end to the compulsory militia system and convict labor; abolition of imprisonment for debt; dismantling of chartered monopolies, including banking monopolies; fairer taxation; the elimination of property qualifications for holding office, and other proposals for more democratic government.[115] Most of these demands were adopted by the Democratic Party.[116]

These early workers' parties disappeared inside the Democratic Party in the next few years, swept into the upsurge of urban
workers and Western small farmers behind Andrew Jackson, "the
foe of monopoly."[117] During Jackson's presidency (1829-37), their
voice was instrumental in winning the removal of most of the property restrictions for voting and outlawing indentured servitude. But
the problems of wage earners and small farmers remained as harsh
as before. Southern planters continued to control the federal government. Only white males could vote, and Jackson was no friend to
African-Americans or Indians.[118]

The experience of these first workers' parties began a pattern
that would recur for independent parties in the United States: upon
their first success after their grassroots beginnings, professional politicians would enter with the promise of short-term gains and entangle
them with one of the "major" parties. The developing "two- party
system" was geared to make it very difficult for independent parties
to get far off the ground.[119]

When these workers' parties broke up in the wake of Jackson's
election, the only labor movement remaining in America was made
up of isolated trade societies in the various cities.

TEN-HOUR MOVEMENT

In 1835, the ten-hour day was won in Philadelphia when
seventeen trade associations went on strike for it, paralyzing the
city.[120] Even municipal employees were given a ten-hour day. Similar successful strikes quickly followed in Paterson, Hartford, New
Brunswick, Salem, Seneca Falls, and Batavia. Ten-hour days were
then granted in other cities without the need of a strike, including
Newark, Wilmington, Albany, Troy, and Schenectady. The ten-hour
day became standard in the skilled trades in the Middle Atlantic
States.[121] However, in New England, where seasons were more extreme, the sun-to-sun system persisted.[122]

The movement for a shorter workday was revived in the early
1860s by the Eight-Hour Leagues, and became a central demand in
the following decades.

3.
The Movements Renewed & the Corporations' Rise 1840-60

By the mid 1800s, economic independence became increasingly difficult to achieve for ever-growing numbers of workers. Technological advances in machinery made many skills obsolete, creating unskilled laborers out of formerly skilled workers. These new machines, and the expense of buying and maintaining them, moved ownership of the means of production out of reach for most "free" workers, and drove them under the domination of the machine owners. With complex machines came the necessity of worker coordination on an ever-larger scale. But the capitalist system decreed that this coordination would take place under the centralized autocratic control of a boss, single or corporate. The work process was being rationalized with crude efficiency, and with little thought to the cost in human life.[1]

One of the most significant developments of the 19th century was the widespread emergence of the modern corporation as a business entity. After the US won independence, the state legislatures took over the right to charter most corporations. In the early years, the states did so sparingly and selectively, with strict but gradually loosened regulations.[2] The states chartered numerous banks. The US Congress could also charter corporations for certain purposes. Congress chartered the First Bank of the United States (1791-1811) and the Second Bank (1816-36) as private corporations.[3]

As transportation and commerce expanded over an ever-widening area, so did the financial power of bankers. Around 1800, large merchants financed by investors and banks began to insert themselves on both sides of small manufacturers, in the supply of raw materials and in the marketing of products. By 1830, these merchant capitalists had gained control of numerous local economies, and drastically cut the profit margins of small producers. This resulted in increased competition among enterprises; masters and bosses pushed the burden down to the workers. The elimination of small enterprises by the creation of ever-larger ones became a dominant trend.[4]

Merchant capitalists became the first organizers and owners of the American factory system.[5] Progress was slow until 1815, when the invention of the power loom transformed the textile industry. Between 1820 and 1860, the Industrial Revolution transformed American society. The textile factories began to dominate the industry, first in Massachusetts, then around Narragansett Bay, upper New York, Paterson, and Philadelphia. They drew their labor from farm families and immigrants, particularly women and children.[6] A regional system developed whereby New England factories and mills, powered by rapid rivers and wage labor, processed cotton from the South, powered by the cotton gin and slavery. As steam engines replaced water power, factories and the wage system spread across the country. The introduction of mechanization into the shoe industry began in 1840.[7] The iron industry was transformed in the same period by new techniques in blast furnaces, refining, and foundries.[8]

In the early 1840s, politicians were heavily promoting the idea of Manifest Destiny to justify the scheme of expanding to the Pacific coast. Manifest Destiny embraced the notion that God had given the US a unique civilizing mission, a concept dating back to the Puritans and Massachusetts Governor John Winthrop's "City upon a Hill" sermon which declared that the Puritans had a pact with God to create a holy community in the New World. Now this was being used as a pretext for provoking a war to annex Texas and the West (the northern third of Mexico), plus the British territory of Oregon.[9]

Before 1860, individual ownership and partnerships were still the most common forms of business, but corporations began to dominate in areas of the economy that required increasingly larger capital outlays, particularly textiles, iron, coal, and railroads.[10] Besides providing companies more capital without really forcing them to relinquish control, incorporation provided limited liability and many tax benefits.[11]

Larger employers increasingly incorporated, using the advantages that this brought and floating faceless pieces of paper between themselves and the factories and mines. Business control over politics and government went hand in hand with increased power, and the employers and financiers themselves wrote the laws making these advantages possible. Meanwhile, they heated things up down at the factory with the newly instituted assembly line. Workers were at a tremendous disadvantage against this yoked team of business and political interests.[12]

Unions grew fast in the years following 1842, after a judicial decision finally declared they had a right to exist at all.[13] The war with Mexico began in 1846, and the South was stunned with a wave of slave insurrections soon after. Northern industrial wage earners were hit with the depression of 1847, bringing a new wave of lay-offs and wage cuts. The workers answered with strikes, and when these failed, the unions turned once again to worker cooperatives as part of their larger strategy.[14] The union worker cooperative movement and the concomitant Associationist communitarian movement of the 1840s were both spurred by Horace Greeley's *New York Tribune*.[15] In this period, unions responded to the industrial and corporate revolutions with the idea that a group of cooperating workers, pooling their resources to buy machinery, combining their skills to become an efficient team themselves, and using the advantages of incorporation, might be able to avoid having to sell themselves into wage slavery. The cooperative movement attempted to establish a permanent structural foothold in the economic system through incorporation.

These movements collapsed when the war with Mexico (1846-48) resulted in the annexation of the West in 1848 and that expansion released much of the social pressure in the East. As the entire country sank back into severe depression in the mid-1850s, the hopes of the cooperators were dashed as many cooperatives failed. The Civil War delivered the final blow.[16]

ASSOCIATIONIST COOPERATIVES

The iron molders of Cincinnati struck in 1847. Their strike, like the recent slave insurrections in the South, eventually lost.[17] But wage earners were "free," and part of the striking group chose not to sulk back at lower pay but instead stalked off to organize their own cooperative foundry. They met with immediate success.[18] A group of Pittsburgh foundry workers, inspired by this Cincinnati cooperative, followed their example later in the year.[19]

By 1849, unions as a whole began forming cooperatives again on an unprecedented scale, beginning with iron molder locals in West

Virginia, Ohio and several parts of Pennsylvania.[20] The Boston tailors soon followed.[21] The next year the tailors' union of Buffalo, New York formed a cooperative for eighty of their members in the wake of a losing strike. In New York City, unions organized cooperatives of barrel-makers, hat-finishers, shade-painters, cabinetmakers, and tailors. In Pittsburgh, they formed cooperatives of glassblowers, silver-platers, puddlers and boilers, and iron molders.[22] Many of these grew out of unsuccessful strikes. In Buffalo, the seamstresses union formed a cooperative, as did the seamstresses of Philadelphia and Providence. Women were now expressing their power in the workforce, and faced questions of how to best organize themselves and their resources, questions similar to those men faced as wage workers.[23]

Albert Brisbane and Horace Greeley, at the core of a group centered on the *New York Tribune,* realized that cooperatives had great potential as agencies for social change, and advocated that workers, particularly strikers, form them.[24] Greeley came up with an "Associationist" formula for their organization that he thought would meet all the needs of the movement, both the worker cooperatives and the related movement of cooperative communities. The cooperatives could variously be either ends in themselves, cell-units in larger industrial organisms, or steps toward gathering resources to eventually form *phalanxes,* the Associationist term for cooperative communities.[25] The *Tribune* did not start or invent the movement of the late 1840s, but gave great aid in publicizing its successes, and Greeley himself reorganized the *Tribune* on a profit-sharing basis.[26]

From an impoverished childhood in a New Hampshire village, Horace Greeley had risen by his own efforts to become a newspaper editor-publisher. Inspired by the transcendentalists, he worked for the rest of his life for "universal justice," which to him included worker cooperation and communalism.[27]

The Greeley formula was essentially the same for both worker cooperatives and phalanxes. It was a profit-sharing system, oriented toward capitalist conditions, with an initial goal of gathering enough resources to get started. They would incorporate and float stock that anyone could buy, not just worker-members. Each stockholder got only one vote, no matter how much stock he or she owned. Cooperatives would pay workers normal market wages or, preferably, a living wage. Over that wage, investor-members would be paid low interest and dividends. The rest of any surplus income would be divided among the worker-members.[28]

The Greeley formula boiled down to an effort to structure the movement to fit inside capital corporate law. Until this time, worker cooperatives had been predominantly unincorporated associations of individual producers. Numerous variations on the Greeley tactic would follow in the hope that some new structural innovation could trump a rigged economic system.[29]

With the coordination of the work-process around machinery in the 1840s, the group as a whole became the predominant entity, and the incorporated cooperative was inevitable under capitalist law. A cooperative, of course, needs a legal structure in order to do business; beginning in that era, many variations (determined by state law) were tried over the following years, with the incorporated cooperative proving itself practical and sophisticated. Besides the usual corporate advantages of capital-gathering and limited liability, the cooperative corporation was a legal way to separate ownership of the cooperative means of production from changing membership.[30]

But the standard corporate structure also brought great disadvantages. It opened the door to non-worker shareowners having a say in management. Most startup cooperatives put tremendous amounts of labor into their shops; this labor accumulated as capital owned as much by the outside investors as by the workers. Being counted too much in dollars and cents stifled the cooperative spirit. This capitalist foothold inside the cooperatives was wedged further open when some groups hired nonmembers as extra help, and paid them at lower wages than they paid themselves. The standard corporate structure was eventually superceded by cooperatives slowly developing their own unique legal frameworks.[31]

At the same time, native-born Americans found themselves competing for factory jobs with the massive influx of new, mostly unskilled, very poor immigrants, predominantly from Germany and France in the wake of 1848's failed revolutions, and from Ireland as the potato famine deepened. Hungarians and Italians soon followed.[32] The population exploded with each new wave of immigration, doubling nearly every twenty years after the American Revolution, at which time it was only about two and a half million. It reached up to twenty-three million in 1850.[33] While real tensions existed over immigration and jobs, these new immigrants contributed greatly to the growth of the cooperative movement. A major demand of the failed French revolution had been large-scale worker cooperatives—

"social workshops"—to be financed by the state.[34] Strong worker cooperative movements among all these new Americans, particularly those from Germany, centered on New York City.[35]

The German immigrants soon had functioning cooperatives in seven American cities. In New York, they attempted to organize a large-scale labor-exchange and barter system around a "bank of exchange," aimed primarily at serving individual producers.[36] But capitalist industrialization had made individual production obsolete in most industries. Experience soon proved that exchange and distribution cooperation would not suffice to keep city artisanal workers self-employed, and most were forced into the factories. The bank of exchange never got off the ground, despite the efforts of Wilhelm Weitling, who had been a leader of the revolutionary workers in Germany alongside Karl Marx.[37] Weitling and some of his comrades formed a communal group, raised financing in part from a German-American labor association, and took off to Iowa, where they started a cooperative community called Communia in 1851.[38]

Many of the worker cooperatives started in the late 1840s and early 1850s lasted only a few years. Besides scarcely having the resources to get off the ground, they met with cut-throat capitalist competition. Businessmen's associations did everything they could to wreck them. They were attacked in legislatures and churches. Some states, including Massachusetts and Pennsylvania, refused to charter them.[39] As one legislator said, "It will not do to encourage the journeymen in such movements; it would ruin the employers."[40] Many Protestant ministers and Catholic priests attacked them openly and aggressively. A common accusation reported in the newspapers was that they were "the first step to Socialism."[41] This was true to the extent that many workers saw cooperatives as a vehicle to transform society, yet many others sought only to improve their lives and had little interest in social reform.[42]

The attack was not confined to worker cooperatives, but was also directed at the Associationist community movement, a more structured renewal of Owenite Socialist communalism. The Associationist community and cooperative movements were closely connected.[43]

MUTUAL CO-OPS

The first "building and loan association" on record in America was opened in Philadelphia in 1831.[44] Building and loan associations were originally clubs formed to facilitate home building, usually by urban workers. They were independent, and not connected with any other organization. Each member would make a monthly payment into a fund that financed construction of the houses, which they built one at a time. The association would hold each mortgage until it was paid off. When all the houses were built, the organization dissolved. These early associations, temporary in intent though occasionally ongoing, were basically small mutual savings banks. Widespread in the 1850s in response to exorbitant rents, their slogan was, "Do your own land lording."[45] Though the Civil War wiped them out along with almost every cooperative in the US, they came back in the postwar period, and were common again in the last decades of the 19th century.[46]

Mutual insurance cooperatives spread quickly among farmers during this period. By 1860, there were over one hundred farmers' mutual fire insurance companies from Maine to Missouri. The first mutual life insurance company was founded in New York in 1843.[47]

PROTECTIVE UNIONS

Between 1845 and 1860, the first organized major American consumer cooperative movement rose and fell in the Northeast.[48] Its members were primarily working people. In the consumer cooperative, as distinct from the worker cooperative, the customers are the voting members who band together to acquire consumer goods directly from producers and eliminate the profits of middlemen. The workers in the cooperative may or may not be members.

John Kaulback, a journeyman tailor and member of the Boston chapter of the New England Association of Mechanics and Workingmen, started a group buying-club of groceries and sundries in 1840 in an attempt to get more people involved in his union.[49] The union was a successor to NEAFMOW, which had organized "cooperative trading" in the early 1830s. In 1845, Kaulback's buying club began meeting weekly at a "dividing store" to distribute the products and produce. Its first purchase was "a box of soap and one-half box of tea" on which the members saved 25 percent by cutting out the middleman.[50] This became America's first successful cooperative store movement. They called it the Working Men's Protective Union (PU).[51]

Albert Wright, who later became Massachusetts State Printer, served as the original PU secretary. Wright wrote its constitution and is given credit for shaping its structure and mission. Kaulback became purchasing agent, working on a small commission based on purchases.[52] The PU began in 1845 during a time of fast-rising prices, but in 1847 the entire economy slipped badly. The PU bought wholesale and passed on products and produce to members at near cost. Members paid an initiation fee and small monthly dues. Three-fifths of this was to be "invested in fuel and groceries, or such other objects."[53] The PU's program was to bring about "the elevation of the laboring classes" through "cooperation, mercantile and fraternal."[54] Its general fund was to be "devoted to the use of sick members," and PU's members formed "visiting committees" to care for them.[55] Local divisions were autonomous, but purchases were expected to be made through the Central Division purchasing agent. Most of the PU's principles were similar to those of the British Rochdale store movement, which developed separately at about the same time (the first Rochdale store was organized in England only months before the first Protective Union).[56] PU stores were at first open only to members, but later opened to the whole community. They sold stock and paid small dividends, but no matter how many shares owned, each member had only one vote in electing the board that managed each store. Stores were locally controlled but federated for wholesale buying and other mutual-aid. Unlike in Rochdale, they sold at near cost instead of giving rebates, and originally sold only to members. Many PUs set up production and service cooperatives for their members. The New York PU, for example, ran a smithy, a wheelwright shop, and a bakery. They had many aspects of a fraternal society.

There were over 3,000 members of Protective Unions in 1847, and 403 divisions in New England, New York, Michigan, Illinois, Wisconsin, and Canada by 1852; five years later, there was almost twice that number. In 1849, the central organization modified its name to the New England Protective Union.[57] The PU was able to grow so large so fast because the practical strategy of group buying to save the expenses of middlemen had great appeal in the situation: workers had not been successful in raising wages to an adequate level, particularly in New England, where many women were employed in factories.[58]

But a schism developed in the organization in 1853 over the commissions that Kaulback was receiving from his job as purchasing agent and chairman of the Board of Trade. Albert Wright and many people involved with local stores stood on one side; on the other side was the Central Division, consisting mainly of Kaulback and his supporters. The locals wanted prices set by the formula cost-plus-expenses, with no profit; Central wanted to change to a fixed profit percentage with dividends to shareholders. The locals wanted the stores to offer credit; Central wanted cash only. The locals wanted to restrict sales to members; Central wanted to sell to anyone. The locals wanted decentralization; Central wanted organizational hierarchy.[59]

Forced to resign, Kaulback took many of his supporters with him, and started a new rival organization, the American Protective Union (APU), which also grew strong quickly, and by 1857 had 350 units in 10 states. The APU in its centralized structure served as an early prototype of the chain store system.[60]

But the financiers panicked again in 1857. As the economy plunged, their capitalist competitors hit both rival Protective Unions with ferocious attacks in many areas at once. They used every weapon in their arsenal: price wars, blacklisting by merchants, employers, and suppliers, etc.[61] Soon neither of the PUs was able to meet members' needs, and the membership simply could not afford to support them. By 1860, the Central Divisions of both rival PUs were gone, but many local groups survived and continued independently. The Civil War devastated most of these locals, though a few hung on and one observer in 1886 was able to unearth four still-functioning PU stores.[62]

The Protective Union's policy of passing on savings directly to consumers by selling at close to cost invoked the greatest wrath of the capitalist merchants. This policy shook up and threatened the market, which the businessmen would not long permit. They saw it in their long-run advantage to hit the PU with unlimited price wars. As soon as they had broken the PU in a locale and gotten it out of the way, the merchants were free to raise their prices again.[63]

Almost every element of modern consumer cooperatives, defined as collectively owned organizations which provide consumer goods, can be found in the early Protective Unions. The American consumer cooperative movement was not imported from England, as is often implied, but was native.[64]

With the coming of the Protective Unions, cooperatives in America took two distinct forms. One, typical of worker cooperatives (industrial production), had all or almost all members working in the cooperative; the other, typical of consumer cooperatives (purchasing and service), had only a small number actually working in the cooperative out of a much larger membership. In the worker cooperative, the workers were their own bosses. In the consumer cooperative, the membership usually elected a board that hired managers who in turn hired and fired workers almost as in a capitalist enterprise. The worker, by this twist, again became a hired laborer.[65]

ROCHDALE PIONEERS

The Rochdale movement was founded in England in 1844 by a group of flannel-weavers who had struck and lost. Their aim was similar to the British Owenite cooperative movement of the 1830s. Indeed, people from this same community of weavers had formed a cooperative back in 1830, but it failed after having overextended credit to members.[66] The English cooperative movement of the 1830s was inspired by Robert Owen, but was really more the work of Dr. William King (1786–1865) who made Owen's ideas workable and practical. Most of these cooperative stores were primarily outlets for members' artisanal products and farm produce, dividing surplus income among member-workers according to the amount of their labor. After several years of mixed success, the movement ran its course and many cooperatives failed.

A decade later and somewhat wiser, the Rochdale weavers gave it another shot. Besides their original store, the Rochdale Society of Equitable Pioneers planned common housing, production cooperatives, common land for collective agriculture, and "as soon as practicable this Society shall proceed to arrange the powers of production, distribution, education and government; or in other words, to establish a self-supporting Home colony of united interests or assist other Societies in establishing such colonies."[67] They admitted women on the same terms as men, beginning with Ann Tweedale, one of the twenty-eight original founders.

The early Rochdale movement and George Holyoake—one of the Pioneers and its historian—became involved with the Christian Socialist movement, which saw social change through an alliance between "self-governing workshops" (worker production cooperatives) and cooperative stores. The worker cooperatives gave the stores sources of supply, and together they formed the incipient structure of a cooperative commonwealth. But many of the early worker cooperatives failed.

Meanwhile, the Rochdale co-op store flourished and became the replicating prototype of an expansive system of stores, a social movement focused primarily on distribution and consumption. The stores were consumer-member owned and run managerially. Workers were hired as employees and were not necessarily members.[68]

Charles Howarth originally proposed and devised the key concept of patronage rebate. The rebate, paid annually to members as a percentage of their purchases, intended to solve the central question of how to keep a social enterprise alive in a market society. In order to avoid destructive price wars, the cooperative would sell to the general community at about market prices and give members periodic rebates and special discounts. Through the means of the patronage rebate, surplus income (profit) would be divided periodically among member-consumers. The patronage rebate was the only really original contribution of Rochdale, but an important one.[69]

In 1854, the group organized the adjunct Co-operative Manufacturing Society, and their first production operation, a calico manufacturing mill. They soon decided that they needed to expand the mill, raising capital from outside shareholders. Outsiders as well as workers could own shares in the mill. Little by little, workers were eliminated from positions of power, and the mill had become a typical capitalist venture by 1862.[70] The English consumer cooperative movement abandoned the idea of worker cooperatives, and went into cooperative production by buying manufacturing plants and running them with employees in the standard corporate way.

The success of the original Rochdale store led all the cooperative stores in England and Scotland to adopt its system.[71] In 1863, a group of these co-ops federated into the Co-operative Wholesale Society, which expanded rapidly and a decade later had 134,000 members.[72] They eventually owned mills, workshops, factories, and even steamship lines. Yet they held onto the idea of a cooperative commonwealth that, in their scenario, did not include worker self-management. The commonwealth was to come about by the co-op movement literally buying the entire industrial economy.[73]

Eventually most of the American consumer cooperative movement would turn to the Rochdale system.

UNION COOPERATIVE ASSOCIATION (UCA)

The true beginning of the Rochdale cooperative movement in America can be dated to the 1859 publication of the first American edition of George Jacob Holyoake's book *Self-Help by the People—The History of the Rochdale Pioneers* (1857), published by Horace Greeley, editor of the *New York Tribune.*[74]

A shoemaker, Thomas Phillips, and a group of his friends came together to organize the Union Cooperative Association of Philadelphia (UCA) in 1862, three months after Lincoln issued the Emancipation Proclamation. UCA was the first American co-op modeled on the Rochdale plan, and the founders took it directly from Holyoake's book.[75] After two years of planning, they opened their first store with twenty-three members during the Civil War in 1864, and met with early success. The co-op was promoted as more than a store: it was a community center, a new way to do business, based on "simple honesty... for we have no interest in deceiving or cheating our customers."[76] UCA had a room for socializing, and set aside a percentage of profits for a library. In their exuberance, UCA members assimilated two other cooperative stores that had opened autonomously in another part of the city, and started a third branch in 1866. Among the members of the UCA were John Samuel and John Shedden, both later prominent in the Knights of Labor, and William Sylvis, later to head the National Labor Union.[77] Phillips and Shedden later also became prominent members of the International Workingmen's Association and the Sovereigns of Industry.[78]

Phillips wrote a series of columns for a weekly national labor newspaper, *Fincher's Trades' Review*, explaining the Rochdale principles and the possibilities of cooperation. This met with an enthusiastic response around the country, and over thirty similar stores connected with unions were begun in twelve states, mostly in industrial towns. More than simply stores and community centers, they were also venues for union organizing.[79] By early 1866, there were similar cooperative grocery stores in Pennsylvania, New York, Massachusetts, Rhode Island, New Jersey, Maryland, Connecticut, Maine, Ohio, Illinois, Michigan, and Missouri. At its peak the following year, "the movement had extended until practically every important industrial town between Boston and San Francisco had some kind of distributive co-operation."[80] A scholar counted fifty-four stores in Massachusetts alone in these years.[81]

The Union Cooperative Association of Philadelphia's three expansion stores were in ill-chosen locations, and always fared poorly. UCA had incurred heavy expenses for its expansion, and although the flagship store continued to be successful, the organization fell deeply into debt.[82]

With the end of the Civil War in 1865, wartime scarcities

vanished, prices immediately fell, and goods at discounted prices became quickly available from many sources. This diminished the cost-saving incentive for shopping at the co-op stores. At the same time, a rash of failed strikes hurt the labor movement in many locations, and this too had a negative impact on the co-op stores. Under these changed conditions in the postwar period, many of these stores faded and died. But the same failed strikes that hurt many co-op stores produced a union movement of worker cooperatives in other places. Overextended by their branch stores, the Union Cooperative Association of Philadelphia collapsed in 1866.[83] Several UCA leaders, particularly William Sylvis, went on to become leaders in that worker cooperative movement.

Despite this stillbirth, the Rochdale system was destined to return and become the dominant form of consumer cooperative organization in America. Approximately a hundred cooperative stores opened during the 1860s, according to an estimate by John Samuel, later founder of the St. Louis Knights of Labor coal distribution and printing cooperatives, a longtime member of the KOL Co-operative Board, and author of its most important pamphlet on cooperation.[84]

Thomas Phillips went on to organize shoemaker cooperatives with the Knights of St. Crispin, and consumer cooperatives with the Sovereigns of Industry. He was the first shoemaker to join the Knights of Labor, was elected president of a KOL cooperative in 1876, and became president of the Boot and Shoe Workers' International Union in 1889.[85]

THE RECEDING FRONTIER

The continual westward movement of the frontier, with the concomitant vision of the West as a land of opportunity, is intimately connected to American history. Struggling Eastern workers could always dream of migrating West, where greater freedom, higher social status, and wealth seemed to await. During the first part of the century, Eastern workers railed at the government's giving away vast areas to speculators and profiteers. Use of the public domain lands became the issue of the century, deeply involving the question of the spread of slavery into new areas. The Homestead Act of 1862 appeared to open a Western utopia, but huge areas went to railroads and speculators, and the Eastern working population wound up feeling angry and cheated once more. Between its enactment and 1890, true homesteaders received only one fourth the acreage gifted to railroads.[86]

As John R. Commons wrote in his introduction to his classic study *History of Labour in the United States* (1918),

> The condition which seems to distinguish most clearly the history of labour in America from its history in other countries is the wide expanse of free land. As long as the poor and industrious can escape from the conditions which render them subject to other classes, so long do they refrain from that aggression on the property rights or political power of others, which is the symptom of a *labour movement*... America, under the constitution of 1787, started off with a... seizure of its western lands by speculators and slave owners. The masses of the people gradually awakened, then resisted, finally revolted, and a political struggle of half a century over the land laws ended in a Civil War, with its homestead act. The struggle was renewed when the railroad land grants of the Civil War brought back again in a new form the seizure by speculators... Free land was not a mere bounty of nature; it was won in the battle of labour against monopoly and slavery.[87]

ABOLITIONISM AND THE CIVIL WAR

The Abolitionist movement, based among wage earners, artisans, small farmers, and homemakers among the "free" population, and of course primarily based among the slaves, demanded immediate and uncompensated emancipation. It sought to change property relationships by overthrowing an oppressive ruling class. Many slave insurrections were organized throughout colonial times with the help of "free" blacks and whites. They began to set up open Emancipation Societies as early as 1775.[88] The earliest members and leaders included Paine and Franklin as well as Richard Allen and Absalom Jones. Societies had formed in eight states by 1792, but as slavery rose to enormous proportions in the early 19th century, they lost heart and disappeared for a couple of decades.[89]

During the entire first half of the century, the plantation owners and the Northern factory owners became locked in a death struggle over whether the vast Western lands should be slave or "free." The slavers needed the land because they had worn out much of the South with agricultural abuse; the factory owners needed the land to constantly dangle before workers as a possibility of escape, a safety valve to keep organized discontent down.[90] The stakes became higher and higher. Property-less workers piled up in the eastern cit-

ies in ever-greater numbers, becoming correspondingly angrier and
more insistent in their demands for decent conditions and control of
their own means of survival. Strikes and slave insurrection broke out
with increasing frequency.[91]

Organized Abolitionism surged forth again in the early 1830s,
stirred by the revolt in Virginia led by Nat Turner.[92] At first, the
Northern unions and the Abolitionists were divided over supporting each other's struggles. Some Abolitionists considered free labor's
struggle against wage slavery to be insignificant in the face of chattel
slavery; some unionists feared that emancipation would result in the
further deterioration of their situation by the increased competition
for jobs.[93] The two movements came together over the threat of the
spread of slavery into the new Western territories. Northern workers
looked to these territories for their own liberation, and experience
had shown that the slave system in an area created near-slave conditions for wage earners and small farmers. Large numbers of Northern workers came around to support the Abolitionist cause.[94]

A number of key leaders were active in the labor movement,
cooperatives, and Abolitionism, including Horace Greeley, Wendell
Phillips, and Frederick Douglass.[95] Phillips worked for "the movement for the eight-hour day, spoke and labored for a cooperative
system of production, and demanded heavy taxation of a profit
economy."[96] George Jacob Holyoake dedicated his classic *History
of Co-operation* (volume I, 1875) to Phillips, "whose intrepid elo-
quence has ever vindicated the claims of the slave, black or white,
in bondage to planter or capitalist."[97] Quartus Grave, a newspa-
perman in Utica, New York, active in the New England Association (NEAFMOW), published *The Co-Operator* in 1832 with articles
about six cooperatives in the area.[98] The paper developed into the
Standard and Democrat, and agitated for Abolitionism; in 1835, a mob
attacked the office and threw the type and furniture into the street.
Abolitionist front lines included many women during an era when
the women's rights movement was also gathering steam.[99] In 1848,
Elizabeth Cady Stanton and Lucretia Mott organized the first Wom-
en's Rights Convention; they were both also Abolitionist leaders.[100]
Abolitionism had become a true mass movement in the North and
West by 1850, with many newspapers and organizations involving
large numbers of people holding huge meetings and conventions.
Their meetings were attacked; their halls burnt down; their leaders and members jailed, beaten, murdered and vilified as "foreign

agents;" their papers harassed and denied use of the mail.

As the country hurtled into another depression, the Abolitionist movement surged to a climax. In 1860, President Buchanan vetoed an early version of the Homestead Act on the grounds that it was "not fair to previous settlers to give away free land, that the government had no constitutional power to do so," and the county couldn't afford it.[101] He called it "communistic."[102] Lincoln's election a few months later on the newly formed Republican Party, (financed by Northern industrialists but with grassroots support of all the "free-soil" and anti-slavery forces) meant that the slavers had lost control of the federal government for the first time since the country's founding.[103] They responded with secession. In 1861, hundreds of thousands of Northern workers and Western farmers poured voluntarily into the Union Army, forcing the union and cooperative movements to almost entirely disband because the workers were gone.[104] The Southern army had to fight with only one hand, as it had to use the other to keep its own workers off its throat. Southern Abolitionism centered in the mountains, where there had almost never been slaves, and the "hillbilly" communities became a haven for runaway slaves and draft resisters.[105]

Ironically, even as "free" workers and slaves struggled against the slavocracy, about 10,000 Asian workers, mostly Chinese, and about 3,000 Irish, slaved for Northern employers as contract laborers on the first transcontinental railroad to the West.[106]

4.
The Aftermath of the Civil War

In 1865, just days before his assassination, Lincoln wrote,

> I see in the near future a crisis approaching that unnerves me and causes me to tremble for the safety of my country... Corporations have been enthroned, an era of corruption in high places will follow, and the money power of the country will endeavor to prolong its reign by working upon the prejudices of the people until the wealth is aggregated in a few hands and the Republic is destroyed.[1]

The Union Army soldiers returned home thinking their side victorious, but numerous veterans found poverty and wage slavery waiting for them. Their response culminated in the Great Upheaval, the national uprising that began with the railroad strike of 1877.[2]

The outcome of the war also threw nearly four million impoverished freed blacks onto the labor market. A few found jobs; most remained destitute and unemployed. The interests who consolidated power as soon as a bullet disposed of Lincoln quickly shelved demands to break up the old plantations and distribute ten acres and a mule to each freed slave. The majority of blacks soon wound up as tenant farmers or sharecroppers in the countryside, almost serfs, and only slightly better off than before. In the cities, they became unemployed or wage slaves in menial jobs.[3]

Although the Homestead Act of 1862 threw open millions of acres for "free" workers, railroad grants ate up gigantic tracts of it. Speculators rushed in, reaping immense profits and winding up with most of the land in the end. Only one out of ten families who went to settle in the West ever actually wound up with a free homestead. This was the ultimate failure of Jeffersonian democracy.[4]

During the Civil War, cooperatives were a major topic of discussion in the labor press.[5] With the end of the war in 1865, worker cooperatives began to appear again in Northern industries in scattered locations and trades.[6] A few, such as the New England cod and mackerel fishery cooperatives, had never stopped operating.[7] Within a year, in 1866, recession hit. The union movement was recovering and reforming. The industrial sector of the labor force had grown almost as large as the agricultural, and would surpass it by 1870. There were over five and a half million wage earners, approaching half the workforce, with over two million in factories. Under the control of Northern capitalists, an all-enveloping national market quickly developed for the first time. This system broke up many regional economies, to the disadvantage of small individual producers, who could not compete with goods made in distant factories. Producers and consumers were separated ever further to the advantage of the middlemen. Small farmers had to ship their produce hundreds of miles to market at freight rates that were often higher than the prices their produce brought. Following nationalization of the market and nationalization of employers' associations, truly coast-to-coast unions sprang up in the various trades for the first time.[8]

As the country slid slowly toward the disastrous depression of 1873, punctuated by the first great wave of American armed interventions abroad, radical movements sprang up among wage earners and farmers, all intimately connected with cooperatives.

NATIONAL LABOR UNION

One of the largest national unions was the Iron Molders. With the leadership of William Sylvis, considered by many to be the first truly great labor leader in the United States, the Iron Molders set up a cooperative stove foundry in Troy, New York, in 1866. It was a fast success.[9] Soon after, the Cincinnati Molders became embroiled in a bitter nine-month strike that wound up a disaster. But the Cincinnati Molders picked themselves up and organized a cooperative foundry. At the urging of union president Sylvis, the entire national Molders union turned to worker cooperatives "for relief from the wages system."[10]

In the fall of 1866, representatives from local unions, city federations, Eight-Hour Leagues and national unions met in a labor congress in Baltimore, and formed the first American union federation on a coast-to-coast scale, the National Labor Union (NLU).

It was a loose federation, like its predecessor the National Trades' Union; it probably had 300,000 members at its peak.[11] The NLU fought for the eight-hour day, for land for settlers, for black and white labor solidarity, for the rights of women, for an end to contract and convict labor systems, and threw all of its weight behind the cooperative movement. To facilitate the movement, the founding congress endorsed cooperative workshops and stores, and called for the passage of cooperative incorporation acts in all the states.[12]

The NLU represented the aspirations of the returned Civil War veterans, and became a primary center of progressive organizing in the years following the war. With extraordinary energy and organizational success, the NLU mobilized the movement on a national scale with goals and membership extending far beyond anything previously conceived. The NLU expanded beyond the trade unions, and attempted to represent the broad extent of working people by including reform organizations of various stripes from anarchist to socialist and suffragist.[13] The war had spurred large numbers of women into the industrial workforce, and many of them stayed in its aftermath, forming Working Women's Protective Unions to agitate and negotiate in their interest. The NLU congress of 1868 broke the gender line by admitting Susan B. Anthony and two other women as Protective Union delegates.[14] Despite its radical agenda, the NLU operated openly and within legal parameters. That transparency was possible because the country was so exhausted by war; a progressive political window had opened. The newly triumphant capitalist powers did not move openly to shut down this national organization. However, employers attacked the NLU on the local and shop level to cut off the roots of union membership. Meanwhile the government, under pressure from business interests and banks, tightened the money system, resulting in the further impoverishment and weakening of the working population. The federal government had issued paper money, not backed by gold or silver, to finance the Civil War, creating "cheap" money. After the war the government began to retire the greenbacks, resulting in scarce money and severe unemployment.[15]

The first congress of the NLU resolved "that in cooperation we recognize a sure and lasting remedy for the abuses of the present industrial system, and hail with delight the organization of cooperative stores and workshops in this country, and would urge their promotion in every sector of the country and in every branch of business."[16]

The second congress elected Sylvis president, and called on all workers to form cooperatives "and drive the non-producers to honorable toil or starvation."[17] Sylvis claimed: "Single-handed we can accomplish nothing, but united there is no power of wrong that we cannot openly defy."[18] The NLU hoped that worker cooperatives would become labor's biggest weapon, a "substitute for strikes."[19] Strikes were not winning bread-and-butter demands, much less liberation. Sylvis wrote, "Of all the questions now before us, not one is of so great importance, or should command so large a portion of our consideration, as co-operation... Co-operation is the only true remedy for low wages, strikes, lock-outs, and a thousand other impositions and annoyances to which workingmen are subjected."[20] At Sylvis' urging, the NLU congress of 1867 passed a resolution petitioning the US Congress to appropriate $25 million to aid in establishing cooperatives, as well as the eight-hour workday and other of labor's demands.[21]

By the end of 1867, NLU newspapers filled with optimism. "Cooperation is taking hold upon the minds of our members," Sylvis said, "and in many places very little else is talked about."[22] Locals of bakers, coachmakers, shipwrights, printers, barrel-makers, mechanics, blacksmiths, hatters, carpenters and other trades formed cooperatives across the country. Many of these were after lockouts by their former bosses, the result of defensive strikes that failed. Sylvis' Iron Molders Union reported eleven cooperative foundries set up between 1866 and 1867, in Troy, Cleveland, Albany, Pittsburgh, Rochester, Chicago, Louisville, Quincy, and Somerset. Others were planned for Buffalo, Syracuse, Peekskill, and New York City.[23]

Most of the NLU cooperatives were organized under a profit-sharing system similar to the one Horace Greeley had devised two decades earlier, under which outsiders could buy stock and departing members retain theirs, although each member could have only one vote no matter how much stock was owned.[24]

TROY & PITTSBURGH FOUNDRIES

The Iron Molders of Troy, New York, one of the leading stove manufacturing centers in the country, were the first local to set up a cooperative in 1866. It quickly began operating at full capacity, with more orders than it could fill. Its fifty members received wages at the going rate plus a share of profits, estimated at $2 per day. After their first eighteen months, they had accumulated $65,000 in capital, including a $17,000 surplus to be divided.[25]

The success of the first foundries formed by locals led Sylvis to put forth a grander plan for a chain of foundries in major cities run by the international union. In 1867, the International Molders Union started a fund from 10 percent of the union's gross receipts; the plan was that when $5,000 accrued, it would be used to aid local cooperatives.[26] But when 150 Pittsburgh foundry workers became locked in a harsh strike, Sylvis took the initiative and prematurely used the fund to set up the first of the projected chain of foundries. The International Union put in $15,000, and the Pittsburgh Cooperative Foundry opened in May, 1868. Sylvis urged every molder to buy at least one $5 share, and almost 2,000 shares were sold. The president and treasurer of the international union were both directors along with those selected by the member-stockholders. No one could own more than 400 shares, and each member had one vote no matter how many or few shares owned. Eighty percent of all profit was distributed to workers in proportion to their wages; fifteen percent was distributed to shareholders, and five percent set aside as a sinking fund to reduce company debt.[27]

But the funds they raised were not enough. They badly needed operating funds, but sources had dried up. A creditor sued for payment, not enough could be raised and the Pittsburgh Cooperative Foundry went bankrupt after only two years.[28]

By that time, however, various local unions were operating fourteen cooperative foundries, and opened two more in 1871.[29]

TROY LAUNDRY WOMEN'S COOPERATIVE

In 1864, Kate Mullaney led 300 laundresses in Troy, New York to form the Collar Laundry Union (CLU), the first women's union in the US.[30] Shortly after organizing, the CLU struck fourteen businesses and won better wages and working conditions. The CLU joined William Sylvis' National Labor Union, and Mullaney was given the mission of coordinating a national organizing drive of working women. In 1869, the Troy collar manufacturers, in an offensive to destroy the union, refused to send collars and cuffs to any laundry employing union ironers, and recruited nonunion replacements. In response, the CLU members opened their own cooperative laundry, but it foundered when the local manufacturers were able to cut off their supply of new collars from out-of-town collar makers. Undaunted, and with the help of Sylvis' Iron Molders' Union, the women started their own collar factory, the Union Line Collar and Cuff Cooperative Manufactory, and lined up a large New York wholesaler to take all of their collars. Just as they were getting off the ground, however, the manufacturers pulled the rug out from under them by introducing new paper collars, which transformed the industry. The CLU dissolved in the next year, but a decade later became the model and inspiration for renewed women's union organizing, including the Joan of Arc Assembly of the Knights of Labor.[31]

NATIONAL COLORED LABOR UNION

Isaac Myers worked with Sylvis and Frederick Douglass to break the color line of the National Labor Union. Myers was the keynote speaker on that topic at the 1869 NLU convention.[32] Encountering opposition, Myers and Douglass organized the affiliated National Colored Labor Union (NCLU), the first national organization of its kind. Myers was elected its first president, and Douglass succeeded him in 1872. The NCLU's program, like the NLU's, backed worker cooperatives. Besides the usual advantages, cooperatives could help remedy racist exclusion from the skilled trades. Cooperation was widespread in black communities across the country, rural and urban. The NCLU led union organizing efforts in Alabama, Georgia, Tennessee and Missouri, and successfully helped organize the longshoremen's union for a wage increase in Baltimore. But on the whole, their pioneering efforts did not result in extensive unionization of African-American workers.[33]

CHESAPEAKE MARINE RAILWAY & DRYDOCK COMPANY

Isaac Myers, a freeborn black, had risen through his abilities as a journeyman caulker to become supervisor of hull caulking for some of the largest clipper ships in Baltimore. As a leader of the Colored Caulkers Trade Union Society, a union and beneficial society, he successfully bargained for better wages and working conditions in 1865.[34] But the end of the Civil War in 1865 occasioned the arrival of a large number of white workers, and the shipyard owners began to replace black caulkers and longshoremen with them. Myers responded by organizing a group of black community leaders to open their own cooperative shipyard. Finding no white shipyard owner willing to negotiate directly with them, they enlisted the help of a white friend as intermediary, and the Chesapeake Marine Railway and Dry Dock Company opened in 1866.[35] Within six months, it was employing three hundred black workers, and operated successfully for two decades despite increasing competition from more automated companies. In the following few years, the Baltimore black community became a center for cooperatives, including stores, coal yards, and various small industries. The Chesapeake Marine cooperative ran successfully until finally losing its lease on the shipyard in 1884.[36]

GREENBACKISM

Throughout the 19th century, employers organized their own associations to buttress the capitalist system and fight the workers. They saw the threat of the NLU and NCLU, and moved in combination to destroy the workers' movement, both the cooperatives and the unions themselves.[37]

During the Civil War, the great demand for labor had placed workers and unions in a position of power. But when the country plunged into the postwar recession, employers attacked the unions, primarily on a local level. They crushed numerous locals by blacklisting, lockouts, and "yellow-dog" contracts that forced workers to sign "iron-clad oaths," swearing they would never join a union. When the NLU tried to respond through worker cooperatives, the employers used their control of the money system to make financing almost impossible.[38]

By 1868, Sylvis was speaking with alarm. Many of the NLU cooperatives were in trouble and failing. The employers were pulling financial strings and this was having a telling effect. Competition had become ruthless. Capitalist manufacturers with deep pockets absorbed losses over long periods, trying to put the cooperatives out of business. They cut the wages of their workers and blamed the competition with the cooperatives.[39]

Sylvis accused "Wall Street's control of money and credit," and urged all workers to get behind the Greenback program of more and cheaper money, to break Wall Street's control.[40] Since the amount of gold in circulation remained fixed while the population was greatly expanding, the gold standard resulted in the continuous enrichment of the rich and the increasing impoverishment of the working population. Money was treated as if it were a scarce or limited commodity, like real estate, and increased demand for any such commodity in an expanding market will always result in price increases. This was passed down to workers in the form of wage cuts so that the gold standard resulted in workers having to labor more for the same pay.[41] Under the Greenback plan, government-issued paper money, backed with silver, would replace the then-current system of bank-issued notes backed with gold. The plan had the government offering long-term negligible-interest loans to all citizens in need, which would provide the cheap capital that workers and unions needed to set up the vast system of cooperatives that they hoped would lead to liberation. Greenbackism was a direct attack on bank control and private ownership.[42]

Through the NLU, Greenbackers organized the first nationwide workers' political party in 1872, the National Labor Reform Party, and set their sights on taking national power.[43]

THE NLU & THE INTERNATIONAL

Sylvis was the first American labor leader to actively try to establish relations with the European and international worker movements.[44]

Sylvis and his group began their movement with little knowledge of the European movement. Indeed, they had almost no knowledge of the history of the movement in America, and were apparently unaware of the worker cooperative movements of the 1830s and 1840s.[45]

In his speeches, Sylvis put forth the success of the Rochdale cooperative movement in Britain as an example to follow.[46] At that time, in 1868, there were over several hundred cooperatives with over 60,000 members affiliated with the English Cooperative Wholesale Society.[47] But Sylvis glossed over the distinctions between worker cooperatives and consumer cooperatives. He apparently knew less about the details of the movement in France, Germany and other countries. The movement in France was primarily based on the ideas of Philippe Buchez, who in the 1830s stressed producer cooperatives, calling for profits to go into a "social fund." Buchez's lead was followed by Pierre-Joseph Proudhon's anarchism and Louis Blanc's state-supported "social workshops." In Germany, the labor leader Ferdinand Lassalle advocated worker cooperatives supported by the state, while Franz Hermann Schulze-Delitzsch led a movement of People's Banks.[48]

Sylvis attempted to steer the NLU into the International Workingmen's Association (IWA), the "First International," to which many NLU members belonged as individuals. Internationalism was an inevitable extension of the NLU's expansive approach, in an era when workers' organizations throughout the Western world were reaching out for ties beyond their national borders.[49]

The IWA, organized by unions in London in 1864, marked the first time that wage earner movements of different countries interpenetrated and coordinated their ideas and actions, creating a supranational character to the movement.[50] The first IWA American sections were formed in 1868-69; their program called for "the adoption of the principle of associative production, with a view to complete supercession of the present system of capitalist production."[51] It was an open organization, basically for educational and support activities, but geared also to give direct leadership in times of mass struggle. The IWA looked to the unions as the centers of struggle. Its greatest strength in America laid in the cities, among the unskilled, the unemployed, and the newer immigrants, mainly German at first but soon also Irish, Bohemian, Scandinavian, and French.

Sylvis died suddenly in 1869 at age forty-two. Shortly afterward, the NLU, inspired to carry on the work he had begun, voted its "adherence to the principles of the International Workingmen's Association," adding it would "join in a short time."[52] But without Sylvis' visionary leadership, the NLU began splitting apart, one wing as a trade union, the other as a political party.[53]

The NLU had tried to be an umbrella for both trade unions and social reform organizations, but fractured over conflicts between the two perspectives. The "pure and simple" trade unionists, with few concerns beyond wages and working conditions, vigorously opposed the alliance with blacks and women workers, traditionally viewing these groups as competing cheap labor. When the reformers brought the NLU deeply into the Greenback movement, the trade unions pulled further back.[54] At the congress of 1870, the reformist majority restructured the organization into two divisions, one industrial and the other political. At the same time they disempowered the annual congress, which had been the governing body, and redefined it as a forum for developing political action programs. In response to this disempowerment, almost all of the national unions pulled out.[55] The next year many unions took great losses in the strike wave of 1871 and 1872. At the first convention of the new political division in 1872, the reformers renamed their division the National Labor Reform Party (NLRP).[56]

NATIONAL LABOR REFORM PARTY

The NLRP was the first nationwide workers' political party. With a Greenback platform, it nominated Supreme Court Justice David Davis (appointed by Lincoln) for president, and set its sights on taking national power but foundered in its first and only campaign. Shortly after their nominating convention, a group of Civil War leaders formed another new party, the Liberal Republican Party, to oppose the reelection of the corrupted Grant. Davis had given a qualified acceptance to the NLRP nomination, because he also sought the Liberal Republican endorsement. Liberal Republicans, however, nominated Horace Greeley, who had been a longtime champion of labor, cooperatives, and national economic reform. Davis dropped out of the race and supported Greeley, leaving the NLRP without a candidate. Greeley won six states and garnered 44 percent of the popular vote in 1872. The National Labor Reform Party, despite its quick death, helped to set the stage for the great Greenback parties that would follow in a few years.[57]

COLLAPSE OF THE NLU

In the aftermath, the political division of the NLU collapsed. The first convention of the labor division, held shortly after the election debacle, was attended by only a handful of delegates, signaling that the NLU was then effectively defunct.[58]

The NLU had enormous influence despite its early demise, bringing into one organization almost every progressive group and issue of its time.[59] Hard on the heels of the NLU's death came the great depression of 1873, which left the trade unions mostly destroyed and wiped out many of the cooperatives started under the National Labor Union.[60] To get a job, most workers now had to sign an "iron-clad oath" against unionization. In the following decade, the Knights of Labor would pick up where the NLU left off, no longer able to operate openly, but as a secret organization.[61]

The Cooperative Stove Works in Troy, New York, founded as the result of a strike led by Sylvis in 1866, disbanded twenty-five years later with six people owning more than half the stock.[62] The Cooperative Foundry in Rochester became a capitalist business in 1887 after twenty years, owned by thirty-five stockholders.[63] Others failed for reasons of every sort: the Cooperative Barrel Works, formed in 1874 in Minneapolis, for example, eventually failed because bags replaced barrels in the nearby mill industry.[64]

Cooperative foundries, however, continued to be organized into the 20th century.

In the successful cooperatives, the contradictions built into their stock system surfaced over time. The unbalanced situation created by the concentration of stock ownership—sometimes in the hands of outsiders—caused many cooperatives to devolve into capitalist ventures.[65] These internal disorders added to the disheartenment that the movement felt over its inability to ward off capitalist attacks. Internal personality clashes of course also wrecked a share of the cooperatives.[66]

In all, during the decade between 1866 and 1876, molders ran at least thirty-six foundries and shoemakers at least forty factories. According to one study, at least 239 industrial worker cooperatives opened between 1866 and 1884, before the great explosion of Knights of Labor cooperatives began.[67]

INDUSTRIAL CONGRESS & THE INDUSTRIAL BROTHERHOOD

After the NLU went into politics, the trade unions went back to organizing a separate federation, disavowing the electoral focus. The Industrial Congress of 1873 called together delegates from six national unions. Also represented were the Sovereigns of Industry, the Grangers, and the Industrial Brotherhood, all of which were secret organizations with brotherhood rituals. The Industrial Brotherhood had ties with the International Workingmen's Association. Robert Schilling, president of the Coopers International (barrelmakers union) and also a member of the Industrial Brotherhood, was elected president of the Industrial Congress. The Industrial Congress debated a permanent structure in 1874, with the two primary proposals involving a merger into either the Sovereigns of Industry or the Industrial Brotherhood. They chose the Industrial Brotherhood, and adopted the constitution of that organization, which had been drafted by Schilling.[68] This took on a greater significance in later years, when the same constitution would be adopted as the constitution of the Knights of Labor. While the Industrial Brotherhood itself disintegrated and merged into other organizations, including the Sovereigns of Industry, Schilling would go on to become an important leader of the Knights of Labor, bringing in the barrel-makers and their cooperative factories in Minneapolis.[69]

CRISPINS

Shoemakers, as we have noted, were pioneers in organizing union cooperatives. Beginning in 1794, they had cooperatives in three cities in the 1830s. Despite being skilled workers, they were increasingly impoverished, primarily because expensive machinery, controlled by employers, increasingly dominated the industry.[70] At the end of the Civil War, shoemakers had neither unions nor cooperatives, but the ground was fertile. In Milwaukee, Newell Daniels organized the first lodge of a new shoemakers' union, called the Knights of St. Crispin, in 1867. Later that year, he organized lodges in New England, New York, and Chicago. By December, 1870, after a whirlwind of activity, there were eighty-five Crispin lodges in Massachusetts, forty-seven in New York, seventeen in Canada, fifteen each in New Hampshire and Michigan, fourteen in Ohio, thirteen in Indiana, twelve in Pennsylvania, ten in Wisconsin, eight in New Jersey, seven in Illinois, and several in California.[71] The Crispins led major strikes in Lynn, Worcester, Philadelphia, Chicago, and San Francisco. In 1870, they probably had 50,000 to 60,000 members, making them the largest union until that time, and one of the most powerful in the world.[72]

The preamble of the Crispin constitution called for "cooperation as a proper and efficient remedy for many of the evils of the present iniquitous system of wages."[73] While they tried to raise wages through control of the labor supply and through strikes, it was really through cooperation that they aimed to solve their basic problems. "We believe the end and aim of all Labor organizations should be self-employment."[74] They proposed that each lodge organize a factory and either a store or buying club. The Crispins organized between thirty and forty stores in 1869 alone. Cooperative supply purchasing clubs were widespread. In 1869, they started their first cooperative factories, in North Bridgewater, Massachusetts, and New Brunswick, Canada. Others followed in New York City in 1870, in Philadelphia and Baltimore in 1871, and two in Newark in 1873.[75] One of their most important leaders was Thomas Phillips, formerly of the UCA store, leader of the Pennsylvania state Crispins lodge, tireless writer and agitator for cooperatives.[76] The core leaders of the cooperative shoe factory in Baltimore, which had a hundred members, also belonged to the International Workingmen's Association.[77] But the Crispins declined as quickly as they had risen, a debilitating blow coming after a disastrous strike in

Lynn in 1872. Soon after, membership plunged to only 52 lodges with 13,000 members. The Crispins revived somewhat in Massachusetts, but after 1878, following a rash of losing strikes, they were in disarray and fading almost everywhere.[78]

As the Crispins faded, the Knights of Labor stepped in and reorganized workers in the shoe industry. The KOL formed many cooperative shoe shops after 1880, particularly in Massachusetts.[79]

NATIONAL GRANGE MOVEMENT AND AGRICULTURAL COOPERATIVES

While mutual aid was inherent in the fabric of life in American rural communities from the earliest settlements, the record of the first formal cooperatives among farmers begins with two dairy cooperatives founded in 1810 in Goshen, Connecticut and South Trenton, New York.[80] A decade later, a group of Ohio farmers formed America's first agricultural marketing cooperative on record.[81] In 1822, Pennsylvania barley farmers set up the first cooperative brewery.[82] The first cooperative wheat elevator was opened in Dane City, Illinois, in 1847. Apart from New Mexican Pueblo Indians and ejidos, the first mutual irrigation cooperatives were begun in 1850 in California and Utah.[83]

As the US expanded ever westward, a central issue in the first half of the 19th century became how the new land would be used, encompassing as it did the struggle over slavery. Eastern workers dreamed of escaping wage slavery and becoming farmers in the West. But time and again the government gave away huge tracts of the public domain to profiteers and speculators, instead of homesteads to aspiring small farmers. By the time of the Civil War, the land issue was enmeshed in the political crisis of whether slavery would be permitted to spread to the new Western territories recently taken from Mexico, and how the vast new public domains would be used.[84] The Homestead Act of 1862, signed by Lincoln during the Civil War, was seen as a great triumph by Eastern workers, and a new path to social justice. George Henry Evans and Horace Greeley were key advocates for its passage.[85] A family could get a 160-acre farm free by living on it for 5 years, or buy it for $1.25 per acre after 6 months. The Act gave an incomparable boost to the morale of Northern soldiers, who saw it as a promise of a new life awaiting in a Western paradise; at the end of the war, many thousands rushed West. Some were fortunate and found the homestead of their dreams: the Homestead Act is credited with creating over 372,000 farms. But as railroads and speculators grabbed vast tracts, including many of the best spreads, numerous aspiring small farmers went empty-handed, and wound up feeling embittered.[86]

Before 1860, small farmers were mostly self-sufficient, producing for their families and nearby markets. But the end of the Civil war saw a great expansion in farmed land and in mechanization. Extension of the Western railroads connected once-isolated communities into a national market. Farm output skyrocketed, pressing prices down. The small farmer became a tiny link in a great chain, dominated and impoverished by bankers, merchants and middlemen. Farmers were obliged to buy overpriced seed, supplies and equipment, and to pay excessively to market their produce.[87]

Oliver Kelly, once a farmer but later a clerk in the US Bureau of Agriculture, founded the National Grange of the Patrons of Husbandry in 1867 as a secret fraternal order of farmers. Patterned after the Masons, it was meant to "to restore kindly feelings" between people in the North and South.[88] Stating "cooperation in all things," the Grangers (named after a farm homestead) soon began organizing cooperatives to meet the needs of their hard-pressed members. They organized openly, while retaining the internal secrecy of a fraternal order.[89]

With the Grange, farmer cooperation changed from being mostly informal and local to a widespread and well-organized movement. The Grange never organized farmworkers, or "hired hands." Until the end of the century, almost all farm work was still done by members of farm families, which were usually big.[90] Farmworkers did not become a large and important group until decades later, and were first successfully organized by the Industrial Workers of the World in the early 20th century.[91]

In 1868, Minnesota Grangers organized their first purchasing and marketing cooperatives, and a state "business agent" was appointed the next year. The local Granges served as mutual aid centers, where information about work and survival were shared, and members helped educate each other.[92] In a few years, Granges had sprung up throughout the Midwest and Southwest. When the economy faltered in 1872 and fell the next year, membership soared.[93]

Their earliest purchasing cooperatives were simply "concentration of trade" plans, with local Grangers agreeing to trade exclusively with a certain merchant for discounts. Montgomery Ward, the original mail order house, started out specializing in Grange orders. This soon gave way to Grange business agents organizing cooperative purchasing, first on a local basis, then statewide.[94]

The Grange organized cooperative grain elevators, warehouses, shipping stations, processing plants, grist mills, bag factories, brick yards, blacksmith shops, cotton gins, rail and ship transport, mutual insurance, irrigation, machine and implement works. By 1875, they had 250 grain elevators in Illinois alone. Together, the Grangers of the West fought a grasshopper plague; in the South, they fought floods. The Grange spread to the West Coast in 1870.[95]

The Grange pioneered cooperative banking in the United States, opening the Grangers Bank of California in 1874, followed by at least four other banks, to provide farmer members with credit, which they particularly needed at certain points in the agricultural cycle. Within a year the California bank had two million dollars on deposit, and was still thriving a decade later. Another Grange bank set up in Kansas emulated its success in 1883.[96] But Grange credit cooperatives never became widespread and the Grange banks faded in the hard times of the later 1880s.[97]

When the monopolists of the machine industry refused to give them wholesale rates in 1872, Grangers tried to have their own line of farm machinery manufactured. The Nebraska Grange manufactured the first attempt, a wheat head reaper. It was a great success, selling at half the price of comparable models, and resulting in price reductions on all machinery in the state. This stimulated the National Grange to manufacture a harvester the following year in Iowa, Minnesota, and Nebraska, but some of these machines proved defective and many were delivered too late for the year's harvest. The project proved a financial loss.[98] Undaunted, the National Grange drew up plans to have a complete line of farm machines and implements manufactured, and bought up patents to that effect in 1874. Manufacturing enterprises were initiated by many state Granges, but most of these immediately stalled on raising the needed capital. By 1875, the Grange drew back from manufacturing and focused its resources on cooperative stores that were proving a surer success.[99]

Until 1873, Grangers just organized cooperative wholesale purchasing. Many local Granges began opening cooperative stores in 1873-74, carrying both farm supplies and consumer goods. In the beginning, the stores sold only to members, but soon opened to their communities. Mostly organized as joint-stock companies with member shareholders restricted to Grangers, they first sold nearly at cost. But capitalists hit them with lawsuits and price wars. Under great pressure and expressing a general dissatisfaction with the joint-stock form of organization, the Master of the St. Louis Grange called for a study of Rochdale and other successful stores. The committee issued a report the following year that included a model set of cooperative "rules" based on the Rochdale Rules. The National Grange threw its enthusiastic support behind the new plan, and stores all around the country switched to the Rochdale system of selling to the general community at about market rates and giving members rebates and special discounts. This threatened the market less and got the businessmen somewhat off their backs. Within a short time, hundreds of stores were started. Throughout the next decade, there were over 500 Grange stores. A decade after the pioneering experience of the Union Cooperative Association in Philadelphia (1862-66), the Grange thus built the first successful widespread movement of Rochdale-type cooperatives in America.[100]

The railroad barons, not satisfied with having been handed a full half of all the Western lands by Congress, used their control of the government to levy enormous taxes to make the people pay the cost of building the railroads.[101] They milked their transportation monopoly for all it was worth, charging huge freight rates. Farmers got little or nothing for their crops, while city people starved because of high food prices. In New York City alone, 40 percent of the labor force was unemployed in the winter of 1873, and 900 people died of starvation.[102]

The Grange struck back. In a typical resolution, the Illinois Grange declared, "We hold, declare and resolve that this despotism, which defies our laws, plunders our shippers, impoverishes our people, and corrupts our government, shall be subdued and made to subserve the public interest at whatever cost."[103] But the combined effects of the railroad barons' tactics and the deepening depression put the Grange in deep financial trouble and many locals were going bankrupt.[104]

The Greenback movement had found its first strong center of advocacy in the National Labor Union. Soon after the NLU dissolved, Greenbackism found a new center among small farmers, and for a time became primarily a rural movement.[105] With the crash of the economy in 1873, "Independent" farmer parties sprang up throughout the West, with Grangers in the leadership, reviving the Greenback movement. These farmers wanted to increase the amount of paper money in circulation because with more and cheaper money, the farmer cooperators, like their industrial counterparts, felt they could get on a more equal footing with the capitalists. The Greenback Party was formed in Indianapolis in 1874, and nominated Peter Cooper for president in 1876.[106]

Due largely to its affiliations with these independent farmer parties and the Greenback issue, membership in the Grange rocketed. In 1875, there were 19,000 local Granges, with 758,000 members.[107] Behind slogans like "Down with monopolies" and "Cooperation!" they allied in 1878 with the Knights of Labor into the Greenback-Labor Party.[108] This same alliance of urban and rural workers into an independent electoral party gathered strength in the decades to follow, and in all successful instances had a base in cooperatives. The party platform expanded in 1880 to include the eight-hour day, women's suffrage, and the progressive income tax.[109]

The Greenback-Labor Party elected fifteen congressmen in 1878, six from the East, three from the South, and six from the Midwest. In the same election, they also elected numerous candidates to state office, particularly in Illinois, Minnesota, Iowa and Wisconsin, tallying over a million votes.[110] In the Alabama coal regions, black Greenback-Labor leaders brought black and white miners together in a common cause.[111] "Repudiationists," demanding cancellation of the state debts, scared the bankers. In parts of the South, some Greenbackers, along with members of several other alternative parties, were met with violence and stuffed ballot boxes.[112] Their elected candidates usually proved ineffectual in making really meaningful changes. Although they passed laws regulating freight rates, they found themselves unable to enforce them. The barons struck back: railroads refused to carry Grange shipments and banks denied them credit. Many gains were overturned by the courts, which remained firmly in conservative hands, and over which voters had little control. It became clear that the basic Grange program could be instituted only on a national scale, because locally it was vulnerable to monopoly capitalists and their allies in government.[113]

But the early 1880s saw the depression temporarily lessen, the Greenback-Labor Party fade without ever becoming strong enough nationally to enact its program, and the Grange grow conservative.[114] By 1883, when the economy slipped again, its leadership was business-oriented and unable to rise to the challenge: no longer meeting small farmers' needs, it was in fast decline within the year. Still, there were numerous successful Grange cooperatives in many areas. The Texas Cooperative Association, chartered in 1878, alone serviced 155 stores across the state in 1887 with $2 million in sales.[115]

In the mid-1880s, a new farmers' cooperative movement—the Farmers' Alliance—was also roaring out of the frontier communities of the West and eclipsed the Grange for a decade.[116]

SOVEREIGNS OF INDUSTRY

The great suffering in industrialized areas wrought by the depression that began in 1873 sparked William Earle, an organizer from the National Grange in Massachusetts, to conclude that the benefits of cooperatives should be brought to industrial workers. In 1874, he called a meeting of sixty like-minded people from eight states (including twenty-one women and Grange founder Oliver Kelly). This meeting founded the Sovereigns of Industry (SI) to serve Northeastern industrial workers, with Earle as president.[117] Like the Grange, it began as a secret society. Its plan was to "unite all people engaged in industrial pursuits," both wage earners and individual producers, into local councils which would set up cooperative stores, ultimately to promote "mutual fellowship and cooperative action among the producers and consumers of wealth throughout the earth."[118]

The SI set up a democratic system of local and state councils, with a national council whose main job was agitational.[119] The national council employed John Orvis, formerly a member of the Brook Farm community, as its national lecturer between 1874 and 1876. Among early members were Albert Brisbane, who had been a key ideologist for the Associationist movement, Victor Drury and James Wright, both of whom would be prominent in the Knights of Labor.[120] Local councils, elected democratically, managed each store. But this sometimes resulted in the hiring of managers and clerks who knew little about the business.[121]

Sovereigns organized 101 councils and 46 stores in their first year mostly throughout New England. They were spread through 14 states by the end of 1875, and had some 40,000 members in 1875-76.[122] Following the Grangers, some stores used the Rochdale system; others sold at cost only to members.[123] In some instances, the Grangers and the SI worked together. Able to grow so fast because many independent labor organizations reorganized as Sovereigns lodges, including lodges of the Industrial Brotherhood, the Sovereigns expanded even as the depression deepened and unemployment swelled.[124]

But the SI grew too large too fast. Merchants hit it with price wars, and wholesalers and bankers cut off credit. Employers turned a part of the labor movement against them: capitalist stores cut their clerks' wages, claiming that competition with the cooperatives forced them to do it, and some unionists joined in the attack, partly in anger because several locals in their unions had dropped out and joined the Sovereigns as lodges.[125] The Sovereigns' only objective, the attacking unionists claimed, was "to buy cheap, if they have to help reduce wages to a dollar a day to do it." The Sovereigns defended themselves, declaring, "we mean to substitute cooperation, production and exchange, for the present competitive system... we war with the whole wage system and demand for labor the entire result of its beneficial toil."[126]

The SI flagship store was in Springfield, Massachusetts. Founded in January of 1874, the "Springfield Plan" became the model of the organization: the local council raised the startup capital and the store sold for cash only to members. Monthly dues were fifty cents for men and twenty-five cents for women. At first they sold at cost, but then changed to a system of 2 percent profit, half of which was to go to the council and the other half into a sinking fund to pay off debts. But by selling at close to cost, they touched off a fierce price war with competitors, who sold below cost to try to put the SI out of business. The Springfield store opened to the general public in 1878, and switched to the Rochdale plan of selling at market prices and giving rebates to members. By this time in a downward spiral, SI dissolved in January 1879.[127]

Ultimately, it was the depression that killed the Sovereigns: as hard times brought them to life, harder times killed them.[128] Few working people had cash, so sales volume in most stores plummeted to next to nothing. Some stores tried a credit system, with disastrous results. After only four years, the Sovereigns central organization went down.[129]

Despite the failure of the Sovereigns and the fading of the Grange, many individual cooperative stores survived, and could be found in scattered communities all over the United States throughout the 1880s. In 1886, an observer noted stores started by the Sovereigns of Industry still functioning successfully in Lewiston and

Dexter, Maine; in Maynard, Worcester, Webster, Lowell, Beverly, and Kingston, Massachusetts; and in New Britain and Birmingham, Connecticut.[130]

FIRST INTERNATIONAL

The International Workingmen's Association (IWA) was a new and different kind of political organization. It did not run candidates for offices in elections, but was an international organization, an umbrella for worker movements in almost every country in the industrializing world.[131]

The International was first organized in 1864 through the initiative of British and French unionists and cooperators to serve as a central medium of communication and cooperation among workers and worker organizations of different countries.[132] The worker movements had all followed a pattern similar to the movement in the United States. As industry, capitalism and wage slavery grew, so grew the resistance organizations of the workers: unions, cooperatives and political parties. The union movements in every country connected to cooperative movements and worker parties.[133]

All schools of thought in the larger worker movement were represented within the International. Its yearly congresses attempted to hammer out a common program for worker movements everywhere. With the IWA, these movements interpenetrated.[134] The largest divisions were between three schools of thought: "scientific" socialists, anarchists, and cooperators. Despite many disagreements about strategy and organization, all concurred that in the end production should be run by a system of coordinated worker cooperatives, and not by private businesses or by an all-powerful bureaucratic state. State socialism, as later understood, was not advocated by any of the factions, not even the early Marxists.[135]

The IWA advocated workers forming cooperatives, particularly production cooperatives. They considered worker cooperatives to be more important than cooperative stores, because they believed that the mode of production is more basic to the system than the mode of distribution that flows from it.[136] The IWA recommended that all cooperatives devote part of their income to supporting and spreading the movement; they suggested that workers, whether members or not, should receive equal salaries, and that excess income should be plowed back into the cooperative instead of divided as "profit." The IWA proposed that all land and resources belong to society;

that mines, public transport and agriculture be operated by worker cooperatives with assistance from "a new kind of state subject to the law of justice;" and that it was the fundamental task of workers to dismantle the wage system and develop a new social order.[137]

"Scientific" socialists, led by Karl Marx, had mainly praise and encouragement for cooperatives. However, they criticized the cooperative movement's early ideologists Robert Owen and Pierre-Joseph Proudhon for not seriously reckoning with the capitalists' use of state power to squelch the movement, for not sufficiently allowing for the needs of increasingly complex machinery in their plans, and for not accurately analyzing the laws of money.[138] Marx saw the economic system of the future to be "united cooperative societies regulating the national production on a common plan, thus taking it under their own control."[139]

But Marx, as general secretary of the IWA, also warned that the experience of the previous thirty years had demonstrated in many countries that cooperative movements by themselves could not defeat the domination of private capital, and that they could not succeed without an allied political movement to change basic property relationships and the general conditions of society. Therefore, he concluded, the ultimate value of producer cooperatives in the present society lay in their conclusive demonstration that wage slaves and a class of employers were unnecessary to large-scale "modern" production.[140]

In opposition to Marx and his allies stood a strong faction led by the anarchist Mikhail Bakunin. Marx and Bakunin basically agreed that society needs to be rebuilt on a foundation of economic social justice, but fervently disagreed about the way to accomplish it and about the hallmarks of social justice. While Marx thought that the establishment of a workers' state would be a necessary historical phase, Bakunin thought that the state should be abolished as the first act of revolution. They also disagreed about how centralized the International should be and how much autonomy each national section should have, with the Marxists stressing unity and the Bakunists stressing autonomy. The International became factionalized around these two poles, eventually leading to a cataclysmic split.[141]

By 1871, there were over 5,000 American IWA members, with sections in New York, Chicago, San Francisco, New Orleans, Newark, Springfield, Washington, and Williamsburg. But events in France would change the course of the movement in America.[142]

With IWA members among the leadership, the revolutionary working people of Paris took and held the city for two months in 1871, establishing the Paris Commune, the most complete and direct democracy the industrialized world had ever known. All public officials were elected, could be recalled at any time, and received the same pay as the average productive worker. Most of the factories were taken over by their workers as cooperatives—the employers having abandoned them and fled the city—and the workers began organizing themselves into a vast cooperative union. The Commune decreed the right of all workers "to their instruments of labor and to credit."[143] Marx called its ultra-democracy "the form at last discovered under which to work out the economic emancipation of labor."[144]

The working people of Paris had formed the Commune in the power vacuum left by the French army's defeat by Prussia. But the old government regrouped with Prussia's help, besieged its own capital city for two months, and attacked. After a week of ferocious street fighting, the Paris Commune was defeated. The IWA was outlawed and persecuted in almost every European country.[145] On top of this, the IWA had become racked by the internal struggles over the methods and program of social revolution, particularly between the factions led by Marx and Bakunin. Most national branches pulled out of the IWA in 1872 and formed a new decentralist organization that they called the International Working People's Association (IWPA) or "Black" International. The old General Council of the IWA left London and moved to New York City.[146]

The Commune of Paris had particular significance in the history of the workers' movement worldwide and was viewed as the prototype of the future society by all schools of socialists and anarchists until after the Russian Revolution of 1917, whose leaders also held up the Commune as their vision, but who created a reality far removed.[147]

WORKINGMEN'S PARTY

In July 1876, during a brutal depression year and shortly after the US national centennial celebration, a large conference of progressive activists in Philadelphia officially disbanded the IWA. They immediately formed the Workingmen's Party of the United States, reuniting the movement in America a few days before the Oglala Sioux, with the leadership of Crazy Horse and Sitting Bull, met George Custer's soldiers at the Little Big Horn.[148]

The program of the Workingmen's Party included the eight-hour day; abolition of prison and child labor; free public education; workers' compensation; public ownership of telegraph, railroads and all transportation; and "all industrial enterprises to be placed under control of the Government as fast as practicable, and operated by free, cooperative trade unions for the good of the whole people."[149] Within a year, the organization had 10,000 members in 25 states, with very large numbers attending their mass meetings and demonstrations. Like the old IWA, the Workingmen's Party was not electorally oriented but looked to the unions as the main centers of struggle for social change.[150]

5.
The Knights of Labor &
the "Great Upheaval"

The great railway strike of 1877 ignited an era of social turbulence known as the Great Upheaval.

During the depression that began in 1873, the employers busted almost every union in the country except those underground. Blacklisting was rampant; employers forced workers to sign "iron-clad oaths," agreeing to immediate firing if they should ever join a union.[1] In 1877, at the height of the depression, the country exploded in America's first great railroad strike that quickly turned into a nationwide confrontation between capital and labor, between the government and the working population. Beginning as a wildcat, the strike quickly spread across the country, involving tens of thousands as large numbers of workers from every trade and the unemployed helped out. Farmers, many of them Grangers (whose organization was based in cooperatives), disgusted at enormous freight rates, poured out of the hills bringing large amounts of food. State militias in many places refused to obey orders to break the strike and instead fraternized with the strikers.[2]

The strikers took control of Pittsburgh, Chicago and St. Louis from the government.[3] In St. Louis, the strikers shut down communication between the East and West coasts for a week. The working people of Pittsburgh held the city for five days and organized survival by neighbor helping neighbor in what has been called the Pittsburgh Commune.[4]

The strike began only months after the inauguration of Republican President Rutherford Hayes. Hayes had reached office through "The Compromise of 1877," also known as "The Great Betrayal."[5] In the election of the previous November, Democrat Samuel Tilden, governor of New York received over 250,000 more popular votes than Hayes and should have easily won the electoral vote. That would have been the first time that the Republican Party lost power since the Civil War.[6] Tilden had been one of a group of anti-slavery Northern Democrats who remained with the party during the war. However, Republican and Democratic leaders secretly cut a deal to hand over the electoral votes of Louisiana, South Carolina, and Florida to Hayes—votes which Tilden had actually won. The ostensible purpose of the deal was to prevent the country from being torn apart again. In exchange for the presidency, the South got a promise of the withdrawal of the remaining federal troops, legislation to industrialize the South, and the appointment of Southern Democrats to patronage positions and to Hayes' cabinet.[7] Soon after his inauguration, Hayes dutifully proceeded to withdraw the occupying army. Withdrawal of the troops meant the abandonment of racial equality in the South and giving the former Confederates a free hand to deal with blacks.[8]

When the great railroad strike spread across the country a few months later, Hayes called out federal troops "to prevent national insurrection."[9] Under his order, the army broke the strike. All told, the government killed over 100 strikers, wounded over 500, and jailed over 1000. This was the first peacetime use of federal troops to suppress a strike.[10] Frightened by an angry population, Congress quickly voted funds to construct large armories in all the major cities to be used for domestic control; these armories still exist today. Many states quickly passed anti-union conspiracy laws.[11]

Members of the Knights of Labor, an extraordinary organization founded eight years previously, played a major role in the railroad strike, and the repercussions transformed the organization.[12]

FOUNDING OF THE KOL

Members of a Philadelphia tailoring cutters local trade union, after being blacklisted for striking in 1869, founded the Noble Order of the Knights of Labor (KOL) in sworn secrecy. They aimed "to secure to workers the full enjoyment of the wealth they create, to harmonize the interests of labor and capital."[13] One of the first principles of KOL was cooperation. When forced out into the open nine years later, the group made their goals public: "We will endeavor to associate our own labors, to establish co-operative institutions such as will tend to supersede the wage-system, by the introduction of a co-operative industrial system."[14] They called for public ownership of railroads and other commercial transport; of telegraph and telephones, water systems and utilities; for the eight-hour day; equal pay for equal work; abolition of contract, convict, and child labor; and "that the public lands, the heritage of the people, be reserved for actual settlers; not another acre for railroad speculators."[15]

> KOL song (c. 1875)
> One sure way to make a cure
> And solve this labor question;
> With heads and hands to tie the bands
> In steps of Co-operation.[16]

Under the early leadership of tailor Uriah Stephens, the Order grew rapidly. The Order was not a trade union, and its members were organized geographically rather than by occupation. Whole trade unions that joined, however, did retain their identity. The Knights attempted to organize all American productive workers into "one big union" regardless of skill, trade, industry, race or sex and were divided into local, district and national assemblies, with a centralized structure.[17] Three-quarters of each new local had to be wage earners; the Knights' membership also included individual and cooperative workers. Despite centralization, the right to strike was given to the locals, not to the central organization to decide. This resulted in locals that were often more radical and active than the central organization.[18] In the early years, the Knights saw the District Assemblies as the units that would organize into cooperatives and become the cells of the future cooperative commonwealth. In practice, they later found that this made the Knights financially vulnerable, since the organization would be liable for any financial failures, and redirected their focus to make the cooperatives more independent, placing more organizational space between the cooperatives and Knights' Assemblies.[19]

The Knights of Labor took the radical step of becoming one of the first organizations to include white and black in the same union. The organization also became one of the first to include women, with over 50,000 women members at its peak, including many housewives, whom the KOL recognized as workers.[20]

> Toiling millions now are waking
> See them marching on.
> All the tyrants now are shaking
> Ere their power's gone.

Storm the fort, ye Knights of Labor
Battle for your cause:
Equal rights for every neighbor,
Down with tyrant laws![21]

Rank-and-file members of the Knights had been an important force in the 1877 railroad strike, along with the Workingmen's Party, formed from the defunct International Workingmen's Association the previous year. Both had been in leadership positions across much of the country, although neither organization had instigated the strike, which had been a spontaneous eruption of long-seething anger. But now both were being blamed for it in the press and from the pulpit. The Knights were charged with being a center for sedition and communism.[22] To defend themselves, they could no longer continue as a secret organization and decided to come into the open. They also felt that secrecy had possibly hurt and hampered their organizing abilities over the years more than it had helped. Until then, their very name had been so secret that members were sworn to never publicly utter it, and outsiders only speculated on their existence.[23]

Upon going public, the Knights quickly went into electoral politics, joining the Grangers' Greenback Party in 1878 to form the Greenback-Labor Party, electing six congressmen from the Northeast, six from the Midwest, and three from the South. They recognized in their Declaration of Principles that "most of the objects herein set forth can only be attained by legislation."[24]

In 1881, the aging Stephens stepped down as Grand Master Workman and the Knights selected Terence V. Powderly to replace him. Powderly had served as a member of the Machinists and Blacksmith's Union, an organizer for the Industrial Brotherhood, and was sitting mayor of Scranton, to which he had been elected in 1878 on the Greenback-Labor ticket.[25] With Powderly's leadership, the center of the Knights moved westward from the coastal cities to the coalfields and the fast-growing industrializing Midwestern cities.[26]

During a fleeting economic upturn between 1879 and 1882, the Greenback-Labor Party faded. The Greenback movement, based on the idea of a monetary reform scheme as a panacea to cure a dire social condition, died when the economy briefly brightened, and many people turned in other directions to solve their problems.[27] The economy, however, didn't stay bright for long. At that point, the KOL, grown to 50,000 members nationally in 1882, backed away from electoral politics and turned its sights to organizing cooperatives.[28]

The Knights' different involvements may seem strangely disconnected today. How could one organization be so involved at the same time with strikes, the Greenback movement, and cooperatives? The answer lies in understanding the American working people at that moment. America did not have a stable working class like Europe. The promise of the Homestead Act had left many people with the conviction that the dream of independence was really within every American's grasp. Most employees did not expect to be employees for the rest of their working lives. They not only thought that they deserved better, but as Americans were entitled to better. The destructiveness of the railroad strikers was fueled by the rage of a dream denied. The working people thought that railroads were by right public utilities that had been usurped by private enterprise. The vision of the KOL updated the American dream to extend beyond the opportunity of becoming a homestead farmer, and offered a path to independence in the industrial age. The same people who felt stuck in oppressive jobs in the railways, mines, factories and mills, thought they could liberate themselves and their families through the KOL's vision and plan of action. They saw themselves in the near future as independent cooperators, no longer employees. And they needed the cheap money and credit proffered by the Greenback program to make that dream come true. While the Knights' three major involvements—strikes, cooperatives, and the Greenback movement—might look tactically disconnected, contradictory, or just parallel, they were strategically connected by the Knights' larger vision. Strikes served as a defensive rejection of an oppressive present, while cooperatives and the Greenback movement were their attempt to construct a liberated future.[29]

THE KNIGHTS OF LABOR AND THE COOPERATIVE MOVEMENT

The early 1880s were a time of industrial expansion, with machinery introduced on an unprecedented scale. The factory system became general and led to an increase in unskilled and semi-skilled workers.[30] The market expanded over an ever-wider area. Domination of wholesalers over smaller manufacturers produced cutthroat competition and pressed wages down.[31] Over five million immigrants, mostly unskilled, arrived in the 1880s; they represented the peak of the flood from Northern Europe and the beginning of the tide from Southern and Eastern Europe.[32] Even while industrial capitalism forced more immigrants into wage slavery, immigrants organized production and mutual-aid cooperatives in their enclaves throughout this entire period. The frontier line disappeared: from Atlantic to Pacific all was at least partially settled. American labor found itself shut in an all-pervading wage system.[33]

KOL locals ran between fifty and sixty stores in 1883. A typical Knight hall had a store on the first floor and meeting rooms upstairs. Members got special discounts. Surplus income swelled war chests for strikes and, in the following years, for starting production cooperatives. With the motto "Cooperation of the Order, by the Order, and for the Order," they aimed to use the stores to create markets for the products of their production cooperatives as stepping-stones to self-employment.[34]

In 1883, a coal mining company in Indiana locked out a group of Knights for refusing to quit the organization. This group leased a forty-acre plot and together organized the Union Mining Company of Cannelburg. When they ran into a financial bind the following year, they turned to the Knights' central organization for help. The Knights took over the project, and Cannelburg became their first major production cooperative, run directly by the central organization. The Knights intended the mine to be the first link in the economic backbone of the new society they planned to build. The KOL spent $20,000 to buy the land, equip the mine, and lay railroad tracks to it. But the railroad company refused to connect their switch to the main track for nine months. At that point the KOL discovered that they would have to wait another nine months before they would have any sales, since their type of coal could be used only in gas manufacturing, and those contracts were issued only once a year. Then the railroad company told them they would have to provide their own switch engine; it would cost another $4,000 that they didn't have. Unable to maintain the cooperative in these circumstances, the KOL leased the mine and eventually sold it.[35]

The Knights quickly switched over to a decentralized plan, urging member initiative. They realized that decentralized cooperatives would be easier to start and be safer from attacks than cooperatives run by the national organization. In most cases, groups of member-stockholders formed and managed the cooperative with financial assistance from their assemblies. However in some cases, the local assemblies themselves organized and managed the enterprise.[36] Under the leadership of John Samuel, the General Cooperative Board became primarily an educational and coordinating organization after the centralized mine project collapsed. The Board published forms of constitutions and by-laws that could be modified for use by almost any cooperative, and numerous articles on the nuts and bolts of different kinds of cooperation.[37] By 1885, enthusiasm was high. "It is to cooperation that the eyes of the workingmen and workingwomen of the world should be directed, upon cooperation their hopes should be centered," urged Powderly. "By cooperation alone can a system of colonization be established in which men may band together for the purpose of securing the greatest good for the greatest number, and place the man who is willing to toil upon his own homestead."[38]

Knight cooperatives sprang up across the United States, concentrated in the East and Midwest. The progress was so rapid in 1885 that Powderly complained, "many of our members grow impatient and disorderly because every avenue of the Order does not lead to cooperation."[39] By the middle of 1886, there were between 185 and 200 Knight cooperatives. Most operated on a comparatively small scale. More than half were mines, foundries, mills, and factories making barrels, clothes, shoes, and soap. There were also cooperative printers, laundries, furniture-makers, potters, and lumberjacks, factories making boxes, nails, underwear, brooms, pipe, and stoves. At the same time, other cooperatives were organized that were unaffiliated with the KOL; according to one study, 334 worker cooperatives opened between 1880 and 1888.[40]

The Knights authorized the KOL label to be put on products produced in cooperatives, and persistently urged the buying public to prefer them.[41]

America's first labor historian Richard Ely wrote that the movement in 1886 was

> national in extent... The only large and powerful organization which has earnestly taken hold of the entire industrial population, with a view to the final introduction of co-operation into all spheres of production, and the complete overthrow of the present industrial and competitive economic order, is the Knights of Labor... While the Knights of Labor have not entirely neglected distributive co-operation, their achievements in productive co-operation are far more remarkable, and are now to be seen in all parts of the land. I suppose that I might, without great difficulty, enumerate one

hundred co-operative undertakings at present in progress under the auspices of the Knights.[42]

Labor historian Selig Perlman has listed 135 KOL worker cooperatives, acknowledging that there were many he had not counted: 22 mining; 15 coopers; 14 shoes; 8 clothing, foundries, soap, knitting, tobacco, and planing mills; 6 cigar and glass; 5 furniture workers; 3 nail mills; 2 tailoring, hats, printing, agricultural implements, painters, matches, baking powder, and carpentering; one each laundries, carpets, bakers, leather, leather goods, plumbing, harness, watch case, pipes, brass works, pottery, wagon, refining, caskets, brooms, pottery, ice, and packing. Total: 135.[43]

From the first, and in most locations, capitalists and competitors hit the Knight cooperatives hard, making it difficult or impossible for them to obtain credit, supplies, and markets. Still, most persisted. The employers tried unsuccessfully to drive a wedge between the wage earner Knights and the cooperator Knights, blaming the cooperatives every time they laid speedup, wage cuts and layoffs on their employees, claiming this was the only way they could compete. But it was not until 1886 that the employers let them have it with both barrels.[44]

Worker solidarity and the embryonic network of cooperatives were great threats to the employers, to their labor market, and to the whole capitalist system. The employers formed associations on an unprecedented scale across the nation, consolidated their strength, and set their sights upon destroying the Knights.[45]

SOLIDARITY COOPERATIVES IN NEW YORK

New York City's District Assembly 49 was one of the most radical of the Knights assemblies, and a number of its key members also belonged to the International Working People's Association. One such was Victor Drury, an immigrant from France who had been involved with the French revolutionary insurrection of 1848, and was a founding member of the First International (IWA) in 1864.[46] By trade a carpenter and stone mason, Drury sat at the center of the "Home Club," a clandestine group which formed the core of District Assembly 49, and organized "Spread the Light" clubs to teach revolutionary ideology to New York and Brooklyn Knights.[47] DA 49 was very powerful in the national KOL in 1886-87; some historians believe that DA 49—and not Powderly—actually controlled the national organization during those key years. Drury held more radical and anarchistic views than Powderly, and they often clashed.[48]

Following the ideas in Drury's influential book *The Polity of the Labor Movement* (1885), District Assembly 49 organized an extraordinary group of cooperatives. A committee on cooperation, chosen by the entire district, managed all the enterprises. The committee appointed foremen for three-month terms. They offered non-interest bearing shares for purchase to individuals and labor organizations that were redeemable after one year. Investors could not determine which cooperative their funds would be used for. No profits went to shareholders, but stock was to be bought back by the cooperatives from profits. Shareholders had no control over management. Of the net profits after salaries and debt payments, 50 percent went to expanding the cooperative chain, 25 percent went for insurance, and 25 percent to a fund to buy land for continual expansion. Seven solidarity companies and a store were started in Manhattan and Brooklyn in 1886-87.[49]

According to Drury's plan, in the store, or *centre of exchange*, products would be sold

> with a very slight augmentation in price, which should only be provisionally and until we could sell at *cost* those commodities which we should produce ourselves as soon as we begin to manufacture. So soon as we could find sale for sufficient of the products of any of the industries we have mentioned to employ a few producers, we should establish a workshop or *centre of production*. For instance, if we sold sufficient bread and pastry to employ four or five bakers, we should immediately establish a bakery... We should then call upon the Trades' Unions to furnish us with the most skilled and capable men in their special industries to direct these *centres of production*.[50]

Historian Edward W. Bemis visited the solidarity cooperatives in February 1887, and described them in *Cooperation in the Middle States*, "Not all were under the direct control of the central committee, but all were managed, in great measure, on the plan just outlined."[51] He went on to say, referring to the unusual situation of investments in the solidarity cooperatives being not based on profit, "Probably the sentiment of class pride and the strong union feeling among many of the New York Knights of Labor assemblies accounts for the fact, and will serve to render these companies somewhat of a success as long as those local unions maintain their strength. Any decrease in the latter must affect the former."[52] This analysis of the cooperatives' success depending on the union's strength would prove prophetic in years to come.

Bemis enumerated the Solidarity cooperatives he visited:

SOLIDARITY FANCY LEATHER GOODS FACTORY [53 Bleecker Street] and AMERICAN FANCY LEATHER GOODS COMPANY [417 Broom Street]. The two fancy leather goods companies named above were doing business, the one with $1,500 capital and the other with $600, on the full solidarity plan, and a growing business was reported.

THE PLUMBERS' COOPERATIVE ASSOCIATION [953 Sixth Avenue] was organized October 1, 1886, as the result of the great plumbers' lockout in New York, due to the effort of the employes to enforce an apprentice law. An assessment of five dollars was levied on every plumber to raise capital for the cooperative enterprise. Over $1,000 has been paid. The distress resulting from the lockout and strike has prevented further payments. No interest is allowed, but all the profits are to go to a cooperative fund to form shops in other towns and to cancel the stock. The number of employes was seventy during the busy season, but very much less during other months. Every employe must own stock as soon as possible...

THE LEADER PUBLISHING ASSOCIATION [184 William Street] had by February, 1887, sold nine hundred five-dollar shares and $1,500 in larger shares. Sixty labor organizations owned one or more shares, and thirty thousand copies were reported to be the average circulation of the paper. Here the solidarity principle was not fully maintained, as each stockholder had one vote.

THE CONCORD COOPERATIVE PRINTING COMPANY [47 Centre Street] reported a paid-in capital of $3,500, on which no interest is paid, but, as in the previous company, stockholders vote. No one of the thirty-five stockholders can own more than ten of the twenty-dollar shares, and each must be a member of the typographical union. The profits since the starting of the enterprise two and a half years ago have been devoted to enlarging the business, which is steadily growing...

THE SOLIDARITY CIGAR FACTORY [10 Chatham Square], started August 1, 1886, has $1,500 capital. Fifty per cent. of the profits will be devoted to redeeming the stock on which no interest is paid, and afterward to a land fund, the building of factories, and extension of other cooperative business; the rest of the profits will be used as an insurance fund, and to enlarge the business. Ten men were employed in March, and the business was rapidly growing. The goods with the Knight of Labor brand are sold in the cooperative store in Pythagoras Hall, the headquarters of District 49, on Canal street, near the Bowery...

SOLIDARITY COOPERATIVE AND DISTRIBUTIVE STORE, 134 Canal Street, which is also the salesroom for the cigar factory last mentioned...

There is also a promising factory in Brooklyn, which is said to produce excellent work, but was not visited, the SOLIDARITY KNIGHTS OF LABOR WATCH CASE COMPANY, COOPERATIVE, 243 Plymouth street...[53]

THE COOPER COOPERATIVES IN MINNEAPOLIS

In the mid-1880s, there were at least thirty-two cooperatives in Minneapolis, including eight cooperative coopers (barrel factories), a cooperative grocery store, laundry, shirt factory, painters' association, house construction company, eight cooperative building and loan associations, and a land association and cooperative colony. Most of these formed between 1882 and 1886, during the precipitous rise of the KOL.[54] The barrel shops lay at the heart of the Knights' cooperative network, with almost 400 of the city's 600 barrel-makers in the cooperatives, producing the majority of the barrels in Minneapolis. In that era barrel-makers were skilled artisans, as machinery was not introduced into the industry until late in that decade. By the mid-1880s virtually all barrel-makers in the city—both cooperators and journeymen employees—belonged to the Knights of Labor, and together constituted an assembly. Knights all over the country pointed to the Minneapolis cooperatives as the flagship of their urban vision. At the same time, the greatest mill in that city, Pillsbury, switched to a profit sharing system.[55]

The cooperative shop movement in Minneapolis originated in 1868, independent of the Knights and shortly before the KOL was even founded. In that year, C. W. Curtis and three other barrel-makers set up a cooperative shop for a season.[56] Minneapolis barrel-makers also organized their first trade union in 1868, and it soon affiliated with the International Workingmen's Association (IWA). Thus the socialistic ideas of the IWA played a key role in the movement.[57]

That first shop was short-lived, but Curtis founded another cooperative shop two years later with a group that included F. L. Bachelder. That shop too had a brief life, but those experiences prepared Curtis and Bachelder for founding the Cooperative Barrel Manufacturing Company in 1874, which had a long-lasting success. Their first contract to supply barrels for a mill was with Charles A. Pillsbury, who had only recently set up in town.[58]

In 1870, Minneapolis was a boom town with 13,000 inhabitants; two decades earlier, it had not even existed. In 1880, its population tripled to 47,000; 130,000 people lived within its boundaries by 1885, many of them immigrants from Scandinavia, Germany, and Ireland.[59] At the heart of the city thundered St. Anthony Falls, the upper end of commercial navigation on the Mississippi and the waterpower harnessed for milling. Minneapolis' first industry was lumber, but its largest industry quickly became flour milling, processing hard Northern wheat. These mills made Minneapolis the largest flour-manufacturing city in the world.[60] While the mills used the highest technology of the time, the barrels were still mostly produced by artisanal methods, although machinery was soon to be introduced. Barrel-makers in search of work poured into the city from all over the country, but employment was sporadic since the work was connected with the harvest season.[61]

Curtis and Bachelder incorporated the Cooperative Barrel Manufacturing Company (CBC) in November 1874, with sixteen worker-members as a joint-stock company. A Minnesota law of 1870—instigated by Grangers—provided for the formation of cooperatives, but they chose to not incorporate under that statute because it was oriented to stores and farmer marketing cooperatives, and didn't serve all of their needs.[62] The CBC by-laws stipulated that all members must be equal shareholders. Distinguishing between two types of profit and loss, they apportioned profits from their primary business of cooperage to members in proportion to the work they had done, and apportioned profits or losses from any other source equally among the members. The latter could have included real estate appreciation and gains from side ventures or even hired help, while losses might have been from fire or default-ing creditors.[63]

Members bought an initial share for $15 apiece, which could be paid by weekly installments withheld from wages. Each was as-sessed $5 weekly to raise capital thereafter. $1,000 was used as down payment on a $3,000 shop on a half-acre of land, large enough for thirty workers, and situated near the railroad. A buy-in was required of new members. Once the cooperative reached an optimum size, new members could buy out departing members.[64] These by-laws served them so well that the seven other cooperative shops that fol-lowed CBC all used the same by-laws.[65]

The Cooperative Barrel Company was very successful. De-spite losing its shop to a fire in 1880, it expanded continually until its membership stood at 120 in 1885 with an accumulated capital of $58,000.[66]

The CBC's success ran parallel to that of the North Star Bar-rel Company, founded in 1877 by Curtis, Bachelder, and several others. They were motivated to organize the new cooperative by the ambition of expanding more rapidly than CBC was willing to undertake, but never fulfilled that goal. North Star reached a peak of one hundred members in 1882.[67]

The industry was based on piecework. In the cooperative shops, no one was allowed to work more than ten hours. Each worker placed his distinctive mark upon every barrel, and so was respon-sible for workmanship. The president and secretary were paid weekly salaries somewhere between the average and the highest earning worker. The president managed the general business and was usually also foreman, supervising the counting and loading of the barrels and the purchasing of materials. The secretary also kept the books.[68]

In 1885, the entire industry began introducing new steam-pow-ered labor-saving machinery. Competition required all the shops to follow suit. CBC invested in several thousand dollars of machinery and cut its membership down to ninety, while North Star reduced to fifty-six. Departing was voluntary and members were bought out at full cash payment of their capital investments. In general, those who withdrew were recent members, bachelors, and renters, and many used this money as a stake to buy land and start a new career as a farmer. For the most part, those who stayed had families and owned homes nearby. Cooperage was becoming less of an artisan industry;

all that was left to do by hand after the introduction of machinery was hooping, heading, and finishing.[69]

There were still 26 flour mills at the falls in 1886, with a 35,000 barrel aggregate daily capacity. After downsizing that same year, CBC had total assets of $58,000 and liabilities of $13,000, leaving a net value of about $500 for each remaining member. Nine out of ten members owned their own homes, about two-thirds of which were financed through cooperative building and loan associations. Many also belonged to the Minneapolis Cooperative Mercantile Company, the local cooperative store.[70]

Beyond the attrition by mechanization, the coopering trade was in decline due to the replacement of flour barrels by sacks and boxes.[71]

Journeymen and cooperators were together in the Coopers Assembly of the Knights of Labor, creating a knotty situation when they tried to work together to raise wages. In 1886, when the going piece rate for a finished hand-made barrel was between eleven and thirteen cents, the KOL launched a campaign to increase it to sixteen cents per barrel. In October, the journeymen walked out and struck. The cooperatives stopped production in sympathy. However, after a week, the cooperative barrel-makers resumed production to meet their contracts, paying fifteen cents per barrel to their members and also paying the striking journeymen full wages for staying out. The strike was finally settled when the four non-cooperative shops agreed to pay fifteen cents per barrel.[72]

In a volatile market, however, economic forces quickly made the agreement come unglued.

In the spring of 1886, the KOL district assembly proposed a plan to regulate the entire industry and take it out of the cycle of destructive competition that plagued the industry. Five cooperative shops and two capitalist shops formed the Coopers Association (CA). Under this agreement, the CA and the KOL would allocate a fair division of trade to each shop, according to their capacities. They would regulate the number of workers and the daily number of barrels per worker. The contract system with the mills would be abandoned in favor of a standard price of labor per barrel. Market price would fluctuate with materials cost. Every worker would be required to become a Knight, and all the shops would be given permission to use a KOL label, which at that time boosted sales.[73]

However, the mill owners led by Pillsbury opposed the arrangement. Three cooperative shops, including North Star, ignored the division of trade agreement. North Star entered into a contract with Pillsbury for as many barrels as they could produce. Until then, the Pillsbury contract had always gone to CBC. The KOL put great pressure on North Star, expelling fourteen members for violating their obligations as Knights, and threatening a boycott. The Knights finally negotiated a compromise whereby North Star divided the Pillsbury contract with the Cooperative Barrel Company. The Coopers Association also cut a deal with the mill owners for thirty-eight cents per barrel, which translated into fifteen cents per barrel to the worker. This contract lasted a year. But managing the pool fairly was complex, and there were constant disputes among the parties.[74]

OTHER KOL COOPERATIVES

Knight locals formed many other notable cooperatives in the mid-1880s.

In Massachusetts, there were KOL cooperative boot and shoe factories in Beverly, Scituate, Spencer, and Lynn, with outlet shoe stores in New Bedford and Clinton, and another shoe store in New Market, New Hampshire. In Chelsea, Massachusetts a KOL company manufactured elastic fabric products such as suspenders. Knight cooperative general stores were located in numerous New England locations.[75]

Baltimore was a center for Knight cooperatives. They organized a cooperative bakery in 1884, but it folded soon after; picking up the pieces, they started another bakery in 1886 with 250 member-stockholders. Knight glass-blowers, after a general strike in the industry, formed the Cooperative Glass Company employing one hundred workers in 1885. After the 1886 May Day strike for the eight-hour day, eighty-five blacklisted joiners formed the Furniture Workers Cooperative Manufacturing Association of Baltimore. In the same period, they organized a shirt factory, a publishing house, and a cooperage.

The Southern and Border states, although primarily still rural, had a number of KOL cooperatives. A tobacco company was started in Covington in 1884, and another in Raleigh in 1886. In Richmond they ran a soap factory and an underwear factory; in Annapolis, a glass works; pottery in Wheeling; publishing in Fort Worth; mining in Hopkins County, Kentucky; laundry in Fort Worth; a match factory in Woodstock, West Virginia; a broom factory in Lynchburg; mining in Louisville and Earlington, Kentucky, and in Salisbury, Alabama. The KOL ran cooperative stores in Danville and Louisville. African-American Knights ran a cooperative cotton gin in Stewart's Station, Alabama. Near Birmingham, the KOL built cooperative villages they called Powderly and Trevellick, today neighborhoods of that city.[76]

The KOL cooperative movement spilled over into Canada. Centered in Ontario, operations included factories producing horse-stays, cigars, and biscuits.[77]

In addition to all the KOL cooperatives, there were numerous other cooperatives organized in those feverish years of the mid-1880s. In the South the Grange also revived to organize new farmer cooperatives.

In response to the workers' agitation in the 1880s, many businesses began to offer profit-sharing to their workers. This system had long been in use in the New England fisheries and other industries, but was recent to manufacturers. Businesses offering profit sharing included Ara Cushman shoes in Auburn, Maine; the Peace Dale wool mill in Rhode Island; Union Mining in Maryland; and, as already mentioned, Pillsbury in Minneapolis.[78]

The 1886 KOL convention elected Leonora Barry to take charge of their new department of women's work and organize new locals, becoming the first woman professional labor organizer in American history. She added her voice to those who proposed that the KOL turn its "whole undivided attention to the forming of productive and distributive co-operative enterprises."[79] In Chicago, St. Louis, and Indianapolis, women Knights set up cooperative garment factories. Barry toured the country for four years, organizing to improve wages and working conditions of women and children, fighting for racial equality, equal pay for equal work, and an end to sexual harassment.[80] Susan B. Anthony was also active in the KOL.[81]

CLIMAX OF THE GREAT UPHEAVAL

The depression of 1883-85 brought great suffering to the working population. Wages fell on average 15 percent, and up to 40 percent in coal mining. Farmers suffered intensely from high railroad charges, exorbitant mortgage rates, and low prices for their produce. Tenant farmers additionally suffered from high rents. Small merchants were hurting.[82] The KOL called on all these "producing classes" to organize "to prevent the benefits being monopolized by the few, and to secure for each member of society a full and just share of the wealth created by the labor of his hands."[83] All of these groups responded to the call to wage a common struggle against monopoly, with a huge wave of strikes and boycotts, the creation of cooperatives, and the formation of political campaigns for progressive legislation. Large segments of the working population, quiescent and unorganized until then, were drawn headlong into the struggle, including the unskilled and immigrant groups. This unprecedented level of activism brought the period that began with the national railroad strike of 1877 to a climax.[84]

In 1885, the Knights won the greatest union victory in American history up to that time, striking against and defeating the Union Pacific Railroad. The KOL forced the railroad magnate Jay Gould, the most powerful capitalist in America, to recognize the union and agree to arbitrate all labor disputes. For the first time in American history, a labor organization dealt with capital on an equal footing.[85] Inspired by that victory, massive numbers of workers began joining the KOL, mostly unskilled and semi-skilled, many immigrants, and many formerly skilled workers now reduced to apprentice level by new machine techniques. By 1886, between 750,000 and a million Americans were Knights, making the KOL the largest labor organization not only in the United States but the world. They had to call a temporary halt to accepting new members due to the organizational chaos this was creating.[86]

THE KOL & THE REVOLUTIONARY SOCIALIST LABOR PARTY

A few months after the great railroad strike of 1877, the Workingmen's Party—with roots in the original "First" International (IWA)—changed its name to the Socialist Labor Party (SLP) and decided to run candidates in the 1878 election. At first primarily made up of German immigrants, the SLP received thousands of votes in many cities, electing several candidates to local office in Milwaukee.[87]

The left wing of the SLP had its fill of electoral politics by 1880. Its members broke away, and formed the Revolutionary Socialist Labor Party (RSLP).[88] The RSLP aimed to establish a "free society based on cooperative production," with cooperative associations federating to take care of public affairs in place of a state-type government. They planned to bring it about through "direct action." The RSLP was a clandestine organization based in cells of nine members; each cell was a partly autonomous collective.[89]

The differences between the SLP and the RSLP were typical of those in socialist movements in many countries at this time, reflecting the ideological struggle between "social-democrats" and "anarcho-communists." The anarchists would attack the capitalist state directly and do away with it immediately; the social-democrats would take over the capitalist state electorally and use that power to socialize the economy, retaining the structure of a centralized government to take care of public affairs until society advanced to the point the structure became unnecessary.[90]

The RSLP saw the trade unions and the Knight assemblies as the basic cells of the new order. Most RSLP members also belonged to one or the other. These would transform themselves into "autonomous communes" once capitalist ownership of the means of production and the capitalist-controlled state machinery of repression were swept away by a revolutionary uprising of workers.[91]

American anarchists considered themselves in the Jeffersonian tradition, as expressed in the Declaration of Independence, which affirmed the equality of all people and justified revolution as a response to the systematic denial and violation of "inalienable rights." In consequence, American anarchist thought demanded the abolition of all laws in conflict with natural rights, particularly laws enforcing privilege and private property, and claimed the right to abolish those unjust laws through revolution. With those laws eliminated, individuals and society would be left "free" to exercise their natural rights, returning to their state of natural equality.[92]

In 1881, the RSLP affiliated with the International Working People's Association (IWPA)—also called the "Black International"—the loose "anarchist" federation of worker movements from different European countries formed by many sections of the old "First" International (IWA) when they split off a decade earlier. The direct-action anarchist followers of Bakunin dominated the "Black" International in Europe.[93] Although both "Black" and "Red" American Internationalists affiliated with the same European "Black" International, the differences between these rival American factions of "Black" and "Red" were more than just alphabet soup. They debated over various positions and, when they were not bickering, came together to fight their common corporate capitalist adversary.[94] The

Icarian communities associated with the "Black" International, as did the core group of San Francisco labor leaders and radicals led by Burnette Haskell who would form Kaweah Cooperative Colony a few years later. Some confusion exists in historical accounts, because distinctly different American "International" organizations in different parts of the country went by similar names. Haskell's California group was commonly known as the "Red" International to distinguish it from the RSLP and its associates, known as the "Black" International. Haskell's group actually called itself the International Workingmen's Association (the exact name of the old "First" IWA).[95]

KNIGHTS VS. AFL

While the Knights were growing, the newly formed Federation of Organized Trades and Labor Unions (FOTLU)—soon to become the American Federation of Labor (AFL)—had an estimated maximum of 140,000 members, at most only a fifth of the Knights.[96] A bitter rivalry flared between the two organizations and their conflicting structures. The Federation, under the domination of former Knight Samuel Gompers, was white-only, skilled-worker-only. They espoused a philosophy of "trade-unionism, pure and simple," and limited themselves to bread-and-butter issues. They were against worker cooperatives not only because of past failures, but also because cooperatives were associated with radicalism and radical movements, of which they wanted no part, and because cooperatives obscured the line between employee and employer. This confused the union's role as bargaining agent, which they saw as the unions' basic identity, with the contract the eternal goal.[97] The Federation harbored no ideas of a Cooperative Commonwealth, and was the first important labor association in America to accept and support the wage system as permanent, and not fight for its abolition. Later, however, the AFL would endorse consumer cooperatives.[98]

The Federation organized with each trade fighting separately against its own employers for its own advantage, while the Knights felt they could not accomplish their goals unless they brought all workers, skilled and unskilled and of all races, into the same organization, to use the tactical strength of the skilled for the benefit of all. So the Knights of Labor, although the older organization, was the aggressor, periodically trying to separate whole unions from the Federation and bring them into the Knights.[99]

HAYMARKET AND THE DESTRUCTION
OF THE KOL COOPERATIVES

By the mid-1880s, the eight-hour movement swept the country. Twelve-hour, fourteen-hour and even sixteen-hour workdays still prevailed in many industries and areas. The Eight-Hour Leagues had originated in Boston with the leadership of Ira Steward, a machinist. They resolved, "We regard co-operation in industry and exchange, as the final and permanent solution of the long conflict between labor and capital."[100] The eight-hour day was to be a first step. They organized nationally and called for a national general strike set for May 1, 1886, to last until all had won the eight-hour day and the forty-eight-hour week with no loss in pay. This act marked the origin of what has become the international workers' holiday, May Day.[101]

While the Federation officially endorsed the strike, the Knight national organization decided to take no official stand; they left each local and regional to decide on its own. Most decided to strike.[102] In practice, many Knights across the country played leadership roles in the movement, and did much more of the local organizing than Federation members. Some Knights were also members of the clandestine Revolutionary Socialist Labor Party (RSLP), which by 1886 had 6,000 members, and branches in New York, Philadelphia and Chicago. The largest was in Chicago, where they had won control of the Central Labor Council. The RSLP became a leading force in organizing the national strike.[103]

Meanwhile, the Knights' settlement with Jay Gould and his Union Pacific Railroad fell apart. Beginning with the discharge of a Knight foreman, the entire Texas and Pacific road went on strike on March 1st, 1886, led by Knight District Assembly 101 Master Workman Martin Irons, a machinist and previously master of the largest Grange in Kentucky. Within a week, the entire system of 5,000 miles of railway through Missouri, Kansas, Arkansas, Indian Territory (Oklahoma), and Nebraska shut down. The strikers took possession of rail yards and disabled all engines. The strike lasted for two months, and was still in progress when the May 1st general eight-hour strike began.[104]

On May Day, almost 200,000 struck for the eight-hour day, with twice that number participating in marches and demonstrations across America. The strike continued the following four days.[105] Tensions around the country grew. No one knew where it might lead. The Union Pacific Railroad strike collapsed on May 3rd. On May 4th, police at the McCormick Harvester plant in Chicago shot six picketing workers in the back.[106]

A large protest meeting was held that evening in Haymarket Square. Police squadrons moved in to break it up. A bomb exploded. Police fired wildly into the crowd, killing and wounding a large number. Police terror swept Chicago and spread across the country, breaking the strike everywhere. Police, goon and vigilante violence were the order of the day wherever organized workers gathered.[107] The employers took the opportunity to hit the Knights with everything they had. They did not touch the AFL though. In New York, Pittsburgh, and St. Louis, police charged Knight leaders with conspiracy. Martin Irons and other leaders of the railroad strike were blacklisted for the rest of their lives.[108]

On August 20th, 1886, a jury in Chicago found eight "anarchists" guilty of the bombing. All of them were associated with the RSLP. The judge sentenced seven of them to death, with their ideas the only evidence against them. Among them stood Albert Parsons, also a Knight of Labor, and the leader of the Chicago Eight-Hour League. The sensational show trial took place during the feverish height of KOL cooperative organization, and the yellow press continually blared "red scare" headlines to a frightened public. An appeal drew out the agony for another year, during which the KOL was constantly wrenched apart. Finally on November 11th, 1887, Parsons and three others were hanged. The RSLP was never heard from again.[109]

Historian Joseph G. Raybeck wrote in *A History of American Labor*, "The first of the Knights' ventures to feel the full effect of the post-Haymarket reaction were their cooperative enterprises."[110] The entire economic system came down hard on the Knight cooperatives: railroads refused to haul their products; manufacturers refused to sell them needed machinery; wholesalers refused them raw materials and supplies; banks wouldn't lend.[111]

The viability of the cooperatives had been tied to the strength and solidarity of the local assemblies and burgeoning organization, and to the goodwill and support of the local communities. Earlier, the KOL cooperatives had great community support. In large part, the public saw the Knights and the labor movement as representing the constructive interests of the American working people, and went out of their way to patronize them.[112] But now as the organization was attacked continually and painted in the press as the source of violence and destructive lawlessness, the cooperatives lost much of their clientele and markets. Now customers stayed away, and some proved afraid to patronize them in an environment of alarm. It derailed and paralyzed their entire operation. "The life of KOL cooperatives was almost always tied to the vitality of the local assemblies. Hard times, capitalist backlash, and shrinking membership ultimately doomed both."[113]

The cooperatives could not stand toe-to-toe against the economic system they had challenged, and that was now throwing its every weapon against them. At a time when the accelerated introduction of advanced machinery increasingly transformed most industries, the great majority of the Knight cooperatives had been started with little capital and obsolescent machinery. Many cooperatives began in the midst of strikes, with their members' incomes cut off. They simply couldn't afford to tool up. They relied instead on the skills of their members, and found those skills no longer adequate. Most cooperatives were not prepared for the cutthroat economics they faced in the marketplace with the competition colluding to destroy them. They pursued their American dream of independence and self-employment, at a time when the economic system was making the fulfillment of that dream impossible for increasingly larger numbers. They held the values of artisans and small farmers, while complex machinery and the wage system were making those values impossible for them to live by. They were humanists in an era of robber barons.[114] As the KOL lost its course and disintegrated, the cooperatives lost their compass and heart. By the end of 1888, most of the cooperatives were forced to close shop.[115] "But let us make no mistake," historian Robert E. Weir wrote in *Beyond Labor's Veil*, "the Knights of Labor did not commit suicide; it was murdered."[116]

Many rank-and-file Knights were angry at the national leadership for not endorsing the national strike and then furious at Powderly when he did not support the call for amnesty for the "Haymarket martyrs." This schism, the violence, and the realization that the KOL did not have the power to solve their basic problems, caused workers to pour out of the Knights as quickly as they'd poured in. KOL membership fell to 500,000 in 1887. The greatest decrease came in the bigger cities. In 1888, the organization fell to 260,000 members, with only 82,000 in the 20 largest cities.

KOL had 100,000 members in 1890 and 74,000 in 1893. After that, the KOL never again released membership statistics.[117] In 1893, a coalition of agrarians and socialists replaced Powderly as Grand Master Workman with James Sovereign, a farm editor from Iowa. They became a secret organization again, based no longer in industrial centers, but primarily in smaller cities, towns and rural areas.[118] Many Knight cooperatives continued in scattered areas around the country, though they ceased to be a major factor in the national economy.[119]

Also in 1893, a new Illinois governor cleared all the victims of the Haymarket show trial and released the survivors, but the damage had long been done.[120]

The Knights gave up attempting to organize the great mass of unskilled workers after 1889. The Knights' defeat and the rise of the AFL marked the ascendancy of business-unionism in the United States. This was the only opposition that the ruling capitalists were now willing to tolerate. Control of the AFL national bureaucracy fell into increasingly conservative hands, despite periodic uprisings of its membership, and the AFL became a "loyal opposition."[121] The eight-hour day was finally won as a universal standard in the New Deal.[122]

The destruction of the Knights' cooperative movement marks the end of the era when the mass of wage earners and labor leaders looked to cooperatives as a strategy for liberating the wageclass from bondage. Experience had demonstrated that industrial worker cooperatives on a national scale could not be achieved under the existing economic system. Apart from vulnerability to financial attack, the cooperative strategy proved impractical because the rising costs of the dominant means of production put them out of reach of even a large group of workers. Never again would the business elite permit worker cooperatives to get a broad foothold in industry, the stronghold of American capitalism. As the KOL waned, the American labor movement continued on a different footing from the European movement.[123] In most of Europe, the socialist movement and workers' parties became an accepted part of the political landscape, while they were excluded from the mainstream in America. As historian Kim Voss wrote in *The Making of American Exceptionalism*, "American industrial relations and labor politics are exceptional because in 1886 and 1887 employers won the class struggle."[124]

OUTSIDE THE MAINSTREAM IN THE 1880s

The movement was pervasive in this era, and workers formed cooperatives in many far corners of society, including cowboys, the Chinese in California, and professional baseball players.

GET EVEN QUICK CATTLE COMPANY

In 1883, Tom Harris, a wagon boss, organized striking cowboys in the Texas Panhandle to form the Get Even Quick Cattle Company, a cooperative "syndicate ranch." Just before the roundup of that year, Harris organized what became known as the Great Cowboy Strike of 1883. They struck over the issues of higher pay and the abolition of a new rule against hands running their own herds on the side. That rule riled them the most. Cowboys until that time had been able to run small herds of their own on ranch land alongside the owner's herd. Because wages were very low, putting their own brand on unbranded mavericks was the only way a cowboy could begin to raise a stake of his own and eventually have his own herd. But large corporations had bought up many of the outfits and outlawed that practice. There were twenty-three original strikers. They set up headquarters at Tascosa, established a strike fund, and organized hands in the surrounding area. Approximately 325 cowpunchers in all went out on strike. A company of Texas Rangers was dispatched to the area. Later the stockmen's association hired Ranger Pat Garrett to head a company of Home Rangers, a private militia, to police the range. Many of the strikers ran out of funds after a month, and were forced to look for work, but found themselves blacklisted. The big ranchers accused the Get Even Quick Cattle Company of being a rustling operation, and fired any cowboy who bought a share. Deeply in debt, the Get Even Quick ranch never lived up to its moniker, but had to fold, and Harris died soon after.[125]

CHINESE-AMERICAN COOPERATIVES

A historian in 1887 noted the prevalence of cooperatives in the economy of San Francisco's Chinatown during that era. All economic activity among the Chinese in California was regulated by community mutual aid organizations, which were highly secretive to outsiders. A board for each industry, appointed by the various cooperative groups, regulated all activities, determining the number of each type of businesses permitted, their location, and number of workers. They ran cooperative businesses in many industries, most prevalently in laundries and shoemakers. All Chinese in California came under contract with one of six Chinese companies, which served to both protect workers and control them. All Chinese workers had to belong to a group. A new group wishing to start a cooperative business would apply to the trade board. Upon approval, each worker would make an investment and receive stock. Before each Chinese New Year, the books were balanced, profits or losses distributed, the books burned, and new books opened for the New Year.[126]

PLAYERS' LEAGUE

In 1889, a large group of some of the best professional baseball players, led by Charles Comiskey and Connie Mack, walked out of both the National League and the American Association, and set up their own organization, the Players' League. The key issue was the reserve clause in contracts, which bound a player to one team until that club let him go. In the new league, the reserve clause was abolished. The Players' League fielded teams in eight Eastern and Midwestern cities in 1890 and played a full season. The league was governed by a "senate," consisting half of players' representatives and half of financial investors. However, the new circuit was hampered by an antagonistic press, which promoted the old leagues and often refused to even report their scores. At the end of the 1890 season, the investors met with the owners of the older leagues and, over the players' objections, merged the circuits and disbanded the Players' League.[127]

6.
"The Bloody Nineties"

FARMERS' ALLIANCE

The Farmers' Alliance flooded across rural America between 1887 and 1890. The organization originally grew out of farmers' clubs that formed spontaneously in many frontier communities of the West and Southwest between 1840 and 1870 for mutual protection from "land sharks" (speculators) and cattle barons. It began as a coordinated movement in 1874, organizing cooperative purchasing and marketing like the Grange.[1] While the Grange was strong, many farmers' clubs were swept into it and disappeared. But some retained their independence and, when the Grange began to fall apart, the Alliance stepped into the vacuum with enormous energy. There were three large separate but connected organizations, one in the North and West, and two in the segregated South by 1890. The Northern Alliance (actually mostly in the West), with Milton George in the leadership, had more than a million members. The Southern Alliance, led by C. W. Macune, had almost three million. The Colored Farmers' Alliance (CFA), founded by J. J. Shuffer, H. L. Spencer, and R. M. Humphrey, had one and a quarter million members, making it the largest-ever organization of black Americans, most of them sharecroppers and tenant farmers.[2]

A complex relationship existed between blacks and whites inside the Colored Farmers' Alliance, as well as between the CFA and the other Alliances. This was the period of "Jim Crow" segregation, and only the lowest economic niches such as sharecropping, tenant farming under the crop-lien system, or field hand jobs were open to blacks.[3] Racism was rampant, and the system pitted poor whites against poor blacks. When landowners evicted white tenant farmers for not being able to meet their crop-lien payments, they often replaced them with blacks. White field hands were told that blacks depressed wages and working conditions. Meanwhile, the property qualifications, literacy tests, and poll taxes that aimed at disenfranchising blacks also disenfranchised numerous poor whites.[4]

The Colored Farmers' Alliance was founded in Texas in 1886 by two African-American farmers named J. J. Shuffer and H. L. Spencer, and a white minister named R. M. Humphrey. Shuffer was the first president, Spencer secretary, and Humphrey general superintendent. Because whites were able to organize openly in areas where blacks would have been met with physical attacks dues to the racist environment, the main task of organizing on the state and regional levels was entrusted to Humphrey and other whites. Black leadership in the CFA was mostly on the local level and low-profile. An exception was William H. Warwick, an African-American who was elected state superintendent of the Virginia Colored Alliance in 1891, despite opposition from Humphrey.[5] Although the Texas Farmers Alliance was white-only, the closely connected Texas People's Party was interracial; the Alliance formed the main constituency of the party. The white Southern Farmers' Alliance controlled the Colored Farmers Alliance by foisting an all-white board on them.[6] Despite this, the Colored Alliance was active, and its pickers struck the cotton fields for a dollar a day wage in 1891, although many of the farm owners opposing them were white Alliancemen. H. S. Doyle, a black preacher working with the Colored Alliance in Georgia and campaigning for the Populist Tom Watson in 1892, was threatened by a mob and sought refuge with Watson, who protected him on his property. Watson sent the word out and 2,000 armed white farmers, supporters of Watson, surrounded the land, guarded the house through the night, and helped Doyle escape.[7] Later however, Watson made it clear that he supported interracial cooperation but not social equality. Nonetheless, their opponents accused the Populists of "treason to the white race."[8]

At first, the Farmers' Alliances did mostly cooperative buying of supplies and machinery, and marketing of cotton and grain. The system through which this was accomplished was known as the "state agency." Like the Grange before them, they soon added groceries and a variety of dry goods. Farmers could purchase supplies on security of their crops. Getting credit from the Alliance freed them from the banks and capitalist suppliers, who would give them crop-liens at huge interest rates, meaning strangulation by ever-increasing debts and virtual serfdom. Under the crop-lien system, the farmer mortgaged his prospective crop in exchange for supplies. The lender received first claim on the harvest, and controlled the price. In practice, the lender was often a local merchant. The farmer usually put up all of his property as a guarantee, and could not trade with any other merchant until he paid the debt off. When the harvest did not erase the mortgage, the farmer was ensnared.[9] The Alliance determined to break that system. Each local Alliance unit usually had a cooperative store, grain elevator, cheese factory or cotton gin, depending on their area. By the 1890s, they'd reached California, where they also operated flourmills and in one location a tannery.[10]

In 1887, the Southern Alliance organized its first big marketing cooperative. Based in Dallas, the Texas Farmers' Exchange dealt mostly in cotton, with C. W. Macune as business manager. The Exchange advanced supplies to member farmers, and was paid back from the sale of the harvest. But the Exchange was hardly able to get off the ground. It desperately needed credit but no bank would advance it, refusing to accept Alliance security notes except at impossibly large discounts. Alliancemen were soon charging there was a conspiracy of bankers, wholesalers, implement dealers and manufacturers set on destroying them.[11] Although the Exchange did a million-dollar volume in its second year, it was hit with a barrage of economic blows, and folded in 1890, with Macune under fire for deficiencies in bookkeeping and in other business practices.[12]

Nonetheless, similar exchanges were soon set up in eighteen other states, trying out several variations on the structure. Unlike the Grange cooperatives, they did not issue shares. They rejected the Rochdale system and preferred to pass on savings directly to members. They were regional in scope, while the Granges were local.[13] In every case, the banking and business interests attacked the exchanges and destroyed them.[14]

Farmers everywhere were losing their land to the banks, merchants, and speculators, and being driven down into tenancy. Half the farmers in the South were tenants after 1890, as were a quarter of the farmers in the Midwest and in much of the East.[15]

"What is life and so-called liberty if the means of subsistence are monopolized?" *The Farmers' Alliance*, the newspaper coming out of Lincoln, Nebraska, asked. "The corporation has absorbed the community. The community must now absorb the corporation— must merge itself into it. Society must enlarge itself to the breadth of humanity. A stage must be reached in which each will be for all and all for each. The welfare of the individual must be the object and the end of all effort."[16]

Farmers' Alliance song (c. 1890)
by Arthur L. Kellogg

I was once a tool of oppression,
And as green as a sucker could be
And monopolies banded together
To beat a poor hayseed like me.

But now I've roused up a little
And their greed and corruption I see,
And the ticket we vote next November
Will be made up of hayseeds like me.[17]

Spurred by the destruction of the exchanges in the midst of the worsening depression, Alliancemen began to run for office to change the laws that permitted the banks to rule. The Alliance worked with the Knights of Labor to write their platform.[18]

Alliancemen and candidates supported by the Alliance won four governorships, took the state legislature in nine states and sent three senators and forty-three congressmen to Washington in 1890.[19] But bringing about real change was harder than electing candidates, as the Greenbackers had found out earlier. Although bills were passed in Nebraska and North Carolina regulating the railroads, they didn't make a dent in the actual freight rates. Bank control remained untouched. Change had to be made on a national scale.[20]

Tom Watson, an Allianceman and newly elected Populist congressman from Georgia, soon presented a plan to Congress prepared by the Alliance and originated by C. W. Macune. Known as the "subtreasury plan," it proposed that the government would become an intermediary in crop distribution, paying farmers 80 percent of market value and storing it for them until it was sold. The government would issue new greenbacks to pay for the crops, whose value would be based on the food itself, not on gold. When this was laughed down as "potato banks" and its advocates as "hayseed socialists," the Alliance turned from both "major" parties and organized a new national party.[21]

ALLIANCE-KNIGHTS COALITION

The coalition between the Farmers' Alliance and the Knights of Labor was forged in the spring of 1886 at the instigation of William Lamb, the first Texas Alliance cooperative purchasing agent and president of the Montague County chapter. It began when Lamb unilaterally proclaimed a boycott in support of the Knights' Great Southwestern Strike against Gould's Union Pacific Railroad. The Texas Alliance president protested that Lamb had no authorization, and a battle ensued over the Alliance's goals and strategy. Lamb believed that farmers in the emerging era were workers and their future depended on a coalition with the labor movement. The membership overwhelmingly supported him. He argued that it was "a good time to help the Knights of Labor in order to secure their help in the near future" because "if the Knights of Labor could receive all they deserve [of] the support of all the laboring classes, they would in the near future bring down the great monopolists and capitalists and emancipate the toilers of the earth from the heavy burdens which they now have to bear on account of organized capital."[22] In 1891, Lamb became the key organizer and chair of the state Populist Party.[23] The KOL at that moment turned to populist electoral politics to try to clear the way for their embattled movement.

POPULIST PARTY

In 1892, the Farmers' Alliance, the Knights of Labor, and several other cooperative organizations including the Agricultural Wheel, the Patrons of Industry, and the Farmers' Mutual Benefit Society united to form the People's Party, known as the Populists.[24]

"Wealth belongs to him who creates it," the Populist program stated, "and every dollar taken from industry without an equivalent is robbery... The interests of rural and civil labor are the same, their enemies are identical."[25] The program called for public ownership of the railroads, telephone and telegraph lines; for abolition of the private banking system; for public control of the money system on a silver standard; for adoption of the Populist "subtreasury" food distribution plan; for reclaiming all corporate-owned land "in excess of their actual needs" and for turning over this land to settlers since "the land, including all natural sources of wealth, is the heritage of the people and should not be monopolized for speculative purposes"; the adoption of initiative, referendum, and recall; and an effective graduated income tax.[26]

"We expect to be confronted with a vast and splendidly equipped army of extortionists, usurers and oppressors," cried James Weaver of Iowa, the Populist presidential candidate, initiating the campaign with $50 in the party treasury. "Corporate feudality has taken the place of chattel slavery and vaunts its power in every state... We have challenged the adversary to battle and our bugles have sounded the march."[27]

The People's Party called for unity between poor whites and blacks. "The white tenant lives adjoining the colored tenant," said Tom Watson. "Their houses are almost equally destitute of comforts. Their living is confined to bare necessities... Now the People's Party says to these two men, 'You are kept apart that you may be separately fleeced of your earnings. You are made to hate each other because upon that hatred is rested the keystone of the arch of financial despotism that enslaves you both.'"[28] Black leaders were most prominent in Texas, but were a factor almost everywhere that Populism was strong. The exception was in South Carolina, where Benjamin Tillman took control of the state Alliance, presenting himself as champion of small white farmers, excluding blacks, and using the organization to inflame racism and get himself elected governor. But everywhere that Populists worked to bring black and white together, the opposition met them with intimidation, fraud, and terrorism, particularly in the South; in Georgia, fifteen were killed.[29] Still, Weaver won in Colorado, Idaho and Kansas, and got over a million counted votes.[30]

The strength of the party continued to grow as the depression of 1893 hit rock bottom. In 1894, a few months after America's second great railroad strike, one and a half million Populist votes were counted, and Populists won governorships in Kansas and Colorado.[31] But as they prepared for a major assault on the presidency in the next election, the left wing of the Democrats staged a coup against renominating the corrupt incumbent Cleveland, and in 1896 nominated instead the upstart William Jennings Bryan on a platform of free silver, part of the Populist program. The Populists and left-wing Democrats had an overlapping constituency. The Populists expected Bryan to take their own Tom Watson as his vice presidential runningmate, but Bryan instead chose a conservative politician. Though terribly split, the People's Party decided to back Bryan, but with Watson for vice president. This alliance possibly saved the Democratic Party from extinction, as it had already been virtually eliminated in the West and Northwest.[32] Meanwhile, the old Democratic machine bolted the party, leaving Bryan without financial support and dependent in many areas on the energy of the Populists. Even though Bryan got almost 47 percent of the vote, the election turned out to be a catastrophe for Populism, as the People's Party was now beyond repair as an independent force. The party never recovered from the strategic error of wedding its broad-based popular economic movement too closely with one candidate and one issue.[33]

With the collapse of the party, the Farmers' Alliance fell too, as did the other farmer cooperative associations. The party had drained off most of their energy; they had run out of strategies.[34]

The Democratic Party soon flopped back under control of its right wing.[35] Most of the local and statewide legislation enacted by Populists was overturned in the courts under the guise of "upholding precedent" and the Fourteenth Amendment to the Constitution. That amendment forbade states to "deprive any person of life, liberty or property without due process of law," and had been set up to protect former slaves. The court turned it around by ruling that corporations were "legal people." At the same time, corporate owners could not be held liable for the criminal offenses of the corporations. In 1886, the Supreme Court voided 230 state laws regulating corporations, primarily freight rates railroads charged farmers, on the grounds that regulation deprived the corporations of their property without due process.[36] Congress passed the first act regulating interstate commerce in the following year, but federal regulation quickly became a tool of the corporations being regulated. Of the 307 Fourteenth Amendment cases brought before the Supreme Court between 1890 and 1910, 288 were about protecting corporate property, and only 19 about protecting people.[37]

When the Farmers' Alliance collapsed, the Grange revived in the Midwest, Far West and North. Its strength was local, not regional. By 1908, it approached the half million mark again. The Grange remained strong until the Great Depression of the 1930s, when it was again unable to meet its members' needs and declined. But the Grange once again made a comeback.[38]

POPULISM AND RACISM

The early Populist movement and the Farmers' Alliance played out the complex pattern of class struggle clouded by race, particularly in the South, a recurring theme in American history.[39]

Between the "Great Betrayal" of 1877 that ended Southern Reconstruction, and the Civil Rights Act of 1964 where the Democratic Party decisively rejected segregation, the racist wing of the Democratic Party controlled the South and enforced "Jim Crow" segregation.[40] The "Dixiecrat" moniker pointed out the party's regional split between northern Democrats who largely supported civil rights, and Democrats of the "Solid South" who supported segregation. The national Democratic Party in this period was a shaky marriage of convenience between these two factions.[41]

Blacks had been primarily Republicans in the years following the Civil War when it was still the party of Lincoln; but when the Republicans handed the South back to the party of the Confederacy—the Southern Democrats—many blacks were attracted to the People's Party as an alternative.[42]

Although Populist politicians like Tom Watson appealed for unity of blacks and whites, Populist nominees were almost entirely white. After the People's Party disappeared into the Democratic Party, many Populist politicians, including Watson, became staunch Dixiecrats. During the last decades of the Jim Crow era, the term "Populist" lost all sense of black-white unity, and became appropriated as a demagogic shorthand for "segregationist."[43]

When the split in the Democratic Party finally ruptured with the Civil Rights Act of 1964, most Southern Dixiecrats changed hats and became Republicans. The Solid South transformed overnight from solid Democrat to solid Republican.

SHERMAN ACT

By the 1890s, most of the major American industries were firmly in the control of "trusts," central boards made up of trustees of supposedly competing companies, giving them monopolistic powers.[44] The enormous spoils in the wake of the Civil War had long been dished out, and financiers and industrialists settled down to ruling different sections of the country like medieval barons from behind various corporate facades, sometimes feuding with each other, sometimes collaborating.[45] The largest contributed heavily to both major parties, the Republicans and Democrats, who had made their peace as twin pillars of the capitalist system.[46]

The Sherman "Anti-Trust" Act of 1890, passed by Congress due to intense lobbying by labor, farmers, and small businessmen, declared illegal any "combination or conspiracy" to restrain interstate commerce. Since the monopolistic practices of the trusts were based on collusion, they were supposedly outlawed. The act supposedly favored small business by curbing monopoly, but it made no distinction between the conspiratorial practices of big business and the cooperative practices of small producers, small businesses, or unions. The Sherman Act outlawed cooperatives engaged in interstate commerce, and unions organizing interstate strikes.[47] Agricultural co-ops requested an exemption, because the very existence of small farms depended on co-ops. Although the farm family remained an American icon, the exemption was refused.[48] The Sherman Act made numerous co-ops illegal. In theory a powerful tool against monopoly, in practice, the Sherman Act was a powerful tool of big business against co-ops and unions. It was used to break strikes twelve times in the decade, but never once to break a trust. As a political observer said, "What looks like a stone wall to a layman, is a triumphal arch to a corporation lawyer."[49]

The economy collapsed again in 1893, the financial panic throwing the country deeper than ever into depression. Morgan, Rockefeller, Carnegie, Harriman, Mellon and other millionaires added immense new holdings to their gigantic fortunes, while farmers got thrown off their land and the unemployed starved.[50]

INDUSTRIAL UNIONISM

There was tremendous labor strife throughout the 1890s. The coalfields of Tennessee constantly exploded in open warfare.[51] 1892 saw the strike at Carnegie's Homestead steel plant near Pittsburgh, where strikers defeated Pinkertons in a gun battle but then met defeat by state militia.[52] A general strike brought New Orleans to a standstill.[53] Martial law was declared in Idaho against silver mine workers.[54]

Unions of a new type were being organized, by industry instead of by trade, and therefore included a broad spectrum of skilled and unskilled workers in their organizations.[55] Eugene Debs, a locomotive fireman, was instrumental in organizing the American Railway Union, in which railroad workers became well organized for the first time.[56] "Big" Bill Haywood at the same time was instrumental in organizing the Western Federation of Miners.[57]

In June 1894, America's second great railroad strike erupted, in support of the workers building rail cars in the company town of Pullman. When the railroads stopped, America stopped. There was

tremendous support for the strike among the general working population; again Populists came to their aid and small farmers helped in
many areas by bringing food.[58] This strike quickly became like the
first great railroad strike of 1877, a nationwide confrontation between workers and capitalists. In Chicago, the hub of the action, the
Central Labor Council voted for a general sympathetic strike, but
before it was to take effect, the corporations flexed their muscles and
President Cleveland ordered out 20,000 army troops to take charge,
crush the strike, and run the railroads. General warfare broke out
between strikers and troops in Chicago.[59] Confronted with overwhelming odds, Debs called for a national general strike, which
Gompers and the AFL leadership refused. Debs wound up in jail for
six months and the American Railway Union was destroyed.[60]

RESURGENCE OF THE SOCIALIST LABOR PARTY, SOCIALIST TRADE AND LABOR ALLIANCE

The Socialist Labor Party (SLP), the electoral party founded
in 1877 and in its first years made up almost entirely of German
immigrants, became slowly Americanized over the next decade. In
1892, with the leadership of Daniel De Leon, editor of the party
newspaper, the SLP nominated its first presidential ticket and garnered 21,000 votes in 6 states, with the majority in New York State.[61]
At that point, the SLP fully expected to win state power through the
political system. But they harbored no illusions that the capitalists
would simply hand over the reins of power and let them socialize the
industries. They likened themselves to Abolitionists before the Civil
War, and expected that if the Left won political power, the Right
would act like the South after Lincoln's election. De Leon worked to
forge an alliance between the SLP and both the KOL and the AFL,
but was eventually rejected by both.[62] The electoral strength of the
SLP continued to rise in the following years, until it garnered 82,000
votes in 1898 and its candidates won local offices in several cities.[63]

De Leon had become powerful in the KOL as a key member of New York City District Assembly 49. From that position,
he worked to construct a close alliance between the SLP and the
Knights, based on the idea that the KOL would provide the vehicle
and structure for socializing the industries. When Powderly opposed
the alliance, De Leon led DA 49 into a coalition with his opponents
and nominated James Sovereign, a farmer and newspaper editor
from Iowa, for Grand Master Workman. In 1893 Sovereign defeated

Powderly and took his place as leader of the KOL.[64] De Leon hoped that Powderly's removal would lead to a radical alliance between the SLP and the Knights, but his hopes were soon dashed. Sovereign had a very different vision. Sovereign's positions, strategies, and agenda focused on cooperators and farmers, while De Leon's focused on industrial workers. Sovereign was centered in the Midwest, while De Leon was in the East. Many KOL leaders saw De Leon as manipulative, and increasingly opposed him. Charging him with conflicting loyalties, the KOL expelled De Leon from the annual convention of the national General Assembly in 1894. In response, De Leon led the entire New York local DA 49 to withdraw from the Knights in 1895. Together with several allied groups, the former DA 49 became the core of a new labor organization, the Socialist Trade and Labor Alliance (STLA).[65] At this same moment, the KOL went into populism and after the defeat of the People's Party lost the last of their bases in major cities, stopped negotiating worker-employer relations, and ceased being a wage earner organization.[66]

The STLA was syndicalist, structured on industrial lines (not trade or territory), and modeled itself internally after the KOL.[67] Unlike the Knights, it had no plans of forming production cooperatives prior to a revolution. Instead of forming new alternative industries, the STLA laid claim to the already existing ones and hoped to expand until it took in the entire labor movement. Seeing cooperativization as the solution to their problems, its members put off instituting their plan until after their sister organization, the Socialist Labor Party, would gain state power.[68]

They planned for the STLA to assimilate the old unions, while the SLP would simultaneously win control of the government through the ballot. According to their plan, the labor unions would take over the industries after the party cleared the legal way, and together the STLA and SLP would bring forth the cooperative commonwealth as a republic of industrial unions.[69]

At its height in 1898, the STLA had 30,000 members and 228 affiliated organizations; some seceded from the AFL and Knights to join them. But the older unions, especially the AFL, effectively attacked them for causing fratricidal warfare—"dual-unionism"—from which all workers wound up the losers.[70]

While the Socialist Labor Party locals were booming, De Leon and the inner party grew progressively more rigid and authoritarian. De Leon's doctrinaire Marxism increasingly isolated the SLP.[71] In

1898, the same year that the SLP peaked in electoral success and the STLA peaked in membership, an ideological struggle rocked both organizations. There was a great internal revolt against De Leon, caused primarily by his inflexible dual-unionist economic policies, and a split emerged. Neither the Socialist Labor Party nor the Socialist Trade and Labor Alliance ever recovered. The STLA lost its momentum and collapsed.[72]

Not long after the STLA's fall, many former members went on to help organize a new, stronger, more independent organization with a similar syndicalist perspective, the Industrial Workers of the World.[73] At the same time as the SLP was falling apart, a new socialist party was forming with a membership predominantly native-born, the Socialist Party of America. Both of these organizations would play important roles for social change in the new century.[74]

OUTSIDE THE MAINSTREAM IN THE 1890s

Two regional movements were significant in this decade, the Cooperative Union of America group of stores in the Northeast and the Labor Exchanges in the Midwest and West coast. Both served as transitions to stronger movements that followed.

COOPERATIVE UNION OF AMERICA

Between 1895 and 1899, a group of scholars, including Francis Peabody of Harvard, instigated the Cooperative Union of America (CUA) in Massachusetts with the goal of organizing a national federation of consumer cooperative stores. At its peak, the CUA had fourteen member stores from Maine to New Jersey. A few of them were old Protective Unions.[75] Its newspaper, *American Cooperative News*, was almost the only source of information among scattered consumer cooperatives in that period. The CUA was the first American cooperative organization to join the International Cooperative Alliance (ICA), which it did as soon as the ICA was organized in 1896, marking the beginning of modern institutional ties between the American and international movements.[76] But the ferocious depression year of 1899 destroyed many stores and took down the CUA.[77]

LABOR EXCHANGES

The labor exchange idea made recurrent comebacks among small producers. Between 1889 and 1906, a labor exchange movement rose and faded. Begun in Sedalia, Missouri, by G.B. de Bernardi, it operated mostly in small towns. At its peak in 1896, it had 6,000 members and over 135 local branches in 32 states, extending into California and Washington, with 22 exchanges reported in Southern California alone. They exchanged both services and products. Members received "labor-checks" for the estimated wholesale value of the products they contributed, and could use those checks to trade for other products. Most of the branches also sold at discount for cash.[78] Some labor exchanges, particularly on the West coast, turned into Rochdale-type cooperative stores, although the national leadership opposed this.[79] In some locations, such as Dos Palos, California, the successor store outlasted its labor exchange origin by decades. Organized in 1896 as Labor Exchange Branch No. 135, the Dos Palos Rochdale Company is credited as the first Rochdale co-op in California, and met with notable success until 1920.[80]

7.
"The Progressive Era": Wobblies & Radical Farmers 1900-29

THE SOCIALIST PARTY OF AMERICA

Eugene V. Debs was released from prison after serving six months for leading the great railroad strike against Pullman in 1897. After his release he and the small group that remained from the wreckage of the American Railway Union got briefly involved with a land colonization scheme, but concluded it was too utopian and decided instead to found a new political party. They joined with a large group that broke away from the old dying Socialist Labor Party, and founded the Socialist Party of America (SP). Within a few years, the SP would unite most political radicals in the country behind its program.[1]

"The earth for all the people. That is the demand," Debs declared. "The machinery of production and distribution for all the people. That is the demand. The collective ownership and control of industry and its democratic management in the interests of all the people. That is the demand. The elimination of rent, interest, profit, and the production of wealth to satisfy the wants of all the people. That is the demand. Cooperative industry in which all shall work together in harmony as a basis of a new social order, a higher civilization, a real republic. That is the demand."[2]

The Socialist Party did not simply advocate government ownership and control of the economic system. Debs, for one, distrusted centralized power. The SP called for a reshaping of government so that it was no longer "above" the people. "Government ownership..." said Debs, "means practically nothing for labor under capitalist ownership of government."[3]

The SP established a Cooperative Information Bureau in Chicago that promoted cooperation as the only solution for the "tremendous waste of the present system of distribution."[4] The Information

Bureau was instrumental in distributing information and in organizing many successful cooperative stores around the country.[5]

In 1900, the first year that the SP ran national candidates, Debs received almost 100,000 votes for president; by 1904, it was up to over 400,000.[6]

Socialist Party poem (c. 1900)

I'll vote for Debs, for the Faith I have
That we'll reach the promised land;
A joyous vote and a splendid vote,
And a clasp of a comrade's hand.[7]

THE INDUSTRIAL WORKERS OF THE WORLD

The growth of the SP was reflected in the growth of radicalism in the union movement. The AFL divided into two camps: the Gompers right wing was still predominant, but the left continually gained strength, supported by about a third of the unions. While many activists worked to turn the AFL to a radical direction, many others thought that the labor aristocracy would never get behind the movement, and the AFL leadership would sink ever deeper into collusion with the employers. A new organization was needed, they reasoned, one to organize the unorganized and unskilled militantly and on an industrial basis.[8]

In 1905, a group of 200 labor leaders and socialists including Gene Debs, Daniel De Leon, Mother Jones, Lucy Parsons, "Big" Bill Haywood and Charles Moyer met in Chicago. Haywood called it "the Continental Congress of the Working Class."[9] There they formed the Industrial Workers of the World (IWW), "one great industrial union embracing all industries...[which would] develop the embryonic structure of the co-operative commonwealth...build up within itself the structure of an Industrial Democracy...which must finally burst the shell of capitalist government, and be the agency by which the workers will operate the industries, and appropriate the products to themselves."[10] They adopted the old nickname of the Knights of Labor, One Big Union, but unlike the Knights the IWW had a decentralized structure. The Western Federation of Miners, led by Haywood, which had withdrawn from the AFL several years before, now became the official Mining Department of the IWW.[11]

Much of the founding convention was taken up debating a clause in the Preamble to the IWW constitution regarding political parties: "Between these two classes [labor and capital] a struggle must go on until all the toilers come together on the political field as well as the industrial field, and take hold of that which they produce by their labor through an economic organization of the working class without affiliation with any political party."[12] The clause was passed, but the controversy continued. The Socialist Party officially dissociated itself, in fear of becoming a victim in the imminent inevitable war between the IWW and AFL, and announced that Debs and the other SP leaders involved with the IWW were acting for themselves and not the party. During this period the IWW still worked informally with the SLP and the SP.[13]

Haywood led a left-wing uprising at the 1906 convention and "revolutionists" took over the organization from "reformists."[14] De Leon was part of the radical group and briefly became the IWW's most prominent ideologue. But within a short time, the IWW split apart internally over questions of the value of electoral politics and the role of violence and sabotage, and eschewed all electoral politics soon thereafter.[15] The same factional differences also divided the Western Federation of Miners, who left the IWW in 1907.[16] The 1908 IWW convention deleted the political action clause in the Preamble and expelled De Leon from the organization.[17]

The IWW denounced elections entirely, relying only on "direct action" in the streets and in the factories, and ultimately on a national general strike. "A strike is an incipient revolution," Haywood declared. "Many large revolutions have grown out of a small strike."[18] They denounced contracts with employers and declared they would never sign one, reserving the right to walk out at any time.[19]

The IWW's structure was geared to transform the organization into the framework of the cooperative commonwealth achieved through "one big strike" on a national level. This transformation reflected, on a grand scale, the strike-to-cooperative transition of early American workers, whose local unions transformed themselves into production cooperatives during strikes.[20]

The IWW program did not include government ownership of the industries; this was a basic difference with the Socialist Party. The Wobblies wanted to do away with the political "state" (that is, power structures above and separated from the actual people) immediately and entirely; the administration of society's survival would be organized from below by the workers themselves through their own coordinated organizations.[21] In this way, they followed in the anarchist and associationist tradition (the French would call a similar movement *syndicalist*). The IWW thought that by turning workplaces into political organizations, organizing all workers industrially, and socializing all industry, the people could gain direct political power and "abolish the state" immediately. The authorities considered this "criminal syndicalism."[22]

Many major industries were totally unorganized at this time, and the AFL was doing little to change it.[23] With great energy, the IWW leaped into the gap and put into practice the slogan, "Organize the Unorganized." In the East, it became strongest among immigrant groups in the ghettos. In the West, it grew strongest among mine, lumber and migrant workers, and in port towns. The Wobblies waged "free-speech" struggles up and down the West Coast, flooding the jails of many towns with great numbers of migrant workers to win the right to speak and organize. Many immigrants, blacks, and women belonged to Wobbly locals. They led strikes of miners in the West, lumberjacks in the Northwest and South, construction workers on the West Coast and in Canada, dockworkers on both coasts and the Great Lakes, steel and textile workers in the Northeast, farmworkers in the West and Midwest.[24]

Wherever Wobbly migrants—*bindle stiffs*—went, they set up large encampments with cooperative survival networks, usually near railroad junctions outside of towns. The word *hobo* probably stems from *hoe boy*, seasonal farm worker. Wobbly hobo jungles were primarily transitory, erected and disbanded as the migrant workers followed seasonal work. The camps were self-governed by rules, customs, and divisions of labor, facilitated by the unifying force of the IWW.[25] The hobo poet Harry Kemp wrote about a camp in 1911,

> It is often a marvel of cooperation. Discarded tin cans and battered boilers are made over into cooking utensils and dishes... There is usually in camp someone whose occupational vocation is that of cook, and who takes upon himself, as his share of the work, the cooking of meals. Stews are in great favor in trampdom and especially do they like strong, scalding coffee. Usually the procuring of food in such a camp is reduced to a system... One tramp goes to the butcher shop for meat, one goes to the bakers for bread, and so forth. And when one gang breaks up, its members are always very careful to leave everything in good order for the next comers... These things are part of tramp etiquet [*sic*], as is also the

obligation each new arrival is under to bring, as he comes, some wood for the fire.[26]

Local organizations were very independent and loose, making an accurate count of IWW membership impossible. At the organization's peak in 1917, the government estimated that about 200,000 Americans were Wobs, although others have estimated half that. Membership tended to soar after a victory, then slip away again, partly due to lack of a strong organizational structure. But from the first the IWW met with goon, vigilante, and government violence. As the Wobs' membership grew, so grew the violence.[27]

IWW SONGS

The Commonwealth of Toil (c. 1905)
by Ralph Chaplin

In the gloom of mighty cities,
Mid the roar of whirling wheels,
We are toiling on like chattel slaves of old,
And our masters hope to keep us
Ever thus beneath their heels,
And to coin our very life blood into gold.
But we have a glowing dream
Of how fair the world will seem
When each man can live his life secure and free;
When the earth is owned by labor
And there's joy and peace for all
In the Commonwealth of Toil that is to be.[28]

• • •

A Song For 1912
(anonymous)

Then up with the masses and down with the classes,
Death to the traitor who money can buy.
Cooperation's the hope of the nation,
Strike for it now or your liberties die.[29]

THE GROWING SOCIALIST PARTY

The Socialist Party, meanwhile, steadily grew in electoral strength. In 1910, Victor L. Berger of Milwaukee became the first ever Socialist elected to the US House of Representatives.[30]

Among his proposals were the social takeover of major industries, the elimination of the president's veto power, and the first old-age pension bill ever introduced into Congress.[31] In 1912, Debs received over 900,000 votes and the SP had about 120,000 members. They elected the mayor of Milwaukee and eighty other cities and towns around the country, and 12,000 local and state representatives.[32] Republicans and Democrats merged in many areas to fight them. The largest single bloc of votes for the SP came from Populist country, small farmers west of the Mississippi; the Oklahoma party had about a third of the state's votes.[33] But in 1914, the national leadership, afraid that too strong a flood of farmers into the party would dilute their wage earner orientation and threaten to alter the nature of the party, chose to delay mass recruitment in rural areas until after the consolidation of the party's urban base.[34] Thus they weakened their forces, while a group of impatient farmers broke away and formed the enormously successful Non-Partisan League in North Dakota.[35]

CHANGES IN RURAL AMERICA

The early 1900s saw enormous changes in rural America. The last years of the 19th century brought telephones—many on cooperative lines—and free mail delivery. By 1910, autos were widespread; by 1920, a good highway network spread across most of the country. The first rural electrical cooperative formed in 1914, and these brought electricity to numerous areas of the United States within a decade. In the same period, the full effects of mechanized farming were first felt.[36] Meanwhile, the percentage of workers in farming declined drastically. While agricultural workers made up half the workforce in 1875, by 1900 they were down to one-third; by 1920, one-fourth; by 1930, one-fifth.[37] Small farmers were continually losing their land and becoming proletarianized. In the South, three out of four farmers labored under the yoke of tenant farming, sharecropping, or cash-lien. Farm labor was replacing the farm family as the basic mode of agricultural production.[38]

INDEPENDENT FARMER CO-OPS

The Sherman "Anti-Trust" Act of 1890 outlawed interstate commerce by cooperatives. It primarily affected farmers' marketing cooperatives because most industrial cooperatives had already been wiped out with the fall of the Knights of Labor. The act declared illegal any "combination or conspiracy" to restrain interstate commerce, but instead of using the act to curb big business, the government used it primarily against unions.

In defiance of the Sherman Act, the number of independent farmer cooperatives continued to grow.[39] Agricultural co-ops were indispensable to small farms, so numerous farmers continued joining out of absolute necessity into co-ops engaged in interstate trade. In 1890, there were about 1,000 of these independent local cooperatives coordinating cooperative buying and marketing, about 700 dairy, and 100 each of grain, vegetables, and fruit. By 1915, there were 5,424 independent agricultural co-ops, most of them in regional federations.[40] Government prosecutions against farmer marketing cooperatives were few. The government chose to look the other way; it would have been politically disastrous to enforce the law against farmer cooperatives because small farmers still formed the backbone of the rural population despite the decline in their numbers.[41]

Successive generations of experience with cooperatives had rooted the ideas of cooperation into the social fabric of rural American life.[42] Farm communities based on the single-family farm needed cooperatives to survive. Cooperatives were part of the infrastructure of community connections. Before, during, and after the Civil War, farmers continued to form independent associations of their own accord for mutual aid in reducing production costs, marketing, and protection from "land sharks." These independents were "pure and simple" practical cooperatives, while the Grange and the Farmers' Alliance were coordinated social movements. In areas where those movements organized, many pre-existing cooperatives became involved or joined while still maintaining some level of autonomy. As historian Joseph G. Knapp wrote, "they would have continued with or without the support of the Grange or Alliance movements."[43]

The Clayton Act of 1914 aimed to help small farmers by exempting nonprofit non-stock co-ops from the Sherman Act. It also established labor's right to collective bargaining. This was the first federal legal protection that specifically allowed farmers to form cooperatives, but its protections were ambiguous and weak.[44]

Prices for agricultural products were down in the postwar 1920s. Agribusinesses that purchased their products held every advantage over farmers in negotiating the terms of sale. Agribusiness could set a price, and farmers usually had to accede. To combat this, the number of farmer co-ops continued to multiply, but with limited success due in part to their still-questionable legal status.[45]

The Capper-Volstead Act of 1922 granted farmers specific legal protection from prosecution under the antitrust laws, and gave farmers the rights of collective bargaining and marketing, placing them on a better footing vis-à-vis agribusiness. It extended the rights given to nonprofit co-ops by the Clayton Act to cooperatives organized on a stock basis. The Capper-Volstead Act was a powerful lever that eventually allowed numerous agricultural cooperatives to grow and prosper.[46]

Meanwhile, in the depression of the early 1920s, many independent cooperatives struggled and many went under. The crisis sparked the resurgence of activist organizations reviving the farmer movement.[47]

NATIONAL FARMERS UNION

Isaac Newton Gresham, a former Populist and organizer for the Northern Farmers' Alliance, founded the Farmers' Educational and Cooperative Union (NFU) in Texas in 1902. He modeled the first Farmers Union on the old Farmers' Alliance as a regional association renewing the militant small farmer tradition. The NFU grew strong over the next decade in the Cotton Belt.[48] It was "built upon the ruins of the Farmers' Alliance. In thousands of communities the locals of the wrecked Alliance still existed as independent units; when the organizers of the Farmers Union came along to offer them a state and national affiliation and invite them to join another crusade, they eagerly accepted."[49] The Farmers Union organized cooperatives for supply purchasing, marketing, credit, grain elevators, and co-op stores. Its early cooperative processing plants were primarily local flour mills, creameries, and phosphate plants. Its members advocated government intervention to eliminate speculation on the commodity markets and to stabilize prices based on cost of production plus a fair profit; worked to improve agricultural education and the standard of living of farm families; opened the organization's membership to farm laborers; and formed an alliance with trade unions.[50]

In its first four years, the NFU started state unions in Texas, Arkansas, Oklahoma, Louisiana, Alabama, and Georgia, and organized in six adjoining states. State unions were granted autonomy in a decentralized federation; by 1905, the Farmers Union had an estimated membership of 200,000.[51] In 1907, the year that Gresham died, the organizing reached to the North Central States. Charles Barrett of Georgia, a farmer and country schoolteacher, became national president, and led the organization for the next twenty-two years. In 1908, the AFL began sending a fraternal delegate to the NFU annual national convention. By that time, the NFU had reached the Rocky Mountain states and the Pacific Coast.[52]

After 1910, the NFU faded in the South following an unsuccessful campaign to hold back cotton for higher prices and the failure of a number of its cooperatives.[53] At the same time, the NFU rose among Midwest grain growers, and the center of its strength slowly shifted to the North Central States of Kansas, Nebraska, and Iowa. The first emphasis here was on cooperative purchasing and stores, but they soon went into elevators and livestock shipping, and then wholesale marketing and purchasing exchanges.[54] Within a few years, dozens of local NFU cooperatives were operating. They formed terminal marketing and purchasing agencies to serve their collective needs, first in Omaha and Kansas City, then in South Dakota, Colorado, and Iowa. The NFU was also instrumental in setting up a farm lobbying coalition in Washington, D.C. in 1915—the National Board of Farm Organizations, chaired by NFU president Barrett.[55]

The decade after World War I brought deflation and depression for farmers. The NFU responded with an increased emphasis on cooperatives.[56] The organization lost members in the early 1920s, but then regained momentum. Farmers Union cooperatives worked with the AFL in the 1920 successful Great Falls, Montana strike for unionization against the Flour Mill Combine. There the farmers bypassed the Combine by grinding their wheat in small mills and shipping them with Farmers Union labels.[57] In 1923, A. C. Ricker, a Union pioneer in the spring-wheat area, worked with A. C. Townley, who had recently left the Non-Partisan League, to organize thousands of spring-wheat farmers into a loose organization, the National Producers Alliance (NPA), which merged into the NFU. Between 1927 and 1930, the NFU organized 60,000 farmers in Wisconsin, Minnesota, North Dakota, and Montana.[58]

EQUITY

The American Society of Equity (ASE) began in 1902 in Indianapolis at the initiative of J. A. Everitt, editor of a farm magazine. Its inclusion of larger farmers as well as small farmers, gave the Equity movement a somewhat different character from earlier cooperative movements.[59]

Equity's original mission was to organize farmers to set minimum prices on important crops, and to hold crops off the market until that minimum was offered. ASE was a democratic organization open to all farmers and "friends of agriculture" for a membership fee of $1 and $1 annual dues. Members agreed "to follow the reasonable advice of the Society regarding crops, prices, and so forth." Equity was "not a farmers' society only, but an American society—that is good for all Americans who want to see better conditions prevail on the farm. It is not a benefit society, but an equity society—benefits are always for an individual or class, while equity is for all."[60] When storage granaries at individual farms were insufficient for holding produce, Equity advocated cooperative elevators, warehouses and cold storage houses. The idea was to get control of prices out of the hands of middlemen and speculators, and into the hands of farmers. They promoted a similar strategy to regulate the prices farmers paid for supplies: ASE would determine fair prices and boycott suppliers who would not oblige.[61]

Equity issued a "Hold Your Wheat" bulletin in May 1903, urging a minimum price of $1 per bushel on the Chicago market, based on the factors of cost of production and "visible supply."[62] The campaign was a great success and resulted in rapid membership growth. The call was extended to corn, potatoes, oats, beans, barley, hay, cotton, and tobacco in the following year. This too met with success. When prices declined in 1905, ASE responded with an intensive regional campaign in six wheat-growing states. Tens of thousands of farmers participated, and brought the price back up in the following years.[63]

Meanwhile, opposition grew to Everitt's centralized leadership and marketing system. In 1906, a group led by M. Wes Tubbs put forth a proposal to replace the centralized marketing system with a decentralized Rochdale-type system. They also proposed a coalition with the labor movement toward "the end that consumers may secure the necessities of life at equitable prices."[64] The convention supported the plan over Everitt's objections and Tubbs' group took over the organization in the following year, instituted the plan, and reorganized Equity itself on a decentralist basis.[65]

The high point of Equity's crop control initiative came with the wheat crop of 1908, when farmers in six states successfully held

out for "dollar wheat."[66] In 1909, they established a Grain Growers Marketing Department to arrange cooperative marketing at the
terminal markets, out of which grew Equity Cooperative Exchange
in Minneapolis.[67]

But the internal conflict did not heal, and the organization
remained in discord. ASE as an organization faded. At the same
time, however, three spin-offs flourished: the Equity Cooperative Exchange (ECE), the Farmers' Equity Union (FEU), and the Wisconsin Society of Equity (WSE). In addition, the Non-Partisan League
(NPL) was organized by Equity members.[68]

The Equity Cooperative Exchange opened in Minneapolis in
1908, a regional terminal marketing association selling members'
grain on consignment. In 1911, they incorporated under North Dakota statutes and applied to the Grain Exchange for trading rights,
but were rejected. The chamber of commerce attacked them relentlessly. Farmers responded with massive support and their volume
doubled in 1912-13 to three million bushels, then doubled again in
1914-15.[69] ECE began setting up local elevators throughout Minnesota and into South Dakota in 1918, and owned eighty of them
in 1922. But owning these local elevators proved nearly disastrous.
A decline in wheat prices in 1921 precipitated great losses for two
years until the Exchange went into receivership in 1923.[70] In 1926,
however, the National Farmers Union took it over and revived it.[71]

In 1910, a group led by C. D. Drayton broke away from ASE
and founded the Farmers' Equity Union (FEU), which operated primarily in Kansas, Colorado, and Nebraska. The FEU's plan was to
promote local marketing exchanges based on the Rochdale system,
and central exchanges to service the locals. Its members promoted the
establishment of cooperative creameries, elevators, and stores along
railroad locations. The first FEU central exchange was opened in
Kansas City in 1916 to market the grain of local exchanges in the adjoining states.[72] The FEU also faded in the depressed early 1920s.[73]

The Wisconsin Society of Equity began in 1903, aligned with
Robert M. La Follette's Progressive m ovement. In 1911, its members
convinced the state legislature to pass legislation for fundamental cooperative incorporation laws.[74] Between 1910-20, WSE's greatest period of activity, members organized over 40,000 farmers in 400 local
purchasing and marketing cooperatives, most of them on the Rochdale plan. Like the others, they had difficulties in the early 1920s, but
hung on and in 1934 consolidated with the Farmers Union.[75]

FARMER-LABOR EXCHANGE

Sparked by the depression of 1921, Charles F. Lowrie founded the Farmer-Labor Exchange (FLE) in Chicago in 1922, a new form of cooperation.[76] Lowrie had previous experience in both movements, first as organizer of the Chicago postal clerks' union and then as president of the Montana Farmers Equity Union and Cooperative Wholesale. The Farmer-Labor Exchange marketed produce, coal, and other products through unions and co-ops in the region. FLE operated successfully through the entire decade. Its first activity was to market honey in Chicago that came from the Progressive Farmers of Idaho, connected with the Non-Partisan League. Members soon added other commodities, including potatoes and poultry. They distributed "union-mined coal from a union-owned mine" in Herrin, Illinois, to members of unions and farm organizations. The FLE operated successfully for a decade, but closed in 1933.[77]

THE NON-PARTISAN LEAGUE

A delegation of North Dakota farmers belonging to the American Society of Equity came home from a trip to the state capital in 1914, where they'd gone to petition for a redress of grievances, and reported to a meeting that their representative had told them to "go home and slop the hogs."[78] In attendance was A. C. Townley, a failed flax farmer and former organizer for the Socialist Party, which had recently rejected recruiting farmers. That night, Townley sat with his friend, Fred Wood, at Wood's kitchen table and wrote a radical political program to address many of the farmers' problems and strengthen them in their ongoing struggle with the regional corporate-political powers. Their objective was to gain political power to clear the way for the goals of Equity. The plan included state-run elevators, packing plants, flour mills, and other industries essential to farming, along with a state bank. It became the platform of the Non-Partisan League.[79] But instead of forming a new political party, their strategy was to endorse candidates from the two dominant parties who would support their program. In 1915, Townley drove around the state in a borrowed Model T Ford organizing, and farmers flocked into the NPL, adopting the slogan, "The Goat That Can't Be Got." Now a large feisty group, they returned to the capital and began to implement their plan.[80]

The NPL slate ran as Republicans in the 1916 elections and won control of the state legislature. Lynn Frazier, a NPL farmer, became governor with 79 percent of the vote. The NPL had a majority in both state legislative houses in 1918, and began to enact its program.[81] Members set up state-run enterprises for agriculture, including the North Dakota Mill and Elevator and the Bank of North Dakota. They instituted a state hail insurance fund, a graduated state income tax that distinguished between earned and unearned income, a workmen's compensation fund that assessed employers, and reformed the electoral system to permit popular initiative and recall of elected officials.[82]

A sharp drop in commodity prices at the end of World War I, however, accompanied by a drought, brought agricultural depression to the region in 1921. A number of NPL industries and the state bank approached insolvency. The NPL wanted the state to issue bonds to support them, but private banks refused help. Business associations attacked them. Newspapers tarred them as incompetent and corrupt. This led to internal fighting. In 1921, Frazier became the first US governor to be recalled. The NPL collapsed almost entirely in 1922.[83]

While the NPL was rising, Townley had become a national political figure. He was arrested in Minnesota in 1921, charged under the Espionage Act with questioning the government's war motives, and served ninety days for "conspiring to discourage enlistments."[84] In the highly charged atmosphere of the time, he ceased being an influence in the NPL and went on to co-found the National Producers Alliance, organizing spring-wheat farmers.[85]

The NPL hung on and bounced back after the economic collapse of 1929, returning to power during the worst depression years of the 1930s.[86]

FARM BUREAU

Between 1900 and 1914, the US Department of Agriculture (DOA) set up an extension program of farmer institutes to educate local farmers on business methods. These institutes helped to organize many farmer cooperatives and led to the American Farm Bureau Federation (AFBF).[87]

The system had its roots in 1903, when Seaman Knapp of the DOA devised a program to teach methods of resisting the Mexican boll weevil to Texas cotton farmers. He organized selected farmers to set up "demonstration farms" using the proposed methods. These were so successful that the system spread quickly in the South.[88] At first the educators were traveling specialists, but this soon gave way to a system of resident county agents.[89]

In 1911, a DOA extension in Broom County, New York, in collaboration with the local chamber of commerce and a railroad, organized a bureau as a department of the local Chamber, and hired a county agent to provide education and information to the local farmers. In 1913, the farmers involved reorganized as an independent organization and became the first Farm Bureau.[90]

The Farm Bureau idea quickly spread, funded by a Rockefeller endowment, railroads, and business associations.[91] In 1914, the county agent system was recognized by federal law and put into nationwide practice. Organizing a Farm Bureau was made a prerequisite for the government installing a county agent in most states.[92] The bureaus included all farmers, rich and poor. They had member control, but under federal guidelines. Some county agents, at the urging of local farmers, started to perform supply buying and marketing services. After businesses complained, the Secretary of Agriculture ruled in 1914 that county agents could not perform business transactions themselves but should help county Farm Bureaus to organize their own cooperatives to perform them.[93]

In 1915, county bureaus began forming state federations, first in Missouri and Massachusetts, and then in seven other states by 1919. These federations started to promote cooperatives in business operations and to lobby for farm legislation.[94] In 1919, representatives from twelve states met and formed the American Farm Bureau Federation, with James Howard as president. Leaders from different regions came with various perspectives. The Midwest representatives were the most radical, and proposed that the AFBF be "an instrument to solve marketing problems on a nationwide cooperative plan."[95] However, the founding convention ratified a more moderate constitution defining the mission of AFBF "to promote, protect, and represent the business, economic, and social interests to the farmers of the nation, and to develop agriculture."[96] They immediately set up a series of departments, including legislation and cooperation.[97]

In 1920, as farmers were feeling early shocks of the oncoming depression, Aaron Sapiro, representing the state grain pooling organizations of the Pacific Northwest, proposed a national marketing plan organized "by commodity—not by locality."[98] AFBF set up committees for grain and livestock, and both set plans in motion for national grain and livestock marketing organizations.[99] In the following years, the Bureau's National Livestock Produc-

ers Association successfully formed a system of commission terminal marketing firms. The grain plan floundered at first on in-
fighting over the question of whether the new system would be
based on existing grain cooperatives or entirely new organizations,
and whether it would be organized from the bottom up or the top
down. In 1922, the AFBF annual meeting resolved "to go all out
for cooperative marketing."[100] A major battle ensued, the organization was split and the AFBF drew back and killed the Sapiro
top-down program of national commodity marketing before it was
ever implemented. After another attempt the following year, plans
for a marketing system collapsed. A more conservative faction took
over the Farm Bureau.[101]

The Farm Bureau allied small and large farmers in the same
organization, and attempted to define the farmers' movement on a
business basis. AFBF worked to preempt another populist-type social
uprising by breaking the traditional alliance between small farmers and wage earners for mutual aid and political action.[102] Larger
farmers, employers themselves, had no economic interests different
from employers in the production industries. AFBF became a bitter
foe of farm labor. The Farm Bureau went on to preside over the re-
lentless closing of family farms and the increasing corporatization of
American agriculture, looking after the interests of big agribusiness
over those of small farmers. Farms had to be ever more mechanized
to survive, the number of small farmers rapidly declined, and small
farmers of one decade often found themselves to be wage earners
in the next.[103]

COMMUNIST FARM ORGANIZATIONS

A number of other farm organizations in the 1920s were largely organized and controlled by the Communist Party (CP). The CP
held appeal for many of the small and middle farmers on the plains
who were badly hurting in the early 1920s. During that period, the
CP mainly organized through front groups, the first of which was
the United Farmers Educational League (UFEL), founded in 1923
and led by Alfred Knutson. The CP also controlled the Cooperative Central Exchange. As the largest consumer cooperative in the
US in the 1920s, this exchange served rural Wisconsin, Michigan,
and Minnesota.[104] The CP dominated the Sharecroppers Union;
the Cannery and Agricultural Workers Industrial Union; the Farmers National Committee for Action; the Food, Tobacco, Agricultur-

al and Allied Workers Union of America (CIO); and Progressive Farmers of America (PFA).[105]

William Bouck founded Progressive Farmers of America (PFA) in 1926 as the national version of Washington State's Western Progressive Farmers (WPF). Brouk had been Washington State Grange Master, but the conservative leadership of the National Grange suspended him in 1921 because of his radical anti-war and pro-labor views.[106] A group of 6,000 farmers left with Bouck and started WPF.[107] In 1926, Knutson recruited Bouck to join the CP's UFEL; in the following months, they organized a convention in Minneapolis with representatives from at least eight states and formed Progressive Farmers of America with several Communists in the leadership. PFA quickly garnered a significant membership in the northern plains states between Wisconsin and Montana.[108] When the Farmers Union staged a massive recruitment drive in the same area the following year, however, PFA's membership faded.[109]

FEDERAL FARM BOARD

The Agricultural Marketing Act of 1929, signed by President Herbert Hoover before the stock market crash, aimed "to promote the effective merchandising of agricultural commodities in interstate and foreign commerce... by promoting the establishment and financing of a farm marketing system of producer-owned and producer-controlled cooperative associations."[110] The act set up a revolving fund of $500 million to be administered by a nine-member Federal Farm Board appointed by the president. The Act directed the Board to use the fund "to encourage the organization, improvement in methods, and development of effective cooperative associations," and to stabilize prices.[111] The act was the first national commitment to use government regulation to provide greater economic stability for farmers. The US Chamber of Commerce attacked the Board, opposing "the use of Government funds in providing capital for the operation of agricultural cooperatives, and for the buying and selling of commodities for the purpose of attempted stabilization."[112]

Hoover appointed a big manufacturer, the president of International Harvester, to chair the Board, but most of his other appointees were leaders in regional agricultural associations.[113] One of the Board's first acts was to call a meeting of the main grain cooperatives to plan for a national grain marketing cooperative. Grain was to be the first test case for similar national marketing cooperatives in other commodities, and a Grain Stabilization Corporation was formed to buy and store quantities to stabilize prices. Soon afterward, the Board organized a Cotton Stabilization Corporation and then a California Grape Control Board. These functioned for two years with some positive effects.[114] At the same time the Federal Farm Board gave financial and technical help to many struggling cooperatives. They had spent most of the revolving fund by the middle of 1931, and little was coming back. It was a case of too little too late. In the conditions of the Great Depression these measures were ineffectual.[115] The Federal Farm Board was abolished in 1933 and its functions taken over by the New Deal Farm Credit Administration.[116]

THE COOPERATIVE STORE MOVEMENT

Between the late 1860s and the turn of the century, many labor unions, including the National Labor Union and the Knights of Labor, ran co-op stores and buying clubs for their members. These rose and fell with their related organizations. While the AFL opposed unions forming production cooperatives, members at the 1896 convention resolved for the first time to support consumer co-op stores: "trade-unionism and co-operation are twin sisters...where one exists the other is almost compelled by nature's inexorable laws to follow...therefore be it Resolved, That [the AFL] recommend to all affiliated bodies...the Rochdale System...and wherever favorable conditions exist to give their aid to such cooperative efforts."[117] But a string of failures led labor for the most part to temporarily lose interest in supporting consumer co-ops by 1897.[118]

The consumer cooperative movement was stalled in the early 1900s. Only in the Midwest and in the Far West were there energetic movements operating wholesales with many affiliated stores. Operating successfully in the Midwest were the Right Relationship League and the Cooperative Wholesale of America. On the West Coast, the Pacific Cooperative League, the Pacific Coast Cooperative Union, and the California Rochdale Company were thriving. There were hundreds of local mostly independent cooperative stores in other parts of the country, but with little communication among them. Many immigrant groups, including Finnish, Swedish, Czech, German, Lithuanian, Jewish, Polish, French, and Belgian immigrants, ran cooperatives in the East and Midwest.[119]

In 1913, several cooperative conferences led to plans for the formation of a national cooperative federation, but nothing was done until 1919, when the National Cooperative Association opened branches in Hoboken, Seattle, and Chicago.[120]

UNION STORES

Beginning in 1912, coal miners of Southern Illinois organized a network of local cooperative groups, at the initiative of John H. Walker and Duncan McDonald, president and secretary of the Illinois State Federation of Labor. The mining areas were depressed and most of the mines only operated part time. By 1916, thirty-two co-op stores were in operation in Illinois and the movement was rapidly extending into neighboring states. Most were returning at least an 8 percent rebate on purchases to members.[121] Some became community centers, such as the co-op at Staunton, which had the store on the ground floor, and upstairs a dance hall, movie theater, restaurant, buffet, and reading room.[122]

In 1915, Walker and McDonald called a meeting that organized the Central States Cooperative Society (CSCS), to promote cooperatives and provide education and exchange of experiences. Within a year, sixteen stores affiliated, and fifty joined the CSCS by 1917. At its urging, Illinois passed a law facilitating cooperative incorporation.[123] CSCS's members set up a wholesale for collective buying and in 1918 there were over a hundred cooperative stores in the area, centered on Springfield.[124]

At that time, World War I was raging in Europe and the US was anxiously gearing up. Prices were rising nationwide but wages were stagnant, and working families needed to stretch their incomes. In response, labor unions looked once more to cooperative stores.[125]

Through the urging of the Illinois delegates, the AFL convention of 1917 passed a resolution urging its members to organize consumer cooperatives, because "the cooperative movement is the organization that is designed to protect the workers in their relations with the merchants and businessmen in the same sense that the trade-union movement protects them from the employers."[126] In the following years, many national unions and state federations recommended that their members open cooperative stores.

Between 1916 and 1921, unions organized consumer co-ops on a large scale: miners of coal, copper, and iron from Minnesota to West Virginia; textile workers in New England; railroad workers across half the country.[127]

Soon, the union co-ops began opening their membership to the larger communities. Most of the union co-ops were separate organizations from the unions themselves.[128] The United Mine Workers (UMW), however, ran their co-ops directly through miner committees. By 1921, there were seventy UMW co-op branches. Centralization and rapid expansion were at first strengths, but later proved to be reasons for failure. Many branch stores were set up without adequate local participation, trained management, or accounting control. The central wholesale was poorly run. During the miners' strike of 1922, money became scarce, quickly exacerbating the situation, and many stores did not have enough cash flow to remain solvent. The centralized system crashed, but twenty-five stores successfully reorganized in 1923 and regrouped into a decentralized federation.[129]

In the postwar depression of 1921-23, most of the union-connected co-ops as well as many other cooperatives around the country collapsed, and the AFL became much more guarded in support.[130]

RIGHT RELATIONSHIP LEAGUE

The Right Relationship League (RRL) began as an informational organization allied to the Cooperating Merchants of Chicago, a group of Midwestern retail storeowners. The Cooperating Merchants had become alarmed at the growth of mass merchandising firms, especially department stores and mail order businesses, and in the middle 1890s, organized a wholesale in Chicago. The wholesale had 450 member retailers, 20 of them cooperative stores, by 1905.[131]

In 1907, the Right Relationship League broke away and became an independent organization based in Minneapolis, with E. J. Van Horn as president.[132] RRL was not itself a cooperative, but tried to operate democratically. Its plan was to collaborate with agreeable owners to transform private stores into cooperatives. A cooperative company would be formed, which would sell stock to the community of the town or county. They would buy out the owner and—if mutually agreeable—hire him as manager. The League would receive a commission for its organizing work.[133]

Fourteen county associations belonged to the League in 1907, along with nearly fifty stores and three thousand members in Minnesota, Wisconsin, North Dakota, and Missouri. Located in farm communities, most local groups ran grain elevators and creameries as well as stores. At its 1910 convention, the RRL reported 54 cooperatives with 86 stores and 7,700 members. It had 140 stores at its height.[134]

From the first, the RRL worked to organize a new wholesale whose members would be entirely cooperative stores, but despite years of work this project never got off the ground. The RRL was instrumental in organizing many successful cooperative stores in the Northwest between 1909 and 1914.[135] But the League lost steam as an effective social movement, and became discouraged by financial problems. The RRL dissolved in 1915 but left behind numerous successful local cooperatives.[136]

PACIFIC COAST COOPERATIVE UNION

In 1899, representatives from cooperative stores around Northern California formed the Pacific Coast Cooperative Union (PCCU) in Oakland. The Oakland member store, Altruria Cooperative Union, had been started five years prior by a group that concurrently organized Altruria cooperative community in Sonoma County. In 1900, the PCCU founded Rochdale Wholesale Co. in San Francisco, and in five years this cooperative wholesale was servicing fifty-one stores, the strongest consumer co-op movement in the country.[137] At its peak in 1902, there were over one hundred cooperative stores in the network. Referring to the PCCU, a historian in 1905 wrote, "In no place (in the United States) is the cooperative movement so strong or successful as it is upon the Pacific coast."[138]

But an economic downturn hit hard soon after, and there were only twelve stores left by 1912. The movement collapsed due to an overextension of credit and other financial weaknesses. Many PCCU stores were formed from the top down, and so had shallow roots in their communities.[139] In an attempt to save the failing movement, the California Rochdale Company was formed as a new organization under central management, and using the Rochdale Wholesale as supplier. Members set up nine branches in the first year, but none lasted past 1912.[140]

With the Rochdale Wholesale in grave danger of failing, a San Francisco group tried to save it by founding the Pacific Cooperative League (PCL) in 1913, and began organizing grassroots buying clubs using the Wholesale.[141]

JEWISH COOPERATIVE LEAGUE

Salesman Hyman Cohn founded the Jewish Cooperative League (JCL) on the New York Lower East Side in 1909. It was made up mainly of trade unionists. The JCL aimed in theory at uniting the entire cooperative movement, but in practice opened a hat store in 1911 and then a hat factory.[142] The word *Jewish* was not actually in its name, but has been added by historians to distinguish the group from the Cooperative League of America (CL), of which the JCL was a precursor. Hyman Cohn and fellow JCL member Albert Sonnichsen went on to play key roles in the founding of the CL.[143] The JCL is also remembered because it initiated the American Socialist Party's opening its cooperative information bureau. JCL joined the International Cooperative Alliance (ICA) in 1912 and sent a delegate to the subsequent ICA congress in Glasgow, Scotland.[144] The JCL hat factory succeeded for several years, but branches in other neighborhoods failed. The organization began calling itself the Industrial and Agricultural Cooperative Association in 1914, and ran restaurants, boarding houses, and a meat market for a decade.[145]

THE FOUNDING OF THE COOPERATIVE LEAGUE

In 1914, a small group of activists in New York, including Albert Sonnichsen, William Kraus and Hyman Cohn, began meeting with the idea of creating a new organization that would unify all the scattered cooperatives into a coordinated movement. Kraus was manager of a co-op in New Jersey. Sonnichsen, originally a San Franciscan, had been a sailor and then a war correspondent in the Balkans for New York newspapers. Calling themselves the Consumers' Cooperative Union (CCU), the group began a newspaper in 1914 called *The Cooperative Consumer*, with Sonnichsen as editor and Kraus as business manager. The paper was received with great interest around the country.[146] In 1915, Sonnichsen called on Dr. James Warbasse in New York as part of a fund-raising campaign, and asked him for $5 in what was to be a historic meeting.[147]

Warbasse had first encountered cooperatives in 1891 as a student in Germany. He became a surgeon in Cuba in the Spanish-American war, and emerged a pacifist. He became editor of the *New York State Journal of Medicine* in 1905, and the chief surgeon in a Brooklyn hospital in 1906. Meanwhile he developed an interest in trying to cure society.[148] In 1910, in *The Conquest of Disease Through Animal Experimentation*, he wrote, "The knowledge and skill which have the power of preventing disease, relieving suffering, and prolonging life should be available to all. They should not be purchasable by some and denied to others, nor bestowed as a charity upon any. Health and life are too precious to be at the mercy of trade and barter."[149]

In 1911, Warbasse joined the Industrial Workers of the World. In 1914, he published an article in the *Journal of the American Medical Association*, "The Socialization of Medicine," in which he advocated doctor-patient cooperatives. This was probably the earliest published discussion of socialized medicine by a doctor in America. He went on to publish similar articles in other medical journals, and began holding weekly meetings with other interested doctors.[150]

Sonnichsen's fund-raising visit with Warbasse led to several organizing meetings at Warbasse's home, where the group founded the Cooperative League of America (CL) in 1916, with the mission of promoting consumer cooperation: "The object of the Cooperative League of America is to spread knowledge, develop scientific methods, and give expert advice on all phases of Consumer Cooperation... It aims to unite into a national league the consumer cooperative societies in the United States."[151] Warbasse was made president.[152]

The CL was destined to become the major umbrella organization of Rochdale cooperatives in the US, and ultimately of all US cooperatives.[153] Joining the International Cooperative Alliance in 1917, CL became the international voice of American cooperatives. It remains that today in its current incarnation as the National Cooperative Business Association (NCBA).[154]

8.
World War I and the Conservative Reaction

WORLD WAR I

By the teens of the 20th century, Woodrow Wilson, elected as a peace candidate, was leading the country into World War I and the enormous clash over world markets. The war was tremendously unpopular among workers and there were great outcries against US involvement.[1]

When the war broke out in Europe, the Socialist Party of America was affiliated with the "Second" International, founded in 1889, and made up of autonomous workers' parties from around the world. All had agreed to try to prevent another imperialist war, and not support war should it break out. Yet when it did, the workers' parties lined up behind their governments, with the exception of the Italians, the Russian Bolsheviks and the Socialist Party of America.[2] The American party split and many "social-patriots" resigned. But the majority stayed firm and the SP chose to "advise" workers everywhere to resist their governments by "mass action," because the war could only bring "wealth and power to the ruling class, and suffering, death and demoralization to the workers."[3]

The IWW resolved, "We as members of the industrial army, will refuse to fight for any purpose except the realization of industrial freedom."[4] After Congress declared war, the IWW took the moderate course of advising members to register for the draft as "IWW opposed to war."[5] The AFL supported the war, and Gompers joined the government, using his position to try to wipe out all opposition to his dominance over the labor movement.[6]

The Russian Revolution of 1917 transformed the socialist movements in the United States and world. The Socialist Party of America along with a large number of people and organizations in America welcomed the Bolsheviks' triumph.[7] A radical group with a socialist ideology had gained real state power for the first time in the history of the world. Widespread cooperatives played an important role in the early Russian revolutionary process, and for a time were almost the only functioning economic sector. A new type of organization, however, was serving as the primary cell of revolution, the *soviet* or workers' council.[8]

In June of 1917, the US Congress, frightened by the repercussions of the Russian Revolution, quickly passed the Espionage Act. It broadly defined "disloyalty," and suppression of dissent came down all over the country.[9] The Sedition Act followed in 1918, and made it a federal crime to make any statement deemed "disloyal." Both acts made free speech illegal, and many were convicted and sentenced to long prison sentences for statements declared unpatriotic. Postal censors examined publications, and any critical of the government were not allowed to be sent by mail.[10]

In August of 1917, several hundred poor Oklahoma farmers of the South Canadian Valley, mostly members of the Socialist Party, rose in arms in the "Green Corn Rebellion," with plans to march to Washington to try to stop the war. Several armed skirmishes resulted in 266 of them being arrested, 150 convicted, and 75 sentenced to jail.[11] In the fall of 1917 nationwide local elections took place. Despite persecution and accusations of treason, the Socialist Party made great gains, with hundreds being elected around the nation.[12]

Soon the Espionage and Sedition Acts were used to jail almost all IWW and Socialist Party leaders, along with activists of many other organizations, for long sentences. At least 2,000 were imprisoned in terrible conditions, many for as long as two years without trial.[13] Free speech was almost totally suppressed. The government shut down the entire radical press, including *The Masses*, possibly the best cultural magazine in the country, published cooperatively for eleven years.[14]

When the Communist "Third" International, or "Comintern," was organized in 1919, the SP asked to be admitted as the US member party. But the Bolsheviks demanded first that all parties reorganize according to their system of "democratic-centralism," with semi-military discipline; that they subordinate their own organization to the Bolshevik International Central Committee; that they give up all participation in elections; and that they lead their working classes to take power "at once" through "mass action" and establish "proletarian dictatorships."[15] When the SP leadership refused, still committed to democratic socialism through elections, the Comintern rejected them and called on the left wing of the SP to either take over or form a new party. The young and idealistic left wing of the SP jumped in with great energy and began winning control of locals all over the country.[16] There were about 110,000 SP members at this time. The old guard struck back, expelled 40,000 members, suspended 30,000 more, and invalidated the elections. Angered at this undemocratic procedure, many additional members quit, and by 1921 the SP was down to 25,000 members and slipping fast.[17]

Many of these former SP members, together with former Wobblies, quickly organized themselves into two parties: the Communist Labor Party (CLP), an open mass party of mostly American-born, and the Communist Party (CP), a cadre organization of mostly Russian immigrants, each with about 35,000 members.[18] Both participated in the great postwar strike wave. They organized workers' councils in many cities, with most success in Portland, Butte, and Seattle.[19] But the government Palmer raids of 1919 destroyed all of these workers' councils, drove both parties underground, and decimated their membership.[20] The CLP and CP, down to about 10,000 between the two, joined forces, reorganized on the Bolshevik democratic-centralist system and affiliated with the Comintern.[21]

The American CP's first Manifesto and Program (1919) proposed to

> organize a workers' industrial republic. The workers must control industry and dispose of the products of industry... The Communist Party propagandizes industrial unionism and industrial union organizations, emphasizing their revolutionary implications. Industrial Unionism... will constitute the basis for the industrial administration of the Communist Commonwealth.[22]

Ironically, the Russian Bolsheviks gave up the call for immediate revolution in favor of the old Second International strategy of working in the unions and participating in elections in 1921, and the new American CP found itself quickly doing the very things it had violently denounced.[23] The CP had both open and clandestine members and, unlike the Socialist Party or the Socialist Labor Party, worked secretly in the unions and in farmer organizations, which made its members susceptible to charges of conspiracy. Its domination by the Comintern also made its members vulnerable to charges of espionage (the Comintern was dissolved during World War II).[24]

In place of the prototype of the Paris Commune's free democracy or visions of a Cooperative Commonwealth, the American Communist Party soon pointed to Soviet Russia as the prototype of "socialism."[25] While the CP was quickly falling into the role of apologists for almost any act of the Bolsheviks, Russia was hardening into a highly centralized state run by the party. The state took control of the Russian unions and cooperatives. With militarized compulsory labor, the "proletariat" was enormously broadened instead of abolished, no longer employees to private bosses but to the all-enveloping state, with "workers' control" relegated to mean indirect control over managers instead of direct collective democracy in the workplace.[26]

1919 STRIKE WAVE

The end of World War I gave the country a brief moment of optimism. But hard on the heels of the armistice came an economic downturn that in turn ignited the great rash of major strikes, shaking the country badly.[27] Over four million workers took part in over 3,500 strikes.[28] In the Northeast 120,000 textile workers walked out; in the anthracite and bituminous coal fields, 425,000 miners struck.[29] On the railroads, 400,000 shopmen nationwide went out, only to be overwhelmed by a sweeping federal injunction.[30] The Great Steel Strike of September, 1919 involved 350,000 workers, shutting down half the industry, including plants in Chicago, Cleveland, Youngstown, Wheeling, Lackawanna, Pueblo, and Johnstown.[31]

SEATTLE GENERAL STRIKE

During World War I, consumer cooperatives mushroomed around Seattle, many of them connected with unions.[32]

In 1918, two cooperatives formed that later would become large citywide cooperative chains. It was in an inflationary period and cooperatives were promoted as a way to stretch income. Carl Lunn, vice president of the Laundry Workers International Union, led the founding of the Seattle Consumers' Cooperative Association (SCCA). By the end of 1918, SCCA had 253 member families, growing from neighborhood to neighborhood.[33] Cooperative Food Products Association (CFPA) began as a cooperative meat stall opened by the butchers' union in the public market, with John Worswick as manager and main organizer, and soon expanded into grocery stores.[34]

On January 21, 1919, 35,000 AFL shipyard workers in Seattle struck to raise wages for the lower-paid unskilled workers. The government sent a secret telegram to the yard owners telling them to resist any raise, but the messenger carrying it delivered it to the union "by mistake." In response, all the city's unions voted sympathetic to the strike.[35]

The cooperatives provided much help during the general strike. For a week the workers ran the city through the Central Labor Council's General Strike Commmittee, providing all the necessities of survival.[36] This was one of America's great worker cooperations. When the Retail Grocers' Association cut off all credit to strikers, CFPA stepped up and offered liberal credit. SCCA gave away 10,000 free loaves of bread in one day.[37] Under orders from the mayor, the police raided the cooperative's offices and seized its books and records. Besides the existing cooperatives adding their forces, workers in each trade and industry organized themselves and made contributions. Twenty-one eating places were set up around town and thirty thousand meals a day served to whoever needed one. Milkwagon drivers obtained milk from small farmers and distributed it. Garbage collection, hospitals, even barbers and steamfitters reopened under worker control. The Labor War Veteran's Guard patrolled the streets keeping order without using force.[38]

The Seattle *Union Record*, a union-owned paper, stated,

> Ninety-five percent of us agree that the workers should control the industries...Some of us think we can get control through the Cooperative movement, some of us think through political action, and others think through industrial action... If the strike continues, Labor may feel led to avoid public suffering by reopening more and more activities UNDER ITS OWN MANAGEMENT. And that is why we say we are starting on a road that leads—NO ONE KNOWS WHERE! [39]

But faced with a military confrontation and tremendous pressure from the AFL International headquarters, the General Strike Committee finally voted to go back to work.[40] Almost immediately, the government raided the IWW, Socialist Party, and the *Union Re-*

cord printing plant, although the IWW and the SP had not even led the strike. They arrested and jailed the SP's city council candidate and thirty-nine IWW members, accused of being "ring-leaders of anarchy." This took place six months before the Palmer raids.[41]

A feverish proliferation of cooperatives continued in the following months. As the area sank into a severe postwar recession, many thousands of unemployed ex-servicemen streamed into co-ops, spurred by the hope that these could lift them out of the economic mire. People were joining co-ops so fast that records were not keeping pace.[42]

By the end of 1919, SCCA had 1,600 families in 8 grocery branches with locations in most working-class neighborhoods, 2 tailor shops, a jewelry maker cooperative, and a cooperative coal and fuel yard.[43] At the same time CFPA had over a thousand members, and its facilities had grown to include three neighborhood groceries, a bakery, a milk condensary, dairy distribution system, slaughterhouse and sausage factory. CFPA women ran an independent exchange in the main grocery, offering sewing services and items such as embroidery, bath towels, laces, and silk hose.[44]

Dozens of other cooperatives opened in 1919.[45] Seattle city employees' and the plumbers' union both organized cooperative groceries. Longshoremen, painters, carpenters, barbers, auto mechanics, shoe repairers, cleaners, and dyers formed worker cooperatives. The Scandinavian community opened a cooperative restaurant, bakery, and reading room.[46]

Lunn of SCCA worked with regional and national cooperative leaders on a plan to start a nationwide wholesale, and they opened the National Cooperative Association (NCA) in June of 1919.[47] At first James Warbasse and the Cooperative League were in strong support. Later, however, Warbasse began to attack NCA for being centralized and based on the chain-store concept rather than Rochdale decentralized federation.[48]

Meanwhile economic forces were working against the movement. In early 1920, the inflationary period ended. Then in June prices fell precipitously, issuing in a period of monetary deflation.[49] The cooperatives had promised lower prices, but now couldn't compete in price cuts with some of the larger merchants. SCCA drained off the assets of its branch stores to fund the NCA wholesale, and now found itself in a deep hole. The wholesale never got large enough to be successful, depleted large amounts of the funds of all its member co-ops, and dragged them down. CFPA also made the fatal mistake of overexpansion. Its milk condensary and slaughterhouse consistently lost money; land that its members bought for ill-conceived expansion had to be sold at a great loss.[50] Most co-ops became dependent on a constant influx of new capital, hoping to reach a point of solvency. When membership dropped and new capital stopped flowing in, they became mired in debt. In 1920, the Seattle Consumer Cooperative Association collapsed, followed by the wholesale warehouse and most of the cooperatives in the area.[51]

COOPERATIVES IN OTHER STRIKES

The American Society of Equity and the Finnish cooperatives helped the IWW strike in 1914 in the Mesaba Iron Range, providing the strikers with provisions on credit.[52] Local cooperative stores became strikers' commissaries during the Tacoma shipyards strike and the San Francisco Machinists and Shipyard Workers' strike of 1919.[53] The National Cooperative Association of Chicago and the Tri-State Cooperative Association ran the commissary for the Great Steel Strike of 1919, providing over half a million dollars worth of food.[54] Six Jewish cooperative bakeries donated 170,000 loaves of bread in the Massachusetts textile strike of 1922. Cooperative bakeries contributed heavily to strikers in the 1924 silk strike in Paterson, New Jersey, and the railroad strike in Los Angeles.[55]

PLUMB PLAN

As part of the war effort, the government took over the railways and ran them, giving full recognition to the unions and improving wages and working conditions. At the same time, the coal mines were strictly regulated by government-negotiated agreements.[56] With the armistice of 1918, the railway unions proposed to Congress that the government permanently acquire the railroads and lease them to a quasi-public corporation controlled equally by representatives of the public, management, and the workers, with the promise of efficient service, low rates, and fair salaries. The government would buy the railroads, federal and local moneys would fund improvements, and profits would retire public bonds. Known as the Plumb Plan (after Glenn Plumb, the union counsel), this economy-sharing nationalization proposal, with union co-partnership and participation in management, reached far beyond the usual trade union demands. The Plumb Plan came before Congress in 1919.[57]

At the same time, the United Mine Workers called for nationalization of the coal mines. With the wartime agreements now defunct, wages were severely depressed, and mines across the country were exploding in strikes.[58]

Congress rejected the Plumb Plan, and the government returned the railways to the corporations` and issued an injunction forbidding coal strikes.[59] The unions continued to lobby for the Plumb Plan in the following years. It was endorsed by the AFL at its 1920 and 1921 conventions. But in Congress the plan was dead. After that year the AFL abandoned socialization and reverted to narrow trade union goals.[60]

WWI AFTERMATH: THE PALMER RAIDS

When the US entered World War I, anti-German sentiment filled the press. This quickly transformed into an attack on anyone suspected of German sympathies, then expanded into an assault on immigrants and minorities, and beyond that into a campaign against any group accused of hindering the war effort, including labor and radicals.[61] During the postwar strike wave and depression, employer groups launched an anti-labor campaign they called "the American Plan," centered around the universalization of the open-shop.[62] Fueled by conservative newspapers and business associations calling loudly for law and order, a mood of fear swept the nation.[63]

During the war, the Department of Justice (DOJ) was given the green light by President Woodrow Wilson to track the activities of any people it considered radical. Any publication advocating for peace or against the draft was under scrutiny. In 1917, the DOJ ransacked the offices of the anarchist Emma Goldman's *Mother Earth* and Alexander Berkman's *The Blast*, and seized a subscription list of 10,000 names.[64]

In 1918, Victor L. Berger of Milwaukee, the first ever Socialist US congressman (out of office at that time) was indicted for opposing the war under the Espionage Act along with four other members of the Socialist Party. Despite the charges hanging over him, he ran for Congress again, and was elected. The House refused to seat him and declared the seat vacant. A special election was held and Berger was elected again. The House once more refused to seat him. Berger was sentenced to twenty years in federal prison. The Supreme Court later overturned the conviction, but the seat was kept vacant for the rest of the term.[65]

J. Edgar Hoover was put in charge of a new division of the DOJ that would later become the FBI, quickly compiled a list of about 150,000 names, and cut his teeth during what is known as the Palmer raids.[66] After the armistice, government repression of radicals did not cease but expanded. Between November 7th, 1919 and January 2nd, 1920, raids were made in thirty cities. Over 10,000 were arrested; most were released without charge but still received severe beatings in the largest mass arrest in American history.[67] Almost half of those arrested belonged to the IWW. About 550 people were deported.[68]

Assistant Secretary of Labor L. F. Post described the raids in New York City, where 700 were arrested:

> Meetings wide open to the general public were roughly broken up. All persons present—citizens and aliens alike without discrimination—were arbitrarily taken into custody and searched as if they had been burglars caught in the criminal act. Without warrants for arrest men were carried off to police stations and other temporary prisons, subjected there to secret police-office inquisitions commonly known as the "third degree," their statements written categorically into mimeographed question blanks, and they required to swear to them regardless of their accuracy.[69]

The IWW, SP, and the newly formed Communist Party were all violently attacked in the Palmer raids. Palmer announced that a Communist revolution in the US was planned for May 1st, 1920, but the day passed uneventfully. That November Gene Debs got almost a million votes running for president from a jail cell.[70]

The IWW was further torn apart in 1924 by an internal rivalry between the lumber and agricultural workers unions, and over the Communist Party's presence in the organization. Despite the schism and the government persecution, IWW members nonetheless went on to lead important strikes in the Colorado coalfields in 1927-28 and Detroit auto plants in 1932-33. Although the IWW never fully recovered, it never disbanded either, and continues today.[71]

COOPERATIVE LEAGUE IN THE 1920s

The first national convention of the CL in 1918, in Springfield, Illinois, had 185 delegates from 386 cooperatives.[72] Only consumer cooperatives could vote, but farmer marketing co-ops and trade unions were also present. They voted to organize a national wholesale, open to all associations operating on the Rochdale plan, and to negotiate with existing regional wholesales to merge into it. Farmer marketing cooperatives were excluded because the CL saw them as having conflicting interests, since they sold produce to the co-op stores. Industrial worker cooperatives were likewise excluded from the CL. Farm supply purchasing cooperatives were considered consumers' cooperatives, and therefore were admitted to the organization.[73]

In 1919, CL secretary Albert Sonnichsen published *Consumers' Cooperation*, the first American book to fully explain the theories of consumer cooperation that had been primarily developed by the British movement.[74] Sonnichsen based his ideas on theories first formulated by Beatrice Potter Webb, later one of the founders of the Fabian Society, in her book *The Cooperative Movement in Britain* (1891). Sonnichsen's book dismissed worker cooperatives and self-management as impracticable. He argued that consumer cooperatives should form cooperative wholesale societies, and purchase farms and factories run with employees to supply them. He held that "consumers' cooperation is an anti-capitalist, revolutionary movement, aiming toward a radical social reconstruction based on an all-inclusive collectivism," and eventually leading to a cooperative commonwealth.[75] Like the CL, Sonnichsen excluded farmers' marketing cooperatives from this scheme, considering them "an integral part of the capitalist system."[76]

However, farmer cooperatives emphatically rejected CL's program of socialization of the land through purchase by proposed giant consumer cooperatives, which would result in farmers becoming employees of those cooperatives.[77] In that proposal, ownership would be vested in the consumers of the farm produce, not in the farmers. At this time, Warbasse insisted that land collectivization in this manner was historically inevitable.[78]

The League took as its mission to become the coordinating center for organizing consumers on a national basis. Its ultimate goal was to take all economic activity under the control of consumers organized in local stores and associations, which would federate regionally and nationally, and take over the manufacturing and service sectors.[79]

Warbasse and the CL soon launched a campaign to create a national cooperative wholesale. Between 1917 and 1918, regional cooperative wholesales were being organized in various parts of the country: the Pacific Cooperative League's Rochdale Wholesale, the Central States Cooperative Society, Tri-State Cooperative Association, Central Cooperative Wholesale, Washington State Society, Cooperative Wholesale Society of America. To Warbasse and the CL the time seemed ripe to try bring them together into a national wholesale. But after initial talks, the existing regional wholesales all backed off.[80]

Warbasse's work with the CL got him suspended from King's County Medical Society in 1918, in the context of the government persecutions of progressives and radicals. The pretext of his suspension was that a letter of his to a medical journal was "antagonistic to the welfare of the United States and the good repute of the medical profession."[81] He wound up retiring from medical practice and devoting himself full time to the CL. (In 1930, the Medical Society offered to reinstate him, but he declined.)[82]

The CL adopted a new alternative strategy for a national wholesale in 1919. It incorporated National Cooperative Association (NCA) wholesale as a clearinghouse for a centralized chain of stores with centers in Chicago, Seattle, and Hoboken. NCA began with great energy and publicity. By the end of 1920 there were seventeen stores in operation in the Chicago area but most of these were losing money. The situation in Seattle and Hoboken mirrored Chicago.[83]

By 1919, the Pacific Cooperative League (PCL) had thirty-two branches and stretched into Arizona. Founded in 1913, the PCL began as a group led by Ernest Ames and A. D. Clump, who were trying to salvage the troubled Rochdale Wholesale in San Francisco.[84] They began organizing grassroots buying clubs that would be using the Wholesale. Some clubs became stores, and sold many things besides groceries, including coal. PCL took over the Wholesale in 1920 and began organizing stores on a large scale.[85] By the next year, it had forty-seven member stores in eight Western states. PCL was promoted at one point by Upton Sinclair, who in the next decade would go on to lead the EPIC self-help cooperative movement.[86]

But the Pacific Coast League became locked in an internecine war with the Cooperative League. Although Warbasse had initially been a strong supporter of both PCL and the National Cooperative Association wholesale, he turned adamantly against the chain-store concept, and began attacking both organizations unceasingly. "Such a central organization proceeds to create societies for its own good."[87] Warbasse promoted a decentralized cooperative movement, and attacked PCL and NCA for their centralized structures. The movement on the West Coast was more politically radical than on the East Coast, the base of CL. When the local Seattle co-ops helped the unionists in their General Strike of 1919, CL disavowed the co-ops even as NCA came to their support.[88]

The CL congress of 1920 refused to seat delegates from both PCL and NCA. A few months later, the National Cooperative Association and its entire chain collapsed. The West Coast movement was cut off from the rest of the country and the whole PCL went down in 1921, having no national support in that depression year.[89]

The Bureau of Labor Statistics reported that in 1920 there were 2,600 cooperative stores and buying associations (including farm supply purchasing co-ops) in the United States.[90] Most of these operated in small towns and served farm communities. But in the postwar depression of 1920-22 and the following years, most co-op chains, wholesales, and federations in the United States went bankrupt, and by the mid 1920s most had failed. They failed primarily because the wholesales had been formed without sufficient local development to support them, forcing the organizers to try desperately but unsuccessfully to form enough groups to provide the needed business.[91] The Cooperative Central Exchange in Wisconsin was the only wholesale to come through the period largely intact.[92]

The 1920 CL congress authorized the formation of "district" leagues, regional organizations to which local cooperatives belonged. Many were quickly initiated but only three lasted, the Eastern, Northern, and Central States leagues. Each of these coordinated education and organization in its territory, and worked to organize a regional wholesale.[93]

One of the CL's most important functions was lobbying state legislatures for adequate laws facilitating the incorporation of cooperatives. Every state had different and confusing statutes. In 1922, the CL got New York State, where its central office was located, to pass the first law authorizing the formation of cooperative federations.[94] This was significant because the federated structure provided the needed framework for democratic decentralization, with one-member-one vote. Until that time CL had run on a somewhat ad hoc basis. The Cooperative League then incorporated as a cooperative federation.[95] The subsequent congress was its first as a really representative member organization. At that time, the CL had 289 member associations with 82,000 members.[96]

Warbasse's book *Cooperative Democracy* came out in 1923. Containing detailed discussions of cooperative philosophy and history, it immediately became a standard text, and had immense impact on the American movement for decades.[97]

From the time of its founding through the 1920s, the CL was financed largely by Warbasse, who was independently wealthy. The number of affiliated societies continually increased, but many of them paid only one dollar a year. At Sonnichsen's initiative, the Board of Directors resolved to take no more grants from individuals in 1930. It was only then that the CL became self-supporting.[98]

In the 1920s, the Communist Party grew to be a strong force in the Cooperative League. Warbasse, in general, supported the socialistic experiments of the early days of the Russian Revolution. As late as September 1923, in an article in *Cooperation*, he approvingly quoted Lenin as saying, "It is incumbent upon us to support the cooperative movement *above all*," adding that Lenin considered the cooperative movement "as an essential step in moving toward a free cooperative society."[99] Radicals dominated the CL congress of 1924 and proclaimed solidarity with the workers of the world. The CP's greatest strength at that time was on the East Coast, in Jewish enclaves, and among Finns in the Lake Superior region. Finnish Communists dominated Cooperative Central Exchange, the wholesale for the Michigan, Minnesota, and Wisconsin region. However, as the Soviet Union became increasingly centralized, a growing group in the CL, including Warbasse, became disillusioned.[100]

The CL was split over the meaning of the Rochdale principle of "neutrality in politics." To some it meant only not supporting candidates for public office; to others it also meant not taking stands on issues.[101] Many Socialists and Communists were involved in the consumer cooperative movement throughout the 1920s. These gained a majority of delegates at the Cooperative League Congress of 1924 and, over objections of the CL board, proclaimed that the co-op movement was part of the general labor movement, with the goal of "cooperation of all workers' movements for the benefit of the exploited toilers."[102]

In the Cooperative League congress of 1928, the "pure and simple" cooperators dug in their heels and brought the issue of Communism to a head. The "pure" cooperators framed it as a question of upholding the Rochdale policy of political neutrality. At the same time a parallel struggle was going on in the International Cooperative Alliance (of which CL was the American member), in which the Soviet cooperatives were transforming all discussions into political debates over economic systems.[103]

In the CL congress of 1928, the "pure" cooperators resolved "in the interest of harmony and unity" to ban any further discussion of "Communist, Socialist, and other political and economic theories." Unless the resolution passed, they threatened to split the Cooperative League into two hostile cooperative federations. The radical cooperators, led by Eskel Ronn, manager of the Cooperative Central Exchange (CCE) wholesale, backed off, abstained from voting, and the resolution passed.[104] In 1930, the Finnish Communist co-ops were forced out of CCE, resulting in the quick economic strangulation of that wholesale. At the Cooperative League congress later that year, all the CP co-ops were stonewalled out, leaving the League dominated by "pure and simple" cooperators.[105] This purge facilitated an alliance between farmer cooperatives and cooperative store systems.[106]

The period of prosperity between 1925 and 1929 gave the country a sense of limitless expansion, and higher incomes during that economic bubble reduced urban consumers' interest in the small savings that could be gained through consumer cooperatives. During those four years, almost 600 cooperative stores and associations went out of business, with the Midwest, Pennsylvania and Washington hardest hit.[107]

During the same period, farm cooperatives expanded. In 1920, there were 1 million members of 9,000 marketing and purchasing associations with a dollar volume of $1 billion. In 1925-26, there were 2.7 million in 11,000 associations, and a dollar volume of $2.4 billion. In 1928, there were 3 million members in 12,000 associations.[108] Much of this increase came from the rapid expansion of large-scale cooperatives, many of them with a centralized internal structure. In 1920, there were only around twenty of these enterprises, doing about a fifth of the total volume of farm co-op business. By the end of the decade some rural areas were dominated by these large cooperatives. By 1932, there were over 200 of them, over half of them centralized, and representing over a third of the total volume of business.[109]

FALL OF THE SOCIALIST PARTY

In the 1924 presidential election, the Socialist Party did not run a separate candidate, but joined forces with almost all the non-Communist left behind Robert La Follette and the Progressive Party. In that coalition were the Non-Partisan League, the Farmers Union, the Farmer-Labor Party of Minnesota, and the AFL, which temporarily abandoned its nonpartisan policy. La Follette garnered a little under 5 million votes for president, 16.6 percent of the total. Nonetheless most of the coalition members considered it a defeat.[110] The Progressive Party quickly collapsed, each group going its own way. The AFL flopped back to its nonpartisan policy. The Progressive Party was a head without a body, never developing the infrastructure to put up candidates for lesser office, and instead supporting "progressive" nominees of other parties. So even though the party was instrumental in electing twenty congressmen and six senators, the Progressive Party got little out of it.[111]

After Gene Debs died in 1926, Norman Thomas, former Presbyterian minister, became the voice of the Socialist Party, and its presidential candidate in 1928. In that election, Secretary of Commerce Herbert Hoover won by a landslide. Thomas garnered fewer than 267,000 votes, while Communist candidate William Z. Foster, leader of the 1919 steel strike, received under 48,000, together adding up to less than 1 percent of the popular vote.[112]

LABOR SCHOOLS

At least six "labor schools" and "labor colleges" operated during this period. Their mission was to teach a curriculum based on working-class culture and history, a perspective distinctly excluded from most American schools of the time. They offered to the upcoming generation knowledge of their families' struggles, and provided ideological continuity to the movement. These schools performed an enormous service to the movement, trained a generation of leaders and scholars, and their influence continues today. Labor schools included Commonwealth College in Arkansas, Brookwood Labor College in New York, Denver Labor College, Seattle Labor College, and Highlander Folk School in Tennessee. Each had a fascinating and important history. Highlander became the Highlander Research and Education Center, still functioning today. We will examine just one here—Work Peoples' College in Minnesota, perhaps the most extraordinary of all.[113]

WORK PEOPLES' COLLEGE

The Finnish Socialist Federation gained control of a seminary in Duluth in 1906 and in the following years transformed it into Work Peoples' College.[114] The burgeoning community of immigrant Finns in Minnesota, Michigan, and Wisconsin flocked to the school. In the later 19th century, thousands of Finns had settled in the region, primarily to work in the mines but most with the hope of becoming farmers. Many had been involved with the labor and cooperative movements in Finland, where there was a strong socialist tradition. Besides the usual college curriculum, Work Peoples' College focused on labor issues, workers' history, class struggle, and socialism.[115]

Politically oriented socialists controlled the school in its early years, but in 1913, after an ideological struggle, industrial unionists took over, and reoriented the curriculum toward the IWW.[116] Under their direction, students studied workers' industrial administration in order to take part in the expected revolutionary transformation of American society. The college turned out a generation of radical activists and working-class leaders, and its graduates built a strong worker-owned cooperative economy in the region.[117]

The Communist Party had a powerful presence in cooperatives in the region, and Finnish Communists dominated the regional wholesale, the Cooperative Central Exchange. Work Peoples' College was one of the first targets of the Palmer raids in 1919. Under the direction of J. Edgar Hoover, agents ransacked the school. Many Finnish immigrants taught at and ran the college, and all of its noncitizens were deported without a hearing or legal representation.[118] School director Leo Laukki was arrested but jumped bail and fled to Soviet Russia. The school struggled to stay afloat in the following years, but never fully recovered, finally closing in 1941. Work Peoples' College was a landmark in its demonstration of the success of education in preparing working people for social activism and cooperative ownership.[119]

OUTSIDE THE MAINSTREAM IN THE EARLY 1900s: UNITED ARTISTS

United Artists film studio began as a cooperative. To gain creative control of his work, Charlie Chaplin formed his own independent film production company in 1917.[120] At that time, however, independent producers remained dependent on a contract with a distribution/exhibition company, with which they split all costs and profits. Two years later, Chaplin's distributor, First National, was suddenly disinterested in renewing their contract. Word came that First National intended to merge with Paramount in a move to monopolize distribution and exhibition, swallow the few independents, and impose complete control over the industry. Chaplin met with his friends Mary Pickford and Douglas Fairbanks, who were suffering similar problems. They partnered with D. W. Griffith and William S. Hart to form United Artists Studios, their own independent company, giving the five partners full control over their work. The studios reacted with disdain, the president of Metro Pictures quipping, "the lunatics have taken charge of the asylum."[121] In the end, United Artists changed the industry from the old studio system to today's system of independent production and distribution. Although UA is today a corporate giant, its early history is closely and dynamically tied to the worker cooperative movement. Chaplin's politics eventually got him banned from the US.[122]

BANKING AND CREDIT UNIONS

The first cooperative credit union anywhere in the Americas was La Caisse Populaire de Levi, organized in 1900 by Alphonse Desjardins in the town of Levi, Quebec. He structured it partly on a model that had been very successful in Germany, and partly on New England savings and loan associations.[123] Cooperative credit unions are based on the idea of people pooling their money and making loans to each other. The idea took off and there were 150 credit unions in Quebec province within a few years.[124] In 1909, Desjardins assisted a group of expatriate French Canadians living in Manchester, New Hampshire, to set up a "people's bank." That same year he helped write the Massachusetts Credit Union Act, which became the legal foundation for credit unions in the US. The political ground for this had previously been laid by a state investigation into the victimization of Boston factory workers by loan sharks.[125]

By 1925, credit union laws passed in 15 states, and over 400 credit unions served over 10,000 members.[126] Credit unions formed statewide leagues, and the Credit Union National Association (CUNA) was created as a confederation of state leagues in 1934. Also in that year, Congress passed a federal credit union act, permitting them to be organized anywhere in the United States, with the option of incorporating under either state or federal law. By 1935,

39 states had credit union laws and over 3,300 credit unions were serving over 600,000 members.[127]

HOUSING CO-OPS

The first urban co-op housing projects in the United States, called "home clubs," were built in New York City in the early 1880s. These were cooperatives for higher income people to give them most of the advantages of home ownership without many of the problems and responsibilities. Incorporated as joint-stock companies, many of the apartments in these buildings were rented to non-owners, with special deals for stockholders.[128]

In 1916, a group of immigrant artisans in Brooklyn started the first working-class housing co-op, the Finnish Home Building Association.[129] In the post-WWI economic boom, home building costs were high, and many urban dwellers turned to joint-stock housing. Over the decade of the 1920s, many housing co-ops were built, some for wage earners, but most for the upper middle class. By 1925, there were co-op buildings in sixteen states.[130]

Hudson View Gardens in upper Manhattan was a middle-class co-op founded by an immigrant German doctor in 1924. In addition to 354 apartments, the cooperative operated a commissary, laundry, restaurant, barber and tailor shops, and other services.[131] In 1927, the New York Housing Act granted tax exemptions that facilitated middle- and low-income cooperatives. One of the earliest was a 300 unit building sponsored by the Amalgamated Clothing Workers Union in the Bronx that eventually grew to 1,400 units. Many union members were housed there.[132] In 1927, a group connected with the Communist Party organized the United Workers Cooperative Colony in the Bronx; it was the largest co-op housing project in the country at the time, with 743 apartments and many service and buying cooperatives.[133] The Queensboro Project, a moderate-income co-op in Jackson Heights, Queens, New York, was built in 1929 to house over 2,000 families.[134]

At this time about half of the co-op buildings in the US were in New York City, followed by Chicago, Detroit, Buffalo, San Francisco, and Philadelphia. The financial collapse at the end of the 1920s brought the cooperative building movement to a standstill. During the depression many suffered foreclosures, including the United Workers Cooperative Colony, where the residents were nonetheless able to retain management control for another decade.[135]

9.
The Great Depression &
the Conservative Advance

The country plunged into the Great Depression in 1929 with massive layoffs resulting in 25 percent unemployment, and many thousands of farm foreclosures.[1] Cooperatives played an important role in helping the nation recover.

There were few consumer co-ops left in urban America in 1929, so city people had to start over almost from scratch. In general, farm cooperatives remained in better shape during the late 1920s, but some rural areas were increasingly dominated by large centralized cooperative enterprises.

The first resurgence of organized grassroots cooperation began with a completely spontaneous movement known as Self-Help, which was totally outside the mainstream movement of the time.[2]

SELF-HELP

When the economy collapsed, the "self-help" cooperative movement, stressing mutual aid and barter, quickly became widespread among the unemployed and underemployed. It was truly a spontaneous mass movement.[3] These cooperatives produced a variety of goods for trade and self-use, and organized exchanges between laborers and farmers, in which people would work for a share of the produce. They sprang up in many locales around the country, and became a part of daily life for many people. Money was scarce. Scrip was sometimes used. By the end of 1932, there were self-help organizations in 37 states with over 300,000 members. A survey in December 1934 counted 310 different groups, about two-thirds of them in California with over a half million members.[4]

Several forms of self-help were usually distinguished, although most groups practiced them all to varying degrees: exchange among members, exchange of labor for goods or services, cooperative production for trade or sale. Exchange among members was the most widespread, and commonly involved partial payment in cash. Only in the later stage of the movement did many groups turn to production, and most never did to an appreciable extent.[5] Of the few large industrial cooperatives that formed during the decade, the most notable were several cooperative plywood factories in the Pacific Northwest that survived the Great Depression and continued to thrive half a century later.[6]

The Unemployed Citizen's League (UCL) organized large-scale mutual aid in Seattle in the early 1930s. Through the UCL, the fishermen's union found boats for the unemployed to use cooperatively; local farmers gave unmarketable fruit and vegetables over to their members to pick; people gained the right to cut firewood on scrub timberland.[7] UCL had twenty-two local commissaries around the city, where food and firewood were available to exchange for every type of service and commodity from home repairs to doctor bills.[8]

In Pennsylvania, unemployed coal miners formed cooperative teams, dug coal on company property, trucked it out and sold it. It has been estimated that at least 20,000 miners participated in this seizure of means of survival. Company police trying to stop them were met with force; not a jury in the state was willing to convict them.[9]

Southern and Northern California co-ops, in general, developed different approaches. The Northern California groups defined their goal as developing permanent production facilities to create an independent survival system for their members, while most Southern groups never developed from simple "vegetable exchanges" into a production phase. Unlike the Northern groups, which distributed items to members according to work performed, many Southern groups also distributed "according to need" in a somewhat indiscriminate manner.[10]

SOUTHERN CALIFORNIA: UCRA & UCDA

Los Angeles County had the largest self-help concentration in Southern California, where about 75,000 people in 107 groups participated in the harvest of fall 1932.[11] Many people in nearby Orange County also formed self-help cooperatives. Among the earliest groups in the state were the L.A. Exchange, the Compton Relief Association—begun by a group of World War I veterans—and the Unemployed Association of Santa Ana. Since farming areas were easily accessible in the South, most of these groups organized large numbers of people to harvest produce in exchange for a share of the crops.[12]

The Southern groups saw their aim as getting food, clothing, and shelter for their members by any means necessary. These means included direct action and what they termed "chiseling."[13] They took to direct action to put evicted members back into their homes, and to turn disconnected utilities back on. They "chiseled" necessities out of farmers, businesses, and local governments. The first instance of chiseling took the form of workers not showing up to perform promised labor, although they had already taken the items exchanged for it. Soon, they began to chisel the local government for grants. Some groups experimented with scrip—in-house currency.[14] These "scrip exchanges" were more common at first in Southern California than in the North, but were usually plagued with problems.[15]

In the spring of 1933, many of the Southern groups came together and set up the Unemployed Cooperative Relief Association (UCRA) with C. M. Christofferson as chairman.[16] Later under "Pat" May, UCRA changed from a loose federation to a highly centralized organization claiming to speak for a combined membership of 200,000 statewide. UCRA took to supporting candidates favorable to its goals in local elections, and packed considerable clout.[17]

Mass "hunger marches" and large demonstrations induced the L.A. County Board of Supervisors and municipal government to grant UCRA gasoline, trucks, and food staples. The focus of the southern groups shifted away from labor exchange and they became primarily distribution organizations. "No more work! We've produced too much already," became a rallying cry.[18] As UCRA became more centralized, a sort of ward-boss and, in one Southern town, a goon squad backed by the local business community took over the group using the elimination of UCRA "radicals" as a lever for its rise to power.[19]

The Northern cooperatives criticized "chiseling," scorned the idea of trying to get "something for nothing," objected to getting involved in electoral politics, and declined becoming relief organizations. Nonetheless, when UCRA moved to become statewide, many of the Northern groups affiliated, including Oakland's Unemployed Exchange Association (UXA).[20]

In January 1933, UCRA parented 5 units in San Francisco with 900 member families, and several other units in the East Bay.

But several factors hindered the San Francisco groups, including long distances to farming areas, intense political factionalization, and comparatively available government "relief."[21] UCRA held its quarterly convention in San Francisco in July 1933 and split into two in the midst of bitter fighting. The San Francisco groups never recovered and four totally collapsed by the end of the year.[22]

In Los Angeles, governmental agencies undercut UCRA by creating and fostering parallel organizations, first the Area Conference, to which most UCRA units became affiliated, and later the Unemployed Cooperative Distribution Association (UCDA), fostered by the New Deal in the fall of 1933.[23] May's group from UCRA took over the administration of UCDA, while UCRA became functionally defunct. Over the year, May managed to preside over both the continued "chiseling" and distribution of $120,000 in federal grants for staple foods and gasoline.[24]

NORTHERN CALIFORNIA

The self-help movement reached its most sophisticated level of development in the San Francisco Bay Area. The Pacific Cooperators' League of Oakland set up the first Bay Area labor exchange in 1930. The summer and fall of 1932 saw the biggest blossoming of organizations and there were twenty-two self-help groups in the East Bay by the spring of 1933, nine in San Francisco and the Peninsula, one in San Jose.[25]

The Berkeley Unemployed Association, at 2110 Parker Street, had sections that included sewing, quilting and weaving, shoe repair, barber services, food canning and conserving, wood yard, kitchen and dining room, commissary, garage, machine shop, woodshop, mattress factory, and painter and carpenter teams. At its height, the Association involved several hundred people and provided full medical and dental coverage.[26] A visitor to the wood shop in December 1934 reported them working on office desks and furniture, as well as fruit lugs for the farm exchange section.[27] Members later changed the name to the Berkeley Self-Help Cooperative, typical of many groups who considered themselves no longer unemployed.[28]

A few blocks away, on Delaware Street, the Pacific Cooperative League (PCL) operated a garage, flour mill, wood yard, store, canning and weaving projects, and ran a newspaper, the *Herald of Cooperation*, later called the *Voice of the Self-Employed*, co-published by Llano colony. The PCL laid claim to having organized one of the earliest labor exchanges of the Depression, when it traded an Atascadero rancher its harvesting labor for part of his apricot crop in September 1930.[29] The PCL was not a new organization like almost all the rest, but dated back decades to when it had been part of the consumer co-op store movement of the same name, which was begun in 1913 and collapsed in 1921. The East Bay PCL group had managed to survive the death of the original consumer co-op store movement. It had staggered along at a low level until sparked to rebirth by the Great Depression and by the other self-help groups nearby.[30]

A group of laid-off cannery workers formed the San Jose Un-employed Relief Council (later called the San Jose Self-Help Co-op). They soon had a wood yard, a fruit-and-vegetable drying yard, a store, laundry, farm, soap factory, barbershop, shoe shop, commissary, and sewing project. The Council contracted for a wide variety of jobs and services, and at its height was about 1,200 strong.[31]

The Peninsula Economic Exchange, in Palo Alto, was organized by a group of unemployed white-collar workers, professionals, and bankrupt merchants. With about a hundred member families, the Exchange had a store, a farm, a cannery, a woodyard, and a fishing boat. Unlike most of the other Northern groups, it issued scrip to members for hours worked.[32]

The most successful self-help cooperative in Northern California was the Unemployed Exchange Association (UXA), started in Oakland.

CASE STUDY:
THE UNEMPLOYED EXCHANGE ASSOCIATION (UXA)
A Self-Help Cooperative in the 1930s

The rise and fall of the self-help movement are exemplified by the life and demise of the Unemployed Exchange Association.[33]

It was July 1932. The economy was stopped. Factories were locked and money was scarce. One out of seven Californians were unemployed. There were almost no social welfare programs. Large numbers were homeless, destitute, hungry. Vacant buildings were boarded up. The fields were rotting with tons of unharvested fruit and vegetables. Small farmers had no cash to pay harvesters, and it didn't matter because there was no market. Many farmers were losing their land. Food prices were next to nothing, but many thousands in the cities and towns had nothing at all. The homeless, including thousands of "wild children," crowded California highways and rails, searching for survival. Over the static of every radio flowed the soothing voice of Franklin Roosevelt promising to bring a New Deal if elected.

"Hoovervilles," shantytowns of the homeless, had sprung up around the country over the past three years. The largest in the San Francisco Bay Area was Pipe City, near the railroad tracks by the Oakland waterfront, where hundreds lived in sections of large sewer pipe that had never been laid due to lack of funds.

Carl Rhodehamel, an unemployed electrical engineer and orchestra conductor, visited Pipe City and talked to the inhabitants. He was a man with an idea. Since the money system wasn't working, he thought, unemployed people should form their own system, not using money at all, and aim at providing themselves with everything they needed to live through barter. He was not the only one with that idea. Barter groups of the unemployed already operated in Seattle and L.A., and were forming all around the country.

He and two Pipe City denizens soon found an abandoned grocery store that could be used for meetings, and a group of unemployed began to gather. All were skilled and experienced workers, but all realized it could be years, if ever, before they'd find work in their fields again. Their first project was going door to door in the neighborhood, the Dimond-Allendale district of East Oakland, offering to do home repairs in exchange for "junk" from people's basements and garages.

They decided to try to gather all the unemployed in the neighborhood into their group, and distributed fliers throughout the area. On the evening of July 20th, 1932, about twenty people organized the UXA, the Unemployed Exchange Association (or Universal Exchange Association, as they later called it). The X stood not only for "exchange," but for the "unknown factor" in a social algebraic equation.

Six months later, the UXA was the most highly developed group in the self-help cooperative movement springing up across America. In a nation of dispossessed, many who were hungry for a new social equation imagined that all that was required to get from the USA to the UXA was a daring leap into the unknown.

Dimond-Allendale was a depressed working-class neighborhood. Little work had been done there in the three years since the crash of 1929, so a great backlog of home repairs remained. The UXA organized residents to fix up each other's houses and to redistribute every variety of article in their garages to where it would be useful. The abandoned grocery became their first storeroom and commissary, soon overflowing with household and industrial articles. Broken items were repaired or rebuilt. The neighborhood, previously choked with despair and immobility, was suddenly bursting with activity and confidence. People poured into the new organization. The UXA soon began sending scouts around Oakland and into the surrounding farm areas to search out salvageable items and make deals with their owners for them. Labor teams followed.

They called it Reciprocal Economy. UXA made no distinction in labor value between men and women, skilled and unskilled. The Association functioned entirely by barter at first; it was all done on the books, without a circulating scrip. Members could write "orders"— like checks—against their account to other members for services provided. Eventually, they began making trades that involved part payment in cash. All work was credited at one hundred points per hour.[34] Members exchanged points earned for their choice of items in the commissary. Each article brought in was given a point value, which approximated the labor time that went into it, with some adjustment for comparable money value. They offered many services for points, including complete medical and dental, garage, nursery school, and barber services. They provided some housing and all of their firewood needs. At its peak, UXA distributed forty tons of food per week to its members.

The General Assembly of members was the ultimate decision-making body. It selected an Operating Committee in semiannual elections, to coordinate functioning. The UXA was divided into various "sections": Manufacturing, Trading, Food, Farm, Construction, Gardening, Homeworkers, Communication, Health, Transportation, Bookkeeping, Maintenance, Fuel, Personal Services, Placement, Food Conservation, Headquarters Staff, Saw Mill, Ranch. The workers in each section decided issues relevant to their work, approved or disapproved Committee and Assembly actions, and determined the admittance of new members into their section. They kept the numbers in each section down to about twenty-five to make decision-making viable; when numbers got much larger, the section split into two.

The Operating Committee met four nights a week at its headquarters on East 14th Street at 40th Avenue. These were open meetings at which plans and decisions were thrashed out in democratic discussions. Outsiders often expressed amazement at how well they functioned without bosses, foremen, or managers. Sitting about a huge round table, the only rule was to speak one at a time. Anybody with an idea, member or not, was welcome to sit in and was heard after the Committee had dealt with the current commitments of jobs which individuals had agreed to do. On Friday nights the coordinators of the sections met with the Operating Committee to form the Coordinating Assembly, the basic ongoing decision-making group. The Operating Committee appointed the section coordinators, with the workers of each section holding veto power. The coordinators had no authority over members, and could be recalled at any time. Power was from the bottom up.

One of the recurring topics at the Assembly and Operating Committee was the question of how to implement barter on a societal scale, so that all people who could not find a place in the failed capitalist economy might join a self-help cooperative and create a whole new American way of life.

Word of the new organization quickly reached certain vigilant ears. The Oakland police department received word that the UXA was a "revolutionary" group with "Communist" leaders. In the fall of 1932, the police "Red Squad" raided their meeting and shut them down. They closed the commissary on the pretext that they were violating an ordinance prohibiting the sale of food and clothing from the same store. Utilities were shut off.

The core group met in secret and decided on an unusual plan, attributed to Rhodehamel. The entire membership, about one hundred people, scattered about the city spreading a rumor that the police and fire departments had changed their minds and were now helping the UXA. They fed that story to the police themselves, then began holding open meetings again. The police came out of curiosity, a dialogue began, the raids stopped, and relations between the local government and the UXA actually became helpful.

By the beginning of 1933, the UXA had a labor force of 600. Anyone over eighteen could join; applicants were screened, but only a small number were rejected. The Association had provisions for expelling people but these were almost never used. According to Rhodehamel, when someone was known to be stealing from the organization, the UXA made it easier for that person to continue stealing, while letting him or her know that the group knew. Before long, most offenders would be shamed to either stop stealing or disappear.

Beyond organizing barter and labor exchange, the UXA began producing articles for trade and sale. Members set up a foundry and machine shop, a woodshop, garage, a soap factory, a print shop, a food conserving project, nursery, and adult school. They had eighteen trucks that they'd rebuilt from junk. They branched outside of town, and maintained a woodlot in Dixon, ranches near Modesto and Winters, lumber mills near Oroville and in the Santa Cruz mountains. At its peak, the UXA was providing 1,500 people with farm produce, medical and dental benefits, auto repair, some housing, and other services.[35]

THE NEW DEAL AND CO-OPS

In 1932, small farmers and wage earners joined once again into their traditional alliance, and together won the New Deal. There was a resurgence of the Left parties too. Norman Thomas became the Socialist Party standard bearer, though the SP was now seriously weakened. Attacks from the government, internal quarrels, disputes with unions, and feuds with the Communist Party had all taken tolls. Thomas garnered almost 900,000 votes in 1932 (about 2 percent), but after that the SP fell into a precipitous decline from which it never recovered.[36] The CP participated in the 1932 election, too, with William Z. Foster receiving over 100,000 votes.[37] But in that election, at the bottom of the Great Depression, Roosevelt swept the nation. The New Deal programs that sprang forth in the following months both united the Left and stole some of its fire.[38]

The Agricultural Adjustment Act of May 1933 was formulated by Roosevelt's Secretary of Agriculture, Henry A. Wallace. The Act set up the Agricultural Adjustment Administration (AAA), and established the role of federal planning in the agricultural sector of the economy. It implemented a plan to withhold produce from the market to stabilize farm prices at livable levels. This was basically the idea that farmer cooperatives had been working to implement for many years, the same strategy as the farmers' strike. The producers themselves would decide on production limits. Included were wheat, corn, cotton, rice, tobacco, dairy products, and hogs. The AAA paid the landowners subsidies to leave a percentage of their land idle. Crop prices were subsidized up to parity. Some crops were ordered to be destroyed and some livestock slaughtered to maintain prices.[39] Marketing cooperatives were at first concerned that they would be marginalized by the government program, but Secretary of Agriculture Wallace insisted that the new system was aimed at strengthening them and putting them on a more secure financial basis. The AAA forced recalcitrant farmers to cooperate in marketing.[40] The program was successful in that farm incomes increased but food prices remained stable. However, no substantive provisions were originally made for the losses that tenant farmers, sharecroppers or farm laborers would sustain due to the program. The AAA was controlled by the Farm Bureau and other big growers, and they had little concern for the plight of poor farmers and farm workers. Because the AAA used the Extension Service to administer the program, it served to enormously increase the influence of the Farm Bureau.[41] In 1936, the Supreme Court declared the AAA unconstitutional, because it levied a tax on processors and passed it on to farmers. In response, Congress passed another AAA in 1938 with financing out of general taxation.[42]

The Rural Electrification Administration (REA) was created in May, 1935 to promote electrification in rural areas. Only about 10 percent of rural homes had service at that time.[43] Private power companies objected that the government had no right to intervene; at the time they were setting rural rates four times as high as city rates.[44] Between 1914 and 1930, at least forty-five electrical power cooperatives had already been organized, primarily in the Midwest. REA made loans available to local electrification cooperatives, which operated lines and distributed electricity. By the end of 1939, REA served almost 300,000 households, or 40 percent of rural homes. The cooperatives forced private power business in many areas to extend service into the countryside and to lower rates.[45]

The New Deal Tennessee Valley Authority Program (TVA), set up in May of 1933, was a regional economic development agency. It planned to use federal experts and electricity to create rapid economic development in an area hard-hit by the Depression, providing flood control, electricity, and fertilizer manufacturing.[46] Headed by David Lilienthal, it was the first large regional planning agency of the federal government. The TVA encouraged many types of cooperatives. Nineteen electrical cooperatives, several soil-conservation cooperatives, and a dozen cold-storage associations, as well as canneries, mills, and dairies were associated with the TVA in 1938. In 1935, TVA also helped set up craft cooperatives such as Southern Highlanders—a craft marketing co-op based in the TVA-planned cooperative community of Norris with outlets in New York City and several other locations.[47]

The New Deal's Farm Security Administration (FSA) of 1935, initially part of the Resettlement Administration, was set up to combat rural poverty.[48] The FSA encouraged every form of mutual aid among participants. The FSA helped organize around 25,000 cooperatives among about 4 million low-income farmers, usually providing loans to get the co-ops started. Besides supply purchasing and product marketing, the FSA backed cooperatives for farm machinery, breeding stock, veterinary services, insurance, water, and medical care. At least 135 of these cooperatives handled consumer goods or provided consumer services; most of the consumer-serving co-ops were small, with fewer than fifty having over one hundred members.[49]

In the South, the FSA stressed rural rehabilitation of poor farmers, sharecroppers, and tenants through "lend-leasing" cooperatives. The government purchased sub-marginal land owned by poor farmers and resettled them in group farms on land deemed more suitable. The relocated farmers leased whole large plantations together and farmed under the supervision of experts using modern techniques.[50] The Farm Bureau strongly opposed this experiment in collectivized agriculture.[51] The FSA was later transformed into a program to facilitate loans for low-income farmers to buy land, and for cooperatives. In its first 8 years, the FSA made over 21,000 loans to about 16,000 service cooperatives, and gave technical advice to over 4,000 rural rehabilitation cooperatives providing goods or services.[52] By the end of 1940, the FSA had sponsored 126 cooperatives at resettlement camps, and had under its supervision 3 greenbelt towns, 178 homestead projects (5 for stranded workers, 25 subsistence homesteads, 73 rural communities, and 75 scattered-farms projects), 58 migratory labor camps, and 69 housing projects.[53]

In June 1933, the New Deal National Recovery Act (NRA) set up a Consumers Advisory Board (CAB) to protect consumer interests.[54] President Roosevelt appointed the Cooperative League's James Warbasse to the board, and Mary Rumsey as chair. Rumsey, though the daughter of a railroad magnate, had nevertheless been active in the Women's Trade Union League and said, "Today the need is not for a competitive but a cooperative economic system."[55] CAB struggled over codes of fair competition for various industry groups. Drafts stemming from business interests were usually antagonistic to cooperatives, and the board was confronted with proposed regulations prohibiting the payment of patronage refunds or rebates of any kind. Through the efforts of the cooperatives, led by Warbasse, Rumsey, and Howard Cowden, who represented National Cooperatives, Roosevelt signed an executive order in 1933 ordering that "no provision in any code of Fair Competition... [shall] prohibit the payment of patronage refunds."[56] The next year he issued another order that no provision should make it a violation "to sell to or through any...cooperative organization."[57]

One of the New Deal's first acts was to set up a Division of Self-Help Cooperatives, providing technical assistance and grants to cooperatives and barter associations.[58] The congressional committees drafting the Federal Emergency Relief Act (FERA) called Carl Rhodehamel of the UXA, H. S. Calvert of the Pacific Cooperative League, and other California leaders to confer on provisions concerning grants to cooperatives to purchase means of production.[59] Due in part to the efforts of these California leaders, the federal government made available badly needed funds, but with strings attached. Rhodehamel argued in vain that they should not be outright grants, but loans repayable in labor exchange. He held that grants would foster dependence on government instead of fostering the cooperative spirit.[60] Furthermore, the law stipulated that production facilities set up with FERA funds could not be used in money transactions, while the self-help groups usually tried to include money in their exchange arrangements whenever possible. In some situations, FERA cooperators could receive pay, but only to produce articles for their own use. This last provision seriously undercut many self-help co-ops' ability to function, since everyone badly needed cash.[61]

The rural FERA program of "community projects" in California included setting up cooperative industries such as a wood mill, a tractor assembly plant, a paint factory, and hosiery mills. But the program was underfinanced and local chambers of commerce usually met the industries with antagonism.[62]

Rhodehamel of the Unemployed Exchange Association tried to prevent his cooperative from applying for a FERA grant out of fear of the strings attached, but the membership decided to anyway. They wrote it into the UXA books as a loan, although the feds considered it a grant.[63]

In two years, FERA distributed $411,000 to 81 groups. The Berkeley Self-Help Co-op received grants for furniture, mattress, and shoe operations. The Pacific Cooperative League received grants for housing, milling, and weaving, and the San Jose Self-Help Co-op for dehydrating and other equipment, and for renting farmland. The UXA received grants for its sawmill, for printing equipment, gardening, and canning.[64]

Because the situation was ostensibly so different in Northern and Southern California, the federal government set up a separate program administration in each location. To become eligible for a production grant, a cooperative was first forced to "demonstrate its managerial ability" by running a distribution program for government staples and gasoline. To administer this program, the federal government set up the Unemployed Cooperative Distribution Association (UCDA) and got the co-ops to join, making the independent UCRA functionally obsolescent.[65] It issued large "blanket grants" for gas and staples to UCDA to be passed on to the affiliated groups. There was a double bind however: acceptance of blanket grant money by a group made it ineligible to obtain an individual federal grant for productive equipment. UCDA applied for a blanket million-dollar production grant, but this was eventually denied. Later, however, after federal blanket grant money stopped, the southern co-ops became individually eligible again. Some did get production grants and turned in that direction, but with less success than those in the North.[66]

The federal government also used money as a carrot to influence the internal affairs of many cooperatives. A typical case of this was the San Jose Co-op, whose grant was held up due to the presence of a "radical faction" in the organization. This touched off a bitter struggle in the group. The "Reds" lost and the grant came through.[67] Thus, FERA money served as a double-edged sword.

DEPRESSION FARM ORGANIZATIONS

During the worst of the Great Depression in early 1932, Milo Reno, charismatic president of the Iowa Farmers Union and head of his own spin-off Farm Holiday Association, led a widespread farmers' strike in the Midwestern states to enforce fair prices.[68] The National Farmers Union program in this period included expansion of cooperatives for the very smallest farmers, division of great farms into family units, and extension of low-cost credit.[69] The New Deal's Agricultural Adjustment Administration (AAA) rejected the NFU's call for cost-of-production price controls, in favor of the Farm Bureau's free market pricing. Nonetheless, NFU spring-wheat farmers headed the first AAA commodity program with crop insurance. During World War II, the NFU battled against the Farm Bureau, which was disregarding social issues, aggressively working to maximize profits, and undercutting small farmer assistance programs of the Farm Security Administration.[70]

During the Great Depression, many small farmers turned to radical actions, and radical farmer organization flourished in parts of rural America.[71] The Dairy Farmers Union (DFU) of the New York milkshed, headed by Archie Wright, was formed in 1936 to establish a fair price for milk and to fight for collective bargaining between producers and distributors. Members held widespread farmer strikes in 1937, 1939, and 1941.[72] Wright was accused of being a Communist, which he denied, but the accusation precipitated a group leaving to join the Farmers Union.[73] In 1942, the DFU affiliated with the United Mine Workers as the United Dairy Farmers.[74]

When the Communist International changed its strategy in 1935 and no longer promoted separate organizations, but instead called for the formation of "Popular Fronts," many groups dominated by Communists or under their influence joined other organizations. Among such groups working with farmers were the United Farmers Educational League and Progressive Farmers of America. Many of their members joined the National Farmers Union. There, they formed a left faction, until most of their members were purged in the early 1950s.[75]

THE SAN FRANCISCO GENERAL STRIKE

After the signing of the National Industrial Recovery Act in 1933, West Coast dockworkers poured into the International Longshoremen's Association (ILA). Dockworkers had to shape up before dawn, hoping to get fingered from the pack. For about $10 a week, they typically worked a twenty-four to thirty-six-hour shift, then got laid off for three or four days. The shipping bosses wouldn't even talk to the maritime unions, so on May 9th, 1934, 35,000 dockworkers up and down the coast voted to strike; with mass pickets in every port from San Diego to Bellingham and Seattle, they shut down the Pacific basin.[76] On the morning of July 3rd, the steel doors of Pier 38 in San Francisco opened and eight squad cars roared out, followed by a convoy of scabs. Thousands of strikers stopped them cold. A police squadron attacked on horseback with clubs, followed by foot squads tossing teargas bombs. The strikers fought back with the two-by-fours stapled to their picket signs, and threw bricks. The battle rampaged for two days, workers swelling the lines from every union in town. The police escalated to vomit gas and shotguns. Scores were injured; two strikers died. The governor called out the National Guard. They sealed off the waterfront with bayonets, barbed wire, and machine-guns, only letting in truckloads of highly paid scabs.[77]

The painters' union called for a general sympathetic strike. Unions all over the city began to vote. The head of the AFL forbade it. But on the morning of July 15th, 130,000 workers struck.[78] The stores were silent, the factories were locked, the streetcars dead. Strikers blocked the highways. For four days, nothing moved in the city without permission of the strike committee. The Oakland and Portland labor councils also voted for general strike in support.[79]

The unions and self-help cooperatives had a history of working together for common goals; many cooperators also belonged to a union. Unionists staffed the San Jose Unemployed Relief Council. The Unemployed Exchange Association members specifically decided that they would not accept any work that would displace any steadily employed worker. So during the general strike while "normal" commerce was blockaded, the self-help co-ops of the Bay Area, including the UXA and the Berkeley Self-Help Cooperative, were able to move about freely. They donated and delivered supplies to the unions and picketers, particularly fruits and vegetables, which the strikers and co-operators had "at a time when money could not procure them."[80]

Meanwhile, gangs of vigilantes appeared at union halls, clubbing and smashing everyone and everything. The police were waiting outside and, when the goons fled, arrested the unionists for resisting arrest.[81] Communist Party members were in the strike leadership, and their newspaper office was trashed.[82] In a close vote, the Central Labor Council ended the strike. By that time, the Employers Association was ready to negotiate, and its members sent representatives to the unions saying that they'd like to talk. Soon, all maritime workers had won union recognition. Longshoremen had a thirty-hour week and a six-hour day, a democratic rotary hiring system, and time-and-a-half overtime pay.[83]

THE CONGRESS OF INDUSTRIAL ORGANIZATIONS

The 1930s were a time of great workers' struggles. The CIO's organization of the giant industrial unions was probably American labor's greatest triumph.[84]

Advocates of industrial unions had long argued that workers in certain industries, particularly ones in which a large number worked a single plant, needed to be all organized into the same union instead of being divided by the AFL system into different crafts represented by separate organizations, each with its own agenda.[85] They maintained that craft unionism weakens the bargaining power of all, and leaves completely unrepresented workers with few traditional craft skills. Some early industrial unions such as Debs' American Railway Union had been quickly destroyed. Others such as the Western Federation of Miners had been able to maintain, and some were affiliated with the AFL. But the conservative AFL national leadership beat down all attempts to stage any aggressive organizing drive.[86]

The drama of the CIO's organizing was set in motion by three victorious major strikes in 1934: the Toledo Auto-Lite workers, the Minneapolis Teamsters, and the West Coast Longshoremen (the San Francisco General Strike). Each of these strikes had Communists and Socialists in their leadership.[87] In 1935, Roosevelt signed the National Labor Relations Act (NLRA) which protected the right of most private sector workers to organize labor unions, engage in collective bargaining, strike, and engage in other forms of concerted activity in support of the common demands. Workers around the country clamored to join unions.[88]

United Mine Workers president John L. Lewis decided that the time was ripe for organizing, and later that year called a meeting of the presidents of eight industrial unions affiliated with the AFL. Together, they formed a new alliance, the CIO, a group of unions within the AFL that supported industrial unionism. They disavowed the syndicalism of the IWW, and declared that they limited their goals to contracts.[89] Yet, industrial unionism was radical by its very nature. The AFL leadership demanded that the CIO dissolve. Instead, the CIO supported striking rubber workers, and formed the Steel Workers Organizing Committee (SWOC) in 1936. The AFL suspended all the CIO unions. Defiant, the CIO ignored them and met with rapid success when SWOC won a collective bargaining agreement with US Steel, and the UAW won a forty-four day sit-down strike—a factory occupation—organizing General Motors. The CIO declared independence and became a rival union federation.[90]

EPIC: END POVERTY IN CALIFORNIA

While the UXA and the other self-help co-ops were on an upswing, Upton Sinclair, long a leading member of the California Socialist Party, suddenly changed his registration to Democrat and threw his hat into the ring for the Democratic gubernatorial nomination in September 1933. Sinclair, the novelistic chronicler of American social reality, campaigned on a program he called EPIC: End Poverty In California.[91]

With "Production for Use" as its rallying cry, the EPIC plan proposed creating state agencies to take over idle farms and production facilities and turn them over to the unemployed, to

> establish State land colonies whereby the unemployed may become self-sustaining, to acquire factories and production plants whereby the unemployed may produce the basic necessities required for themselves and for the land colonies, and to operate these factories and house and feed and care for the workers...[to] maintain a distribution system of each other's products...thus constituting a complete industrial system, a new and self-sustaining world for those our present system cannot employ.[92]

Public bodies would preside over rural, urban, and barter exchange. The plan included proposals for a series of social welfare programs (virtually no state programs existed at the time), and for a general redistribution of the wealth downward through changes in tax laws. Sinclair offered workers the thirty-hour week.[93]

EPIC took its immediate inspiration from the self-help cooperatives, with the UXA as the classical model. Here was living proof that these were not idle utopian dreams, but ideas that could actually work. Sinclair said later of self-help: "Of course it was 'production for use,' and those people automatically became EPICs."[94]

Nearly 2,000 EPIC clubs sprang up around the state. The *EPIC News* reached a circulation of 1.5 million.[95] Self-help, union, and unemployed workers formed the core of Sinclair's election workers. Hjalmar "Hans" Rutzebeck, personnel coordinator of the UXA, took a leave of absence and became a key aide in the campaign.[96]

But most of the co-ops, considering themselves economic and not political organizations, decided it was out of their sphere to endorse electoral candidates, even though much of Sinclair's core support came from them and from the unemployed who had created them. Some were wary of political entanglements because of past experiences. The support of local candidates by UCRA in L.A. and by the Unemployed Citizens League in Seattle had led to betrayal in the first case and defeat in the second. The co-ops decided it was better left to members to participate individually. The unions, like the co-ops, declined to get directly involved in EPIC, though Sinclair had the support of most union workers.[97]

Sinclair, who had garnered 50,000 votes running as a Socialist for governor four years previously, now swept the 1934 Democratic primary with 436,000 votes, more than the other six candidates combined. But the California right wing, entrenched for decades, had not yet begun to fight.[98]

Most of the Democratic old guard defected to the Republicans; the state Democratic Party organization declined to be of any support. The news media, which at first had usually reported favorably on the self-help movement and on Sinclair, now turned around and attacked without quarter. Almost every newspaper and radio station came out against him. An anti-EPIC newsreel was shown in every theater in the state. Gigantic sums of money (for that era) were spent to defeat Sinclair, in probably the most vicious and libelous campaign in California history up to that time.[99]

Sinclair countered by going to the New Deal for support. Roosevelt, in office only a year and a half, had decided not to single out any particular Democrats for special endorsement. Sinclair noted that this did not exclude his endorsing any particular plan. He conferred with Harry Hopkins, the Relief Administrator (later to set up the Works Progress Administration). Hopkins announced his readiness to work with EPIC; he presented it to FDR as a potential hothouse for a national plan. Sinclair met with Roosevelt, and recounted the conversation in his *Autobiography*: "At the end he told me that he was coming out for production for use. I said, 'If you do that, Mr. President, it will elect me.' 'Well,' he said, 'I am going to do it.'"[100]

FDR indicated that he would announce his support for the plan during a nationwide radio address scheduled for the week before the election, and Sinclair hinted publicly that this would happen. On the night of the broadcast, the entire EPIC movement was glued to the radio. When Roosevelt signed off, few could believe the speech was over and he'd said nothing about production for use. A mood of doubt suddenly permeated the organization, where joyous optimism had reigned.[101]

Sinclair's main opponent was incumbent Republican Governor Frank Merriam. Seventy and somewhat senile, Merriam had saved himself from being dumped by his own party by violently suppressing the San Francisco General Strike a few months previously. This made him the darling of the reactionary Right, which threw all its forces behind his reelection campaign. In the end, Sinclair garnered almost 900,000 votes, 37 percent, to Merriam's 49 percent, while a liberal third-party candidate got the difference.[102]

The EPIC uprising, even in electoral defeat, took much of the bite out of the state's right wing for decades afterwards. The reflection of many of EPIC's proposals can be seen in later New Deal programs. Sinclair went on to offer a national version of EPIC, win a Pulitzer Prize for fiction, and be nominated for a Nobel Prize by a group that included Mahatma Gandhi, George Bernard Shaw, and Bertrand Russell.[103]

THE WPA AND THE COLLAPSE OF SELF-HELP

The Works Progress Administration (WPA) of 1935, promising a cash job at a decent wage to every unemployed person able to work, ironically undercut the entire self-help movement.[104] The government had cut off cash incomes for cooperators using FERA-funded production facilities, and now dropped the other shoe. Members could not be in two places at once, and had to choose between the limitations of barter or an assured cash income. The New Deal was not willing to implement policies that could have made self-help cooperatives a permanent part of the economy. Sinclair wound up calling WPA "that arch-enemy of self-help."[105] Rhodehamel tried to prevent a mass exodus from the UXA by arguing that these government programs would be temporary and, if they let the UXA collapse, members would have no cooperative to come back to when the WPA was shut down. Nonetheless the exodus took place. Hundreds of groups around the country collapsed. The UXA, like the rest, found itself in a sudden labor shortage. It now had difficulty delivering on work promised, and fell deeper and deeper into a hole.[106]

Rutzebeck from the UXA traveled to Washington to try to convince the Roosevelt administration to fund self-help and to let work in the cooperatives count as WPA hours. This would have saved the co-ops. He spoke with Resettlement Administration head Rexford Tugwell, Relief Administrator Harry Hopkins, and finally got an audience with Roosevelt himself. But Hopkins was turning away from support of independent co-ops, becoming increasingly committed to the centralized WPA bureaucracy, and advising Roosevelt in that direction.[107]

It is an irony of history that at the same time that Adolph Hitler was destroying the German cooperative movement just as Mussolini had done earlier in Italy, Roosevelt's New Deal programs were simultaneously promoting cooperatives and helping to destroy the self-help movement.

PROBLEMS OF SELF-HELP

The New Deal was far from the only problem of the self-help movement. Besides the usual personality clashes and leadership disputes that are a fact of life in all organizations, especially democratic ones, the co-ops were beset by a number of particular difficulties.[108]

In production-oriented groups, such as the UXA, productivity proved an ongoing problem. When members decided that all work would be worth the same on a time basis, they hoped that spirit and education would make up for the inevitable unproductive attitudes in some members. Despite weekly classes, the UXA School of Reciprocal Economy could never overcome the "employee mentality" of some members, who tried to put in as many hours as possible with no care for productivity. This resulted in the piling up of more points on the books than the organization had products to redeem them with, a problem common to all the groups that kept track of hours.[109] The Southern California cooperatives that distributed "according to need" circumvented this problem on paper but in reality had a similar affliction. The scrip exchanges were hit with particular severity, as the groups tended to issue too much and it quickly depreciated in value. State law prohibiting the using of scrip to pay wages further hampered them.[110]

The cooperatives' field of scavenging operations also slowly diminished. Their work eventually decreased the surplus products in their areas. This was a natural and unavoidable process as the depression was brought on in part by "overproduction," and time depleted surpluses over a few years.[111] High turnover rate of younger members was another problem. Younger members tended to move on when they found job openings, while the older members, largely "unemployable," tended to stay in the cooperatives for the long run.

The result in some instances was a dearth of muscle power. The median age of the UXA was forty-eight.[112] And finally, many cooperatives were "entered into" by members of radical groups who were more interested in turning the cooperatives to political ends then in the actual day-to-day work. Since by their very nature cooperatives have a radical aspect, this was inevitable; many cooperatives were founded by social revolutionaries. Outsiders guilty of disruptive "entrism" were usually isolated and soon gone.[113]

CL AND THE NEW DEAL

Through 1932, the organizational membership of the Cooperative League consisted of individual consumer cooperatives, cooperative wholesales, and District Leagues. The majority of members were urban worker families. League organizations were limited to handling consumer items such as food, clothing, or other family-oriented goods or services.[114] That changed when a nationwide wholesale was organized, National Cooperatives, Inc. (NCI), that both urban and farmer wholesales could join.[115]

NCI wholesale was incorporated in February, 1933 by five regional farm organizations, Central Cooperative Wholesale, Farmers Union Central Exchange, Midland Cooperative Wholesale, Indiana Farm Bureau Cooperative Association, and Union Oil. NCI was set up with parameters specifically permitting cooperatives handling consumer goods to join. The Illinois and Michigan state Farm Bureau Associations declined to join because they were opposed to the inclusion of consumers, and wanted the new national wholesale to serve only farmers.[116] The formation of National Cooperatives brought farmer cooperatives within the CL sphere, although the CL constitution excluded NCI at first from actually joining.[117]

When E. R. Bowen became CL's General Secretary and CEO in 1934, he quickly toured the Midwest and enlisted the support of the regional wholesales and NCI, which was based in Chicago. He won the support of the Ohio Farm Bureau Federation by assuring Murray Lincoln that he disagreed with Warbasse's position that the farms should eventually be owned by consumer cooperatives.[118]

In his report to the 1934 CL Congress, Bowen maintained that "cooperative purchasing [of farm supplies] and consumers cooperation are one and the same thing."[119] Bowen also believed that the economic area suitable for cooperative development was limited to a sector, while Warbasse promoted universal Cooperative Democracy. Over Warbasse's objections, the Cooperative League redefined the basic aim of the movement as "not to supersede other forms of business but to see that they are kept truly competitive." CL dropped its original goal of socialization of the land and changed its policy to support individual land ownership, replacing "the cooperative commonwealth" in its program with "the cooperative sector of the economy."[120] Thus CL bought a truce with both farmer cooperatives and business interests. With this alliance, National Cooperatives became a member of CL and opened to urban stores. The two leaders also disagreed in that Bowen believed that education and business should be combined into one organization, while Warbasse supported separate organizations for the League and the wholesales. Bowen's group predominated by 1938 and CL became increasingly closely coordinated with National Cooperatives. By that time the majority of CL members were no longer urban worker families, but farm families.[121]

SOUTHERN TENANT FARMERS' UNION

The New Deal did not help all farmer cooperatives. The Arkansas Cotton Belt was dominated by huge plantations, and mostly worked by black and white tenant farmers and sharecroppers. The agricultural production limits of the New Deal Agricultural Adjustment Administration (AAA), formed in 1933, under which planters were paid by the government to leave a percentage of their land idle, resulted in hardships for tenants and croppers. Planters plowed up crops that the tenants and croppers had planted, and very often kept all the government payments. Many planters evicted them, so increasing numbers became homeless with their only recourse to become farm laborers.[122]

In 1934, a group of eleven blacks and seven whites in Poinsett County, Arkansas formed the Southern Tenant Farmers' Union (STFU) in semi-secrecy for mutual aid and to protest the hardships and displacement caused by the AAA. Important early black leaders included Will Davis and John Handcox. Founders H. L. Mitchell and H. Clay East, both white, belonged to the Socialist Party.[123] The membership and concerns of the STFU quickly enlarged beyond tenants and croppers to include farm laborers and small farmers. The STFU championed cooperatives, organized buying clubs and ran a large cooperative farm. It called for redistribution of the land to the actual workers, and also negotiated agreements with planters for higher wages and better working and living conditions.[124] It appealed to the AAA, but the latter was controlled by the Farm Bureau and big growers, and met STFU's concerns with a blind eye.[125]

In 1935, when the going rate for picking cotton was an unlivable forty to sixty cents per hundred pounds, the STFU led a strike for one dollar per hundred. It was met with violence and terror. Vigilantes and police attacked and disrupted their meetings, beat and threatened them with guns. A group of a hundred evictees moved into a tent colony. Someone threw a stick of dynamite at them, but the local sheriff declined to investigate.[126] For greater safety, STFU moved its headquarters to Memphis. The violence received national publicity, bringing them widespread sympathy. A governor's commission held hearings and under public scrutiny the violence subsided. The STFU expanded into neighboring states. In 1938, it had more than 35,000 members.[127] But forces were also working to split the STFU internally. A dispute erupted over whether or not to join the Congress of Industrial Organizations (CIO), involving members affiliated with the Communist Party. Mitchell, who opposed joining, was briefly driven out of the organization. The STFU fell apart, due in part to these internal disputes, but also to mechanization and the Great Migration that drove many black people from the rural South and into Northern cities.[128]

NON-PARTISAN LEAGUE IN THE 1930s

In 1932, the NPL's "Wild" Bill Langer was elected governor of North Dakota, and corporate farming was prohibited by state-wide initiative.[129] Accused of pressuring government workers and government aid recipients for donations, he was found guilty of a felony after a contentious trial and the North Dakota Supreme Court ordered him removed from office in 1934. Langer, with a group of supporters, barricaded himself in the governor's mansion and declared North Dakota independent from the US. He eventually acquiesced and went to prison, but was retried the following year, exonerated, and elected governor again in 1936.[130] In 1940, Langer became US Senator, and remained in that position until he died in office almost twenty years later.[131]

While most of the NPL projects had limited success, some continue today, including the state bank and state mill. Corporate farming is still prohibited in North Dakota, and remains today a keystone in preserving the family farm in the state economy.[132] Although the NPL started as a bloc in the North Dakota Republican Party, it eventually merged with the North Dakota Democratic Party.[133]

The NPL spread to adjoining states, but never became dominant there. Just over the border in Canada, a parallel struggle took place as Canadian cooperators, led by J. S. Woodsworth, formed the political party known as the Cooperative Commonwealth Federation (CCF) in 1932 with a radical agenda promising public ownership of key industries, universal pensions, universal health care, unemployment insurance, and workers compensation—all radical ideas for the time. Taking over the NPL's slogan, "The Goat That Can't Be Got," members declared as a basic principle "the abolition of the present system of capitalistic robbery and the establishment of a real cooperative social system controlled by the producers."[134] They won seven seats in Parliament in their first election in 1935. After a decade of struggle, the CCF took over the government of Saskatchewan in 1944, and became the first avowedly socialist government in North America. At that time, it had membership of over 90,000, and instituted the universal health care system that would become national.[135] In 1961, CCF entered into coalition with the Canadian Labour Party and formed the New Democratic Party, which continues today.[136]

BANKS FOR COOPERATIVES

The New Deal Farm Credit Administration (FCA) of 1933 set up Banks for Cooperatives. This program had a very significant effect on the farmer cooperative movement. It set up a central bank and twelve district banks, under a cooperative bank commissioner. Banks for Cooperatives became a member-controlled system of financing farmer cooperatives, as well as telephone and electric cooperatives. After having been set up with government seed money, the FCA became self-supporting.[137] During this era the banks were not permitted to give assistance to consumer or industrial cooperatives. Banks for Cooperatives became an indispensable institution for organizing and stabilizing farm cooperatives for the rest of the century.[138]

The decade of the 1930s saw an unprecedented growth in farm cooperatives. The number of farm cooperatives held steady at around 12,000 during the first 3 years of the Great Depression, 1929-32, though the dollar volume shrank about 20 percent to $2 billion. As the New Deal programs took hold, a large number of regional and district wholesales formed, as well as federations for various services and the manufacture of various products. By 1939, half the farmers in the United States belonged to cooperatives, and most were large and incorporated. But the number of small farms was actually still shrinking, and along with it the farmer movement.[139]

CONSUMER CO-OPS AFTER EPIC

After the 1934 electoral defeat, EPIC leaders split on what to do next. While Sinclair took off on a national speaking tour, a group led by Frank Taylor set up a Production for Use Committee and worked to turn the EPIC energy into a consumer co-op movement, hoping that the consolidation of buying power would be a step toward gaining control of the economy.[140]

A large number of EPIC groups planned consumer co-ops. Over the following eight months, they organized at least fifty buying clubs and thirty stores, with thousands of members. Among the most successful at first were New Day Co-op in Oakland, with about 1,000 members, and Producers-Consumers Co-op at 668 Haight Street in San Francisco.[141] But these and the great majority of the others quickly collapsed. Most had formed hastily, with little knowledge or capital, and sank shallow roots in their communities. Most organizers had overestimated the capacity of enthusiasm to compensate for a sustainable business plan.[142] However, some members of these failed EPIC co-ops went on to become leaders of the next generation of cooperative stores.[143]

END OF THE NEW DEAL

Roosevelt's programs alleviated some of the problems of the Depression, but as the 30s progressed, the economies of California and the nation slumped back into lethargy. The WPA ended, but the self-help movement did not revive, as the country and the world braced for war. Finally, World War II snapped the country and the economy out of the depression, created "full employment," and gave birth to the mighty industrial machine that emerged at the war's end.

Many people had hoped the New Deal would lead ultimately to a form of democratic socialism, but Roosevelt's programs served to save and strengthen corporate capitalism in the end. "Bread and butter" demands were acceded to, heading off any mass independent movement of wage earners and small farmers, while radicals were assimilated and co-opted.

As soon as the United States entered World War II, almost the entire American Left enlisted, the opposite of its action in World War I.[144] Ironically, while unionists and small farmers were dying overseas, rightists stayed behind and took control of the unions, and agribusiness dismantled the Farm Security Administration.[145]

WARTIME COOPERATIVES

There was a boom in co-op stores during World War II, and many farm-supply regionals began handling groceries as well. The United Auto Workers (UAW) in Detroit and the United Rubber Workers in Akron organized store systems. But retail prices of consumer goods dropped with the war's end, and there were widespread failures, including several Midwestern regional wholesales and the UAW group. This rise and fall followed a pattern similar to that around World War I.[146]

POSTWAR

At the end of World War II, wages in numerous non-war industries were quickly cut an average of 10 percent. In September 1945, just a month after the war ended, 43,000 oil workers responded by going on strike in 20 states. In the following weeks, 200,000 coal miners went out; in the Midwest, 7,000 teamsters; in the Northwest, 44,000 lumber workers; in the Bay Area, 40,000 machinists; on the East coast, longshoremen and flat glass workers; in New England, textile workers. The basic cause of almost all these strikes was the sudden drastic wage cut. In November 1945, 225,000 auto workers struck GM. In January 1946, 174,000 electrical workers went out, followed by 93,000 meatpackers and 750,000 steel workers. In April, 340,000 soft-coal miners struck; in May a nationwide railroad strike brought national commerce to a halt.[147] In the first 6 months of 1946, 2,970,000 workers struck in over 250 disputes, "the most concentrated period of labor-management strife in the country's history," according to the US Bureau of Labor Statistics.[148] Historian Jeremy Brecher called it "the closest thing to a national general strike of industry in the 20th century."[149] Over the year 4.6 million workers were involved in strikes.[150]

President Truman responded by seizing basic industries, using wartime powers to do so, even though the war had ended. He seized half the oil refineries in October 1945; in January 1946, he seized the packinghouses; in May, he seized the railroads and bituminous coal mines. Federal troops brought the great postwar strike wave to a cold stop.[151] All except for the miners returned to work, and their union was fined $3.4 million for contempt. The government set up "fact-finding boards," and the unions reluctantly accepted their decisions.[152]

At the same time, big business launched the home front of the "cold war," purging the few remaining militants out of the unions entirely, instituting anti-communist oaths, kicking thousands out of jobs and blacklisting many thousands more. The Taft-Hartley Act of 1947, written by the National Association of Manufacturers, virtually repealed the New Deal's Wagner Act; it went far towards destroying internal union democracy and paralyzing the progressive movement.[153] Veterans returning home often didn't know what hit them. The unions that workers had fought so hard to win were now often being used against them. Under the Internal Security Act, freedom of speech was restricted and the FBI compiled lists of "risks" to be rounded up "in event of a national emergency."[154] A million "radicals" were purged from the CIO when it merged with the AFL in 1955.[155]

The Cooperative League was on the defensive in these years, although it worked successfully with the international cooperative community, helping European cooperatives to recover from World War II.[156] Murray Lincoln, the farm cooperative leader who replaced Warbasse as president in 1941, promoted combining the educational and business functions of the Cooperative League and National Cooperatives Wholesale into one organization. The merger came to fruition in 1946. Centralization quickly showed its defects, however; shortly thereafter, National Cooperatives transferred all educational functions back to CL, and they reverted to separate organizations.[157] Under Lincoln, CL helped to create CARE (Cooperatives for American Relief Everywhere). A cooperative organization, CARE's relief efforts were at first directed toward Europe, then became worldwide. Lincoln became the first president of CARE.[158]

At the end of World War II, the National Farmers Union had some 350,000 members in cooperatives, about half in Wisconsin, Minnesota, the Dakotas, and Montana. Its Grain Terminal Association in Saint Paul was the country's largest cooperative grain-marketing agency. American farmers were principally represented by three organizations: the NFU, which primarily looked to the interests of the small family farm; the Grange, which was dominated by wealthier farmers in Ohio and the Northeast; and the Farm Bureau Federation, which chiefly represented large farmers in the South and Midwest.[159]

In the postwar years, the NFU lobbied Washington strongly in support of domestic social equity and for a US foreign policy based on anti-imperialist policies and world peace through international cooperation and the United Nations.[160] In opposition, the Farm Bureau and the American Legion accused the NFU of having communist sympathies. This precipitated an internal conflict in the NFU between Fred Stover of the Iowa Farmers Union, who advocated no accommodation on these principles, and national NFU president James Patton, who wanted to compromise in order to remain a player in formulating postwar farm policies. Between 1950 and 1954, Patton's faction engineered a series of purges, and expelled many of the NFU radicals.[161]

By 1949, there were very few consumer co-ops anywhere in the US, and the 1950s remained a period of decline for nonagricultural cooperatives everywhere in the United States. To most consumer cooperative activists, many decades of urban work seemed lost. Only agricultural cooperatives maintained any vitality.[162]

10.
Case Study:
The Berkeley Co-op

When I moved to Berkeley in 1971, one of the first things I did was join the Co-op. The Berkeley Co-op was much more than a store. It was a community center and a nexus of social activism, a place where you saw many of your friends. Every progressive concern of the time was hotly debated in the Co-op, and the organization lobbied Sacramento and Washington on numerous hot-button consumer issues. I remained a member until the Co-op's demise in 1987. During its final year, its fiftieth anniversary, the editors of the *Co-op News*, Michael Fullerton and Paul Rauber, asked me to write a series of articles on its history, and opened the archives to me to research it. I spent many hours reading through fifty years of newspapers, pamphlets, and other materials. The standard history of the time, *California's Uncommon Markets* (1971, 1982) had the strengths, insights and limitations of being written by an insider and stakeholder, Robert Neptune, the Co-op's very first employee and long-time manager. My history, in four parts, was published in the paper between April and August 1987.[1] I also served as a member of the committee that proposed a last-ditch attempt to save the Co-op by restructuring it as a hybrid worker-consumer cooperative.[2] The encapsulated history presented here is based on my research at that time, along with *What Happened to the Berkeley Co-op?* (1992), the post-mortem collection edited by Fullerton.

Consumers Cooperative of Berkeley (CCB) began with the merging of two groups, the Berkeley Buyers Club and the Berkeley Cooperative Union (BCU).[3]

The Berkeley Buyers' Club formed on January 27th, 1936. According to the secretary Catherine E. Best,

> A small group of families, all more or less connected with the EPIC and Democratic clubs of Berkeley, banded to buy their

groceries cooperatively... Supplies are bought at wholesale
and 10 percent added for handling, 5 percent of which goes
to Rev. Wilson for gasoline and handling, the rest to Mr. Darling for delivery expenses... Consumer education is to be part
of our program... There is little use paying 2-3 percent pre-
mium for an advertised name when the same merchandise is
put up under other labels as well... We plan to use services of
the new Consumers Union.[4]

The group thrived, operating out of the basement of the par-
sonage of Roy Wilson, a Methodist minister in nearby Alameda,
and working in cooperation with other buying clubs in Oakland and
adjoining areas. The Oakland club had been the first, formed about
seven weeks before the one in Berkeley, with former members of
New Day Co-op as leaders. But the Berkeley branch quickly became
the largest. Delegates from the various clubs, totaling about sixty
families, joined to form Pacific Cooperative Services (PCS), to do
joint operations. The Berkeley Club soon hired its first employee,
Robert Neptune, at $30 per month and in April 1937 Consumers
Cooperative of Berkeley (CCB) opened its first store, ten by twenty
feet in dimensions, at 2491 Shattuck Avenue.

The store was a quick success, withstanding an attack by a
nearby grocer. Its first recycling program was begun in the very first
months with egg cartons, offering a half cent per carton rebate. The
members formed a Quality Committee to test generic canned foods
and other goods to go under their own Co-op label. Finishing 1937
with eighty-one member families and a total of $7,260 in member
purchases, they relocated to larger quarters on University Avenue.
Over the following years, the Berkeley group flourished while the
other units of PCS languished and faded away.

Meanwhile, Berkeley's Finnish community was forming a
similar organization, the Berkeley Cooperative Union (BCU), opening a gas station on San Pablo Avenue in 1938. This station was
among the very first to offer unleaded gas because, as *Co-op News*
pointed out, "lead is a cumulative poison." But the gas station came
under attack. The wholesaler announced it was cutting off supplies
because the station was a cooperative, forcing the BCU to find a
smaller independent wholesaler.

In February 1938, the CCB began its first campaign to promote strong consumer protection laws, urging members to write
letters in support of expanding the Food and Drug Act to cover

advertising and cosmetics. It joined with the rest of the Northern California Co-operative Council in a resolution that they sent to President Roosevelt condemning destruction of oranges near Los Angeles, and urging that the oranges being destroyed should instead be distributed to those on relief.

BCU and CCB had increasingly overlapping membership, and the two organizations worked closely together.

From the earliest days, the Berkeley Co-op declared its solidarity with the labor movement. In 1937, CCB agreed to "the handling of union-made goods as far as possible for the purpose of creating a closer rapprochement between the labor union and the cooperative movements." The early co-op relied largely on volunteer labor, but when it opened a new larger store, CCB signed its first contract with the Retail Food Clerks Union.

In 1939, the Co-op incorporated. At that time, it had 225 members, sales of $700 per week, and was going strong.

BERKELEY CO-OP IN THE 1960s

World War II produced hard times for the Berkeley Co-op, but the war's end signaled a quick financial recovery. By early 1947, the Co-op was swinging into a period of expansion. CCB and the neighboring Finnish co-op group merged. The postwar decade saw uninterrupted expansion. The Co-op continued pioneering with a full-time education director and home economist, wholegrain breads, a supervised "kiddie korral" for shoppers to leave small children. Members debated nuclear energy and endorsed legislation calling for regular inspection and testing of foods for radiation. Membership rolls, dollar volume, and patronage refunds kept doubling. A second Berkeley store, and another in nearby Walnut Creek opened. By 1957, the Berkeley Co-op had become the second largest urban cooperative in the United States. Further expansion resulted in a pharmacy, an arts and crafts co-op, a co-op bookstore, and a credit union.

But along with expansion came problems. The *Co-op News* debated the issue, "How do we keep democratic control and participation while we continue to expand?" The Co-op had 6,000 member families, but an increasingly smaller percentage took an active role in Co-op affairs. Semiannual meetings were immobilized by lack of quorums, and board members were elected by low turnouts. In 1959, members set up an experimental parliament of sixty delegates, a portion elected by each shopping unit district, to discuss policy and make recommendations to the board. But low voter turnout resulted in the parliament's dissolution. In the following years, the Co-op developed a system of autonomous Center Councils.

The dawn of 1960 found Berkeley a quiet Republican town, and the Co-op a venerable 22-year-old institution with 15,300 members on a course of steady quiet growth. It found a site for a third Berkeley store, making Co-op shopping accessible to almost everyone in town. Plans were underway for new stores in El Cerrito and Marin County, and there was talk of Oakland and San Francisco. Sites were proposed farther and farther away, so the Board decided to set a twenty-five-mile limit.

CCB had close ties with two other cooperatives in the Bay Area: the Palo Alto Co-op and the regional wholesale, Associated Cooperatives (AC). Both had been founded at about the same time as CCB, and involved some of the same people. Berkeley was the flagship of AC, providing most of its sales volume and having more members than the other eight AC co-ops combined; Palo Alto was second largest. In 1960, the general managers of Berkeley, Palo Alto, and AC made a joint proposal for merger of the three cooperatives. The stores already had overlapping managements, with a number of key people in important dual roles, including the three general managers. A study purported to show that the entire system had to expand and integrate if it was going to remain competitive economically. Constant growth was axiomatic, because cooperatives were more than businesses: they were a social movement. Indeed, the executive director of the Cooperative League, Jerry Voorhis, in his influential book *American Cooperatives* (1961) included "constant expansion" as one of four basic "cooperative practices." AC's objective was to be the wholesale for an integrated chain of consumer co-ops throughout California, and the Berkeley Co-op's expansion was considered key to the plan.

In 1962, the board suddenly announced it had bought a small chain of five stores from a competitor, three in Berkeley and one each in Walnut Creek and Castro Valley. Many members were stunned. Instead of the normal process of full open discussion and member participation, the decision had been made after a series of secret negotiations. The move was hotly debated. Was it financially sound? Some of these stores were already failing, and they were not in areas where a base of Co-op members already existed. Would such rapid growth mean more central planning and less center autonomy? Only professional managers could handle this scale of operations, while the Co-op had always been small enough to involve members intimately. Members began to accuse the board of "empire building ambitions."

The board and management hoped to make the new stores profitable quickly, but all except one suffered constant losses. Most of the many new employees knew nothing about cooperatives. Membership swelled to 30,000, but member education and participation sagged hopelessly behind. Management found little time for member input. The patronage refund rate sunk to the lowest in over a decade. For the first time, serious clashes occurred between workers and management.

On the positive side, the addition of the store at Telegraph and Ashby Avenues made CCB truly citywide, serving one third of the families in Berkeley as customers, and earning the Co-op recognition as a city resource truly belonging to the Berkeley community. With this sense came new assumptions of social responsibility and, as the issues of the 60s heated up, the Co-op became an arena in which they were played out. For the first time, members formed electoral slates to get on the board. The "progressive slate" held that Co-op leadership had become "entrenched...institutionalized...inflexible,"[5] and that the supermarket chain purchase had been a grave mistake. President George Little, spokesman for the conservatives, thought the Co-op "shouldn't try to take on all the world's problems;" that "pro-employee militancy" was the problem; and that the rebels were "trying to democratize a situation that can't readily be democratized."[6] Larry Duga, a progressive, responded, "When some people say 'no politics' they really mean no free speech tables... If we can't run the Co-op as a co-op, then we have no reason for existence."[7] Bob Treuhaft, another progressive, avowed, "The war in Vietnam is the number one consumer issue today."[8]

Irv Rautenberg represented a third force, who asserted, "The Berkeley Co-op's fate lies in the hands of the Center Councils—not in the hands of the board of directors, not in the hands of management, not in the hands of any factional group."[9] Board member Maudelle Shirek also supported center autonomy: "a management contract for each Center with a central warehousing and accounting division becoming the helpers rather than the arbiters."[10]

In 1967, under heavy fire, President Little stepped down, and the following year the progressive slate won a Board majority for the first time.

Meanwhile, the Berkeley Co-op's social accomplishments continued to mount. Its members instituted "free speech tables" near entrances for literature and petitions in 1962. In 1963, they debated milk contamination from a proposed nearby nuclear power plant; supported a local anti-discrimination housing ordinance; and stopped stocking products boycotted by the Central Labor Council. In 1964, they increased minority employment; held a food drive "to aid persons suffering Civil Rights discrimination" in Mississippi; and pioneered biodegradable detergent with Co-op label. In 1965, they packaged meat with the better side down; lobbied for a bread and cereal enrichment law; and educated on peanut butter additives. In 1966-67, they lobbied for a Fair Packaging and Labeling law; contributed to the United Farm Workers Union (UFW) co-op in Delano; instituted unit pricing on all shelves; lobbied for regulation of diet foods and for a unit pricing law; agitated against a phone rate increase; labeled all Dow products as boycotted because of the company's napalm production; and assisted the legal defense fund for besieged integrated Southern co-ops. In 1968, they authorized centers to ban smoking; removed all nonunion grapes; and withdrew from the Chamber of Commerce because of its consistent opposition to consumer legislation. In 1969, they battled against utility rate hikes; donated food to the Black Panthers children's breakfast program; demanded the "immediate termination" of the military occupation of Berkeley by the National Guard (ordered by Governor Ronald Reagan because of People's Park); posted statements in all Co-op centers condemning the war; and closed in solidarity during a People's Park protest march and on Vietnam Moratorium Day.

At the same time, the Co-op was continuously drained by the failing expansion stores, and profits continued to spiral down. The patronage refund rate dropped to its lowest in over twenty years. As the tumultuous 60s ended, the Berkeley Co-op's political pendulum swung again and conservatives retook control of the board. Over the following years, that political pendulum would continue to swing as the Co-op groped for ways out of its deepening financial crisis.

DECLINE AND FALL

The Berkeley Co-op's long list of consumer accomplishments continued to roll on and on. In 1970, the Co-op began selling organic produce. On the first Earth Day that spring, volunteers from the Co-op, the Ecology Center, and Ecology Action (both of the latter only recently organized) banded together at the Co-op Garage on the corner of Sacramento and University to begin recycling in Berkeley and set the tone for a new decade. The Co-op put forth a bold and far-reaching consumer legislative program, and lobbied vigorously in Sacramento and Washington. Members petitioned for the first bottle deposit law, and lobbied against electricity rates increases. They opened a separate natural foods store in 1971, removed enzymes from Co-op brand detergent, banned smoking, and distributed condom information. That's the year I became a member. In 1972-73, members were instrumental in passing a law requiring all foods processed in the state to list ingredients, got the FDA to codify nutrition information on food labels, and were the first store in the country to sell nitrite-free hotdogs.

But while this was happening, internal problems disrupted the Co-op, and eventually consumer issues were superseded by questions of sheer survival. Apart from several factions struggling for power within the Co-op's board, there were also the workers, the management, and the members.

THE BOARD

Throughout the 1970s, the board was badly split between more progressive and conservative factions. Their differences often revolved around the question of political neutrality. Led by conservative president Lew Samuels, the board set a policy in 1970 "to take action only on consumer issues, not on general political, social and community issues. The board intends to interpret what is or is not a 'consumer issue' in the narrow rather than the broad sense."[11] The progressives argued that taking stands on issues and legislation was well within Co-op principles, and that political neutrality meant not endorsing electoral candidates.[12]

Two letters from the *Co-op News* of January 4, 1971, give an inside glimpse of what was going on at board meetings. Future president Jane Lundin wrote the first:

> In the absence of one member of the conservative majority...
> the Board of Directors took two significant and progressive
> steps at the December 28 meeting... The board adopted...
> an affirmative action program for fair employment. This
> program, which I helped draft, is the first in California to
> provide for hiring and promoting more women as well as mi-

nority group members... The board also agreed to continue Co-op support of the United Farm Workers... by refusing to reorder five Dow Chemical products. Dow is part owner of Bud Antle, the giant lettuce growing firm whose court actions have jailed Caesar Chavez... Dow formerly made napalm and now supplies herbicides to poison Vietnam as well as the lettuce fields of California... It is against just such amoral businesses that a Co-op should use its economic power...

Here is a perspective on the same meeting by president Samuels:

Hello again, disruption and confrontation politics, and good-bye, logic and democratic Co-op government!... The irresponsible motions by Duga and Thompson concerning employment policies and the boycott of Dow Company products at that meeting reversed all attempts by the Co-op to reach logical policies... The board minority took advantage of the absence of two regular board members and literally played to an audience of screaming, stamping women's libbers...[13]

In a Pyrrhic victory, Samuels and the conservatives briefly got their revenge on Lundin, restoring Dow to the shelves (but with "product controversy" labeling) and toning down the affirmative action program.

THE WORKERS

The board and management treated employees below management level much as workers anywhere are treated. The Co-op was a "good boss" by industry standards, which were not high. They negotiated with unions, and signed and abided by contracts. The job did not require interest in cooperatives or even knowledge of them. Many employees were not Co-op members. Board after board made repeated promises of more worker input, but the workers, like the center councils, remained without a real voice. Through the decade, store-level morale sunk ever lower.

THE MANAGEMENT

Management stayed on track with the plans of Associated Cooperatives, the wholesale, for constant expansion until a size might be reached where the Co-op could be more competitive with the chains. For the most part, both Co-op board factions accepted this analysis and acted on it. The Co-op was deeply committed to AC, which in 1970 was still being managed by Robert Neptune, the Berkeley Co-op's very first employee and first manager. Although AC acted nominally as a regional wholesale, the number of consumer co-ops in California outside the Bay Area had dwindled drastically in the two previous decades. The Berkeley Co-op increasingly became AC's main hope. By the 1970s, expansion of the Berkeley Co-op became the main strategy of the consumer cooperative movement in the state, just to create enough volume to keep the wholesale alive. Management blamed many of the Co-op's problems on the Board, complaining that "staff feel that member leadership is not working with them toward a common goal. They feel variously ignored, pressured, attacked."[14] Management's complaints about the board were similar to the workers' complaints about management.

THE MEMBERS

There were 50,000 members in 1970, with people joining at a pace that would double that number by the end of the decade.[15] But the average Co-op member was no longer a very active participant, except as a shopper. Of course, just choosing to shop at the Co-op was a political act for many, and in those days of patronage rebates, one could always give the number of one's favorite cause or charity at the checkout stand, thus sending the year-end dividend to support social activism. Some members shopped at the Co-op believing they were supporting a social movement, while other members were interested solely in consumer quality and low prices. Center councils remained advisory bodies, without real powers. The Co-op did not have a member work program, as the majority of successful co-op stores do today.[16] In such a program, members receive a discount in exchange for a certain amount of weekly or monthly labor, typically 15 percent for 2 hours of work per week or 10 percent for 4 hours per month. Without a member labor program, the Berkeley Co-op limited a member's opportunity to participate in the work of the cooperative as more than a shopper.

In the fall of 1971, two events shook the Co-op: Gene Mannila, general manager for twenty-five years, retired, and the first operating loss since World War II was announced. Mannila had been the rudder. A chaotic year followed in which a new manager came and went, leaving a $294,000 loss. Finally another manager was hired. His experience lay entirely outside the cooperative movement, but operations pulled together, and the Co-op again showed a profit and offered a patronage refund to members by 1973. This manager proposed solving the Co-op's financial problems by even further expansion, doubling the number of Co-op centers within the decade. "Whether you like it or not," the *Co-op News* quoted the manager as saying, "you're in the supermarket business up to your ears."[17]

Early in 1974, another conservative board purchased a North Oakland store from another failing chain without member knowledge or input. Because there had been talk for decades about expanding into Oakland, there was very little opposition. In an almost identical procedure four months later, the board bought two more of the chain's stores. The next year, the Co-op opened its first San Francisco store, making thirteen centers in all. A short time later, the manager and several "conservative" board members proposed that the Co-op take over the management of two more privately owned stores, part of a chain of twelve, and, if this should prove successful, the Co-op would take over management of the entire chain. The stores would remain privately owned. This Management Contract Proposal touched off an enormous storm.

Two new groups were formed: Concerned Co-op Employees (CCE) and Concerned Co-op Members (CCM). *Co-op News* reported, "The Co-op's problems are seen by CCE and CCM as stemming largely from an erosion of member control and employee rights, vis-à-vis increasing management control and the emergence of what they have called the corporate image."[18] CCE and CCM demanded a stronger role in selection of a new general manager, and employee representation on all governing bodies, including the board of directors. When the smoke cleared, the Management Contract Proposal was dropped and the manager was gone, leaving behind a $217,000 loss for 1976. All of the new stores, losing operations when they were bought, continued to lose money as co-ops. The workers won an Employee Advisory Council, but the next board election bolstered the conservative board faction, and the Employee Advisory Council complained of being ignored.

Morale kept sinking with a $760,000 loss in 1978. In the emergency, Robert Neptune, the Co-op's very first manager, was called back. He came through and produced a profit in 1979 and even a small patronage refund in 1980. But Neptune retired in 1980 and as soon he was gone, the losses came in great waves.

The truth had to be faced: expansion had failed. There were ten losing stores scattered around the Northern Bay Area, supported by the three still-thriving Berkeley Co-ops. "Just as the arrow was shot into the air, it fell back to earth," said president Fred Guy, "and in 1983 one by one all the losing operations were closed, at great financial loss, and the Co-op remained briefly with only the centers in Berkeley left, just being a community cooperative, which was perhaps what they should have remained all along."[19]

The members showed that they still cared by coming to the Co-op's financial aid with well over $200,000, and by voting overwhelmingly to open the board to employees, the Co-op's only remaining great untapped resource.

I was a member of the "structure" subcommittee empowered to put forth a radical restructuring proposal to transform the Co-op into a new organization, a "hybrid" owned and controlled half by consumer members and half by employee members. The concepts of worker ownership and self-management, pioneered in America by the "new wave" collectives of the 1970s, were merging with the largest consumer co-op in the United States. The unanimous consensus of our subcommittee was that changing to a joint consumer-worker co-op was both feasible and highly desirable. We proposed the following structure: there would be two classes of membership, consumer members and worker members. Each class would elect one half of the board and one half of each Center Council. Worker members' investment in the Co-op would come from recycling a percentage of future salaries. All Co-op employees would be members. A percentage of yearly profits would be returned to workers according to amount of time worked, and to consumers according to amount of patronage. There would be more center autonomy, through consumer-worker Center Councils making policy decisions affecting individual centers, and selecting and overseeing center managements. Day-to-day operation of centers would be the responsibility of workers' committees. Continued fine-tuning of the new structure would be by ongoing consumer-worker committees. Worker participation would be a flexible mix of salaried and volunteer time. The Co-op would state and stress our identity as a community development resource for all of Berkeley. Our goal would be to become more of a cooperative, both among our worker and consumer members, and to the general Berkeley community, and not "a river eight miles wide & one inch deep."[20]

In the spring of 1987, the year of the Berkeley Co-op's fiftieth anniversary, all the stakeholders debated this last chance for a rebirth. If the employees, the unions, and the board could work out a viable plan that summer, they would ask the membership to vote on it in the fall.

But it was not to be. The organization was too wounded and split. So in 1988, after exactly a half-century, the Berkeley Co-op reluctantly gave up the ghost.[21]

For the community, it was as if a dear old relative had died after a very long illness. It took a while for it to sink in. The list of Co-op activists who for five decades made important contributions to the City reads like a who's who of the local progressive community during those years. The Co-op's legacy remains indelible in Berkeley history.

11.
Cooperatives & Counterculture: the 60s & 70s, Part I

The 1960s began with cooperatives in a state of dormancy and decline in America, but the explosion of movements for social justice in the 60s infused a great burst of new energy into the movement. Almost every social justice movement had a component of collective work and cooperation, and through this collectivity a new generation struggled to find its identity. In the 1970s these movements peaked; then declined in the chilling climate of the Reagan era in the early 1980s.

This section is focused on the San Francisco Bay Area, partly because it was a center of concentration, and partly because that is where I participated in the movement. Using history itself as a primary source, I will not attempt to document by references to secondary sources.[1]

SOCIAL JUSTICE ORGANIZATIONS

Numerous activist groups struggling for social justice included cooperatives and collectivity as part of their strategies and programs, creating the environment in which the mass youth movement that became known as the counterculture exploded on the national scene.

Farm workers remained almost totally unorganized in 1962 when the National Farm Workers Association (soon to become the United Farm Workers) was formed in Delano, California. Some of its first acts were to set up several community mutual aid associations that included a cooperative store and a credit union. Full-time boycott workers usually lived in union-run communal houses.[2]

In 1965, a former field worker of the Student Nonviolent Coordinating Committee (SNCC) organized the Poor People's Corporation in Jackson, Mississippi. Within four years, it was running thirteen producer cooperatives and a marketing co-op, producing sewing, leather crafts, wood crafts, and candles. The Corporation had over 800 members, mostly former sharecroppers.[3] The 1964-65 black voter registration drives and the Selma to Montgomery "March for Freedom" led by Martin Luther King resulted in the formation of the South West Alabama Farmers Cooperative Association. Within a few years it included 1,800 families, making it the largest agricultural cooperative in the South. Originally eight of the families were white. But harassment by racist politicians and businessmen followed, and banks and suppliers refused to deal with them until the white families withdrew.[4]

In 1967, twenty families in Northwestern New Mexico formed La Cooperativa Agrícola del Pueblo de Tierra Amarilla in the wake of an armed raid on the local courthouse by the Alianza de Mercedes to secure the return of stolen ejidos (land grants guaranteed by US treaty to traditional groups of cooperative settlers). The Cooperativa pooled over 600 acres of land for collective farming and grazing, for self-consumption, and soon had a clinic, law office, job service, and shoe store.[5]

The "inter-communalist" Black Panther Party, first organized in Oakland in 1966, ran a host of "survival programs pending political revolution."[6] In Oakland, this included a health clinic, free shoe factory, plumbing service, food and clothing, communally built and owned housing, job-finding service, transportation for elders, breakfast program for children, pest control, busing to prisons for visitors, and a prisoners' commissary. All goods and services were free. The Panthers ran communal houses for full-time party workers. Through boycotts, they convinced many businesses to recycle some of their profits back into the community through the Panthers' social projects. In a 1971 interview, Panther Chairman Bobby Seale averred:

> We must evolve a humane people's communalism... Here, while the revolutionary struggle is going on, our survival programs will exemplify what the people want and need.

Seale defined a "communal society" as one which has adequate wealth but is organized around its equal distribution. The people control the technology, but on a local level rather than having resources controlled and allocated by a centralized authority. He said the most immediate task for the Black Panther Party was the implementation of the "survival programs," which he called "the people's fuel for revolution."[7]

COUNTERCULTURE

Starting in the mid-1960s, large numbers of young people worked to create a survival network outside of and against the capitalist system with a common ideological base of working to build a new social system based on cooperation and sharing "within the shell of the old."[8] At first the mass media called it the "counterculture" or "alternative." It was an era when many people, particularly young people, were searching for a better way to relate to the world and to each other. Many thought that they found it in collective and cooperative work. The world they rejected was based on hierarchy, power, and competition. They wanted a world based on equality, democracy, cooperation, sharing; a way to live and work that could liberate.

Large numbers of young people felt there was no place for them in American society. The schools taught that freedom and democracy had triumphed over fascism in World War II, yet where in the daily lives of working people were they to be found? And now the country was hurtling into a new war in Vietnam. With nowhere else to turn, young people turned to each other. In the mutual aid and support they found there, they saw the embryo of a new society in which the promises of America could at last become reality.

The earliest rumblings of the counterculture probably came with the Left's rediscovery of the collective form of organization in the freedom rider groups of the early Civil Rights Movement, and in the anti–Vietnam War and student movements. This was an era when large numbers were actively trying to make social change, and felt that their internal processes and methods needed to reflect the goal. For those who claimed that there really was a better alternative to the status quo, collectives were the proof of the pudding.

COLLECTIVES

A collective is a democratic work group. Based on equality and direct participatory democracy, a collective works toward consensus and strives to be unbureaucratic and unhierarchical. Many American Indian tribes have traditionally used the collective form in their councils. Kids all over the world naturally form collectives to play games. Musicians have always formed collective groups. Groups such as the Quakers and Mennonites have used the collective form for hundreds of years. It is the traditional form of the anarchist affinity group, and was widely used in the IWW.

A collective can be formed for almost any purpose, short or long term, and can take on a loose or a formal structure. Different structures work better for different sizes. Most collectives are small by nature. Most early work collectives were small independent units of no more than twenty or so people; this smallness can be a strength. The larger the group, the more difficult it is to reach consensus, usually defined as less than unanimity, but greater than a simple majority. At some point in growth, a collective ceases being a collective. Larger groups become cooperatives, with more formal and hierarchical structures. But over the years, in some situations, larger collective groups have been formed through a decentralized system of small groups sending delegates to larger council meetings, facilitating hundreds of people being able to participate in consensus planning of an event.

The collective form of organization gained great popularity and stimulated the movement so much because it helped break through formalistic "democracy" at a moment when a new energy was bursting forth through the social fabric. Within a few years, dozens of these groups sprang up in numerous fields such as the women's, ecology, and anti-nuclear movements. Collectives were used to organize almost every activity from education, childcare, art, communications, and counseling to legal services and recycling. Almost all the early countercultural forms chose the collective form because participants wanted their means to reflect their ends. These forms ranged from freestores to communes, from "underground" newspapers to collective gardens, including cooperative houses, food conspiracies, and "free" schools and universities. They developed the organizational technology that laid the base for the producer and merchant worker collectives and cooperatives that appeared in widespread areas.

Many of the early collectives tried to provide basic social services that capitalist society did not supply. Primarily young professionals formed the free clinics, law collectives, and free schools. Others were connected to political movements, like the Young Patriots' clinic in Chicago and the Black Panthers' clinic in Oakland. Most clinics functioned through collectives of physicians, paraprofessionals, and volunteers. Almost all had some combination of control by the worker collective and the community. Most of these social service collectives survived through donations and grants.

The roots of the counterculture went back to the underground cultural centers of the late 1950s, particularly to the two most prominent centers, Greenwich Village in New York and North Beach in San Francisco. Increasing numbers of young people were drawn from everywhere to these centers, where they formed loose communities helping each other survive. In the early 1960s, new centers sprang up in other locations in those same cities, in the Lower East Side (part of which became the East Village) and the Haight, both inexpensive working-class neighborhoods that became the early urban nuclei of the counterculture.

BAY AREA COLLECTIVES

Young people from all over the country were drawn to the San Francisco Bay Area, where conditions, including inexpensive housing, seemed ripe for a new consciousness. By the summer of 1966 the community of young people had grown to such proportions that it began to gather national attention in the news media. Communal households were widespread. A newspaper expressing the new consciousness appeared, the *Oracle*. The first "Human Be-in" happened that fall in Golden Gate Park. The Haight became the hothouse in which the national movement called the counterculture was born.

The group known as the Diggers helped to channel the enormous energy that was exploding into the rudiments of a survival system outside of the old society. They began gathering necessities that were being wasted or hoarded, and redistributed them, organizing free food giveaways and a freestore. Duplicated around the country, the freestore was run entirely on collective energy. The idea was simple: people could bring and take what they wanted and needed.

But national attention brought a flood of people from all over the country to San Francisco in the summer of 1967, overwhelming the community and making it impossible to continue as it had been. Entrepreneurs looted the freestore, coming at favorable hours to clean out anything sellable. This resulted in the store being replaced by a free box on the street.

Moving beyond the limitations of the Diggers' approach, people soon began setting up more organized structures. "Alternative" news media, primarily "underground" newspapers, grew to mass proportions around the country by the late 1960s, filled with information impossible to come by in the mainstream media. Collectives doing community service work were often "open," and almost anyone could join or participate as an unpaid volunteer. The open collective was for projects that attempted to draw in as much community energy and input as possible. In numerous university towns "free universities" were set up, with courses in subjects ignored by the schools. These eventually gave way to a large variety of "alternative" educational organizations.[9]

Numerous collectives of every sort came out of the women's and feminist movements. A small collective group started the San Francisco Women's Center in 1970. Over the following years, numerous women inspired by feminist ideology came together spontaneously into small consciousness-raising groups. Out of these developed many service projects, such as the Health Collectives and the Switchboard, to fill gaps not provided for by society; and many women' work collectives, such as Seven Sisters Construction, the Juice Bar, A Woman's Place. The San Francisco Women's Center, housed in the Women's Building, became an umbrella organization of about eighteen collective projects. The collective structure was a natural form, as it provides group empowerment for previously disempowered people.

Collectives hit the airwaves. In the Bay Area, listener-sponsored KPFA radio, begun back in 1949 as the flagship of the Pacifica network, struggled and experimented with the issues of collectives and internal democracy in these years. Like the Berkeley Co-op, KPFA earned recognition as a community resource.

Collective groups also played an important role in the development of the Bay Area's gay and lesbian communities. The San Francisco Gay Men's Chorus, for example, self-organized in the days following days the assassinations of Supervisor Harvey Milk and Mayor George Moscone in 1978, after an impromptu gathering the night of the tragedy to sing on the steps of City Hall.

WORKER COLLECTIVES IN THE 1970s

The earliest collective businesses were mostly connected with radical communication media: presses, bookstores and film. This reflected the explicitly political movement from which they emerged. They were followed by food-related cooperatives in the late 1960s, and artisan/industrial collectives and cooperatives beginning around 1970 both in urban and rural areas. These differed from earlier American industrial cooperatives and co-op stores mainly in that they chose worker control through the collective consensus decision-making system, rather then the majority-rule managerial system predominant since the early 19th century. With few exceptions, their organizational motives included an overt idealism. Most considered themselves to be part of a larger movement, even when they had no organizational relationship to it. They explicitly committed their work to high craft standards and affordable prices, not just whatever the market would bear.

Worker collectives and cooperatives represented the embedding of the counterculture in the working population; their revolutionary meaning was workers' control and self-management.

They took two basic forms. Some collectives were centralized, with each worker paid through the enterprise. Others, such as artisan cooperatives, were decentralized, maintaining the studio space or the means of production that the craftspeople used.

These early cooperative and collective work groups sprang up in many areas around the country. Almost all were small. The workers involved formed most of them with few resources, and in fields that required no great outlay of capital for machinery and raw materials. The workers in many started out semiskilled. By pooling energy, resources, and skills they found that they could do together what few could have done alone, and gain at least partial economic independence and freedom. There were soon collective and cooperative bakers, teachers, truckers, mechanics, farmers, carpenters, printers, food-handlers, cabinetmakers, taxi-drivers, medical workers, sellers, artists, technicians, machine-operators, cooks, editors, etc. Cooperatives operated successfully almost everywhere in light production, distribution, and services.[10]

They existed under a variety of legal forms: incorporated cooperatives, joint-partnerships, nonprofit corporations, unincorporated associations. Many had no legal existence at all, and operated in the fringe areas of the economy. Since capitalist law requires all group "enterprises" to conform to a corporate or partnership structure, the collective structure was often forced into an underground existence.

Cities where the largest concentrations of worker collectives and cooperatives could be found included the San Francisco Bay Area, the Boston area, Seattle, Portland, Minneapolis, New Haven, Austin, and Madison.

Not surprisingly, many found that the price of freedom was often very hard work for low pay, at least until they got their skills and organization together. The dominance of wage slavery in an area depresses working conditions for all workers.

Among the earlier work collectives in the Boston area were the New England Free Press, Red Book store, and Newsreel films. These were followed by New Hamburger Cabinetworks, Walrus Woodworking and Cambridge Auto Co-op, around 1970. In 1980, there were over fifty worker collectives in and around Boston.

In Berkeley-Oakland, one of the earliest collectives was Taxi Unlimited, collectivized in 1965, in time to play a role in the Free Speech Movement; others included Uncle Ho's Mechanix Rainbow, Movement Motors, Build carpenters, Alternative Food Store, and the Cheeseboard, all formed between 1970 and 1972, followed by Uprisings and Nabalom Bakeries, and the Brick Hut and Swallow restaurants. Every loaf of Uprisings bread included a small flier announcing progressive political and cultural events. By the end of the decade, there were over 150 collectives and collective-cooperatives in the San Francisco Bay Area.

Due to their underground nature, estimates of the total number of worker cooperatives in the US in this period differ widely. One study published in 1980 estimated between 750 and 1,000 small worker cooperatives in the US at that time.[11]

COLLECTIVE DIRECTORY GROUP & INTERCOLLECTIVE

In 1976, a small autonomous Bay Area circle called the Collective Directory Group began a project of networking among collectives. The first edition of the *Collective Directory* was published in 1977. Updated editions came out in the following years. Besides listing information about groups, expanded *directories* included articles on history and theory of the movement.[12]

In 1980, workers from a wide variety of Bay Area collectives came together and formed the InterCollective, an association for exchanging ideas and information, promoting networking, and striving to develop the movement. The InterCollective had no centralized leadership or organization, but gathered in open monthly meetings and held political and cultural events. I was a member of both the Collective Directory Group and the InterCollective. We organized a well-attended Collective Conference in 1982, weekly classes and workshops between 1981 and 1986, a Collectives Fair in 1983, and sponsored an anti-nuclear action collective for the 1982 nonviolent blockade and civil disobedience at the Livermore Weapons Lab.

The InterCollective Statement of Purpose defined the group as

> an association of people working in collectives, cooperatives
> and communes formed for the following purposes: to pro-
> mote and support collectives, cooperatives, communes, and
> networking and exchange among them; to provide a forum
> to facilitate exchange of information and ideas concerning
> them; to work for the right of all people to self-manage their
> work situation, and to collectively own and control their
> means of survival; to promote collectivity as an integral and
> organizational part of the movement for progressive social
> change; to work for a society free of oppressed classes and
> not dominated by the commodity form of exchange or the
> wage-slavery form of work organization; to support the de-
> velopment of *appropriate* technology, for human needs and
> the protection of the natural environment; to support the
> struggles against imperialism, racism, sexism, homophobia,
> ageism, and all other forms of oppression; to oppose war and
> the proliferation of nuclear power and arms; and to promote
> recreation and socializing among members.[13]

The *Collective Directory* became a project of the InterCollective.
Updated editions came out in 1983 and 1984. The 1985 edition was
the most extensive, listing almost 150 collective groups in the Bay
Area and over 350 on the West Coast.

But by that time the collective movement had already peaked
and, like most progressive movements in the country, succumbed
to the wave of capitalist triumphalism and cultural individualism
that engulfed the country during the Reagan era. The 1985 *Collective
Directory* was the last, and in the following years the InterCollective
faded and disbanded.

Although the 1980s saw the slow attrition of the collectives,
not all 70s collectives succumbed, and some continue up to today.

THE FOOD SYSTEM

Collectives and cooperatives connected with food cut across
rural-urban lines. Of all the countercultural organizations, they
became the most interconnected, the most developed ideologically
and—apart from music groups—had the most far-reaching effects.
In the late 1960s, "food conspiracies" formed in cities and towns
across the country. Basically buying clubs, they called themselves

conspiracies to indicate that they aspired to more than just stretching dollars, and aimed at overthrowing the established food distribution system. Most had literature and newsletters that publicized their larger motives along with local food news. Most were based on member energy and labor requirements, and run through democratic and collective systems. Many connected with small local and regional organic farms, and made "natural" foods available in their areas for the first time, while providing the farms with needed outlets. According to the Cooperative League, between 5,000 and 10,000 of these clubs had formed across the country by 1975. The Bay Area was a West Coast nexus.

The Haight-Ashbury Food Conspiracy began in 1968 as a buying club, reaching 150 member houses in 1973. At the same time across the bay, the Berkeley-Oakland Organic Food Association had some twenty-one affiliated neighborhood conspiracies. The conspiracies were organized around member participation. They got food from regional farmers as well as at the farmers' market, and were organized so that each neighborhood conspiracy was responsible for one job each month.

In the early 1970s, "new wave" co-op stores began appearing, run by worker collectives and many stemming from conspiracies. They differed from the earlier co-op stores in that they were non-managerial. In some, the worker collective comprised the entire membership, while in others workers and member-customers shared control. Meanwhile, natural food stores began to appear, and chain supermarkets also began stocking organic and natural food lines, providing competition at the alternative system's strongest point. The Cooperative League estimated in 1979 that between 5,000 and 10,000 small "new wave" food co-ops of various structures had formed in the past decade, and several thousand were probably still functioning with a $500 million annual volume.[14]

When natural food stores began appearing in an area, the buying clubs generally took a dive as the stores were providing most of the same products almost as cheaply and with more convenience. Some of the most active people in the old food conspiracies were instrumental in starting some of the stores, and many of the former conspiracy members formed their customer base. By 1976, both the Haight-Ashbury Food Conspiracy and the Berkeley-Oakland Organic Food Association had lost most of their membership and were in a state of near collapse.

The conspiracies and collective stores found that due to their small size they could usually only compete with the supermarket chains in the area of natural foods. In response, the collective stores began forming alternative wholesales, some run by independent collectives, some by federations of stores and conspiracies. Trucking collectives connected the whole into broad interlocking networks on both coasts and the Midwest. Citywide and regional "Food Systems" attempted to grow large enough to create a stable economic base for the whole movement and to create a viable alternative to the supermarket chains.

From the Seattle Workers' Brigade and the Portland Area Food System down to the Southern California Cooperating Communities across to the Tucson People's Warehouse, the Austin Community Project, Minneapolis People's Warehouse, the Federation of Ohio River Cooperatives (extending over a six-state area), and the New England People's Cooperatives, regional Food Systems soon overlapped coast to coast.

The collective movement made its greatest impact in the Food Systems. Here the counterculture actually made a frontal challenge to the dominant system in one of its most vital spots, food. It was a real and serious attempt to provide a large-scale collective alternative to the corporate food system, weaving worker-run production units into a larger organism reminiscent of the old Cooperative Commonwealth. Because food is essentially a political issue, many of the most volatile of forces of the 1970s met in the Food Systems, and clashed.

The Food System movement became based in the "new wave" wholesales and regional federations around the country. As such, these became the center of ideological struggle over the aims and strategy of the counterculture movement by the mid-1970s. Some saw the movement as primarily part of an overall struggle against the capitalist system, and advocated more political involvement. In general, these people thought that the movement should be focused to serve the working population, that it should be anti-profit, that its capital accumulation should not be privately owned by groups of workers or consumers, and that the movement should be more unified and centrally structured. Others saw the movement as primarily economic and personal, and in general supported decentralization, structural diversity, and federation, with each group deciding questions like capital accumulation, profit, or political involvement as it saw fit. There were not two clear-cut camps, as each organization had its own variation of worker vs. consumer control, federation vs. centralization, etc., and there were many different viewpoints within each organization.

The mid-1970s was a time of crisis for Food Systems around the country. When many small collectives and cooperatives attempted to federate into larger organizations, they came up against the problem of how to grow large enough to be economically viable without becoming managerial bureaucracies like many of the co-ops started in the 1930s. This, together with the economic recession and runaway inflation, caused most to remain on shaky foundations.

The Austin Community Project was begun in 1972 to develop alternative distribution of natural foods. In 3 years, it expanded to include 2 co-op stores, 2 buying clubs, 4 organic farms, and collectives doing distribution, baking, canning, recycling, a restaurant, etc, with 1,000 to 1,500 members. But the project collapsed from over-extension and disbanded in 1976. Many of the member groups fell along with it, but others carried on.

In Seattle, the Workers' Brigade, formed in 1974, brought together a group of collectives into a joint organization, including ones doing baking, food distribution, bookkeeping, maintenance, and trucking. It nearly collapsed a year later, but managed to stay alive and continue.

Some, like the Federation of Ohio River Cooperatives and the Arcata Co-op in California, became consumer-owned and collectively operated, combining worker control and social responsibility in a democratic manner.

The San Francisco Common-Operating Warehouse took a democratic-centralist structure. Democratic-centralism—first devised by Lenin—in theory tries to combine hierarchical democracy with efficiency. Structurally, democratic-centralism means elected and recallable representatives forming a central committee with a wide latitude of powers, its majority decisions binding on all members. But all too often on the left, "democratic-centralism" has in practice meant real power residing in a self-perpetuating clique atop a bureaucratic pyramid. Democratic-centralism places extraordinary power in the central committee, and discipline upon the membership to carry out their decisions. Small groups describing themselves as "democratic-centralist" attempted to take control of Food Systems in several cities, and to turn the System into part of their programs.[15]

By mid-1975, the movement had reached an ideological crisis in many areas, and exploded first in the Minneapolis People's Warehouse. The ideological issues were quickly buried in a fog of conflicting personalities and rhetoric, involving a "collective" which probably wasn't really very collective, and a "democratic-centralist" group which demanded worker control, used force to get it, then took on three new workers but soon fired them when the latter demanded that worker control include them, too. While the "democratic-centralist" group occupied the Warehouse, many of the member co-ops and collectives left and formed a new competing warehouse. Food Systems and warehouses around the country took sides, with each or both of the Minneapolis warehouses being boycotted by various other groups in different cities. The store movement in the area was not big enough to support both, and they tottered on the verge of financial extinction. After about six months, a court order and the local police reinstated the former group. The movement in the area and around the country was badly shaken.[16]

The San Francisco People's Food System was formed in 1973 by some of the most active people who had left the old Food Conspiracy and organized the first collective stores. The Food System centered on the SF Common-Operating Warehouse. It was not long before the Common-Operating Warehouse's democratic-centralist system of limited representative democracy and central committee power collided with the autonomy and consensus system of many of the member work collectives.

In early 1975, SF Food System workers began gathering in regular All–Co-op meetings ("the Forum") to try to develop and better organize the system. By 1976, the System was growing large and strong, with member collectives and co-ops on both sides of the bay. Internally, an ideological battle was brewing over organization between anarchists and Marxists. In April, members decided that there would be an elected Representative Body (RB). This happened at nearly the same time as preparations for the alternative People's Bicentennial celebration on July 4, 1976, which the Food System was instrumental in organizing in San Francisco. Over its short life, the Food System had actively and materially supported a number of progressive struggles. Internally, there was a stress on struggling with racism and sexism. By the end of the year, the Representative Body had drafted a "Basis of Unity", which was approved by all the collectives, and the RB elected a steering committee in January 1977. But at that point internal disagreements and problems rushed to a head.

External forces were also at work. A number of people began acting strangely disruptive. Rumors flew that Nixon's Cointelpro agents, who had destroyed many other progressive and radical groups, had infiltrated the Food System, too. A number of the food collectives were involved with the prisoners' rights movement. The California system at the time used "indeterminate sentencing:" a prisoner with a promise of a job on the outside could get an early release. The collectives offered that promise. However, there were competing radical prisoner organizations, in violent conflict with each other, each accusing the other of being led by police agents. These prisoner organizations began to battle for power in the Food System.

Meanwhile, the steering committee decided to rewrite the Basis of Unity, without approval of the collectives. The new draft de-emphasized the politics of food and declared "democratic-centralism" to be the organizational structure of the Food System. There was an outcry of opposition from many of the collectives; many workers thought that the steering committee was usurping power. Some wanted to return to the all-worker Forum or set up a delegate assembly with limited powers as the decision-making group.

An all-worker conference was called for April 1977 to discuss these issues. The fate of the Food System was at stake. But on the first day, a small group disrupted and shut down the conference, some of them outsiders from radical groups. Hard on the heels of this, a gun battle broke out between former prisoners belonging to feuding prisoner organizations at Ma Revolution natural food store on the corner of Telegraph and Dwight in Berkeley. The San Francisco Food System came crashing down and, as it did, a countercultural dream shattered and died.

With the SF Food System functionally defunct, the numerous small autonomous collectives again became the main base of the movement in the Bay Area. The following year, the old Food Conspiracy was reorganized and revived as a communal enterprise, with all member-customer energy requirements removed; under this system it grew to sizable proportions again in the Bay Area for a few years. The San Francisco Common-Operating Warehouse hung on for a few years, then closed its doors in February 1982.

Outside the Bay Area, there were still about two dozen "new wave" warehouses around the country and about a thousand stores in 1980, doing a half billion dollars annual volume, with statewide federations in many areas, and interstate cooperation. A network of connection and federation among food collectives, co-ops, and small organic farms still extended nationwide. But the movement remained on a shaky financial basis, and continued to be kept alive more by people's energy and visions than by accumulated capital.

COLLECTIVITY AND NONVIOLENT MASS ACTION

The Civil Rights Movement, the anti-war movement, and the anti-nuclear movement of the 60s and 70s all had deep connections with collective organizing and nonviolent mass action. Alongside co-operative movements, they worked toward a more democratized society with greater social equity, which almost all organizations tried to bring about through nonviolent mass methods and tactics.

Some of their forebears, including Abolitionism and the early women's movement, employed nonviolent mass demonstrations, marches, disruptions, boycotts, hunger strikes, vigils, civil disobedience. The "free speech" campaigns of the IWW in the West in the early 1900s in Spokane, Fresno, Aberdeen, San Diego, and other locations followed this pattern. When street meetings were outlawed, the IWW held them anyway, and when a speaker was arrested, a large number of others followed, until authorities had to arrest more than the city jail and budget could handle. Over 500 Wobblies went to jail in Spokane in 1909, including Elizabeth Gurley Flynn. Industrial unionists organizing the CIO used a different tack. In the Flint, Michigan, sit-down strike to organize General Motors in 1937, the workers voted to occupy the factories and to live inside until their demand for union recognition was met. During the factory occupation all strikers met together daily to plan and organize the tasks that had to be done. The sit-downs spread rapidly to other GM plants and, with much outside support, the strikers achieved their goal. The Congress of Racial Equality initiated the modern civil rights movement with sit-ins and a freedom ride in the 1940s. The 1956 Montgomery bus boycott drew national attention. Other organizations joined the struggle in the early 1960s with sit-ins at lunch counters and other facilities, freedom rides, and similar acts. The 1963 March on Washington drew 250,000 participants. Through mass nonviolent actions, the Civil Rights Movement abolished Jim Crow segregation. In the 1960s and '70s, groups opposed to the Vietnam War used nonviolence to radicalize public opinion and force American withdrawal, including sit-ins, blocking induction centers, draft card burnings, draft file destruction, draft and tax resistance, and mass marches and demonstrations. Following that tradition, the anti-nuclear movement grew in the mid-1970s, with nonviolent mass actions at the nuclear facilities at Diablo Canyon, Seabrook, Trojan, Rocky Flats, Comanche Peak, and also at the Pentagon.

LIVERMORE ACTION GROUP

In 1981, the Livermore Action Group (LAG) formed in the Bay Area. According to its statement of purpose, the ultimate goal of LAG was "to further the cause of (1) global nuclear disarmament, (2) the de-militarization of American society, and (3) a redirection of economic priorities that provides for a more equitable distribution of wealth and resources at home and abroad."[17] LAG's immediate goal was to organize a mass blockade to shut down the nuclear weapons laboratory in Livermore, California. To plan and carry out the action, LAG decided to use a decentralized, collective organizational structure.

The system was based on affinity groups that functioned through a feminist process. The *Blockade/Demonstration Handbook* defined an affinity group as composed of five to fifteen people sharing a specific interest, issue or philosophy. The name goes back to the anarchist movement in Spain in the early part of the 20th century. Feminist process meant small autonomous groups, consensus decision-making, skill sharing, diminishing adversarial thinking, and rejecting hierarchies. Every affinity group needed to start with reaching consensus on a statement of principles of unity, deciding how the group would make decisions and what it wanted to do at the blockade. Consensus was defined as a process of synthesizing ideas to arrive at a decision acceptable to all. A dissenter who felt strongly enough could block consensus or withdraw from the group. Each affinity group would send a spokesperson to a spokescouncil, which tried to consolidate, synthesize, and arrive at proposals agreeable to all. The spokespeople then relayed any new proposal back to the affinity groups for further discussion. The process was repeated until consensus worked out. Through this process, hundreds of people were able to successfully participate in consensus planning.[18]

The blockade came off without a hitch, drew nearly 10,000 participants at the lab's gates, and made a powerful statement. The

InterCollective had an affinity group there, to which I belonged; we built a float on a windmill theme at Heartwood. With 1,475 arrested, it was one of the largest mass arrests at a political protest in US history. It was also a high-water mark for the organization. Although after the blockade LAG faded without achieving its goal of shutting down the weapons lab, it was a paragon of empowering its members and demonstrating the viability of a large, activist organization with a decentralized structure.[19]

12.
Case Studies:
Bay Warehouse Collective &
Heartwood Cooperative Woodshop

I was a member of both of these Berkeley groups. One emerged from the other. They were both successful in their own ways, Bay Warehouse for only two years, and Heartwood for over three decades.[1]

BAY WAREHOUSE COLLECTIVE

Bay Warehouse Collective was founded in Berkeley, California in 1972. A centralized collective, Bay ran an auto repair shop, a print shop, a woodshop, and a theater out of a large warehouse near Gilman Street between 5th and 6th Streets. All shop income went to the central collective, which paid workers salaries based on need: "rent money, food money, emergency money, and that is all there has ever been."[2] At our height, we had about thirty-five to forty members in the core group. Eighteen thousand square feet were much more than the shops needed, so the warehouse also housed and rented space to a number of independent operations that were not part of the collective proper and had separate finances: a pottery shop, an electronics shop, a typesetting group, a photographer's darkroom, a legal collective, and a candle factory. We hoped that eventually they would all join the larger collective. The theater troupe—Stoneage Theater—was considered part of the collective, but paid no rent, took no salaries, and brought in almost no income. Bay Warehouse also provided free space to a food conspiracy, a collective garden, and a worm farm. Numerous people who did not belong to the core collective were involved with all these operations, keeping the Warehouse a lively place. The woodshop kept busy making speaker boxes for rock and roll groups, including Santana. Being part of Bay Warehouse was the most fun I'd had since I lived in the artist commune Drop City in Colorado between 1966 and 68.

An article that we collectively wrote for the "underground" newspaper *New Morning* in 1973 describes Bay Warehouse pretty well:

> We are trying to approach work and work-relationships as creative processes, attempting to create work situations that are unalienating, where the work is not fragmented, the worker not estranged from the product of her or his labor. This is only possible where the workers run their own shops and no individual 'owns' the tools. We pool our income and share our skills and resources. We take individual money according to need, and each individual determines his or her needs. Each separate shop has its own organization, each slightly different, but all within a leaderless structure, attempting to make decisions collectively, by consensus, as equals... We have come together from many places, each looking for some alternative... to either exploiting or being exploited, oppressing or being oppressed. We are attempting to turn work into a liberating force in our lives... We try as much as possible to keep our shops open to people, to share our skills and tools. We want to relate to our machines not as individual or even collective possessions, but as the social products that they are. We want to use our machines in ways that help provide for real human needs...
>
> Bay Warehouse is one of the first glimpses of what is taking place as the 'counter culture' finally attempts to deal with the realities of living and working... [W]hat we are attempting to do, [is] what could be possible if only the workers got together, if only the workers were in control... create a truly free society, controlled from below, by the people themselves, through their collectives and communes and councils, a society based on economic equality, communal ownership of the means of survival, of the air, oceans and land, a society where exploitation is outlawed and crime unnecessary, where we can all stay alive in harmony, and grow.[3]

Bay Warehouse formed out of the wreckage of Bay High, an "alternative" trade high school created in 1970 and funded in part by a grant from *The Whole Earth Catalog*. The school was structured as a typical Berkeley "free school" of the era vis-à-vis the students, with few academic or even attendance demands. The students were mostly kids who had not thrived in public school, and whose parents could afford the tuition. A 1973 collective document from my archives describes in part what happened: "After two years it became obvious that the arrangement was little more than high-priced babysitting... we decided to stop collecting tuition and work with anyone of any age who wished to learn on a one-on-one basis."[4] But that's only part of the story.

The school was nominally structured as a democratic collective with everyone having an equal voice. But a sharp struggle soon developed between shop workers and administrators—who were also the academic teachers—over real control and over the refusal by the administrators to do manual maintenance work, such as sweeping the floors and taking out the garbage. The shop workers thought they were doing all the work. It felt like class struggle. The shop workers took over the school, dismissed the administrators, disbanded the school proper, and, shortly after I joined, organized Bay Warehouse Collective.

I first got involved with Bay when I was doing carpentry with my partner Vern when he arranged to borrow a scaffold from Bay for a job we were doing. After a taste of what was happening at Bay, I was sold and joined. This happened right before the school imploded.

Those were heady times. We felt like we had staged an insurrection and won. The workers had seized the means of production and now we had the power to reshape our world. We held meetings almost daily. Eric made what he called an *ostrakon*, which in ancient Greece was a potsherd used as a ballot on which people wrote their votes, but at Bay was a carved wand decorated with feathers and leather, which was passed to the speaker so only one person could speak at a time. Meetings would go on until everybody was satisfied, or at least tired of talking.

Bay Warehouse didn't live long enough to write a constitution and bylaws, but we did apply for a grant once, and wrote a description and mission statement for that occasion. We described Bay as

> a collectivized institution for the research and development of non-exploitive relationships. It is a community resource center providing facilities in which we can develop alternative methods of life support, provide a center for learning, develop and practice skills and crafts, maintain open access to information and tools, and provide low cost services to the community. The social, political and economic relationships

developing in Bay High Warehouse can ultimately serve as a model to be duplicated and improved upon throughout the community.[5]

Each shop made internal decisions that affected its separate functioning, as a smaller collective inside the larger one. Bay Printshop made decisions affecting the print shop, and likewise did auto and wood. New members were taken in by each separate shop. We were about equally divided between women and men, with men the majority in auto and wood, and women the majority in print. There was a lot of struggle revolving around sexism; the women were very supportive of each other, and only the men seriously trying to struggle with the problems were around for very long. Our average skill level was not high; far too many were scarcely beyond an apprentice level, but together we combined our knowledge, corrected each other's mistakes, and turned out reasonably professional work.

The print shop did a lot of work for many progressive groups in our area, some free, some almost free; all three shops contributed our skills to the community at times, and provided supervised access to tools to many people. In the grant proposal and article we described each shop:

> The printshop is operated by a collective of three women and two men. We emphasize low cost high quality work for groups we feel we most want to support and encourage. We operate an open shop Monday, Wednesday and Thursday nights for people we feel are doing valuable work for the community who need access to cameras, plate makers, presses and a paper cutter... We encourage people who want to learn printing skills to participate in the work and decision making of the collective. For projects we wish to support and encourage, our prices are absolutely subjective. We encourage people to participate in any and all aspects of their job, thus keeping prices down, allowing us to handle more work, and involving them in the printing process.[6]

> The auto shop provides low cost automobile repair to all members of the community. Space is available on a limited basis to all people who want to work on their own cars. Energy exchanges can be worked out to reduce the cost of repairs. The collective presently consists of nine people... Volkswagen and a few other foreign cars are our specialty, but we

work on most Detroit cars. We have even worked on a 1959 Edsel and a 1956 Studebaker. We hope someday soon to be able to function more as a teaching facility to demystify auto mechanics, but presently can only work on a very limited basis with patient people.[7]

The woodshop offers custom cabinets, carpentry, toys, play equipment, home and garden furniture, geodesic domes, fine woodworking of all sorts at people's prices... We share our facilities with those who need to use woodworking tools, on a labor exchange basis. One of us makes guitars.[8]

As in most countercultural organizations, there was no one ideology, at least in words: the organization itself contained most of the ideas. For some it was enough to work in a non-bossist non-sexist shop, although salaries were pathetically low. Others saw us becoming more communal and buying large houses to live in, eventually branching out into the country. Still others saw us growing large and strong enough to become, in federation with other collectives and cooperatives, a challenge to the capitalist order. We did not have a share system: members who left had no claim to a share, and new members did not have to "buy in."

But the warehouse that Bay Collective inherited from the school was too costly for our needs and abilities. We did not find ways to make enough energy flow back transformed into dollars. Weekly salaries in August 1973 averaged less than $90 per person (not including ten or fifteen people who received nothing at all), and in September averaged about $57 per person. Our bank balance on October 1st was $60.40. We finally decided to disband the larger Collective into three autonomous worker collectives, and in early 1974 each collective found a smaller space. The print shop retained its centralized collective structure, becoming Inkworks. The auto shop became CarWorld, a joint-partnership. The woodshop became Heartwood, an artisan cooperative. All the shops became successful businesses. Other Bay Warehouse alumnae and alumni went on to co-found at least three other collective enterprises: Nexus (an artisan and artist collective in Berkeley), Seven Sisters Construction (also in Berkeley), and Coastfork Artisans Guild (in Cottage Grove, Oregon).

HEARTWOOD COOPERATIVE WOODSHOP

Heartwood is today a cooperative of custom woodworkers sharing a well-equipped three-thousand-square-foot shop in Berkeley, where we have been for over thirty years. We share machines, knowledge, skills, energy, resources. Some of us specialize in cabinetry, some in furniture. We are self-employed, maintain our independence by keeping overhead down, and get a lot of perks from working in a democratic egalitarian situation with peers.

The cooperative operates the shop, owns most of the equipment, provides basic woodworking supplies such as glue, dowels, biscuits, nails and sandpaper, and provides insurance. We are each responsible for a share of the upkeep, maintenance and improvements. Each member is self-employed with his or her own business, and contracts jobs separately. We help each other when needed. The shop is a nonprofit incorporated cooperative today, but for many years it was an unincorporated association. We have full-time and part-time members. New members have a buy-in of two months rent. Members do not own shares, so departing members are not bought out. We are incorporated under the same California statute as consumer cooperatives. But we do not issue shares, and we do not pay dividends or rebates, since the cooperative makes no profit. The central purpose of the cooperative is running the shop.

Important decisions are made at weekly meetings. We strive for consensus but also vote when necessary. No one has any permanent shop job or position of power. One special job is shop manager, which changes monthly in rotation.[9] The shop manager makes sure all the basics are taken care of related to overall shop functioning, and also chairs meetings. Other special jobs are bookkeeping and insurance.

On the first Wednesday of each month we have Shop Day, when we spend a half day doing clean up, maintenance, and improvements, followed by a meeting. In mid-month we have shop clean-up, followed by a meeting if we need one. This second day usually takes only an hour.

Most of our machines are owned by the cooperative and some belong to individuals, but all are used and maintained collectively. The shop is responsible for replacing any machine used by the shop that has been worn out or damaged. Each of us has individual hand tools. When we need help on a job, we occasionally hire each other, but jobs are usually limited to a size that one person can handle.

Full-time members have unlimited use of the shop; part-time members can use the shop up to twenty hours per week. "Ghost" members have minimal use of the shop; this status is limited to former members.

Our cooperative system is typical of groups of artisans, in which the means and methods of production are basically individual. The artisan cooperative is clearly distinguishable from the industrial worker cooperative, in which both the means and methods of production are collective. The artisan cooperative is usually an association of self-employed members, each with their own business, while in the industrial worker cooperative the members are employees and owners of the business at the same time.

Heartwood is now over thirty years old. Over the years, more than fifty woodworkers have been members of our shop. The median average stay has been around five years. We have been able to maintain a cohesive center, while membership has slowly changed. Our longevity can be attributed partly to our system being very simple, practical, and flexible, arising from our actual needs and the conditions of the industry itself. Our policy of maintaining an affordable buy-in has kept our shop open to new members with limited financial resources. If we had shares that accrued value, the shop would probably become unworkable over time, since most incoming members do not have extensive financial resources to buy out departing members. Much of the turnover in the shop has come because people move around a lot these days, because the cost of living is very high in the Bay Area, and because unfortunately even in a cooperative it is still not easy to make a good living doing custom woodworking. Many former members have gone on to different better-paying professions. Woodworking is rewarding but not very lucrative. As quality increases, fine woodworking becomes increasingly skilled and labor intensive, yet financial compensation does not always rise in proportion. Mid-quality cabinetry often pays better than high-end. Part of your motivation has to be the craft itself.

I am the only remaining member of the original group of six who founded the shop in early 1974. The founding group of Bob, John P, Sherry, Eric, Curt, and myself had already been working together for several years in Bay Woodshop. We started Heartwood because none of us individually had the financial resources to start a shop, because we wanted to work with others in an equal and democratic situation rather than becoming an employer or an employee, and because individually our technical knowledge was not always adequate, but together we managed to fill in the gaps and do professional work.

I had started my career as a professional woodworker several years previously, in 1970 in what is known in the trade as a production shop, a small kitchen cabinet factory in Albuquerque, New Mexico. There were around twenty employees. I started at the bottom, a sander. The work was hard, dangerous, and low-paying, and there was no union, but the worst part was my shattered expectation that I would learn woodworking there. I soon realized that in a production shop my skill level would never get beyond journeyman. The workers were always limited to particular operations, and large segments of the process were beyond the scope of my job. I realized that I might enjoy being a woodworker if I could do it in a different context. I got that context first at Bay Woodshop, then at Heartwood.

While we were Bay, our average skill level was around journeyperson. The shop would take in a job and the group would collectively figure out how to build it. But we were constantly improving, as well as learning how to run a business. By the time we formed Heartwood, we were all capable of making the leap from workers to artisans. The shop, and not the job, became our common project.

An enormous amount of excellent work has passed through Heartwood over three decades, but the real story of the shop has been the human story. A rich cross-section of humanity has also passed through the shop, with all the same human foibles as the rest of the world. The shop has taken different flavors in the various mixes of people. Sometimes it has been a good sitcom, sometimes a melodrama. There have of course been personality conflicts and struggles in the shop over the years, dramas have been played out, and on occasion someone has had to leave. In the end, so far at least, it has always turned out okay, and the shop has survived.

While Heartwood has had a lot of continuity, it has also had several distinct incarnations. The shop would periodically lose key people and be on the brink of falling apart, but then new people would join and the shop would reform. The early group included Jean and Priscilla. In the late 1970s and 80s the group included Liz, Jed, Rick, Bill, Tom, Michael, Robert, Lynn, Lauri, Sara, Stu, Trent, Steve, Shelly, and Closetman Dave. By the 1990s and 2000s, Heartwood members included Laurie, Steven, Mike, Brad, Kim, Debi,

Jim, Jason, Moses, Real, Gerard, Joseph, Kristen, Susan, Chickie, Peter, Elizabeth, Michael#2, Josh, Gren, Gus, Phil, Ron, Andrew, Nick, Jamie, and Jay. Every one of these people interacted, struggled, laughed, shared good times and hard times, and made contributions. Every person was coming from somewhere in his or her life and going somewhere.

People don't miraculously change when they join a cooperative. However, a successful cooperative is structured to function around and to bring out the better parts of human nature. While all people have tendencies such as territoriality, competitiveness and envy that, when unchecked, can destroy a cooperative, some people have worse cases than others. Extremely competitive people cannot work harmoniously in a cooperative. There have been a few members who simply did not have cooperative personalities, who were overly self-serving or opportunistic. One or two played the system for what they could get out of it. But for most people, working in a situation that stresses cooperation, sharing, and trust serves to temper and minimize the opposite qualities.

Despite personality difficulties such as occur in every group, the great majority of Heartwood members have always worked things out and had productive stays. A good number of former members stay in contact, and appreciate their time in Heartwood as well spent, although they have moved on in their lives.

In woodworking, as in many fields, while advanced technology has greatly expanded capabilities and productive powers, it has at the same time narrowed the number of worker s able to make a living at it independently, due to the expense of machines and competition from mass production. The market forces set in motion by advanced technology in a very competitive industry make it very difficult for workers to be productive enough using simpler machines and tools. A cooperative such as ours helps to reverse this process by democratizing access to the means of production.

Personally, after thirty-plus years, one of these days I know I'll have to retire from woodworking, but I still enjoy working in the cooperative and I still get a lot out of the work. You don't always get to know everything about people's lives when you work with them, even in a cooperative, but you find appropriate spaces for those relationships. You get to know them as work friends. If the work situation is harmonious, as it can be in a well-functioning cooperative, you retain fond memories of those work friendships for the rest of your life. The process of woodworking is meditative and creative. Wood is a wonderful medium. The democratic interactive process of a cooperative is also a wonderful medium to pass your work life in.

13.
Cooperatives in the Mainstream: the 60s & 70s, Part II

COOPERATIVES AND COLLECTIVES

At the same time as the collective and communal movements of the 1960s and 1970s brought together many young people, the older cooperative movement continued along a parallel track. Interactions between the newer and older movements were due more often to overlapping membership than to organizational connections. I'll give a few a personal examples. In the 1960s, when I belonged to the rural commune Drop City in Colorado, we got water and electricity from cooperatives that had been set up by the New Deal in the 1930s. In the 1970s, many members of Bay Warehouse Collective, Heartwood, and the InterCollective also belonged to the old Berkeley Co-op (CCB) grocery store. In turn, the CCB newspaper *Co-op News* publicized worker collectives and InterCollective events. When CCB fell into desperate straits, it invited ideas from the collective movement in a restructuring attempt. On the whole, however, the newer and the older movements remained separate, partly because the new movement was based in young people and oriented toward small groups, while consumer cooperatives were based in the larger working community, and farmer cooperatives were of course geared toward that focus.

UNIONS, CO-OPS AND INDUSTRY

Contemporary labor unions have organized and supported food co-ops, housing complexes, credit unions, and various service co-ops, but virtually no worker production cooperatives. Their attitude is mainly the long-standing AFL-CIO policy of opposing any clouding of the line between employer and employee, accepting basic control of the workplace by employers in exchange for contracts. They hold that any clouding of employee-management lines confuses their own role as bargaining agent and weakens the union. They point to the many profit-sharing schemes that employers have offered workers over the years, the primary purpose of which has often been to accomplish precisely that confusion and weakening. Opponents of union production cooperatives also point out that numerous large industrial cooperatives have failed, demonstrating how risky they are in a capitalist market economy. Lastly, some unionists oppose democratization of the workplace, which has been acceded to in limited degrees by some companies from time to time, because some of these experiments have ironically resulted in layoffs due to increased production.[1]

The United Auto Workers is one of the few unions that raised any of the issues of worker control in the decades following WWII, notably in the Lordstown assembly plant strike of 1972, and that supported several experiments in workplace reorganization.[2] Chrysler workers at one point attempted to take over the company. In the late 1970s, an experiment in limited self-management was tried at a General Foods plant in Kansas with great success for the workers. It was shut down because it was too threatening to management.[3]

Most large industrial cooperatives in the 20th century have been the result of workers taking over bankrupt or near-bankrupt companies; this is, of course, a shaky situation to begin with. The hope is that the industry can continue to support its workers when there is no longer any necessity to provide owners with profit on top of that. Historically many have proven to be in dying industries that continued to go down, with bankers winding up the only real winners.

PLYWOOD CO-OPS

By the end of World War II, very few true worker cooperatives remained in large industry, but a handful continued and flourished. In the Pacific Northwest, several cooperative plywood factories started in the 1930s made it through very difficult times and continued. They were structured with workers electing managers to oversee the operation, but still retaining much control. They gave themselves salaries 35 percent higher than workers in comparable capitalist factories, better safety conditions, health and dental care, lunches, insurance paid by the cooperative, gasoline at wholesale rates, and other side benefits. By 1980, there were 18 of them, producing about 12 percent of the plywood in the United States.[4] However, they suffered a sharp decline in the following years. One of the few remaining worker cooperative factories in 2003 was Hoquiam Plywood, in Washington, with ninety-seven worker-owners.[5]

ESOPs

In the decades after World War II, "employee-owned" firms became increasingly common. Today, approximately 2,500 companies in the US are 100 percent employee-owned. Four thousand are majority-owned by employees. In all, 11,500 companies in the US have significant employee ownership today, with 10 million employees, about 10 percent of the private workforce. About 25 percent of these are in the manufacturing sector.[6] The most widespread system of employee-ownership is the Employee Stock Ownership Plan (ESOP). ESOPs are not true cooperatives. Employee ownership is a shareholding system, differing from a standard corporation only in that it includes a method to allow employees to become owners of the business through company stock invested in their retirement plans. As in any corporation, shareholders have as many votes as shares. Most ESOPs are not majority-owned by their workers. Few ESOPs have employees on their board of directors. Not all the workers are necessarily stockholders. Workers cannot sell their stocks, and get profits from any gains in the value of the stock only in retirement benefits. Stock earnings over the years of the employee's tenure are not accessible until retirement.[7] In the great majority of ESOPs, workers have not become significantly empowered. Only a few majority-owned ESOPs have done any workplace reorganization to increase democratic input by employees. In these situations, workers have gained some power in electing managers, and in creating good salaries, job security, safe working conditions, and side benefits.

A typical ESOP firm on this scheme is McKeesport Steel Casting, in Pennsylvania, set up in the late 1970s. To provide employees with enough capital to buy the stock, 25 percent of salaries went into a trust, which borrowed money to buy the stock; the stock was transferred to a retirement fund in the name of each employee; workers could not draw proceeds for at least ten years, and not then unless all debts of the company were paid.[8] Other examples of that time period are Yellow Cab in San Francisco; South Bend Lathe, in Indiana; Saratoga Knitting Mills and Herkimer Woodworking in New York; and the Vermont Asbestos Group. Most of these were taken over by their workers after shutdowns, or after long strikes.[9]

When the largest taxi company in San Francisco, Yellow Cab, went bankrupt in 1977, the workers organized a cooperative to take it over. After long negotiations with banks for financing, it was set up under an Employee Stock Ownership Plan, but with much of the control relinquished to the bankers. By 1980, fewer than half of the workers were co-op members and only about one out of four workers owned stock.[10]

It has not been easy to get banks to finance even the moderate ESOP system. The community of Youngstown, Ohio, for example, tried to take over the shutdown Youngstown Sheet and Tube steel company in the late 1970s, the largest enterprise in the city, as a worker-community joint enterprise, but the bankers refused adequate funding.[11]

However, the Carter administration sometimes attempted to facilitate ESOPs, and in a few instances induced government agencies such as the Farmers Home Administration and the Urban Development Grant Program to help with loans. In this way, employee-owned Bates Fabric in Maine and Rath Packing in Iowa were set up.[12]

The government wrote ESOP advantages into the tax code in 1984, making ESOP financing somewhat more viable.[13]

INDUSTRIAL COOPERATIVE ASSOCIATION

The Industrial Cooperative Association was formed in 1978 in Boston to develop worker-owned-and-controlled cooperatives on a model of self-management. A nonprofit, the Industrial Cooperative Association expanded the concept to include community-owned businesses and ESOPs.[14]

The Industrial Cooperative Association defined an industrial worker cooperative as self-governing, with one vote per member-worker, and based on the principle that all workers should receive the fruits of their labor within the framework of social and community responsibility for the resources used. It made an exception to all-worker-ownership with retail stores, for which it supported the option of the decision-making structure extending to community representation.[15] With ICA's guidance, the workers took over the shutdown Colonial Press in Clinton, Massachusetts in 1978, and transformed it into the first true large industrial cooperative formed in the United States in twenty years. The following year, the Industrial Cooperative Association helped the workers of International

Poultry in Willimantic, Connecticut, to become the next. In collaboration with a neighborhood Community Development Corporation in Dorchester, they transformed a shutdown supermarket into a community-worker cooperative, with each group having 50 percent control. The Industrial Cooperative Association continued its work in the following decades.[16]

FARMER CO-OPS IN THE 70s

The Capper-Volstead Act of 1922 encouraged the growth of ever-larger farm cooperatives, which continued to merge into multistate and national federations. By 1950, most independent local cooperatives were in federations.[17] These federations and the larger cooperatives embarked on significant business ventures. Cooperatives expanded services in processing, warehousing and transportation. There were 8,100 farmer co-ops with 7.6 million more members in 1955.[18] By the 1960s, the growth of large agricultural cooperatives through constant mergers was well underway. For cooperatives such as Land O'Lakes, Ocean Spray, Welch's, and Sun-Maid, vertical integration became achievable from production to grocery shelf. Meanwhile, the number of small farms was still falling precipitously in the 1960s and 1970s, despite the efforts of the Farmers Union and the Grange. Both of these progressive small farmer organizations remained active.

By 1979, there were only 7,500 farmer cooperatives with fewer than 6 million members. Despite these setbacks, cooperatives did about a third of the total farm production and marketing in the United States in 1980.[19]

There were some success stories during this period, such as the Cooperativa Central, down in the California Central Valley near Salinas, made up of seventy-five Chicano families, many of them former farmworkers displaced by mechanization. The Cooperativa looked to the United Farm Workers union as a source from which it sprang. Begun in 1973 as a semi-cooperative organization marketing strawberries, the Cooperative had become California's largest farm production cooperative by 1980, with a large, collectively worked, diversified vegetable farm.[20]

The number of small farms shrank continually through the 20th century, although the population multiplied almost six times. There were fewer freeholding farmers in 1980 than a hundred years before.[21] Most rural people were no longer independent farmers, but wage earners, part of a fast-growing "rural proletariat." The agricultural Banks for Cooperatives, originally set up with government seed money from the New Deal, was helpful to some, but the smallest farmers were still continually driven off their land, while agribusiness reorganized farming to suit themselves.[22]

Still, the major farm organizations remained connected with cooperatives. Besides the National Farmers Union and the Grange, the National Farmers Organization, the United States Farmers Association, and the American Agricultural Movement, were all fairly progressive organizations. The National Farmers Organization was formed in the 1960s, handling collection, dispatch, and delivery services nationwide for grain, livestock, milk, and other products.[23] The Grange had a resurgence beginning in the 1950s, and by the end of the century had 300,000 members, providing services to agricultural and rural communities in 3,600 locales in 37 states.[24] The Grange still supports cooperatives for economic development and education in order to strengthen and preserve a sustainable life in rural America.

Aligned against the small farmer organizations remained the American Farm Bureau Federation (AFBF), still serving to pave the way for agribusiness.[25] The Farm Bureau was much larger than the other organizations, due mainly to the side benefits it offered through the support of bankers. AFBF remained acceptable to corporate America because it was a big corporation run by a giant managerial bureaucracy far above its average members. The same was true of large agricultural cooperatives such as Sunkist and Farmland, seven of which were listed among the "top 500" corporations. In the 70s, huge Midwestern dairy co-ops were exposed giving enormous bribes to the Nixon administration.[26] Business cooperativism ultimately served corporate interest.

FARMER-UNION ALLIANCE

Two nationwide strikes began in December 1978, one by small farmers of the recently-founded American Agriculture Movement (AAM), the other by bituminous coal miners of the United Mine Workers of America (UMW). The primary issue for the farmers was saving the family farm; for the miners, it was the right to strike over local conditions.

The farmers' strike meant that they would stop planting, selling produce and buying supplies until government came to their support. The previous year had seen a drastic drop in farm income, and many small farmers were in danger of losing their land. The AAM demanded that the government guarantee "parity" prices, high enough prices to produce a reasonable profit.[27]

The UMW strike became the longest miners' strike in American history, eliciting sporadic violence in several states. The Indiana governor called out the National Guard, and the Virginia governor declared a state of emergency.[28]

In March 1978, 250 striking small farmers of AAM left Campbell, Missouri, in a mile-long caravan of trucks, vans, and cars packed with food, and drove across the Mississippi River. The trucks were loaded with produce, meat, and canned foods collected from farmers in fourteen states. They were welcomed in Central City, Kentucky the next day by 7,000 striking bituminous coal miners belonging to United Mine Workers of America, whose food stamps had been cut off. The farmers distributed the food to the miner families at the county fair grounds. Many of the miners came from farm families or had once been farmers.[29]

A *New York Times* story quoted miner Rondal Staples, as his wife, Diane, stood nearby holding a ten-pound bag of flour a farmer had just given her, "We came off the farm and went to coal mining because of this 100 per cent parity that the farmers are trying to get today... It's all labor organizing and we need to support each other."[30]

Thus the traditional mutual-aid alliance between farmers and unions was renewed once again.

The day after the rally, President Carter declared a national emergency, invoked the Taft-Hartley Act, and ordered the miners back to work, but they ignored the injunction.[31] The following week, 30,000 AAM farmers marched down Pennsylvania Avenue in a "tractorcade" to the Capital demanding higher price supports. UMW and mine companies eventually reached a compromise; Congress passed and Carter signed an emergency farm bill.[32]

CONSUMER CO-OPS IN THE 1970s

In 1976, 48 million Americans—about 25 percent of the population—belonged to a cooperative. Most of were members of credit unions or utility cooperatives such as electrical or water.[33]

The 1970s were a time of both advance and retreat for consumer co-op food stores. Areas of concentration included Northern California (particularly the Bay Area), Baltimore-Washington, Minnesota, Wisconsin, Chicago, and Greater New York. The Berkeley Co-op was the largest in the United States, the flagship of American co-op supermarkets, followed by Greenbelt Cooperative in the District of Columbia.[34] But the movement was plagued by internal and external problems. Internally, the exigencies of running a grocery store often clashed with the commitment to democratic processes. Externally, huge chains increasingly dominated the industry with enormous stores that sold merchandise far beyond the traditional supermarket.[35] The larger co-ops attempted to keep pace with the increased giganticism of the industry, believing that they needed to grow ever larger to remain competitive. Some co-op leaders believed that part of their mission was continuous vertical centralized growth, as distinct from the horizontal growth of smaller autonomous co-ops.[36]

CREDIT UNIONS

The end of World War II brought a spurt of growth to the credit union movement. In 1945, there were 8,683 credit unions in the country. This almost doubled by 1955. By 1969, there were nearly 24,000 credit unions. The 1970s brought a wave of mergers of smaller credit unions into larger units. Meanwhile, the number of members soared to over forty-three million by the end of the decade, and up to eighty-two million in 2004.[37]

CO-OP HOUSING AND URBAN HOMESTEADING

A number of housing co-ops were built in the Bay Area in this period, the largest being St. Francis Square in San Francisco, founded in 1964 by the International Longshore and Warehousemen's Union with 297 units for low- to moderate-income people.[38] In New York, Co-op City was built at around the same time in the Bronx, and became the largest cooperative housing development in the United States, with 60,000 residents and many cooperative services. It was also the scene of a prolonged struggle between tenant groups and management.[39] Many other housing co-ops were constructed around the country in this period; outside the New York City area, almost all were financed in part through the US Department of Housing and Urban Development (HUD).[40]

In the mid-1960s, many New York landlords in low-income neighborhoods abandoned their apartment buildings because they considered them not profitable enough, averaging 38,000 abandoned units a year in the late '60s.[41] The city foreclosed for non-payment of taxes and serious code violations, and assumed ownership as "landlord of last resort." In 1969, a group of mainly Puerto Rican neighbors on East 102nd Street in Manhattan took over two buildings by direct action and started rehabilitating them through sweat equity as cooperatives.[42] This touched off a direct action tenant movement in other neighborhoods. In 1970, groups of squatters took over vacant buildings on West 15th, 111th, and 122nd streets, and along Columbus Avenue around 87th Street, proclaiming the community's right to possession of a place to live.[43] The city reacted by evicting most of the squatters, but public outcry resulted in community organizations being granted management control of some of the buildings for rehabilitation by the tenants themselves. Several cooperative development nonprofits were formed including the Urban Homestead Assistance Board (UHAB), which became the most effective organization. In 1973, 286 buildings were slated for urban homesteading, but funding obstacles undercut their efforts. Forty-eight of these buildings were actually completed as homesteaded, low-income, limited-equity co-ops.[44]

NATIONAL COOPERATIVE BANK

In 1978, under the administration of US President Jimmy Carter and at the instigation of the Cooperative League and many other organizations, Congress set up the National Consumer Cooperative Bank (NCB), stating that:

> The Congress finds that user-owned cooperatives are a proven method for broadening ownership and control of market participants, narrowing price spreads, raising the quality of goods and services available to their membership and building bridges between producers and consumers and their members and patrons. The Congress also finds that consumer and other types of self-help cooperatives have been impaired in their formation and growth by lack of access to adequate cooperative credit facilities and lack of technical assistance. Therefore the Congress finds the need for the establishment of a National Consumer Cooperative Bank which will make available necessary financial and technical assistance to cooperative self-help endeavors as a means of strengthening the nation's economy. [45]

Started with government seed money, the plan was for NCB to become independent, following the pattern set by the agricultural Banks for Cooperatives. Through NCB, capital would be far more easily available to help cooperatives get started and to help existing ones get through difficult times. There were provisions that at least 60 percent of loans would go to consumer co-ops, no more than 30 percent to housing cooperatives, and no more than 10 percent to producer cooperatives. The bank was to try to make 35 percent of all loans go to low-income cooperatives or cooperatives primarily serving low-income people.[46] Congress also set up an Office of Self-Help Development and Technical Assistance to provide information and technical help. This included producer (artisan and craft) marketing co-ops.[47]

But almost as soon as the bank's door opened, the incoming Reagan administration wanted to shut it down. The bank's many friends rallied around, stood firm and kept it alive, but with much less funding.[48]

A 1979 SNAPSHOT

The Cooperative League remained the main educational, coordinating, and lobbying organization of the cooperative movement. Its members included consumer stores, and farm supply, housing and insurance cooperatives, and it was also supported by credit unions, health, and rural electric cooperatives. The League represented the US in the International Cooperative Alliance, attached to the United Nations, with a membership of cooperatives from most countries in the world.[49]

According to Cooperative League statistics, one out of four Americans belonged to a cooperative in 1979. About 6 million of them were members of farmer cooperatives; 1 million belonged to consumer goods cooperatives (with 900 stores); 40,000 were members of handicraft co-ops; 5.6 million belonged to health care, 9 million to rural electric, 1 million to rural telephone, 1.5 million to housing, 40 million to credit unions, and many more to service cooperatives such as childcare, auto repair, insurance, cable TV, legal services, funeral, optical care, and student services.[50]

There were probably some 750 to 1,000 small worker and producer cooperatives and collectives in 1979, most of them averaging fewer than fifteen members. There were also a few larger groups, including the 18 plywood co-ops with between 80 and 350 members, and the Hoedads reforestation co-op with about 300 members. In total, there were probably some 17,000 members of worker cooperatives in America in 1979. This was a peak, followed by a precipitous crash in the Reagan era. Only a small fraction remained by 1989.[51]

14.
Surviving: From the 80s through the Millennium

Reagan era economics meant aggressive capitalism and intense competition. In the summer of Reagan's first year, 1981, the country plunged into the worst recession since the Great Depression, peaking in 1982 with 10.8 percent unemployment.[1] Reagan's response was to throw big tax cuts to corporations and the wealthy, severely reduce government regulations, cut back government spending for social programs, and infuse massive amounts of money into military contracts. This brought enormous profits to the wealthy, escalated the arms race to a feverish pitch, and almost tripled the national debt. It produced overall growth in the economy, but this prosperity was not shared beyond a narrow elite.[2] The "me decade" intensely fostered an extreme individualism, with fabulous rewards for the few at the top. To working families, it dangled promises of "trickle down" benefits that almost never arrived. For small businesses, the environment of ruthless competition meant a high casualty rate. Cooperatives were among the numerous small businesses that failed not only in the US but around the world.

As the generation of the counterculture aged, it merged with the general population. The competitive climate engulfed and bankrupted many of the most successful of the worker collectives. Some groups self-destructed. In those years, few new collectives or cooperatives were being formed. The InterCollective disbanded in 1986.[3]

The 1980s were also generally disastrous for consumer co-op supermarkets in the US. As the decade progressed, most of the larger co-ops found themselves in increasingly dire financial straits, and cut back, closing many stores. By the end of the decade, the Berkeley Co-op had closed, Greenbelt was closing stores, and the cooperative supermarket movement was in full retreat. But the collapse of the larger supermarkets did not mean that the entire co-op food store movement collapsed. Many of the smaller natural food store cooperatives continued to thrive, and became the most common form of food cooperative in America.[4]

The decade of the 1990s opened with a few worker cooperatives celebrating several decades of existence on a terrain devoid of start-ups. But as the 90s progressed, the heritage of the 60s and 70s, the last period of growth for cooperatives, provided fertile soil for a new generation.

New worker cooperatives took shape here and there in the early 1990s. Some established groups, such as the Cheeseboard collective in Berkeley, aided in replicating their economic success in other communities. Perhaps the most significant developments in the early 90s were the linkages formed between co-ops on a regional basis, in the Northeast, the Northwest, and Northern California. In the San Francisco Bay Area, home to the highest concentration of worker co-ops in the country, almost thirty groups organized into the Network of Bay Area Worker Cooperatives (NOBAWC).[5]

The rise of new technologies, in both electronics and energy, gave impetus to cooperative development. Programmers, Web designers, and digital support staff explored cooperative arrangements. The Linux operating system developed as a collaborative effort from the start so that it could be the best system available, unencumbered by proprietary enclosures.[6] As the old energy technologies increasingly presented untenable futures due to environmental degradation and resource depletion, small ventures in alternative energy technologies arose in the solar, wind, and bio-fuels areas.[7] Bicycle culture all over the country became linked with cooperatives, from engineering and manufacturing facilities like Burley Design in Oregon, to maintenance and retail outlets, and messenger services in urban complexes.[8]

A significant advance that some cooperatives adopted was the training of members in basic skills of democratic group processes. Most Americans have had very limited personal experience with these skills due to the utter disconnect between the promotion of American democracy as exemplary, and the reality of its absence in almost every facet of American economic and daily life. Cooperatives have learned to bridge this gap and open up a world of possibilities to people.

The success of Mondragon, the cooperative industrial complex in the Basque region of Spain, demonstrated how economic enterprises of a very high order of technical competency and coordination can function democratically. In the 80s, information about Mondragon was increasingly disseminated in America, inspiring cooperatives here as around the world, and contributing to a renaissance of thinking about economic development.

Meanwhile, the Reagan program continued, promoting corporate consolidation and mergers, privatization of public services, deregulation of corporations from governmental restraints, offshoring of industries, and weakening of unions. Reagan's economics forced cooperatives and unions to struggle for survival. Since the late 19th century, and particularly since the New Deal, the federal government had been a moderating counterbalance between profits and social welfare, but now government used its power primarily to leverage maximum private profits.

While social and environmental responsibilities have always been integral to the cooperative structure and vision, they have been largely absent from the corporate agenda. During the 1980s and 90s, the American public became increasingly sensitive to antisocial and anti-environmental corporate practices. Nongovernmental organizations (NGOs), regulatory agencies, organized socially conscious shareholders, and ethical investments advocates had some successes fighting these practices. Some corporations established offices of corporate responsibility to analyze their practices and report to shareholders, and a few actually took constructive measures.

GLOBAL CONTEXT AND GLOBALIZATION

Since the age of colonialism, the European powers competed for control of world resources, each through its own national corporate capitalist system. The challenge of socialism changed that dynamic. In the decades after World War II, both the American and Soviet governments courted emerging nations with the promise of the superiority of their respective economic systems. Capitalism and socialism were both touted as best able to promote prosperity and social justice. The competition of course ended suddenly with the collapse of the Soviet Union in 1991. The consequent globalization of unchallenged capitalism proceeded at a breakneck pace. The capitalist system now aimed directly at almost every spot on earth, with the goal of capturing raw materials, cheap labor and national markets worldwide. In many places, globalization meant the replacement of self-sufficient local economies with sweatshops, privatized essential services, increased poverty, mono-crop agriculture, environmental destruction, and a precarious dependency on the international market.

In America, globalization meant deindustrialization and the importation of products cheaply produced abroad and sold in malls and mega-stores. Approaching the 21st century, American communities faced the disappearance of good paying blue collar jobs, replaced at best by low-paying service industry employment. Civic life was plucked from the heart of towns and cities, and deposited in malls, with many old city centers becoming ghost towns or, in more fortunate cases, historic districts with upscale boutiques.

Some American communities fought back to protect their local economies, for example, by organizing to halt mega-store expansion plans. A profound distrust of corporations runs deep in the American consciousness. The most far-reaching resistance struck at the very heart of the corporation: its charter. Licking and Porter townships in Pennsylvania adopted ordinances that eliminated a corporation's ability to claim any constitutional rights as a "person." They then revoked corporate charters on the grounds of the constitutional right of local governments to protect health, safety, family farms, and the environment.[9] Another positive direction was indicated by several Midwest towns, which invested in community economic ventures to re-circulate wealth locally and keep jobs.[10]

A grassroots economic response to globalization began to emerge in many locales around the world, by people organizing into worker, artisan, farmer, and community cooperatives. In 1994, the Zapatista uprising in Southern Mexico spectacularly brought grassroots opposition to globalism to the world's attention. Landless peasant movements in Brazil, Peru, India, the Philippines, and elsewhere, adopted an ethic and strategy of community-based economic democracy. Argentina's economic collapse at the hands of the World Bank and International Monetary Fund inspired peasant land seizures and the reclaiming of 200 self-managed workplaces.[11] Worker and peasant occupations of under-utilized land and abandoned factories multiplied in Brazil, Venezuela, and other locations. One of the central goals of this anti-globalization opposition has been to supplant "free trade" with a system of "fair trade" based on the concept of people before profit. Since cooperatives reflect and incorporate the values of economic and social justice, they inevitably became one of the strategies and goals of the movement.

The annual World Social Forums support the development of a social economy as an alternative to globalization, an economy from the bottom up that provides for people's needs instead of one from the top down that marginalizes those who don't fit in. The social economy concept has had great success in parts of Europe and in Quebec as a superior alternative to privatization of social services. Social co-ops incorporate both the workers and the community in democratically managed firms providing services in health care, education, recycling, and other socially responsible areas. They are initially funded in part with public monies, and in part from bonds, foundations, or clients. The social co-ops in the Emilia-Romagna area of Italy are particularly renowned, and the social economy sector (including cooperatives) in Quebec employs an estimated 100,000 workers.

COMMUNITY ECONOMIC DEVELOPMENT

In the US, in response to the increasing threat of community dissolution from debilitating economic forces, and no longer hoping for significant help from the government, some progressive social activists in the Community Economic Development (CED) sector took a fresh look at worker cooperatives as a possible means of creating sustainable healthy communities. In the Bay Area, Women's Action to Gain Economic Security (WAGES), a development group that created several toxic-free house-cleaning co-ops, has been a successful example of this model.[12] Another successful social co-op is Cooperative Home Care Associates in New York City, founded in 1987, today a 500-strong self-managed agency.[13] This approach has nonprofits developing businesses in trust for the workforce, avoiding the pitfalls facing workers with little business experience, and transitioning to worker ownership over time. Members of a community worker co-op are committed to their enterprise because it belongs to them. While there may be substantial capital investments in the co-op on the part of the members, these are made not for speculative purposes, but for security, like money in a bank. Rooted in a community, they provide decent jobs and vital services.

ESOPs OR WORKER COOPERATIVES?

In 1984, Congress provided tax incentives to owners of businesses that sell their companies to their workers in the form of a cooperative or an ESOP (Employee Stock Ownership Plan). This measure has led to the creation of thousands of ESOPs, but until now to no worker cooperatives, because of organizational complications. Conversion to an ESOP is costly, particularly for a smaller firm. Under federal law, ESOPs must comply with complex requirements and regulations, and the costs involved are a deterrent for small business owners to sell through an ESOP. But research by the Ohio Employee Ownership Center suggests a more favorable financial arrangement for many small businesses might be selling the company to their workers as a cooperative rather than an ESOP, because the seller can defer capital gains. Special regulations of retirement plans apply to ESOPs but not to worker cooperatives, making the latter less expensive to establish and maintain.[14]

URBAN HOMESTEADING

Other community activists focused successfully on limited-equity co-op housing. In the 1980s, tenant groups in New York City led many squats, renewing the direct action movement of the previous decade by taking over abandoned buildings (illegally at first) and rehabilitating them. By 1981, the city had become the owner by foreclosure of about 8,000 buildings with around 112,000 apartments; 34,000 of the units still occupied.[15] At the urging of housing activist groups, particularly the nonprofit Urban Homestead Assistance Board (UHAB), the city instituted urban homesteading programs to legally sell the buildings to their tenants for sweat equity and a token payment, with a neighborhood organization or a nonprofit development organization often becoming manager during rehabilitation. By 1984, 115 buildings had been bought as limited-equity tenant co-ops under the Tenant Interim Lease Program, with another 92 in process.[16] UHAB provided them technical assistance, management training and all-around support. Autonomous groups of squatters continued to take over buildings in New York in the 1990s, with an estimated 500 to 1,000 squatters in 32 buildings on the Lower East Side alone. Hundreds of Latino factory workers and their families squatted in the South Bronx.[17] The city's response changed with the political winds. Some city administrations curtailed the homestead program and evicted many of the squats, but some squatter groups successfully resisted eviction. The city renewed its support of tenant homesteading in the 90s, and over 27,000 New York families were living in homesteaded low-income co-ops by 2002.[18] Over the last 30 years, UHAB has worked to successfully transform over 1,300 buildings into limited equity co-ops, and 42 more buildings containing 1,264 units are currently in their pipeline, most of them in Harlem and the Lower East Side.[19]

INFRASTRUCTURE OF THE MOVEMENT TODAY

US FEDERATION OF WORKER COOPERATIVES

Established in 2004 by over 115 representatives from around the country, the US Federation of Worker Cooperatives (USFWC) is the result of many years of organizing at local and regional levels. At the founding conference in Minneapolis the Federation set goals and elected a board of directors representing four regions of the country and some at-large members. Its members have joined the international worker cooperative organization CICOPA, and are currently exploring joint health insurance plans, retirement funds, educational resources, a national database, and a development fund. The founding board includes members of SACCO (Southern Appalachian Center for Cooperative Ownership, in North Carolina), People's Co-op (Portland), GEO collective (Washington, DC), Arise Bookstore & Resource Center (Minneapolis), Blue Moon Café (Asheville), People's Grocery (Oakland), Rainbow Grocery (San Francisco), Green Worker Cooperatives (Bronx), Seward Community Café (Minneapolis), and the Federation of Southern Cooperatives (Epes, Alabama).[20] Affiliated with USFWC are the Eastern Conference for Workplace Democracy (ECWD) and the Western Worker Cooperative Conference (WWCC), nonprofit cooperative organizations established to aid and develop worker-owned enterprises and the workplace democracy movement regionally and nationally. Both hold biannual conferences bringing together worker-owners, employees of democratically run ESOPs, support organizations, and others interested in the workplace democracy.[21] Other federation partners are the Federation of Workplace Democracies in Minnesota, and the Association of Arizmendi Cooperatives in the Bay Area.

NETWORK OF BAY AREA WORKER COOPERATIVES

Founded in 1994, NOBAWC (pronounced "NoBOSS") grew out of monthly meetings between several Bay Area groups to discuss their experiences and common problems. A USFCW federation partner today, NOBAWC's mission is to encourage information and resource sharing among worker co-ops, and to build a movement for worker self-management. In 2005, it transformed from an all-volunteer group to a dues-paying membership organization of over thirty diverse self-managed workplaces located mostly in Oakland, San Francisco, and Berkeley, some in business over twenty years. Its member groups include manufacturing, retail, and volunteer groups. NOBAWC has published a facilitating guide for new cooperatives, instituted a 10 percent discount for members at each other's cooperatives, and organized conferences to address issues in depth.[22]

THE VALLEY ALLIANCE OF WORKER COOPERATIVES (VAWC)

VAWC started in 2005 to facilitate the growth and development of worker-owned cooperatives and a local sustainable economy in the Pioneer Valley of Western Massachusetts and Southern Vermont, with the goal of focusing on low-income and minority communities. A federation partner of USFWC today, VAWC consists of ten member cooperatives in Brattleboro, Putney, Amherst, Florence, Greenfield, Belchertown, Northampton, and Haydenville. Its operations include a yarn spinnery, renewable energy system installations, Internet hosting, natural skin care products, bike delivery and hauling service, auto parts sales, technology, copy shops, nonprofit fundraising, and home improvements.[23]

COOPERATIVE DEVELOPERS

Organizations that are dedicated to developing and funding cooperatives and social enterprises include Northcountry Cooperative Development Fund (MN), Cooperative Development Institute (MA), Green Worker Cooperatives (NY), Interfaith Business Builders (OH), and the Cooperative Fund of New England.[24]

INDUSTRIAL COOPERATIVE ASSOCIATION

ICA continues to develop worker co-ops, community-owned businesses, and Employee Stock Ownership Plans. In the 90s, the Association focused on community-based enterprises, and in the past decade its members have created or saved an estimated 7,000 jobs in 51 diverse companies. ICA has helped form cooperatives in new immigrant low-income neighborhoods, including an office cleaning company in Dorchester, in collaboration with Viet-AID, a Vietnamese-American community center. Overall, its members have helped form twenty startup worker cooperatives, twelve buyouts by workers, and eleven employee stock ownership conversions.[25]

CENTERS FOR COOPERATIVES

These university-based organizations have been vital sources of research and teaching. The first and largest was founded 1962 at the University of Wisconsin. It was joined by centers at Kansas State University in 1984, at the University of California at Davis in 1987, and at North Dakota State University in 1994. While North Dakota and Kansas were focused on agriculture, Wisconsin and Davis cast their nets more broadly over the entire range of cooperatives. When marketing, housing, and financial co-ops languished, the longevity and linkages of worker cooperatives caught the attention of the Davis and Wisconsin centers in the '90s, and they increasingly included this previously neglected sector in their activities. Both of these centers along with co-op developers in the field began, for the first time, to provide assistance to cooperative ventures in immigrant and disenfranchised communities, particularly to the women of these communities. On the West Coast, home and office cleaning co-ops were formed, and on the East Coast home health-care groups started. Due to state budget cuts, the center at Davis closed in 2004. However, rural California cooperatives continued to be supported through a new Rural Cooperatives Center. New centers and programs that have opened recently are the Cooperative Enterprise Program at Cornell (Ithaca, New York), and the School of Community Economic Development at Southern New Hampshire University.[26]

NATIONAL COOPERATIVE BUSINESS ASSOCIATION

The Cooperative League (CL) changed its name in 1985 to the National Cooperative Business Association (NCBA). This underscored a change in focus away from education and toward business. It continues to use the name CLUSA in its international program. Originally CL excluded worker and agricultural marketing cooperatives, but today NCBA includes all types, urban and rural, and is the national voice for cooperatives internationally, although worker co-ops are still a very secondary focus. Its mission is "to develop, advance and protect cooperative enterprise."[27] Toward that end, members conduct programs of education, co-op development, communications, public policy, member services, and international development. They lobby for co-ops in Washington, and propose legislative and regulatory changes. NCBA is organized according to cooperative principles, with a membership open to all cooperatives and co-op associations. In 1991, NCBA successfully lobbied Congress to establish the Rural Cooperatives Development Grants program, creating a new source of funds. Today, NCBA helps new and existing rural cooperatives through a partnership with Cooperation-Works, a network of 17 rural co-op development centers which have helped develop 117 new cooperative businesses with over 27,000 members, and more than 1,700 new rural jobs. The NCBA Urban Cooperative Development Initiative for the inner cities "seeks to expand the role of cooperatives in creating economic opportunity through both self-help and legislative solutions." NCBA works closely with the Cooperative Development Foundation, a nonprofit promoting self-help, mutual aid, and economic and social development through cooperatives. In partnership with USAID, NCBA-CLUSA's International Program has served 3,500 co-ops and farmer associations in 79 countries in East Asia, Africa and Central America, managing over 200 long-term projects and over 1,000 short-term consultancies with an annual international development budget averaging $16 million. In 2005, there were twenty-five current projects operating in eighteen countries.[28]

COOPERATIVE GROCERS' INFORMATION NETWORK

Cooperative Grocers' Information Network (CGIN) was organized in 1997 "to strengthen all retail food cooperatives by creating community and facilitating the sharing and development of resources among members." A nonprofit cooperative, CGIN helps food co-ops to "maximize their collective resources and keep them, as independent groups, from being put at a competitive disadvantage." CGIN hosts several listserves, which facilitate discussion and research of topics of interest. The main listserve is a forum, open to anyone, where any issue related to food co-ops can be discussed. The other listserves are for special interest groups and staff, currently "membership and marketing," and "human resources." CGIN also has a "Resource Exchange," consisting of secured-access web pages that allow food co-ops to share information, ideas, and resources. CGIN has developed a "Livable Wage model" to help co-ops calculate the livable wage for their communities and the rate needed to be paid in wages by the co-op after factoring in key employee benefits. CGIN's web site includes job openings in food co-ops.[29]

NATIONAL COOPERATIVE BANK & COBANK

The National Consumer Cooperative Bank, now simply the National Cooperative Bank (NCB), organized and promoted by the Carter administration, officially opened for business in 1980, together with the connected Office of Self-Help (OSH), which was set up to provide startup and development aid to new cooperatives. In its first year, the bank originated almost $10 million in loans, mostly to natural food co-ops and several housing co-ops, including a university's student housing co-op. But in 1981, the incoming Reagan administration tried to cancel the bank's charter, then moved to privatize it, and to lever it away from its original mission. In 1985, the bank dropped the word "Consumer" from its name "to symbolize a transition from an organization in the public sector to a competitive market-oriented private financial institution."[30] The Office of Self-Help became the National Cooperative Bank Development Corporation. Today, NCB is owned and democratically controlled by the 1,800 cooperatives that are its member-stockholders, and has more than $1 billion in assets. Over the last two decades NCB has provided a broad range of financial services to co-ops, with a goal of "spurring economic growth and community development in urban and rural America."[31] Its focus has been housing, purchasing, ESOPs, grocery wholesalers, Alaska Native enterprises, community development corporations, nonprofit community-based health care, senior living, and mom-and-pop hardware stores. But there are very few worker cooperatives on NCB's client list. Instead, it has helped more business franchises and fast food chains like Best Western, Carpet One, Dunkin' Donuts, Church's Chicken, Popeye's, Togo's, Baskin-Robbins and A&W, all of which qualify as business cooperatives under its definitions.[32]

In a parallel development, the agricultural Banks for Cooperatives originally started by the New Deal, became CoBank, a cooperative whose customers are local, regional, and national agricultural cooperatives. Rural cooperative utilities use the National Rural Utilities Cooperative Finance Corporation, a nonprofit providing low-cost services to member utility co-op systems, most of which are of New Deal vintage.[33]

NATIONAL COUNCIL OF FARMER COOPERATIVES

NCFC, formed in 1929, still serves as the national representative and advocate for farmer cooperatives in Washington. NCFC has been instrumental in maintaining laws favorable to agricultural co-ops, in face of renewed corporate attacks. Still, in 1995 the number of farmer co-ops was down to 4,006 (about half of 2 decades previously), and the number of small farms continued to decline. There were some 3,400 agricultural co-ops in 2005, with membership still made up of a majority of America's 2 million farmers and ranchers. Co-ops continue to be indispensable today for the continued existence of small farms.[34]

ESOPs

Resources for ESOPS include the National Center for Employee Ownership in Oakland, the Vermont Employee Ownership Center, and the Ohio Employee Ownership Center (at Kent State University).[35]

NATIONAL ASSOCIATION OF HOUSING COOPERATIVES (NAHC)

Formed in 1960, NAHC is the only national organization representing and serving the nation's housing co-ops. It is a nonprofit federation made up of housing cooperatives, mutual associations, other resident-owned or controlled housing, housing organizations, and individuals promoting co-op housing. In the face of today's housing crisis, NAHC encourages cooperative homeownership as a better way to deal with large-scale single-family foreclosures and threatened foreclosures.[36]

THE NORTH AMERICAN STUDENTS OF COOPERATION (NASCO)

Since 1968, NASCO has provided education and technical assistance to help students, worker-owners and community members to organize and sustain cooperatives, particularly in affordable group equity co-op housing. NASCO works to educate the public in cooperative principles and practices, and promotes the community oriented cooperative movement.[37]

CICOPA

The International Organization of Industrial, Artisanal and Service Producers' Cooperatives (CICOPA) is the worker co-op branch of ICA, the International Cooperative Alliance (see below). The main mission of CICOPA is to represent worker cooperatives at the international level. CICOPA now has a membership of over fifty-seven organizations from thirty-nine countries. With globalization of the world economy, the numbers of worker cooperatives have increased in both industrialized and developing countries. Once considered marginal, worker cooperatives are now looked at by many in the international community as central to the hopes of economic progress in numerous communities around the world. In Europe alone, there has been a leap from 2,500 worker co-ops in 1980 to 85,000 today, with a membership of one and half million. Mondragon in Basque Spain alone employs over 66,000 people. In Italy, more than a quarter million members belong to worker-owned co-ops.[38]

INTERNATIONAL COOPERATIVE ALLIANCE

ICA is an independent, nongovernmental association with the mission of promoting and strengthening autonomous cooperatives throughout the world and in developing countries in particular. Today, about 750,000 cooperatives belong to ICA, with over 800 million members. Of that total, 182 million are in the Americas, 118 million in Europe, 9.5 million in Africa, and 414 million in Asia and Oceania.[39]

US GOVERNMENT & COOPERATIVES

The federal government continues to provide rural cooperatives with significant support, but still offers only minimal aid to worker and producer cooperatives, as it has done ever since the New Deal in the 1930s. Due in part to this supportive legal and regulatory environment, agricultural cooperatives in particular continue to be prominent in America. Federal and some state governments provide financial support, technical assistance, extension services, and some favorable legislation to cooperatives doing agricultural supply and marketing, rural electrification and telecommunications, community credit unions, housing, independent retailers, and local consumer services.[40]

US law exempts cooperatives from corporate income tax, since their business objectives are nonprofit, and they provide members with goods and services at cost. However, rebates or dividends to members are taxed as individual income. The Capper-Volstead Act continues to exempt agricultural cooperatives from monopoly legislation. The mission and mandate of the Department of Agriculture includes promoting and supporting existing and new cooperatives.

Its Rural Business and Cooperative Services division offers help from specialists in commodities, management, law, and regulation. The National Credit Union Administration is a regulatory body. The Rural Utilities Service finances the creation and expansion of rural electric cooperatives. The Farm Credit Administration provides a wide range of support to cooperative financial institutions.[41]

Internationally, the US assistance program has funded international cooperative development organizations since 1962. The Overseas Cooperative Development Act of 2000 expanded that mandate. In 2000, the government provided about $175 million to that program, promoting credit unions; agricultural supply, marketing, and processing cooperatives; rural electric and telecommunications cooperatives; insurance cooperatives; and community-based cooperatives that advance self-help housing, environmental improvements, and job creation.[42]

WORLD SOCIAL FORUM

Today, a worldwide network of grassroots movements struggles for social change and against globalized capitalism. Of key importance in this network is the World Social Forum (WSF), brought together annually since 2001. The WSF is

> an open meeting place where social movements, networks, NGOs (non-governmental organizations), and other civil society organizations opposed to neo-liberalism and a world dominated by capital or by any form of imperialism come together to pursue their thinking, to debate ideas democratically, to formulate proposals, share their experiences freely and network for effective action... It proposes to facilitate decentralized coordination and networking among organizations engaged in concrete action towards building another world, at any level from the local to the international.[43]

The WSF contests the idea that the globalization of capitalism is inevitable, and proclaims that Another World is Possible. It is "a permanent process of seeking and building alternatives," and aims to replace the globalization of capital with the globalization of solidarity. At the core of the WSF is a worldwide network of organizations whose goal is not profit but to make the world work for everyone through mutual aid, self-management, and cooperation.[44]

Fishing in Chesapeake Bay

Copper mining near Lake Superior

Indian town gardens in Virginia

Buffalo hunt,
Great Plains

NATIVE AMERICAN COOPERATION

Colonial industries

Community
harvest

Fire
fighters

EARLY SETTLER COOPERATION

Thomas Paine

Horace Greeley

THE TRIAL

OF THE

BOOT & SHOEMAKERS

OF PHILADELPHIA,

ON AN INDICTMENT

FOR A COMBINATION AND CONSPIRACY

TO RAISE THEIR WAGES.

TAKEN IN SHORT-HAND,
BY THOMAS LLOYD.

PHILADELPHIA:
PRINTED BY B. GRAVES, NO. 40, NORTH FOURTH-STREET,
FOR T. LLOYD, AND B. GRAVES.
1806.

Unions prosecuted as conspiracies

Working Man's Advocate.

NEW YORK:
SATURDAY, OCTOBER 31, 1829.

WORKING MEN'S TICKET.
ASSEMBLY.
ALEXANDER MING, senior, Printer,
FREDERICK FRIEND, Brass Founder,
THOMAS SKIDMORE, Machinist.
CORNELIUS C. BLATCHLEY, Physician.
ROBERT M. KERRISON, Whitesmith,
ALDEN POTTER, Machinist.
AMOS WILLIAMSON, Carpenter.
EBENEZER WHITING, Cooper.
SIMON CLANNON, Painter.
EBENEZER FORD, Carpenter.
BENJAMIN MOTT, Grocer.
SENATE.
SILAS WOOD, of Suffolk.
EDWARD J. WEBB, of New York.

PROSPECTUS.
In issuing the first number of our paper
without first circulating a prospectus, we
have departed from long established custom;
but we imagine that neither our readers nor
ourselves will suffer any inconvenience from

Worker protest, New York, 1837

WORKERS' EMERGING STRUGGLES

Mill and factory workers

FREE SOIL,
FREE LABOR, FREE SPEECH,
AND
Free Men.

The Democrats of Berkshire, and all others, who are in favor of maintaining Freedom in the Free Territories of this Union, and preserving the dignity, and the rights of free labor, are requested to assemble at Stockbridge, on the fourth day of July next at 3 o'clock in the afternoon.

Mr. CHAPMAN, of Wisconsin, Mr. D. D. Field, of New York, and Mr. Fitch of Sheffield, and other Democrats, will address the meeting.

Gershom M. Fitch,   B. Palmer,
F. O. Sayles,   R. F. Barnard,
Charles Sedgwick,   J. E. Field,
John C. Wolcolt,   L. C. Thayer,
John R. Bulkley,   William O. Curtis,
James S. Davis,   Harvey Holmes,
F. Eddy,   Benjamin Coles,
Marshal Warner,   H. J Bliss,
William Darbe,   D. B. Fenn.

Anti-slavery poster

Working Men, Attention!!

It is your imperious duty to drop your *Hammers and Sledges!* one and all, to your post repair, *THIS AFTERNOON,* at *FIVE* o'clock P. M. and attend the

GREAT MEETING

called by the papers of this morning, to be held at the *CITY HALL,* then and there to co-operate with such as have the GREAT GOOD OF ALL THEIR *FELLOW CITIZENS at Heart.* Your liberty! yea, your *LABOUR!!* is the subject of the call: who that values the services of HEROES of the *Revolution* whose blood achieved our Independence as a Nation, will for a moment doubt he owes a few hours this afternoon to his wife and children?

HANCOCK.

Union card

Working Men's ticket

BEGINNING OF INDUSTRIALIZATION

National Labor Union: Frederick Douglass, William Sylvis, Isaac Myers

NLU Boot & Shoe Cooperative

Thomas Phillips, IWA
& Union Cooperative Assn.

Victoria Woodhull, IWA leader
in New York, demands to vote

International Working Men's
Association membership card

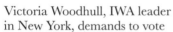

IWA & NATIONAL LABOR UNION

Oliver Kelly

"Ceres" Adams

John Trimble

The Grange awakening the sleepers, 1873

Sovereigns & Grange publications

Grange rally

NATIONAL GRANGE

Uriah Stephans

Terence Powderly

Frank J. Ferrell

Leonora Barry

Barrel label

Victor Drury
Solidarity Cooperatives

Joseph Buchanan
Great Soutwest RR strike :

KNIGHTS OF LABOR

Farmers Alliance flag

Posters

Tom Watson   C. W. Macune   H. S. Doyle   Mary E. Lease

Alliance parade

Farmers Alliancemen

FARMERS ALLIANCE & POPULISM

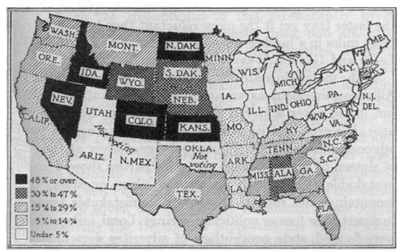

The vote for Weaver, Populist Party, 1892

James Weaver
for president
1862

William Jennings Bryan
literally on the stump
1896

POPULISM

Debs button

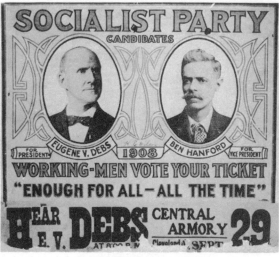

Gene Debs for president

Edward Bellamy,
author of *Looking Backward*

Farmer-Labor Party
Minnesota, 1920

Victor Berger, Socialist Party
US Congressman, Milwaukee

Non-Partisan League rally, North Dakota

RADICAL POLITICS

"Mother" Jones   Gene Debs   "Big" Bill Haywood

Daniel De Leon

Industrial Workers of the World

S.T.L.A. membership certificate

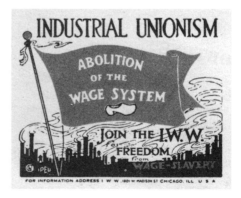

INDUSTRIAL UNIONISM

Carl Rhodehamel, U.X.A.

Unemployed Exchange Association
outpost in Oroville, CA

Upton Sinclair, E.P.I.C.

Unemployed Citizens
League Commisary
Unit 239
Santa Monica, CA

SELF-HELP IN THE GREAT DEPRESSION

Farmers Union
Co-op Creamery,
Oregon, 1935

Co-op cannery, Orange County

Southern Tenant Farmers' Union

Cooperative quilting, Los Angeles

Pacific Cooperative League, Berkeley

COOPERATIVES IN THE DEPRESSION

James Warbasse

Albert Sonnichsen

Berkeley Co-op, c. 1938
1715 University Avenue

Grange co-op store, c. 1950
Cadmus, KS, founded 1876

Berkeley Co-op Flea Market, c. 1970

International Cooperative Alliance,
Basel, Switzerland, 1921

Dos Palos Rochdale Company, CA
Labor Exchange, Branch No. 135,
founded 1899

CONSUMER COOPERATION

Cambridge Bike Repair Collective, c. 1975

Uprisings Bakery, Berkeley, 1975

Panther Free Breakfast Survival Program, c. 1974

Jamaica Plain Food Co-op, c. 1975

Taxi Unlimited, Berkeley, 1965

Bay Warehouse Print Shop, 1973

David Food Co-op, 1972

Diggers, 1967-68

Newspaper, SF, 1970

SF, 1978

COLLECTIVITY IN THE SIXTIES & SEVENTIES

Food System workers
at the Peoples Bicentennial, 1976

Women's Center Newsletter, 1982

Food System Newsletter, 1976

InterCollective conference, 1981

Collective Networker, 1982

Heartwood Cooperative Woodshop, 1974

COLLECTIVITY IN THE SEVENTIES & EIGHTIES

A. J. Wayland, Robert Owen, Albert Brisbane, George Ripley

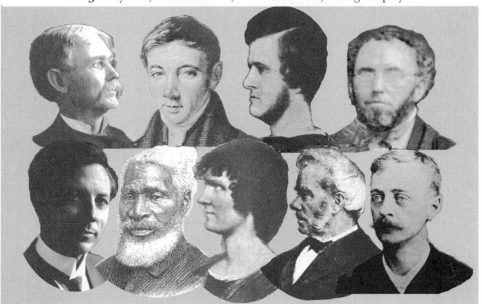

Job Harriman, Josiah Henson, Frances Wright, Josiah Warren, Burnette Haskell

New Harmony, 1825

Brook Farm, 1841

Nashoba, 1826

Communalist publications

COMMUNALISM

Kaweah, 1886

Equality, 1897

Llamo del Rio, 1914

Drop City, 1966

INTENTIONAL COMMUNITIES

Penn-Craft, PA
subsistence homestead

Mountaineer Craftsman Co-op
Arthurdale, WV
homestead community

Norvelt, PA
subsistence homestead

Westmoreland
Homesteads, PA

NEW DEAL COMMUNITIES

2

COMMUNALISM

In the future days, which we seek to make secure, we look forward to a world founded upon four essential human freedoms. The first is freedom of speech and expression—everywhere in the world. The second is freedom of every person to worship God in his own way—everywhere in the world. The third is freedom from want—which, translated into world terms, means economic understandings which will secure to every nation a healthy peacetime life for its inhabitants—everywhere in the world. The fourth is freedom from fear—which, translated into world terms, means a world-wide reduction of armaments to such a point and in such a thorough fashion that no nation will be in a position to commit an act of physical aggression against any neighbor—anywhere in the world. That is no vision of a distant millennium. It is a definite basis for a kind of world attainable in our own time and generation... Since the beginning of our American history, we have been engaged in change—in a perpetual peaceful revolution—a revolution which goes on steadily, quietly adjusting itself to changing conditions... Freedom means the supremacy of human rights everywhere. Our support goes to those who struggle to gain those rights or keep them. Our strength is our unity of purpose. To that high concept there can be no end save victory.[1]

—Franklin D. Roosevelt, January 6, 1941

15.
Cooperatives & Communalism

The communalist and cooperative movements have shared a long intertwined history in America. Many of their leaders have played important roles in both. The history of one cannot be clearly understood without a study of the other. Both are movements for social justice and personal liberation. Both offer very practical benefits to participants, and make that the core of a broad social justice mission. While cooperatives are limited to particular functions, however, communalism invites members to join in more intensive and inclusive ways.

Communalism is a recurring social movement that touches a nerve near the center of the early American experience. Indeed, the notion of a group of idealistic like-minded people breaking away and emigrating to a frontier to form a community where they could live as freely as they choose and create the society of their dreams resonates closely with the mythology of American history. These ideas are functionally identical to many of the motivations behind the Declaration of Independence. The very concept of the federal system embodies the idea of states being places where populations could choose to live in different ways, and at the same time serve as testing grounds for social constructs that might have wider applications. One study counted 281 intentional communes founded in America between 1683 and 1937.[2] These formed the fertile soil in which the thousands of intentional communities of the 1960s and 70s sprang up.[3]

Communalism offers groups the opportunity to experiment in finding better ways of living than that offered by mass society. At the same time, communalists have tried to inspire a larger social movement by demonstrating the advantages of cooperation. Early cooperative communities provoked widespread debate about their larger applicability. In 1822, Thomas Jefferson wrote to Cornelius Blatchly, author of the popular pamphlet promoting cooperative communities, *Essay on Common Wealth*, and offered cautious support: "That, on the principle of a communion of property, small societies may exist in habits of virtue, order, industry, and peace, and consequently in a state of as much happiness as Heaven has been pleased to deal out to imperfect humanity, I can readily conceive, and indeed, have seen its proofs in various small societies which have been constituted on that principle. But I do not feel authorized to conclude from these that an extended society, like that of the United States or of an individual State, could be governed happily on the same principle."[4]

The communitarian experience of the Pilgrims and other early religious sects had both a spiritual and a secular form. When separation of church and state was embodied in the Constitution, communalism separated into two distinct streams, one secular and one religious. Both involved movements for social justice, as each saw it. A shared millennial spirituality was central to all the religious or spiritual communalists, who formed a parallel and related movement to political or social communalism.

We will look at social and spiritual communalism separately, with the understanding that there was a dynamic reciprocity between the two.

The 19th century saw a succession of secular social movements aimed at creating rural colonies where urban people—particularly but not exclusively working people—might escape oppressive conditions and find liberation. These experimental communities were also seen as hothouses of social innovation, and fulcrums to release forces of change and reform the larger society.

There were several distinct waves of the recurring communalist movement in the 19th century. The Owenite Socialist phase (1825-28), involved at least ten communities; the Associationist phase (1841-46) at least twenty-eight colonies. There were several Abolitionist colonies (1830-65), in the US, and across the border in Canada. The "Modern" Socialist communal movement (1886-1919) directly involved at least twenty communities, most of them large. Communalism even touched the Knights of Labor. All of these community movements were connected to larger social movements, and rose and fell with the vicissitudes of those larger movements. At the same time, many other cooperative communities formed that were not part of these major waves, founded without the immediate impetus of the surge of a mass movement.[5]

Spiritual communalism parallels the secular movement. Some spiritual communal groups focused on charismatic leaders, and turned to separatism and cultism. The opposite tendency can be seen in Christian Socialists and similar groups, whose history spans both communalism and cooperatives, and who took it as part of their mission to spread cooperation into the larger society.[6]

As the US expanded, many groups established intentional communities along the Westward-moving frontier, which offered inexpensive land and few social restrictions. Many workers in eastern cities joined a cooperative community as a stepping-stone out of wage slavery and into the promise of a new and better life in a farm community. Numerous urban workers—many of them recent immigrants—were only reluctant industrial workers, and dreamed of becoming farmers. Many saw communalism as a way to achieve that dream. Those who stayed in the Eastern cities organized cooperatives to improve their lives and try to achieve their liberation without leaving home. American urban workers, struggling for social justice in the face of the aggressive growth of the capitalist system, organized themselves time and again into movements of unions, cooperatives, and political parties; many of these same workers also organized themselves into communalist groups. When each strategy met with limited success, they turned in a recurring sequence from one organizational form to another. When new communalists arrived in rural America, they usually found a society of small farmers already in place, whose struggles for a better life paralleled those of wage-workers in the cities. When communalists left their intentional communities, or the communities disbanded, they often joined the larger existing farm and town communities, and tended to blend right in. Others went on to join another intentional community, and many communalists lived in a succession of intentional communities.

Communalism before the Civil War can be said to have culminated in the Homestead Act of 1862, which briefly offered land almost free. After the Civil War, farm communities in both the Midwest and West were largely populated by families only recently drawn there by the Homestead Act. Most of these had previously been wage-worker families in the East. Like industrial workers, farmers organized cooperatives to try to solve their economic problems.

When the economic system stymied them, both groups formed political organizations to try to change the rules of the system. Indeed, cooperatives bridged farmers and urban workers, the two parallel tracks of the American working people. Both workers and farmers rose up regularly in response to economic inequities, and their trajectories followed the economic cycles. The two groups shared common roots, and often worked closely in coalition, sharing common goals. The Grange and the Farmers' Alliance worked in close coalition with the Knights of Labor in the Greenback-Labor Party and then the Populist Party.

The communalist movements did not succeed in reforming society by stepping out of it, or by creating a parallel social system of colonies, but they did succeed in demonstrating the principles of cooperation to those who stayed in their existing communities and attempted to reform them through cooperatives or political means. The first two communalist movements—Owenite Socialism and Associationism—began at the rise of greater social movements and helped to inspire those efforts, while the "Modern" Socialist communal movement was initiated by failures of the larger social movement. This shows very different dynamics in their rise and fall. Both the Owenite Socialist and the Associationist communal movements took place before union movements of worker cooperatives and fertilized the soil they grew in with ideas of the benefits of cooperation.[7] Leaders such as Albert Brisbane and Horace Greeley played key roles in communal as well as cooperative movements. "Modern" Socialist communalism began soon after the closing of the frontier around 1880, channeling pent-up social forces similar to the early movements; it was strongest on the West Coast, where it involved many labor activists who had given up on reforming society by direct means after a series of defeats of the labor movement. That wave of communalism was laid to rest by the repression surrounding World War I. The New Deal offered government sponsorship of cooperative communities as a strategy for solving deep social problems. Twentieth-century communalism culminated in the great explosion of the 1960s, which again preceded and inspired a widespread cooperative movement.

Comparing the longevity of communities formed as part of a wave with those formed at other times, one can see that many communities started during peaks tended to be shorter-lived. While the Owenite and Associationist groups disbanded and vanished, some of the more successful later groups assimilated into larger communities that were growing up around them.

In practice, the vaunted advantages of cooperative communities did not always materialize. The history of intentional cooperative communities has shown them to be far from immune to conflict. On the contrary, they hold a mirror to society and human nature in many ways. People joining or forming intentional communities are ordinary people, and carry with them life experiences that affect the situation. Rather than being static *end results,* they have been schools of cooperation for like-minded people. So while it is more likely that a small intentional group can treat each other decently and care for each other than a group arbitrarily formed, unfortunately that has not always been the case. Marriages that begin with vows of eternal love do not always end that way; it is just a sad fact of human nature and the current human condition.

Cooperation, cooperatives, and communalism are not magic pills. They do not abolish human conflict. Whether dealing with a society or the whole world, there are always a great variety of people, with very diverse intentions, not all of them cooperative. Cooperatives offer structural ways to minimize and resolve conflicts, but they do not always prevent it. Communalism has also proved itself very limited as a strategy to change society. Cooperative communities appeal to only a comparatively small number of people; the world is for the most part still organized on the basis of the biological family and the single family unit. So for most people, belonging to a cooperative rather than to a cooperative community is a far more viable option. With a cooperative, the commitment is limited to areas where a co-op can make a significant practical improvement in members' lives. That usually involves a far less intense and encompassing form of cooperation than a cooperative community.

Cooperative communities have also shown that they are not self-perpetuating. Most participants eventually move back into the larger society. Children raised in a secular communalist situation (although there are exceptions) are usually unwilling to limit their lives by the explicit separation and typically do not renew the community beyond the first generation.

Yet communalism is so deeply embedded in American history and mythology that it will almost surely attract and inspire future generations curious to experiment in better ways of living.

16.
The Early Communalist Movements

COMMUNITARIAN SOCIALISM

Between 1825 and 1830, groups of urban workers made their first concerted attempt to escape deteriorating city conditions by acquiring land cooperatively and setting up cooperative communities based primarily on agriculture. Many urban wage earners had the goal of becoming farmers, but the skyrocketing price of land was putting that goal out of reach for ever-growing numbers. This development mirrored the skyrocketing cost of the means of production in manufacturing, which made the transition from wage earner to self-employed out of reach for ever-growing numbers of industrial workers as well. Workers turned to both production cooperatives and rural cooperative communities for the same reasons. The transition to cooperative community proved more difficult, as it also necessitated a change from city or town to country, and usually also a change of occupation. Urban workers generally knew little about farming, and tried to overcome this by pooling their knowledge, skills and resources.[1]

America's first full industrial depression sparked the new communalist movement, as it ravaged the working class communities in the Eastern cities beginning in 1816, then became a general economic collapse with the panic of 1819.[2] Cornelius Blatchly laid the movement's ideological base in his *Essay on Common Wealth* (1822). He proposed solving the problems of the depression by asserting society's right to withdraw its "gift" of private property and restore to people their "natural equality."[3] To bring this about he advocated the formation of "pure communities" where collective good and cooperation would replace selfishness and competition. These could be formed from small beginnings and eventually spread to take in the whole population, giving rise to a new America while the repressive and obsolete old society faded away. Toward that end, he founded the New York Society for Propagating Communities.[4]

Blatchly's essay contained long excerpts from a work by Robert Owen, a Welshman with whom Blatchly had been in touch while making his own preparations. In *A New View of Society* (1813), Owen originated the idea that the capitalist system could be transformed by the creation of cooperative communities everywhere. Part agricultural and part industrial, all the unemployed could settle in them along with all former wage earners who wanted their freedom, producing for each others' needs and for exchange with the outside world. These cooperative villages would grow, spread and federate "in circles of tens, hundreds and thousands," eventually transforming the whole of society around the world. From inside the shell of "the old immoral world" a "new moral world" would arise, where all were free and equal and where true democracy would rule.[5] He called this Socialism, adding a new word to the languages of the world, and founded the Association of All Classes of All Nations to try to bring it about through peaceful means.[6]

Owen had been a wage earner starting from the age of nine, as a shop assistant at a draper's. Keeping his eye on the boss, he figured out the capitalist system. He briefly ran his own spinning mill factory, got a job as manager of a spinning mill, married the daughter of the owner of the largest cotton-spinning business in Britain, and bought the New Lanark mills from his father-in-law. Under his management, Scotland's New Lanark became famous as the only mill in England where a large portion of the income was plowed back into high salaries, good working conditions and fringe benefits for workers.[7] In 1817, Owen went to the House of Commons, unveiling his plan to replace capitalism and requesting government assistance to set up the first of these Villages of Cooperation or Home Colonies, as he called them. He claimed they would not only solve the problems of poverty and inequality, but would also rejuvenate all of society.[8] He estimated the best size as being about 1,200 people on 1,000 to 1,500 acres. According to his plan, the government would help set the communities up then get out, leaving them autonomous and self-supporting.[9]

The capitalists in control of the House of Commons rejected him out of hand.[10] Scarcely five years had passed since their former colonies in America had whipped them in a second war; now this former wage earner wanted to set up home colonies right in Britain. Owen turned to wealthy individuals, appealing to their "moral sensibilities," but got the same response.[11] He decided that a self-supporting movement could be created, without any further outside help, once the first few got off the ground. He and his friends began gathering resources to start one in Scotland.[12]

NEW HARMONY

Blatchly soon convinced Owen that America was the most fertile ground for developing Socialism. At that moment, it happened that George Rapp and his group of a thousand German immigrant religious communalists decided to sell their home of Harmonie, Pennsylvania, and move to a new site in Indiana. Owen put his money on the line and set sail for America. And so the first movement in the world to call itself Socialist was about to take place in the United States, while Karl Marx was going to kindergarten.[13]

In America, Owen quickly became a celebrity. He went on a meandering tour to Indiana, and was greeted with excitement and press coverage everywhere along the way. His rejection of Britain in favor of America as a more convivial location for liberty and equality flattered the national ego. On February 25th, 1825, he spoke in Washington, D.C.'s House of Representatives, and he was warmly received by a crowd that included president-elect John Quincy Adams, outgoing president James Monroe, Speaker of the House Henry Clay, and numerous senators, congressmen, and Supreme Court justices.[14] Owen's speech has been preserved:

> The whole trading system is one of deception... a better system might be, with far less labor, and without risk, secured in perpetuity to all... In the new system, union and cooperation will supercede individual interest... The very imperfect experiments of the Moravians, Shakers and Harmonites, give sure proof of the superiority of union over division, for the creation of wealth... For when the new arrangements shall be regularly organized and completed, a few hours daily of healthy and desirable employment, chiefly applied to direct modern mechanical and other scientific improvements, will be amply sufficient to create a full supply, at all times, of the best of every thing for every one.[15]

In the spring of 1825, New Harmony opened to any and all. Within a short time, over 900 mostly urban working people had crowded in. Many of New Harmony's inhabitants traveled long distances to join, while others came from the surrounding area. The community thrived for a year. It had 20,000 acres, with large tracts under cultivation, a cooperative silk factory, woolen mill, brickyard, distillery, oil mill, and die works. Members worked under a cooperative system, each person being responsible for balancing debits from the community store with work-credits on an annual basis. This plan was to be in effect two years, under direction of a committee, at the end of which the community would work out a permanent constitution.[16]

Owenite Socialist hymn (c. 1825)

Brothers, arise! behold the dawn appear
of Truth's bright day, and Love's Millennial Year!
...
Mankind shall turn from Competition's strife,
To share the blessings of Communal life.
Justice shall triumph—leagued oppression fail—
And Universal happiness prevail.[17]

Between 1825 and 1826, the prospering New Harmony received nationwide publicity along with Owen's theories, which inspired the founding of other cooperative communities across the Northern states into the Midwest. Many expected New Harmony to act as both a seedpod and a bank for the movement, gathering capital that could be used to start numerous other communities. All of the other new communities, however, were financed entirely by their members combining their own resources.[18] Fragmentary histories of at least nine are recorded, the most successful being Kendal and Yellow Springs in Ohio, Valley Forge in Pennsylvania, Blue Springs in Indiana, Franklin and Coxsakie in New York. At least 2,000 people were members. Apart from New Harmony, most of the other cooperative communities were formed by local townspeople and small farmers already living close to site. In the case of Kendal, twenty-nine locals put up their existing farms for the down payment on the larger cooperative tract.[19]

Owen himself was not at New Harmony during most of the first nine months. Instead, he toured the country speaking about Socialism, leaving the people at New Harmony space to work out their own destiny. When he returned, the community was functioning so well that he decided to spring early what he had expected to present at the end of the two-year trial period. He offered a plan for a "community of equals." All would be resolved into a democratic family of equals, holding means of survival in common and working all for each other's needs. They would switch from a cooperative community, with each receiving material benefits according to work performed, to a commune with each receiving according to need.[20]

The people of New Harmony, excited at the prospect, decided to dive in headfirst. They met with disaster. The community was barely on its feet as a cooperative, a great achievement for 900 people who for the most part did not know each other at the start. The 900 also included a wide range of people from the most varied backgrounds: working families, middle-class intellectuals and *lumpen* vagrants. The transition to commune was premature at the least, and resulted in factions and feuds as the open struggle among people of differing class backgrounds, outlooks, and economic resources split the community beyond repair. Even after they retreated back into a cooperative system, the personal wounds could not be healed. New Harmony split into at least five groups, forming separate independent communities on different parts of the land.[21]

Without New Harmony for a center, the movement lost direction and dissipated. New Harmony's failure was reflected and replicated in all the other communities. Most of the communalists were unprepared for the personality problems that they encountered, and the real benefits of communal living never met their high expectations. One by one, they became discouraged, and all of the communities dispersed. The longest lasting was Kendal, which dissolved after less than three years.[22]

Apart from common land ownership, the communalists' situation did not differ significantly from that of other settlers in rural areas. Their cooperative culture added little new to the already-existing cooperative networks in much of rural America. The communalists from urban areas found that moving to the countryside did not solve their economic problems. Farm communities all around the country were being squeezed dry by banks, middlemen, and land speculators. It was becoming increasingly difficult for people who'd known farming all their lives to make a living, much more so for former city and town people. For most of the intentional communities banks still owned the land, so the communalists suffered under large mortgage payments for many years. The worsening of the depression and the disheartenment of New Harmony's collapse brought a temporary end to socialist communalism as a movement. While money was scarce and getting scarcer, not even the best paid amongst the working population could afford land even when collectivizing resources. It would be another decade before economic conditions would permit the movement to burst forth again. By 1830, all of the Owenite communities had faded into the rural landscape and were gone, some of their members absorbed into the surrounding farm communities and others migrating to urban areas.[23]

However, the New Harmony movement left a strong legacy in the larger society. A number of people involved in the early period became activist leaders in the labor movement and in the struggle for free public education. Owen's freethinking philosophy and rejection of organized religion left a heritage that others carried on. The failures of the movement did not discourage the similar Associationist movement a decade later. An early New Harmony member, Frances Wright, went on to found Nashoba Community, initiating the Abolitionist community movement.[24]

MUTUALIST COMMUNITIES

Josiah Warren, who had been a participant during New Harmony's first year, became America's major exponent of mutualism, the strategy of reorganizing society through mutual aid. After the success of his Time Store in Cincinnati beginning in 1827, he founded several mutualist cooperative communities: Equity in 1834 and Utopia in 1846, both in Ohio, and Modern Times in 1850 on Long Island, New York. These communities had no government from above but simple mutual aid structures from below. Equity community was soon struck with malaria, and closed. Utopia and Modern Times both lasted over twenty years, never disbanding but simply merging with the surrounding communities that had grown about them.[25]

ASSOCIATIONIST COMMUNALISM

Associationism in America started in 1840 with the publication of *The Social Destiny of Man* by Albert Brisbane.[26] This book introduced the ideas of the Frenchman Charles Fourier (1772-1837) to this country in a manner similar to the way Robert Owen's ideas had been introduced. Fourier had lived through the violence of the French Revolution, and set out to devise a new social system in order to prevent another upheaval. Brisbane was the editor of the most widely circulated newspaper of the time, the *New York Tribune*—a radical Abolitionist paper published by Horace Greeley. Brisbane and Greeley both thought that the earlier Socialist community movement had not succeeded, partly because a successful formula had not been developed for workers to collectivize their resources, gather capital, buy land, and start their cooperative communities. They did not see the cooperative community as a short transitional step to the full commune as Owen did before New Harmony's disaster. For them, the cooperative community was the end in itself. Fourier and the Associationists felt that all people could be emancipated and the inequalities and injustices of capitalist society cured by a vast network of cooperative villages, phalanxes or associations as they were variously called in Fourier's plan.[27] Once the restraints imposed by capitalism were removed, people would naturally work together in a spirit of cooperation. A nurturing environment in which all were free to follow their passions would lead to social harmony. They hoped that phalanxes would spring up all over the country, and gradually federate like cells into a growing organism that would eventually transform America and the world. While the movement of the 1820s had been more oriented toward agriculture and handicrafts in practice, the Associationists stressed industry in keeping with the times. They felt that collective production for trade or sale was necessary for a phalanx to survive. They encouraged the production cooperatives that many union workers were already forming in the 1840s. These could become parts of larger industrial organisms or steps toward phalanxes.[28]

Greeley developed a formula for gathering resources to start phalanxes and to operate them. They would be incorporated; each member would have one vote no matter how many shares owned; and surplus income from their industries would be distributed as dividends. Members received survival needs plus money income varying with the amount of work performed. Outsiders could also buy stock. Associationism was more of a middle-class movement than Owenite Socialism, as shown by its focus on the contract form. The Fourierist phalanxes were joint-stock companies, with detailed formulas for protecting every financial interest.[29]

The Associationists, like the earlier Owenites, saw these communities as levers for wide social change. Brisbane wrote, "The whole question of affecting a Social Reform may be reduced to the establishment of one Association, which will serve as a model for, and induce the rapid establishment of others."[30]

But while the *Tribune* supported Associationism, other papers denounced it, as did legislators and various church leaders, as a threat to the social system.[31]

Between 1843 and 1850, at least thirty-four phalanxes, averaging well over a hundred members apiece, sprouted across the Northern states from the Atlantic to the Mississippi. By 1844, the movement was progressing so rapidly a National Convention of Associations was held. The Wisconsin Phalanx, founded in 1845 deep in the previously uninhabited prairie in the Fond du Lac region, grew to 180 members within a year. In isolation, they built a successful agricultural community centered on a large communal building or "phalanstery." Even more successful perhaps was the North American Phalanx near Red Bank, New Jersey, which began in 1843 with $1,000 in capital and a membership of about eighty that included Greeley. They quickly built a gristmill, other workshops, a three-storied, 150-foot long central phalanstery, and planted 70 acres of orchards and large fields of vegetables.[32]

The most celebrated community of the decade was Brook Farm in Massachusetts, begun in 1841 not as an Associationist phalanx, but as a spiritual commune originally named West Roxbury Community. It was founded by transcendentalists coming out of the Unitarian tradition and led by George Ripley and William Henry Channing, whose uncle had founded Unitarianism. In 1845, the Brook Farm Institute jumped headlong into Associationism, becoming Brook Farm Phalanx. Channing predicted in *The Harbinger*, the primary newspaper of the movement, that the example of Brook Farm's "associative unity" would inspire the nation "like one man" to "organize into townships on the basis of perfect justice."[33] Ripley looked toward Associationism in the expanding West for social change, and wrote that "an Association which would create but little sensation in the East, might produce an immense effect in the West."[34] Brook Farm residents included Nathaniel Hawthorne, who wrote a fictionalized history of it in his novel, *The Blithedale Romance*, and Charles A. Dana. Regular visitors included Margaret Fuller, Ralph Waldo Emerson, and Bronson Alcott. Brook Farm planned for a great expansion and members focused most of their energies and resources on building their phalanstery. One hundred seventy feet long and three stories high, it was expected to house a very large number of new people. But in 1846, when almost completed, the building burned to the ground.[35]

Other Associationist communities included LaGrange (Mongo, Indiana), Alphadelphia (Galesburg, Michigan), Trumbull (Trumbull County, Ohio), Claremont Phalanx (Cincinnati), and five communities near Rochester, New York: Clarkson, Bloomfield, Sodus Bay, Mixville, and Ontario. In all, at least 3,000 people were members. As in the case of Owenite communities, many of the Associationist communities were formed by local townspeople moving onto land just a few miles further out into the countryside.[36]

Meanwhile, the same problems that had stopped the movement in the mid-1820s remained to stop it again. Most poor and working people simply could not afford to form phalanxes, even after combining resources. Furthermore, the Greeley system stressed profit sharing at the expense of simple communal sharing. The phalanxes usually remained poor, often strangled by debts they had undertaken. Outside investors had as much say as community members; they equally owned the enormous amount of work members put into the phalanxes, leaving members feeling exploited by their investors. In the end, most workers were not convinced that phalanxes were the answer to raising the quality of their lives. Rather than move out of their communities in separationist fashion, most working people saw a more solid road to progress in staying home and trying to transform their communities.

The Associationist movement rose in response to the depression that had begun with the panic of 1837. When the economy picked up due to the imperialist war against Mexico, the movement was shaken. The rush for gold in newly annexed California deflected much of the pent-up social energy that had been behind Associationism. At the same time, the new flood of immigrants into the East Coast helped the new Associationist worker cooperative movement to rise, which was also publicized and supported by the *Tribune*.[37]

Brook Farm folded in 1847, demoralized by the fire and at the end of its resources. In 1850, after five years, the Wisconsin Phalanx lost heart and disbanded. Most of the smaller phalanxes were also gone by that time. The North American Phalanx lasted longer than any other, and appeared to thrive until 1854, when its mills and workshops were also devastated by fire. Its closing the next year effectively ended the Associationist movement.[38]

OTHER COMMUNITIES OF THE PERIOD

In this same period, several communities were formed outside of the Associationist movement. Skaneateles, in upper New York, was a community founded by socialists involved with Abolitionism. Northampton, on Long Island, was secular and cooperative. Both had well over a hundred members, but both disintegrated after four years. Other non-Associationist communities included the mutualist communities started by groups founded by Josiah Warren in this period, Utopia and Modern Times. Both contained many former Associationists, and both made it through these hard years. The bare simplicity of their social structure, nothing more than a basic agreement to mutual aid and cooperation whenever possible, provided a flexibility that helped pull them through.[39]

IMMIGRANT COMMUNES: ICARIA & COMMUNIA

New immigrants continued to bring new communitarian models to America. Social upheavals, working-class uprisings and attempted revolutions in France and Germany in 1848 brought on government repression and waves of political exiles. In both cases, groups of former revolutionaries fled to the US and set up communal colonies.[40]

Refugees from the attempted revolution in Germany began arriving in New York in 1848. Led by Wilhelm Weitling, a leader of the German insurrection, they first attempted to organize a cooperative bank of exchange. When that project failed, Weitling led a group which bought some land in Iowa with funds raised in part from a German-American labor association, and traveled West to found a commune called Communia. However, the land proved impossible to farm, and the group disbanded after several poverty-stricken years.[41]

In 1849, 260 French political refugees, led by Etienne Cabet (who'd been a member of the Insurrection Committee of the earlier 1830 Paris uprising), bought the old Mormon community of Nauvoo, Illinois. There, they formed a commune they called Icaria, after a socialist utopian novel Cabet had written between the two French working-class insurgencies. Cabet, like others before him, envisioned a federation of socialist colonies in America involving millions. Icaria grew eventually to a population of about five hundred. But as it grew, Cabet became authoritarian and created many enemies; the commune expelled him in 1856. A large group followed him to St. Louis.

Cabet died soon after, but the other St. Louis Icarians ran several cooperative houses there for many years. The original Illinois group, forced to leave the state due to debt, moved to Iowa. More French refugees poured into both of these Icarian communities after the defeat of the Paris Commune of 1871. Clashes between older and newer residents in each Icaria caused further splits. One break-away group founded Icaria Esperanza in Southern California in 1884, which lasted only a few years. Icarians went on to found co-op stores in Cloverdale, California. The Iowa Icaria continued until 1895.[42]

COMMUNALISM IMMEDIATELY AFTER ASSOCIATIONISM

After the collapse of Associationism, communalism lost its credibility for a generation among the American-born as a method of social change. While the Owenite Socialists could point to New Harmony's collapse as the key failure that brought down the movement, the Associationists did not really have one particular community as their focus, so their failure was clearly the failure of some basic assumptions of the entire movement. The movement assumed that communal colonies, once started, would easily maintain themselves. But experience showed that they were fragile and dependent for success on a large variety of difficult factors. The movement assumed that they would offer a quality of life so superior to mass society that participants would have no motivation to leave. But experience showed that communal living offered no panacea for many of the problems and discontents of everyday life, and even added new levels of complexity to them. Participants often burned out, and many were relieved to return to the comparative simplicity of the single family household of mass society.

The movement never grew large enough to become an imminent threat to the established order, and most people became convinced that it never could. As it lost heart in thinking of itself as a mass movement, it lost its center. The secular movement for social justice was central to the communalist movement; once it became clear that the movement could not achieve a great enough scale to create real change, most people turned to other methods to achieve social justice.[43]

BLACK & ABOLITIONIST COMMUNITIES

The Underground Railroad, a network of secret routes and safe houses used by slaves to flee to free Northern states and Canada with the aid of Abolitionists, permitted over 30,000 people to escape enslavement between 1810 and 1865.[44] Communalist colonies were involved as an Abolitionist strategy (Nashoba), as Railroad stops (Northampton), and as destinations (Dawn, Elgin).

NASHOBA

One of the participants at New Harmony during the successful first period was Frances Wright, one of America's early women's suffragists. A few months after leaving New Harmony in 1825, she founded Nashoba Community in Tennessee, a slave state. While Owen's concept strove toward the liberation of all people from wage slavery, Wright tried to apply the concept to chattel slavery. She considered communalism a stratagem for the liberation of black people, an alternative to violent insurrection. Communes of blacks and whites would produce for their common needs and raise funds to found new colonies and liberate more slaves. To that end she published *A Plan for the Gradual Abolition of Slavery in the United States* (1825), urging Congress to set aside tracts of land for the purpose. The Marquis de Lafayette, hero of the American Revolution and an honorary citizen of the US, served as a trustee of Nashoba. Wright freed the blacks living at the community. She wrote to Thomas Jefferson, trying to get him involved. He answered with encouragement and support, saying, "The abolition of the evil is not impossible... Every plan should be adopted, every experiment tried, which may do something towards the ultimate object."[45] Jefferson—who never freed his own slaves—went on to say that this was a job for young people, while he was near his end. Nashoba succeeded for three years, despite harassment from local racists, but the 1828 depression hit the community hard, and the next year members could not meet their land payments. In 1830, the freed blacks moved to "liberated" Haiti, while Wright, together with Owen's son Robert Dale Owen, became active in the New York Working Men's Party, giving up the socialist communalist strategy as impracticable at the time.[46]

NORTHAMPTON

In Massachusetts, the Northampton Association of Education and Industry was begun in 1842 by a group of abolitionists, farmers, and silk workers. One of the founders was George Benson, brother-in-law of abolitionist William Lloyd Garrison. Another prominent resident was Dolly Stetson, who had been president of the Brooklyn

Anti-Slavery Society. Underground Railroad leader Sojourner Truth joined the following year, and was living at Northampton when she dictated the classic *The Narrative of Sojourner Truth*. She was joined there by black abolitionist and Underground Railroad leader David Ruggles.[47] Northampton regularly hosted anti-slavery lectures, and grew renowned as a center of radical Abolitionism. Among its visitors were Frederick Douglass and Garrison. The town of Florence formed nearby, and became an important stop on the Underground Railroad. Over the next four and a half years, over two hundred people belonged to the community. They were governed by a constitution that detailed their vision of an egalitarian America. They supported themselves by a silk farm and milling industry. However, the silk industry failed, and near the end of 1846 Northampton disbanded. Sojourner Truth moved to another Associationist community, Harmonia, in Michigan.[48]

DAWN

In 1830, Josiah Henson, with his wife Nancy and four children, escaped from slavery in Maryland, and crossed the border into Canada. Finding shelter in rural Ontario, an area of refuge for an ever-growing number of African-Americans, Henson took employment as a farm laborer, and became a minister. He saw that many of the blacks in the area never really advanced economically beyond bare survival. Officially free, they were still not their own masters. Henson organized a dozen black families with a plan to pool their resources with his family, buy land and colonize it. They discovered a good cleared plot near Colchester, a government land grant that the grantee was renting to settlers. They leased it in 1834, moved onto it, and put in wheat and tobacco. Henson discovered that the grantee had not complied with certain conditions of his grant, and therefore was not legally entitled to rent. They appealed to the legislature, and after two years of legal battle, won and took over the grant. After that, they lived rent-free. They farmed the land collectively for the next seven years, but remained painfully aware that the government could put the land up for sale at any time, even as all their improvements increased the land value out of their own reach. They realized that they needed to own their land, and started to raise money to buy another plot.[49]

Henson began working with a group of Abolitionists and Quakers to gather funds to start schools in the US and Canada.

Having raised $1,500, Henson organized a convention of blacks in Ontario in June 1838 to decide how to spend it. At the meeting, he proposed to use the money to establish a school for their children, a manual-labor-oriented school in which mechanical and domestic arts would be taught along with academic subjects. The proposal passed unanimously. The group purchased 200 acres near London, Ontario, and in 1842 opened Dawn school, which also became the name of the town that sprang up around it. Many of the original Colchester group moved to Dawn.

Over the following years, Dawn became a self-sufficient community of over 500 black people, many of them fugitives from US slavery. They purchased more land, raised wheat, tobacco, corn and oats, started a lumber industry, and built a community saw mill and gristmill. In addition to the communal land, town residents individually bought another 1,500 acres in the immediate area. Dawn became the center of a territorial black renaissance, with about 20,000 blacks prospering in settlements throughout the surrounding region. For many, Dawn was the promised end of the Underground Railway. But its success was short-lived. In 1849, Henson published his autobiography, *The Life of Josiah Henson, Formerly a Slave*. It had only a small circulation until it inspired the novelist Harriet Beecher Stowe to appropriate parts of it loosely in *Uncle Tom's Cabin*.[50] Stowe acknowledged her debt to Henson's book, and he became an international celebrity. While Henson traveled on Abolitionist speaking tours, Dawn suffered from management problems back home. The community languished and sank into a deep financial crisis. Henson made a series of efforts to get things back on track, but both the school and town continued to fade. The final abolition of slavery in the US led many residents to leave Dawn and return to the states. The school closed in 1868. Josiah and Nancy Henson, however, lived at Dawn for the rest of their lives, and their house still stands.[51]

OTHER BLACK COMMUNAL COLONIES

Several other colonies of free and fugitive blacks organized in the Northern US and Canada. Like Dawn, all were aided and some were initiated by Abolitionists, clergymen of several denominations, and Quakers. These formed a network, and some of the same people were involved in helping several of the communities. According to historian Cheryl Janifer LaRoche, "Dozens of flourishing black farming settlements were founded in Ohio and Indiana between

1808 and the Civil War, many of them by emancipated slaves from Virginia and North Carolina. Moved by their success, the Black National Convention, held in Buffalo in 1843, recommended formation of black farming settlements in Michigan, Illinois, Iowa, and Wisconsin and, as a result, sizable black farming settlements were established in Southern Illinois by 1860."[52]

In 1836, Augustus Wattles, white headmaster of a school for blacks in Cincinnati, organized Cartagena Colony on a tract he purchased in Mercer County, Ohio. Cartagena became a rural cooperating community of independent black farmers, and Wattles transferred the land title to the settlers two years later. With a grant from a group of Quakers, Wattles started the Emlen Institute, a "manual training" school there with one hundred students in 1840. The settlers grew corn, rye, oat, hay, cattle, and experimented with mulberries for a silk worm farm. It was similar to other frontier communities in its informal institutions of house-raising, community harvesting, corn husking bees, and similar activities. After six years, they had a community gristmill, saw mill, and brickyard. Cartagena residents included a variety of artisans and craftspeople comprising shoemakers, weavers, masons, a blacksmith, tanner, wagon maker, and hatter. However, racists in the surrounding area undercut and harassed the community, and ultimately forced the entire colony out. In 1857, Emlen school closed.[53]

In 1836, Robert Rose organized the Silver Lake Community in Susquehanna County, Pennsylvania, in collaboration with the African Methodist Episcopal Church of Philadelphia. Nine free black families and several single men settled on the land under a share-cropping system. A three-man committee managed the general affairs. However, little is known of how they fared, and they disappeared from record after a short time.[54]

Wilberforce Settlement in Ontario, Canada, was begun in 1829 by a group of blacks from Cincinnati, in reaction to abuse and discrimination in that city. Financed by a group of Quakers, they sent an agent who purchased 800 acres. About 500 to 1000 blacks left Ohio for Canada, and around 200 settled at Wilberforce. The community was primarily agricultural, with individual homesteads and cooperative social structures. Austin Steward, once a grocer in Rochester, became chairman of their board and their primary leader. By the end of 1832, the group owned a hundred head of cattle, pigs, and horses, a sawmill, gristmill, general store, and school. But the community had ongoing disputes with the agents supposedly raising funds for them in the States, and Wilberforce had deteriorated by 1836. In 1838, a visitor saw them as still eking out a poor subsistence, but soon after the community failed and disbanded.[55]

ELGIN & THE REFUGEE HOME SOCIETY

In 1849, William King, a minister in the Free Presbyterian Church, organized the Elgin Association in Toronto, Canada. The Toronto Synod of the church purchased 4,300 acres at Buxton, and by the end of the year a small group of fugitive blacks moved onto the land. Predominantly farmers and artisans, each family had fifty acres to farm. They mostly practiced subsistence farming with a variety of crops and livestock: wheat, corn, oats, buckwheat, hay, potatoes, tobacco, cows, horses, sheep, oxen, and pigs. A few years later, they added several thousand more acres. At Elgin's height in the late 1850s, the population was about 200 families and 1,000 people, cultivating 1,500 acres.[56] The colony had its own stock of artisans in specialized trades, a soap factory and a sawmill. Elgin school was so successful that by 1858 the neighboring whites integrated it by enrolling their children there and closing their own school.[57]

But Elgin also suffered setbacks from poor management. From its inception, the community was under constant attack and pressure from racists in the Provincial Assembly who were trying to prevent black settlement in the area. For many years, certain Conservative members of Parliament accused the community of malfeasance and finally secured an official investigation into Elgin's finances. In 1861, Elgin was cleared of all charges. Internal problems were never enough to cause the community to disintegrate, but it eventually declined as members returned to the United States. With the advent of the Civil War, at least seventy joined the Union Army. During Reconstruction, a number of former Elgin residents became doctors, lawyers, and educators in the US; one became a member of the US House of Representatives and another of the US Senate. The Elgin Association, after two decades of success, closed in 1873.[58]

The Refugee Home Society was a joint project of Abolitionists in Canada and Michigan, modeled on Elgin and founded for fugitives. It purchased about 2,000 acres in Ontario in 1851, and soon had 150 settlers. The society later bought and distributed another 290 acres. One of the leaders of the organization was Josiah Henson, although he never lived at the settlement. The Society resold plots to blacks at cost and helped provide housing. They established a school and provided new settlers with tools, supplies, and training. But because the land was scattered in different plots, they never had the cohesion of Elgin, and the Refugee Home Society disintegrated with the end of the Civil War.[59]

COLONIZATION OF KANSAS

When the US first opened Kansas to homesteading settlers in 1854, Abolitionist organizations in the North staged a massive organizing drive to colonize the area for free labor, facilitating groups of free-staters to migrate there. In the South, pro-slavery groups and state governments did the same for slavery supporters. The most important Abolitionist group was the Emigrant Aid Company (EAC), formed in Boston by Eli Thayer, A. H. Bullock, and Edward Everett Hale. A great rush of colonists to the area ensued, free-soilers primarily from New England, and slavers from Missouri and Arkansas. At stake was whether Kansas would enter the Union as a free or a slave state. EAC organized 2,000 settlers. Its members founded Lawrence and Manhattan, and were key in establishing Osawatomie and Topeka. After six year of turmoil and violence between the two groups, the Abolitionists triumphed and Kansas entered the Union in 1861 as a free state.[60]

PORT ROYAL EXPERIMENT

On November 7, 1861, the Union staged a naval invasion of Port Royal, center of the Sea Islands of South Carolina. The local white Southerners fled to the mainland, leaving about 10,000 blacks who were no longer slaves but still not really free. They were primarily Gullahs, the group closest to its African roots of all American blacks.[61] In that rice-growing region, endemic tropical diseases had led white masters to leave their plantations under the sole supervision of black overseers for long parts of the year. Taking advantage of that unique situation, the Gullahs developed a culture in which many elements of Western African languages, cultures, and community life were preserved.[62]

The occupying Union government sponsored a group of about fifty Northern philanthropic workers, directed by Boston Abolitionist Edward Pierce, to organize and oversee the education of the former slaves and help them become self-sufficient.[63]

Although the Port Royal Experiment was never a true self-governing cooperative community, it involved self-management by former slaves transitioning into free society. Many organized their own daily tasks as wage workers in the fields, grew their own crops on the side, selling the surplus, and supplied some of their own needs through hunting and fishing. By the end of the war, thousands of blacks had bought land on the islands. Port Royal was a model of what Reconstruction might have been, and was probably the first federal involvement in adult education.[64] However, Lincoln's successor Andrew Johnson ended the experiment abruptly in 1865, and returned most of the land to the former slave owners. Johnson used all the powers of the presidency to reverse civil rights and beat freedmen down into segregated second-class citizens.[65]

FREEDOM TOWNS & VILLAGES

In areas of the South occupied by the Union Army during the Civil War, numerous freed blacks "established freedom villages and freedom towns on abandoned and confiscated plantations."[66] Beginning as refugee centers, many of these became self-governing communities, protected by black regiments. This process continued to some extent after the war, despite the reestablishment of control by planters in partnership with Northern investors. The most well-known freedom village was Davis Bend, near Vicksburg. It was patched together from six plantations and managed by former slave Benjamin Montgomery, and later by his son Isaac. After the war, thousands of freed blacks migrated to other areas and founded all-black rural communities across the South and in other regions.[67]

BLACK TOWNS IN OKLAHOMA

The largest concentration of "freedom towns" was in Oklahoma. For a half century, between the end of the Civil War in 1865 and 1915, a movement took place of Southern blacks migrating to first to Kansas and Arkansas, and after 1890 to Oklahoma and Texas. Some considered it an attempt to create a black territory. Seven towns were established in Oklahoma by 1892, and at least twenty-five by the early 1900s. The movement was assisted by the Five Civilized Tribes, and most of the towns were on land that had formerly belonged to those tribes.[68] The black towns functioned through "close communal life and cooperation," as one resident put it.[69] But the area was poor; they were largely surrounded by

Indian land with inescapable competition between the two groups. Still many hung on and their descendants are there today.[70] The leaders of the movement included W. H. Boley, Lake Moore, and E. P. McCabe. Boley, a railway roadmaster, arranged for his eponymous town to be a train stop and for the railroad to employ many inhabitants. McCabe, the publisher of the *Langston City Herald*, was another key figure. The oldest town was Tullahassee. Boley had the first black-owned bank, telephone and electric companies, a college, and acquired the largest population, with 7,000 inhabitants in 1911. Grayson's industries included mining coal and other minerals. Redbird and Taft were known as centers for black farmers' markets. Wewoka was first inhabited by Seminole freedmen.[71]

COMMUNALISM IN THE 1870s

Groups of new immigrants still commonly formed cooperative colonies. In California alone, there were new colonies of Swedes (Kingbury), Danes (Solvang) and English (Rosedale) in the early 1870s. Usually an advance party was sent to buy the land and make all the arrangements; the colonies would be very collective and cooperative at first, but almost invariably divided up the land into individual lots when they became well settled, choosing to assimilate into the surrounding society rather than remain permanently set apart.[72]

Union Colony was founded in 1870 in the South Platte River valley in Northern Colorado, by a group financed and promoted by Horace Greeley, and organized by Nathan Meeker, the agricultural editor of Greeley's *Tribune*. The colony successfully organized cooperative irrigation for its 600 agricultural homesteaders, with every cooperative member responsible for maintenance of at least one irrigation ditch. Two years later in 1872, some Union residents split away to found the Fort Collins Agricultural Colony. Union Colony's success also resulted in its demise as it eventually lost its character as a colony, became absorbed into its surroundings, and was incorporated in 1886 as the city of Greeley.[73]

"MODERN" SOCIALIST COMMUNALISM

Radicals continued to form communities, but most of them redefined their ideological meaning in the late 19th and early 20th centuries. Most social radicals (in all their varieties from social-democrats to communists to cooperators to anarchists) began to see them as attempts to demonstrate the viability of the principles of cooperation and socialism, and therefore adjuncts to the mass movement rather than its basic stratagem. Many communities in the late 19th century were formed in separatist fashion by participants in failed mass political movements; but rather than aiming for personal escapes, these communalists were trying to create living visions that they hoped would stimulate new mass movements. Members invariably found their communities harassed and attacked by the same forces that wrecked their political organizations. Only in the far West did communitarians still have serious dreams of transforming society through their cooperative communities.[74]

KNIGHTS OF LABOR COMMUNALISM

In the 1880s, the Knights of Labor dabbled in communalism with limited success.

The most successful KOL venture was undertaken by the Knights in two cooperative villages of Powderly and Trevellick near Birmingham, Alabama. In 1887, three Knights formed the Mutual Land and Improvement Company for that purpose, and within a year both villages' plots were bought and laid out on 60-by-120-foot lots. By the end of the first year, Powderly had 200 inhabitants, with a school, general store, and free reading room. Houses were built at half the cost of buildings in Birmingham. An early industry there was the Powderly Cooperative Cigar Works.[75] Over time, Birmingham expanded and eventually absorbed both communities; today Powderly and Trevellick remain as neighborhoods of that city.

In 1880, Knights from New York City began Eglinton Colony in Missouri; they called their group the Grand Cooperative Brotherhood. They bought a thousand-acre cattle ranch, with plans to become a self-sufficient agricultural colony. They had about a hundred members in 1883 and joined the KOL as a district assembly.[76]

In 1884, several Minneapolis KOL leaders organized an association to promote an agricultural colony, sold shares to fellow Knights to raise money, and bought 153 acres fronting on Bay Lake in the Mille Lacs region for $675 to be repaid by the settlers. In the spring of 1886, the Pioneer Cooperative Company moved onto the land with seventeen members, including children. Two of the men had been barrel-makers in a cooperative shop, and all had farm backgrounds. They purchased horses and farm implements, planted beans, corn, potatoes, and other vegetables, and refurbished an old sawmill.[77]

Both the Eglinton and Pioneer colonies struggled to survive, and folded after a few years.[78]

KAWEAH

Kaweah Cooperative Colony, in the Sierras near Visalia, California, was organized in 1886 by a group of socialists affiliated with the "Red" International Workingmen's Association who were very active in the San Francisco area between 1882 and 1886. After the Haymarket disaster of 1886, the Red International disbanded, and many members and leaders, including Burnette Haskell (leader of the KOL in San Francisco) and J. J. Martin (founder of the local seamen's union), organized Kaweah Colony "to improve the health, secure the happiness, and perfect the well being of each and every member. And as well to propagate and extend in the world at large the idea of universal and just cooperation."[79] Their concept of the aim of socialist communalism was strongly influenced by Lawrence Gronlund's *The Cooperative Commonwealth* (1884), generally considered the first book to put many of the ideas of Marxist "scientific" socialism into a truly American idiom. Gronlund called colonization "one way to bring a State to the threshold of Socialism."[80] The Kaweahns, ranging at times between 50 and 300 in number, homesteaded a tract of 600 acres in Tulare County. However, two months after they filed their claims under the Homestead and Timberland Acts, the land office in Washington withdrew the area pending investigation regarding suspicions of fraud. The colonists proceeded with their plans, sure that the matter would be quickly resolved.[81]

By 1890, they'd built homes, orchards and gardens, constructed an eighteen-mile long road and a ferry, published a weekly magazine, and had an operating sawmill. They functioned under a system of labor-checks based on the amount of time worked; the checks were convertible for any item at the community-run store.[82]

But the major state newspapers barraged the public with articles attacking Kaweah, and reactionary forces moved to shut it down on the pretext that the original homestead filings had been technically deficient. At the initiative of these forces, in 1890 the US Congress created Sequoia National Park out of Kaweah's core, and designated much of the adjoining area as national forest. Labeled as illegal squatters, federal troops were sent to clear them off the land. Most of the local population supported the colonists; many town residents jeered the soldiers and some shot at them in the woods.[83]

A few acres remained to the colony, and the decreased number of Kaweahns crowded onto them. Soon after, the trustees were hit with stiff fines for unlawfully cutting five pine trees on public land. While the state's major newspapers ran lengthy articles attacking the colony, the local press supported them. The *Tulare County Times* called Kaweah "a prosperous and harmonious colony" that was suffering from "unwarranted prosecution by the government."[84] In 1892, Haskell and the other trustees were arrested for illegal use of the mail in a scheme to defraud by sending out information about the colony and receiving donations. They were finally acquitted, after the trial drained the last of their meager energies and resources. By that time, everyone had abandoned the land.[85]

PUGET SOUND COLONIES

Between 1881 and the early 1900s, a series of cooperative communities sprang up in the Puget Sound area of Washington. These included Washington Colony, Puget Sound Cooperative Colony, Glennis, Equality, Burley, and Home.

Twenty-five Kansan families migrating west formed Washington Colony in 1881-83. They bought an old lumber mill and surrounding lands near Bellingham, and built Colony Mill. They operated the mill and constructed a mile-long wharf out into deep water for shipping. However, with attrition the colony wound up with an insufficient population, and faded.[86]

The Puget Sound Cooperative Colony was founded in 1886 by a group similar to the one that organized Kaweah. Almost all were working people from Seattle and neighboring cities, many previously involved with labor struggles, the Knights of Labor, and the International. After martial law was declared in Seattle during a labor dispute over the importation of Chinese contract laborers as strike breakers, many of the leading union agitators led a large group into communalism. By the end of Puget Sound Colony's first year, there were 400 colonists, and 500 at its peak. Its main industry was lumber, and the colonists soon had an operating sawmill; they also built and operated their own steamship. They used a system they called "Integral Cooperation." The colony was incorporated and managerial with officers holding wide powers and only limited worker control; meals were in common but each family had separate sleeping and living quarters. The immediate problems caused by growing so large so fast were made worse by differences between workers and managers. The colony sparked a boom in the nearby town of Port Angeles, and some members moved there, disillusioned by too much bureaucracy at the colony. This ultimately resulted in the town dominating the colony. Puget Sound Colony became insolvent and dispirited; it first changed into a joint-stock company, and finally dissolved in 1894 to be swallowed by the town as a neighborhood of homesteaders. Many members went on to participate in the populist and socialist movements.[87]

SOCIALIST COMMUNALISM IN THE 1890s

The mid-1890s saw a revival of socialist communalism as a mass movement, tied directly to another renewal of the mass political movement. Both were stimulated by the ideas of Edward Bellamy and Julius A. Wayland, as well as Gronlund. Bellamy's novel *Looking Backward* (1887) predicted a benevolent managerial state socialism in America, brought about peacefully. There were soon over 160 Bellamyite Nationalist Clubs around the country, with thousands of members. These clubs were basically educational groups aimed at helping the new Nation to be born. Activists such as Daniel De Leon, Gene Debs, Helena Blavatsky, and J. A. Wayland were all early members of different Nationalist Clubs.[88]

RUSKIN COLONY

In 1894, J. A. Wayland helped gather a group to form Ruskin Cooperative Colony near Cave Mills, Tennessee. There they opened the world's first socialist college and published *The Coming Nation*, a weekly that soon had a circulation of 60,000, the largest of any radical newspaper in the country.[89] Ruskin Colony was the only voting member from the US at the second annual congress of the International Cooperative Alliance in 1897 in London.[90] But the colony crumbled after five years in a rash of personality clashes. Its newspaper nonetheless continued, and became instrumental in uniting forces for social change into a new national organization in 1897 with a communalist program, the Social Democracy of America.[91]

BROTHERHOOD OF THE COOPERATIVE COMMONWEALTH SOCIAL DEMOCRACY OF AMERICA

Ruskin Colony allied with a group called the Brotherhood of the Cooperative Commonwealth (BCC), who planned to colonize a Western state, introduce socialism there, and use it as a base for a national movement. The members compared themselves to the free-soilers who colonized Kansas prior to the Civil War. The Brotherhood was first conceived by two Maine Populists, Norman Lermond and Ed Pelton.[92]

Soon after its founding, the BCC connected with a small group around Gene Debs, all that was left of the once-great American Railway Union after its crushing defeat in the Pullman strike of 1894. Through *The Coming Nation*, the BCC organized a convention in Chicago aimed at founding an umbrella organization to house the scattered American workers' movement. Unionists, socialists, communitarians, nationalists and radicals of every sort attended and set up the Social Democracy of America (SDA) in June 1897, with a program that was essentially the Brotherhood's. In the following months, Debs worked to raise money for the land, but eventually he joined a growing group inside the organization who felt that the colonization project was quixotic and wanted to form a new electoral party instead.[93] The next year, when the BCC and SDA communitarians went off to Washington State to found two cooperative communities, the Debs group stayed behind and gave birth to the Socialist Party of America.[94]

The BCC and the SDA were closely connected but retained separate identities. The BCC was larger than the SDA, with 130 local unions of supporters around the country, and about 3,500 dues-paying members by 1898; at its peak, the SDA had about 1,200 member-supporters. Both organizations founded colonies in close proximity on Puget Sound. The BCC created Equality Colony in 1897 and the SDA founded Burley Colony a year later.[95]

GLENNIS, EQUALITY, BURLEY, & HOME
While remnants of the Puget Sound Colonies still abounded in the area, yet another group began operations, the Glennis Cooperative Industrial Company. Glennis was a highly structured cooperative community founded in 1894, but by 1896 it fell into discord and declined due in part to anarchistic dissidents protesting its tight organization. From Glennis' disintegration came the anarchist Home colony in 1898.[96]

The Brotherhood of the Cooperative Commonwealth bought 600 acres for Equality, and over 300 colonists quickly poured in. They lived in large communal houses, with success in farming, milling, fishing, dairying, and other small industries. They started a newspaper called *Industrial Freedom*, edited by Harry Ault, which reached a circulation of 8,000 (Ault would go on to edit the *Seattle Union Record* and play an important role in the 1919 Seattle General Strike). But dissension soon rose between the colonists and the national BCC organization that saw Equality as just the first of many colonies to be organized. However, the national BCC came to realize that the larger project's survival required the success of this first colony. Equality gained complete autonomy. It was structured democratically, through general assemblies. One major debate was whether "Voluntary Cooperation" or "Business Methods" should prevail. The former stressed individual freedom, while the latter stressed systemic organization based on the necessities of production. Although some wanted work assignments to always be voluntary, new members were required to sign contracts agreeing to work wherever foremen or department heads assigned them.[97]

The national program remained the sphere of the BCC but, depleted of resources to start further colonies, it soon ceased to exist as a national organization. Equality's population declined to about 120 by 1900 and continued to fall, due mainly to poor economic conditions in the colony and greatly improved ones outside, with promises of higher income elsewhere luring workers away. Equality was not close enough to its markets to create any thriving industry, and so produced insufficient income; it was also hampered by too many unproductive members. An anarchist group took over Equality in 1905, quickly transforming it from a centralized colony to a community of voluntaristic small groups, and changed its name to Freeland. But this structural change caused strife that was never resolved and led to the dissolving of Equality-Freeland in 1907.[98]

Meanwhile the Social Democracy of America changed its name to the Cooperative Brotherhood, purchased 260 acres nearby, and founded Burley in 1898. Like the other groups in the area, Burley focused on logging. By 1900, Burley had 145 residents. But Burley was having problems similar to Equality: strife arose between local and national organizations, as well as between directors and workers. The workers included a large group of anarcho-communist miners from Colorado, who saw things differently from the social-democratic oriented organizers. Burley Community, losing its spirit, reorganized partly as a joint-stock company, with a Rochdale store in 1904. Stagnation continued, and the community dissolved in 1913.[99]

A spin-off from Equality was Freeland Island, begun in 1900 as a group of homesteaders committed to mutual aid and free community cooperation. Freeland soon had sixty members and a Rochdale store. Over time, Freeland shed most of its socialist orientation and evolved into an ordinary suburban community.[100]

When Glennis fell apart, several former members, Oliver Verity among them, founded the anarchist community of Home in 1898. They formed the Mutual Home Association for landholding and mutual aid, with a single-tax plan. Home had 120 residents by 1905 and almost double that 5 years later. But when US president McKinley was assassinated by an immigrant who considered himself an anarchist, a wave of persecution hit the colony, both from local vigilantes and the US government. One Home leader, Jay Fox, was jailed for two months for mailing "obscene" literature advocating "free love."

Many important activists in the mass movement, Wobblies and communists as well as anarchists, visited and stayed at Home, including William Z. Foster, Emma Goldman, Elizabeth G. Flynn, and Bill Haywood. Foster was a frequent visitor, worked regularly on its newspaper *The Agitator*, married a Home resident, then went on to lead the Great Steel Strike and become a leader of the new Communist Party. In 1919, the Mutual Home Association was ordered dissolved by a judge for financial insolvency. The larger Home community continued, about 300 strong, becoming a more conventional settlement that continues today.[101]

OTHER COMMUNITIES

Topolobampo Colony was a debacle of North Americans on the West coast of Mexico organized by Albert Owen on his "Integral Cooperation" system between 1886 and 1895.[102]

Roycroft Community was an artisan colony founded by Elbert Hubbard near East Aurora, New York in 1894 after he visited William Morris' printshop in England. Roycroft produced fine books, furniture, lamps, and metal and leather work. Hubbard, a retired businessman, started with the printshop, publishing a magazine and pamphlets containing his own philosophical writings. These were based on the pre-industrial ideals of the Arts and Crafts Movement, stressing the role of craftsmanship and art as agents of social change. Some of the finest craftspeople of the era lived at Roycroft, which became a self-supporting cooperative community, with Hubbard as somewhat of an overlord until his death in 1915. The community declined after that, and dissolved in 1938.[103]

The Co-operative Brotherhood of Winters Island was founded in 1893, when Mrs. Kate Lockwood Nevins, formerly a Farmers Alliance organizer, led one hundred members from the Bay Area to the Sacramento River delta. They got off to a good start building levees, but were devastated by the depression of 1893, and were last heard of shipping onions in 1898.[104]

SINGLETAXER COLONIES

Henry George published *Progress and Poverty* in 1879, in which he held that the root cause of poverty in the midst of plenty stemmed from land owners increasing rents to capture the increased wealth generated by technological advances that should benefit all. To correct this injustice, George advocated that the government impose a single tax on land that he claimed would make all other taxation unnecessary. This tax would be equal to the land's "natural value," as distinct from its improved value. He claimed that this would make speculation and landlordism unprofitable, and result in the eventual socialization of the land, which the government would make available to all. "We must make land common property."[105] The single tax, he claimed, would be all that was needed to run the federal government. In 1886, Henry George ran for mayor of New York on a coalition party formed by the Socialist Labor Party and several trade unions. The fiery George mayoral campaign took place in the heat of the eight-hour-day movement. In an election tainted by fraud, George probably got the most votes, but Tammany Hall was counting.[106] After his narrow defeat and after Haymarket, a number of his supporters went off into communalism. "Singletaxer" colonies formed at Fairhope, Alabama (1893), at Arden, Pennsylvania (1900), and at Berkeley Heights, New Jersey (1910).[107]

Fairhope was founded by E. B. Gasto, when he proposed to the Des Moines Single Tax Club the idea of a colony based on George's principles. The colony would be organized on *cooperative individualism*: "that which Nature provides is the Common Property of all God's children; that which the individual creates belongs to the individual; that which the Community creates belongs to the Community."[108] Members bought 135 acres of land in Alabama, and 33 members were living there by early 1895. Colonists built their own homes and were expected to find their own employment. The land was marginal for agriculture, but most farmed their plots, while others had trades or small businesses. By 1900, there were a hundred colonists. Fairhope was incorporated as a town in 1908, retaining its unique system of taxation. Its population rose to almost 850 in 1920.[109] A large town today, Fairhope is still strongly influenced by its origins.

17.
Communalism in the 20th Century

In the early years of the new century, the central current of communalism continued the movement of the previous decades. The Puget Sound colonies were fading during these years, but a new major initiative was begun with Llano and Nevada City. Both of these foundered in the state repression surrounding World War I. The next great upsurge took place in the Great Depression of the 1930s, when the government became a backer of community experiments as a way to fight unemployment and entrenched poverty under the New Deal. Most of the New Deal colonies were disbanded during World War II. The final wave of the century arose in the mid-1960s, with the "hippie" and "countercultural" communal movement. While most of the early 60s and 70s communities were short-lived, others continued, leaving a continuous legacy from that era until today.

HELICON HOUSE
In 1906, Upton Sinclair, author of *The Jungle*, started a commune in New Jersey called Helicon House, but it was destroyed by fire after only two years. Sinclair would go on to lead the EPIC movement in California in 1934.[1]

LLANO DEL RIO & NEW LLANO
Llano del Rio Co-operative Colony organized in 1914 on a large plot of land in Antelope Valley north of Los Angeles. One of its main founders was Job Harriman, who had been Gene Debs' running mate on the Socialist Party in the 1900 presidential election, and in 1911 narrowly missed being elected the mayor of Los Angeles. A year after its founding, Llano had 150 members, and by 1917 about 1,000. Llano sold shares, like the old Greeley system,

and had a managerial structure. Its members operated shops and industries that included a print shop, shoemaking shop, cannery, laundry, machine shop, blacksmith, rug factory, soap factory, cabinet shop, brick maker, and bakery. They also planted crops, managed a fish hatchery, and raised animals such as cattle, hogs, and rabbits. Under continual harassment by the authorities, they faced constant organizational and managerial problems from overextending themselves, and letting the community grow too large too fast. They also found that they did not have the water needed to support the colony in that location, making it impossible to stay.[2]

In 1918—while the American Left was being torn apart for its opposition to World War I—the colonists left California and founded New Llano in Louisiana. There they had their ups and downs, finally disbanding after 20 years in 1938.[3] The share system, managerial structure and internal factionalism, all factored into their undoing. Even more, Llano's demise reflected the failure of the larger mass movement. Of those who remained in California, a group of former Llano colonists became activists in the Self-Help cooperatives of the Great Depression and Upton Sinclair's EPIC campaign.[4]

NEVADA COLONY

In 1915, Job Harriman and others from Llano organized a second community, Nevada Cooperative Colony (Nevada City), on 320 acres of farm land in the isolated but fertile Lahonton Valley near Fallon. A group moved onto the land in 1916. With Harriman busy elsewhere, an Oklahoman named C.V. Eggleston became the group's main leader. He used the colony as a base to organize for the Socialist Party, which proved strong in Nevada when its candidate for US Senate garnered almost 25 percent of the votes in 1914.[5] Fred Warren, formerly of the newspaper *Appeal to Reason*, edited *The Co-operative Colonist*. With the winds of war all around, they began to promote the colony as an antiwar and pacifist refuge. At its height, Nevada Colony had about 200 inhabitants, but only a few dozen homes were ever finished. In the spring of 1918, the local sheriff came to arrest resident draft resister Paul Walters. The sheriff was shot and killed, and a group of bounty hunters in turn killed Walters. Most of the colonists left in a mass exit, and by the end of the year only a few remained. The property was sold in 1919.[6]

YAMATO, DURHAM, & DELHI

In 1904, Kyutaro Abiko founded the cooperative agricultural colony of Yamato for Japanese immigrants near Livingston, California. It had thirty members by 1908. By 1910, the colony had a food- buying cooperative; by 1914, a marketing cooperative; by 1917, a packing shed. The colony did so well that state planners soon proposed that the state promote the founding of non-Japanese colonies nearby. The new colonies were to be populated by veterans returning from World War I, who were militantly demanding a share of America's wealth and land. An underlying motivation, patently racist, was apparently to limit the expansion of Japanese immigrant farmers in the area. The state of California sponsored two cooperative land settlements near Yamato in 1919, Durham and Delhi, under the auspices of the state government and with the planning of the state university. But the economic planning of the "experts" was inadequate. The land was very poor, and turned out to be incapable of supporting the colonists. The postwar deflation brought the colonies to ruin, and Durham and Delhi both disbanded in 1931 as the country was sinking toward the bottom of depression.[7] The Japanese-American farmers however continued to flourish. By 1940, 69 Japanese families worked more than 3,700 acres in the Livingston area. During World War II, all members of Yamato Colony were sent to internment camps. A land manager handled the properties during this terrible period, but after the war a new generation took over the farms and made them flourish again.[8] Today the area is still agricultural, primarily fruit and almond orchards. Most of the original colony is now part of the city of Livingston, an ethnically diverse town of about 10,500 in 2000.[9]

EMIGRANT COLONIES

Bill Haywood, the Wobbly leader who spent some time at the anarchist Home colony, was convicted in 1918 for calling for strikes during wartime. He skipped bail to escape prison, and took off to revolutionary Russia, where he was welcomed as a revolutionary hero. There he joined with 200 other American citizens to found Kuzbas Autonomous Industrial Colony in 1921 in Siberia. He clashed almost immediately with others on the Management Board, resulting in Haywood's expulsion from Kuzbas and in other colonists leaving with him. Haywood patched things up with the new "workers' state," and some of his ashes are buried under the Kremlin.[10]

In 1922, a group of eighty-seven Americans from Washington and Oregon, many of them IWW and Communist Party members who had been arrested in the Palmer raids, emigrated to Soviet Russia and formed Seyatel ("Seattle") Commune in the Caucasus. The core group was Finnish, and one of the leaders was Victor Saulit, a founding member of the Communist Labor Party in 1919. Seyatel became one of the most successful revolutionary communes in Russia, renowned for its highly mechanized farming techniques.[11] It reorganized as a collective farm in the 1930s, eventually devolved into a farming community, and as such continues today.

According to at least one account, members of both Kuzbas and Seyatel were victimized during Stalin's purges of 1934-38.[12]

NEW DEAL COLONIES

The New Deal homestead colony program, created in the depths of the Great Depression, involved at least 99 communities through 3 different agencies, and about 11,000 families, totaling around 50,000 people.[13] The basic idea was to give people in need the prerequisites for looking out for themselves: a house, some land, a way to make a living, and assistance to get started. It was also an attempt to bridge the boundaries between rural and urban, between agricultural and industrial. Of all the major New Deal programs, it was the smallest. Although burdened with undercapitalization, it touched numerous lives. Constantly attacked in Congress and the conservative press as socialistic, it was also critiqued from the Left as paternalistic and bureaucratic. The program came out of several schools of social and economic planning, particularly John Dewey's radical empiricism. An immediate stimulus was the back-to-the-land movement touched off by Ralph Borsodi's book *Flight from the City*, published in 1933, describing his family's discovery of the agrarian lifestyle of homesteading as a way to escape the troubles of urban living.[14]

Beginning in 1933, the Federal Emergency Relief Administration (FERA) created 28 communities for 2,426 families. The Division of Subsistence Homesteads (DSH), initiated in 1934, built 34 communities with 3,304 family units. The Resettlement Administration (RA), started in 1935, founded 37 communities with 5,208 families. In all, the government invested over $108 million in the project. The leading figures were Harold Ickes and Rexford G. Tugwell.[15]

The Federal Emergency Relief Administration, headed by Harry Hopkins, was the first relief operation of the New Deal, providing assistance for the unemployed and their families. Set up in May 1933, FERA gave states and localities $3.1 billion for local work projects and transient programs, provided work for over 20 million people and built facilities on public lands around the country over the next two-and-a-half years. FERA started 28 largely agricultural communities for 2,426 families. Among its more successful colonies were Cherry Lake Farms, FL; Dyess Colony, AR; Pine Mountain Valley Rural Community, GA; and Matanuska Colony in Alaska. FERA also had an "infiltration" project, in which the individual homesteads were scattered in ones, twos, or small groups through several counties. In May 1935, the FERA colony programs were taken over by the new Resettlement Administration. As we have seen, its Self-Help Cooperative Program also helped groups start cooperatives, assisted existing grassroots cooperatives to produce goods for themselves, and facilitated barter for needed goods that could not be produced within the group.[16]

The National Recovery Act (NRA) of 1933, one of the most basic pieces of New Deal legislation, established the Division of Subsistence Homesteads (DSH). Placed in the Department of the Interior, the project's director was M. L. Wilson, an agricultural economist. The department's mission was to create new rural communities where unemployed and underemployed industrial workers could relocate and support themselves by combining part-time farming with work in nearby industries. DSH funded several types of communities: twenty-four industrial communities for unemployed urban workers; four colonies for stranded workers in rural areas where the primary employers had left the area, particularly unemployed coal miners; three farm communities for submarginal farmers; a cooperative industrial community for a group of New York garment workers; and subsistence gardens for urban workers. The number of families in each community varied from 20 to 287, and the average cost per unit was $9,114.[17]

The industrial communities were considered the most successful because of their proximity to industrial employment, and they were built on fertile soils providing successful subsistence farming. Duluth (MN), El Monte (CA), San Fernando (CA), Granger (IA), and Longview (WA) homesteads were considered the most successful.[18]

The stranded communities, such as Arthurdale, WV, were considered the least successful. The DSH was not able to attract new industries to the areas and Congress did not provide funds to build its own factories.[19]

In 1935, the new Resettlement Administration (RA), headed by undersecretary of agriculture Rexford G. Tugwell, consolidated programs relating to land use planning and rural relief, and took over most of the community programs, including the DSH colonies. RA was charged with resettling farmers from sub-marginal lands and retiring those plots from agriculture. It encouraged clients to form cooperatives for purchasing supplies, machinery, or breeding stock; organized innovative small group medical plans and funded a number of forest homesteads and cooperative farms. RA was itself replaced by the Farm Security Administration in 1937.[20]

RA's Suburban Resettlement program added Greenbelt "garden cities," cooperative communities for low-income families on the fringes of cities. The Greenbelt villages would be surrounded by wide belts of common land to be left permanently undeveloped. RA projected building a hundred of them, but only three were begun: Greenbelt, MD; Greendale, WI; and Greenhills, OH. The Greenbelt program was attacked in the press as costly and subversive. None of the villages was ever finished. The project was abruptly shut down in 1939 and much of it was sold off to speculators. However, the cooperative traditions in some of the towns remained. In the 1970s, the Maryland project was home to the largest concentration of consumer co-ops in the United States.[21] As late as 1960, Tugwell called Greenbelt, MD, "still the most beautiful and efficient suburb in the US for low income families."[22]

The Great Depression ended with the launching of the war economy. During World War II, the right wing attacked all the New Deal social programs under the cover of patriotism. As some level of prosperity returned, attempts to create a new society fell out of popular favor. An antagonistic congressional investigation into the resettlement program resulted in a directive by Congress to dismantle it. As the Cold War set in, the scrapping of the New Deal homestead colony program was completed under Truman.[23]

SEVERAL NEW DEAL COLONIES
DYESS COLONY

In May 1934, FERA sent 1,300 Arkansans on relief into a 16,000 acre tract of swampy bottomland and put them to work digging ditches to drain it. They then built roads and 500 small five-room houses. The land had been purchased by FERA for a resettlement colony for tenant farm families. The colony was conceived by W. R. Dyess, Arkansas's first WPA administrator, and funded with $2 million in federal aid.[24]

It was laid out as a wagon-wheel with a community center at the hub surrounded by farm homesteads of twenty to forty acres. A few months later, the families began to arrive, selected from relief rolls because of their farming backgrounds. Each would get to own their own land by homesteading it for about three years. They drew a subsistence advance to buy their plot and house, plus a mule, a cow, and supplies until the first year's harvest. They cleared the land, planted cotton, corn, and soybeans, and set up pastures for livestock. The farms were worked individually, but the colony functioned as a cooperative, with seed purchased and crops sold as a group. Colony members often performed community tasks on a cooperative basis. Each family received a share of profits from the selling of the harvest, and from some of the other town businesses, including the general store and cannery. The town center grew to include a cotton gin, blacksmith shop, feedmill, sorghum mill, furniture factory, print shop, ice house, library, theater, newspaper, school, hospital, and community bank. They used a local scrip called a "doodlum." In 1936, there were about 2,500 residents. Singer-songwriter Johnny Cash grew up in Dyess. A dispute between state and federal governments resulted in the colony being placed under the Farm Security Administration (FSA) in 1940. By that time many of the farmers were fighting interference in community affairs from government administrators. During World War II, about half the residents left. In 1964, it was incorporated as a municipality, and over time became a small stable community with 550 residents in the year 2000.[25]

GRANGER HOMESTEADS

Granger Homesteads was begun in Iowa in 1933 by Luigi Ligutti, a Catholic priest and outreach leader. With a loan from the New Deal's FERA, he bought 225 acres and divided it into fifty small plots for a community of mostly urban miners. The plan was to work their homestead plots as a supplement to seasonal mining incomes. Granger Homesteads developed an agricultural school and a horticultural field laboratory as well as farmer cooperatives. No longer homesteads today, Granger's estimated population in 2003 was 638.[26]

CASA GRANDE

By 1934, three New Deal subsistence homestead colonies were in partial operation in the Southwest. Casa Grande Valley Farms, in Arizona, was the largest of these, with sixty families. The land was farmed through a centralized cooperative, though each family had its own subsistence plot. They had cooperative handicrafts, food processing, and other forms of mutual-aid. The government retained ownership of the property and controlled planning.[27] The colony became insolvent in 1943 and was dissolved and sold off in 1947.[28]

JERSEY HOMESTEADS

Jersey Homesteads was started in 1935, funded by DSH at the initiative of Benjamin Brown, as a self-sustaining community for urban Jewish garment workers. It was to be a combination of subsistence farms and a cooperative garment factory. The community built 200 red Bauhaus-style houses in clusters with common open space in the middle of each block. Members formed a Protective Association to negotiate with the government, safeguard settlers' interests, and support the cooperative character of the settlement. One of its residents was artist Ben Shahn. Only 120 of the 200 houses were purchased by homesteaders, and the remaining 80 were rented. The garment factory and farm lasted only a few years. Jersey Homesteads became the municipality of Roosevelt, population 900 today.[29]

MATANUSKA COLONY

In May 1935, FERA set aside 260,000 acres in the fertile Matanuska Valley, Alaska, for a homestead colony, and erected a tent city near the rail stop of Palmer. Soon arriving were 203 families from depressed areas of Minnesota, Wisconsin, and Michigan, regions with a similar climate. The colonists were chosen based on backgrounds in farming as well as skills in carpentry, blacksmithing, machinery, and leadership. The government brought in a workforce to build houses, barns, and infrastructure, spending $5 million on the project.[30] A drawing was soon held for forty-acre tracts; those who drew poor parcels were permitted to draw an additional forty acres. Some traded parcels. The colonists got to choose from five house designs, some log and some frame construction. Facing short growing seasons, high freight prices, and fairly distant markets, the farms had a high failure rate, and over half the population had left by 1940. But some met with success. Many maintained their homesteads by working in nearby military projects that were begun for World War II. Palmer became the only community in Alaska that grew from an agricultural economy. Twenty of the original families were still farming in the valley in 1965. Some of the farms are still operating today, while many in the area work in Anchorage. In 2005, the population of the town was around 7,000.[31]

BLACK HOMESTEAD COLONIES

At least fifteen black homestead projects were approved by the RA, but protests from groups of local white racists killed projects in several areas, including Dayton and Indianapolis.[32]

Aberdeen Gardens, begun in 1935 in Virginia near Newport News, was a Greenbelt town and the first New Deal African-American colony, funded by RA. Its 158 two-story brick homes were built by a black WPA work crew, and the colony manager was William Walker, an African-American. Each family had a tract for raising food as a supplement to a cash income from work, primarily in the shipyards.[33]

Blacks took part in five FERA projects. The first was Tillery in North Carolina, where 10,000 acres were divided into 200 units. Forty homes were finished when RA took over FERA. The new administration combined Tillery with a nearby white project, Halifax Farms, together making Roanoke Farms. The segregated sections were maintained, Tillery with 149 black families and Halifax with 145 white families. Each unit had a house with four to six rooms, indoor plumbing and electricity, a barn and poultry house.[34]

FERA included blacks in its "infiltration" project of disconnected parcels. Alabama Scattered Farms was a successful project involving thirty black families. Florida Scattered Farms, Arkansas Central Valley Farms, and Coffee Farms in Alabama all included both blacks and whites.[35]

Under the Farm Security Administration, there were nine black projects in seven Southern states, including Desha Farms, Lakeview, and Townes Farms in Arkansas. In Alabama, Prairie Farms and Gee's Bend would become world famous for their quilts, produced by their quilting cooperative. Beyond that, blacks participated in twenty-six integrated projects in the South.[36]

TVA

The New Deal Tennessee Valley Authority (TVA) planned a total regional cooperativization of the area beginning in 1937.[37] The first TVA head, Arthur Morgan, initiated one of group's first projects to build the town of Norris for employees at the dam. Norris was to become totally cooperative, a demonstration project to train people in cooperative principles and provide leadership for the vast cooperative movement the New Deal projected for the mountain people. But Norris never got past being a government project and a company town.

CELO

Morgan went on to found Celo Community in the mountains of North Carolina. This time, he arranged private financing to buy the 1,250 acres. Morgan set up an initial governance system, and gathered a cooperative-oriented group to get it started. The American Friends Service Committee (AFSC) was involved. The Celo vision saw members initiating economic enterprises doing non-exploitive work, preferably in partnership with other members. The group soon instituted a labor exchange, a cooperative store, and various social services. The community owned the land, but lifetime leases were granted to members (this system is more developed today as a community land trust). Any matter affecting the common interest remained controlled by Celo community as a whole. They instituted work days when the members worked together for their common interest. Celo's pacifism during World War II created great strains with the surrounding local populace, but the community struggled along and saw a revival in the 1960s. As generations aged, they became more conventional while retaining their landholding system. Celo continues today as a lively progressive community.[38]

BAYARD LANE & THE SCHOOL OF LIVING

Tired of struggling to survive in New York City in the 1920s, Ralph Borsodi left and built a rural homestead in Suffern, New York. His book, *Flight from the City* (1933), which advocated homesteading, influenced the New Deal. In 1934, he founded the School of Living (SOL) to research and teach a more balanced self-sufficient and fulfilling lifestyle centered on the ideas of healthy living based in the home and the land. He was soon joined by Mildred Loomis. Two years later, they began Bayard Lane Community on forty acres

extended families, as some of the early ideologists had predicted. There was continual turnover and, contrary to some forecasts, most people living communally continued to couple off. Many of the life-style innovations went into the mainstream, and the struggles over gender roles and equality in the family reshaped the average family household. Despite the turnover, new collective and cooperative living groups continued to form and remained widespread through the era. There were deep connections between the early communes and the other movements of the social upheaval of the 1960s. They were a haven for draft resisters, formed part of the underground railroad of resisters to Canada, and served as a sanctuary for refugees from numerous social and political struggles.

Communalism became a mass social movement. Many people had deeply rejected what America had become, yet retained an equally deep faith that something better was possible, something more in harmony with the planet and with the best in human nature. They had a conviction that if enough people decided it should happen, they could make it happen. There was a millennial atmosphere about the movement at first. The commune movement of the 1960s had elements of both separatism and social revolution, both secular and spiritual.

In its separatist aspect, 1960s communalism embraced the philosophy of "dropping out," having as little dependence as possible on the dominant system. In its social revolutionary aspect it saw large numbers abandoning the dying cities and moving out onto "liberated" land, interconnected communes around the country, where people could go who wanted out of the old culture and into something better. The communes could be decompression chambers from the old into a new society, where the best in people could be freed and permitted to blossom into a truly revolutionary force. They could be test-tube societies of the future and cells of the new society, bases for the spread of revolutionary ideas as well as bases for the people practicing them. The old oppressive system could die of its own dead weight if a new generation chose not to join. However, the concept of "dropping out" as a stratagem to transform society was patently flawed in underestimating the large pool of people ready to jump in and take the place of anyone who dropped out.

The first open commune of the 1960s was Drop City, begun in the spring of 1965 as an artist colony near Trinidad, Colorado. From the first, Drop City saw itself as part of a mass movement that was arising spontaneously all around, created by the same forces for social change that were forming the other movements of the '60s. Communes quickly began sprouting up in the Southwest and around the country. In New Mexico, Drop South, the Lower Farm, and New Buffalo all begun in the following year. They were open communes like Drop City. All the New Mexico communes were also very influenced by the Indian pueblos and the Chicano ejidos.

Tolstoy Farm, in Washington State, which had begun earlier in 1963 as a cooperative community based on the principles of Gandhi and Tolstoy, was swept up in the commune movement, and declared open land in 1966. Soon, a large communal group and many smaller ones and individuals were scattered on the land.

The open land concept was different from that of the open commune in that anyone could move onto the land without a communal commitment. Residents could share and cooperate as they chose. The next year, Morningstar in Sonoma County, California, was opened, and nearby Wheeler Ranch followed. Soon all of the open lands became enormously overcrowded.

Almost all the early communes and open land used the collective consensus system for decision-making (to the degree that they had any identifiable system at all). Most tried to retain what was useful and humane from modern technology, while returning as much as possible to basics and to the soil. While most had gardens or farms and small craft industries, probably all maintained outside incomes by members working or by other means. Few developed an adequate and reliable source of income.

Many of the communities made connections with older cooperative structures in the larger communities in which they were situated. Drop City got its water and electricity from the local cooperatives that had been serving the area since the 1930s. Without the help and mutual aid of neighbors and friends throughout the local population, many successful communities would never have survived their first year. Intentional communities established regional cooperative relations. Drop City helped New Buffalo with planting and harvesting, and New Buffalo gave Drop City use of its tractor. Some communities engaged in shared wholesale buying. Members crossed over regularly between groups.

The concept of openness started out as a strength in the movement but eventually turned into a weakness. Open communes proved to be generally unlivable in the long run because they were too unstable. Since people did not all choose each other, they were often not committed to each other. Not every two people can share the same bathroom and kitchen in peace. The communes attracted not only people willing to work for their survival, but also people looking for free trips.

Within a couple years, all the open communes decided to set population limits, declared the land closed and began taking in new members by invitation only.

But the momentum was not lost and a new wave appeared by 1968. These were mostly closed from the beginning. A similar progression had taken place 140 years earlier: New Harmony had been open at first and had attempted to go to the extreme sharing of a commune; when this proved an unworkable combination, they retreated to closed cooperation. The second wave of communities in both the earlier and the present movement ranged from full communes to land cooperatives.

Among these second-wave communities were Libre in Colorado, Twin Oaks in Virginia (with an elected managerial system), Reality Construction Company, Morningstar East and Lorien in New Mexico, Mullein Hill in Vermont, Wooden Shoe Farm in New Hampshire, The Farm in Tennessee, and Cerro Gordo in Oregon.

A new generation of communities inspired by the School of Living sprang up, including Heathcote Center in Maryland and Deep Run Farm in Pennsylvania, both of which helped to develop the landholding system of the community land trust, designed to give the community a true permanence set apart from the individuals participating in it at any given time while retaining member-control.

The Community for Non-Violent Action, an offshoot of the Committee for Non-Violent Action (which originally developed in the late 1950s in opposition to the spread of nuclear weapons and plants), ran a communal farm called Voluntown on its forty acres in Connecticut during these years, and took in many draft opponents and resisters during the Vietnam war. In 1968 the community was attacked by a squad of armed Minutemen, but held its own during a pitched battle.[43]

The communal movement reached a numerical peak around 1970, with probably about 3,500 land cooperatives and communities. By 1978, the number had declined to about 1,000.[44] The Farm was the largest, with over 1,000 members. Twin Oaks, Libre, Mullein Hill, Tolstoy Farm, U and I (Missouri) and Renaissance (Massachusetts) all continued strong. Twin Oaks, together with East Wind and a few smaller communities, formed the Federation of Egalitarian Communities. Drop South, Morningstar, Wheeler, and the Lower Farm each lasted only two to four years. New Buffalo went through several turnovers, but stabilized and developed a steady income as a dairy farm.[45]

Many communities met with friction in their surrounding regions. They were seen as a sort of advance-guard for a wave of newcomers squeezing in where there was hardly room already, depressing conditions either because they were willing to work too cheap, or because they didn't seem to work at all and lived on food stamps, welfare, or without any visible means of support. The FBI made regular rounds of them; many were harassed by their local authorities, business establishments and vigilantes; some were bulldozed, some raided. But in general, those communities that made friends and connections in their areas thrived, while those that didn't became isolated in a new type of alienation perhaps as bad as what they were trying to escape.

During this same period, communal living among young people was also common in urban areas, and most participants considered it part of the same movement. In the Bay Area, a communication network among collective and communal households sprang up through a series of collectively produced free magazines, beginning with *Kaliflower* in San Francisco, published in small editions monthly between 1969 and 1972. *Kaliflower* was succeeded by *The Grapevine* and then *The Networker*. The Berkeley Tenants Union organized a chain of cooperative-communal houses in the late 1960s stemming from a rent strike, some of which continued for over twenty years. Another group combining personal and political struggle was the Movement for a New Society, a network of small autonomous living collectives in seven cities, working for nonviolent radical social change. They came out of the antiwar movement in 1971 and were active in the anti-nuclear movement. Their largest center was Philadelphia, with about a hundred members in twenty communal houses in 1979.

While cooperatives and communes structurally embody nonviolent social change, some groups based in communal houses and deeply involved with collectivity, such as the Weather Underground and the Black Panthers, were also stirred by social injustice and the war, and worked to turn the system's violence back on itself.

Panther Houses, where many party members lived, provided for all the survival needs of the activists, who were expected to devote themselves fully to Panther Party work. Like all communal groups at the time, they struggled with issues of sexism. As Bobby Seale wrote in *Seize the Time* (1970), "In our Party, the sister is not told to stay home... But the very nature of the capitalistic system is to exploit and enslave people, all people. So we have to progress to a level of socialism to solve these problems. We have to live socialism. So where there's a Panther house, we try to live it. When there's cooking to be done, both brothers and sisters cook. Both wash the dishes... But a real manhood is based on humanism, and it's not based on any form of oppression."[46]

The Weather Underground, an offshoot of Students for a Democratic Society, organized communes that became safe houses when many of them went into hiding after the "Days of Rage" riots of 1969, during which they confronted Chicago police in response to the trial of the anti–Vietnam War activists known as the Chicago Eight.[47] A Weather Underground communiqué (1974) declared, "We create the seeds of the new society in the struggle for the destruction of the empire. For our generation that has meant the birth of communalism and collective work in the most individualist, competitive society in the world. Revolution is the midwife bringing the new society into being from the old."[48]

CASE STUDY: DROP CITY

The following is a brief synopsis. I present a more extensive personal account in my novelistic memoir, *Memories of Drop City*. I lived at Drop City from 1966 to 1968.[49]

I met Gene and Joann Bernofsky in New York City in the summer of 1965. They, along with Clark Richert, had founded Drop City in Southern Colorado a few months previously, and were back visiting their families in Queens and Brooklyn. I was living on the Lower East Side, an old immigrant neighborhood that a lot of creative young people had invaded and were starting to change into the East Village. This was during the early years of psychedelics. We weren't hippies—the concept hadn't yet been invented—and we were too young to be beats or beatniks.

Gene, Joann, and Clark had bought a small plot of former goat pasture for $350. They moved onto it, and declared it open to anyone to live there with them as a communal family with no preconceived or permanent rules, leaderless in structure, and sharing resources, work, and survival. They planned the entire community to be built of domes, and had completed one small one; this was the first use of domes for community housing. They invited me to come and stay for as long as I liked.

Joann and Clark were both painters, and Gene was an artist too, but his main canvas was Drop City. The three had met several years previously in college art classes. I thought Gene and Joann were both smart and funny. To give you a fuller picture, I need to say that Gene and Joann's families were working-class Jewish and Communist, and Clark's were Kansas Mennonite farmers. My dad was a mailman, my family was ethnically mixed, mostly New Deal Democrats, and grandpa, a union guy, called himself a communist. My mom called us "lower middle class," which I think meant to her that my dad had a job. Most of the other future Droppers, I would later find out, also came from families with few economic resources, and had some college education.

The idea of Drop City really blew me away. I'd never heard of anything like it. I was urgently looking for an alternative to New York where I'd grown up. Survival was just too hard there, and I felt I had to get out. I was a somewhat alienated outsider, working at marginal jobs and trying to avoid the Vietnam draft. I was planning to check out the West Coast, where many of my friends said that life was easier, and decided to stop at Drop City on the way.

I arrived the next spring. There were nine people there, including two kids. It looked like a space colony out on the high plains of southern Colorado, not far from the Purgatory River. Two domes were completed and two others under way. A fence surrounded the land, which seemed weird to me at first, but they had decorated it with art objects, and it formed a sort of protective ring of art, sheltering Drop City from the dangers out in the surrounding desert and mass society. An exciting, creative atmosphere enveloped the place. They were actually trying to "live the Revolution," as people used to say in those days. It was primarily an artist colony, but you didn't have to be an artist to live there. Everybody took Dropper names. I made friends with Clark ("Clard"), Richard ("Lard"), and the others. They were all visual artists except for "Rabbit" and his wife "Poly Ester," who were writers. I stayed for two weeks. We did a lot of construction, spending our free hours immersed in conversations and creative projects. It was hard work but also a lot of fun. I loved it, and they asked me to stay. But I also wanted to see the West Coast, and had a plan to meet my girlfriend "Patt" in San Francisco. I told the Droppers that I would be back in the fall with money to build a dome.

San Francisco was an exhilarating place in 1966, the year before the "summer of love." This was a moment when the counterculture was forming and the 60s were being invented. The Haight had been a somewhat depressed working-class neighborhood. Rents were cheap and young newcomers were beginning to take over large units and to live in groups. My girlfriend and I stayed that summer in a residence hotel called the Greta Garbo Home for Girls. San Francisco at that moment was so great, that word went out around the country and ignited that deluge of young people the next year. But even in '66, it was starting to turn hard-edged, and by the end of summer I wanted out. I arrived back in Drop City again in September of that year.

Another family had joined and one person had left, bringing the population up to twelve including me. A strange pallor hung over the place. I soon found out that there had been a fight between Rabbit and the new guy, Alteresio. It was complex. Rabbit was also not getting along with Gene and Joann, and they wanted him to leave. And I had thought things were going to be different here.

Things actually were different, but not in all the ways I had expected. I'd hoped that the Droppers would somehow be beyond personality conflicts, which in reality are going to be with us as long as there are people. Drop City was like a growing extended family, with all the interactions that implies. It was also democratic, and democracy can be messy. But there were so many positive, creative, stimulating activities going on that I could easily put up with the downsides. Over the next two years, I mostly had a great time. My girlfriend wasn't as enthused as I was. She cared more about comfort than I did, didn't take to sharing kitchen and bath, and was upset by the separation between Drop City and the surrounding society.

Because the domes were a technological innovation arguably better for housing than traditional construction, they came to very visibly symbolize a new and better society of which Drop City's communal social system and collective democracy were the microcosm. The domes also referred back to the ideas of R. Buckminster Fuller, inventor of the geodesic dome and advocate of the rational use of technology for the common good of all people and the planet. That fall, Fuller gave Drop City the Dymaxion Award for 1966, "for remarkable initiative, spirit, and poetically economic structural accomplishments." Drop City was utopian in that its declaration of openness to all was in direct contradiction to its small physical size, which could not possibly hold very many. But Drop City also advocated that others start similar communes and communities, which could be done on a shoestring, on inexpensive land, using scavenged and recycled materials, and connecting with the good will and survival cooperation of the people in the surrounding communities.

Drop City made decisions collectively: nothing was considered decided until everyone was satisfied enough to go along with it. It worked pretty well, even when the group grew larger. There were frustrating times, usually when two individuals had an ego problem, but over all, most things got straightened out. Drop City treated all objects except very personal possessions as common property. There was a common clothing room where any traveler in need could be supplied. In the fall of 1966, we formed a nonprofit corporation to hold the land, with outside friends as officers to look after the long-term preservation of the community, and with the directors changing with the current membership. We wrote into the deed that the land was to be forever free and open to all people.

In the spring of 1967, Drop City began receiving national and international attention, first in the underground press, then in the mass media. This publicity helped touch off the explosion of communes and communities in the following years. It also brought a flood of visitors, first as a stopping place for people traveling to the West coast for "the summer of love." In response, we set a population limit of fifty (when we were already over that) and in effect changed from an open commune to a closed community. But that did not stop the unending stream of visitors the publicity brought. The rule was that somebody had to invite you to stay, and the single Droppers, particularly the guys, were constantly inviting visitors to stay. People would couple up just long enough to get their foot in the door, then break up and couple again briefly with another new person. We had made an early decision never to throw anyone out, and that created a thorny situation when difficult people moved in.

It didn't take long before the Bernofskys had enough. They had wanted it to be a quiet family place, and it had become anything but that. They left soon after the flood of people started. Clark was offered a job designing art posters for a New York company, and he and his new wife Suzi Sunshine moved there temporarily, but never returned. Rabbit went on to start another community, Libre, with several other people.

Over the two and a half years that I was there, many things happened, both good and bad. In the early days, the main spirit had been hard work for collective survival, but that gave way to a carnival atmosphere that was smothering us; notoriety brought an easy cash flow, hindering us from developing some self-supporting industry and becoming a stable extended-family type community, as most members of the early group had wanted. Drop City never recovered the unity of spirit it once had.

For a while, I thought I'd found a home in this world and would live there for the rest of my life. But Patt and I moved to New Mexico in 1969 and started a family. Lard was the only Dropper remaining who had been there when I first arrived, and he left soon after. Drop City continued as a commune until 1973, going through a continual turnover of residents before it was finally abandoned, never having overcome the instability that the open concept fostered.

A few years later, Clark, Lard, and Alteresio convinced Patt and me to agree to sell the land and turn the money over to Criss-Cross, an artist cooperative they were involved with in Boulder. In order to sell it, they had to remove the phrase from the deed that it was to be forever free and open to all people. I found out later that the Bernofskys were opposed. Gene had retained the idea that, once all the furor burned itself out, he and Joann would return and start Drop City again. It was not to be.

Drop City was an episode in all our lives. With few exceptions, we all would have moved on, no matter what had happened there. In retrospect, I have to say that it was a great place despite its short-comings. If I were in my twenties again and had the chance, I'd do it again without hesitation.

COMMUNALISM TODAY

After a down period in the 1980s, many people began to organize communal living groups again. Motivations are the same today as they have ever been, a combination of lifestyle and involvement in a movement for progressive social change. In the new millennium, communalism has not yet reached a level that could be called a resurgence of the mass movement, although Communities Directory currently lists over 900 intentional cooperative communities in North America, and over 1,200 internationally.[50]

Communalism has been ingrained in the American experience since colonial times and has played an important role in numerous social reform movements throughout our history. We can expect periodic renewals of the communalist movement in America's future.

18.
Spiritual Communalism

The tradition of spiritual and religious communalism begins with the Pilgrims and runs along a track in American history that parallels the history of secular, socialist, and anarchist communalism. Although most religious communal groups have been theocratic— and therefore not true cooperatives, which are by definition democratic—their history is illuminating to this complex story. Analogous social forces and dynamics fueled both communalist tracks, and the mythological concept of America as a promised land permeates the historical perspective taught to almost every American child.

In Native American tradition, the indigenous nations and tribes all hold fast to a spiritual connection with the land. Tribal land is almost universally considered sacred, usually the place of origin, given to the tribe or nation by the Creator. The proper way of life is one lived in harmony with the land, caring for it with respect for future generations. The land itself could be called the beginning and end of tribal and native religion.[1]

Christian communalism is part of a larger social movement usually known generically as "Anabaptism." European Anabaptism had two wings, one separationist (or separatist) and the other political. The separationists went off to live among themselves in the little worlds they created and hoped to inspire others to imitate them; the politicals tried to take over state power and transform the whole of society to fit their vision. This duality was reenacted in America. Numerous religious sects formed separatist colonies while mainstream religious fundamentalists, despite separation of church and state, struggled to take state power. The distinction between the two groups was bridged by the concept that separationism was not an end in itself, but a strategy of social reform. Even as a sect separated from mainstream society, it also called on society to reject its old form and join it. The lure of America included the promise of a place where like-minded people could band together and live in the manner of their choice, and numerous persecuted religious groups came here seeking the fulfillment of that promise. In later periods, spiritual communalism continued to parallel the secular movement, and its focus on charismatic leaders continued to lead to separationist cultism. The opposite tendency took place in Christian socialism and similar movements, whose mission involved spreading the so-called "social Gospel" of cooperation into the larger society, and whose history spanned both communalism and cooperatives.[2]

ANABAPTISM

European Anabaptism began as a medieval heresy advocating an imitation of the communal living of Jesus' band and early Apostolic Christianity, which in turn took as its role model the communalist structure of the tribes of Israel in the Wilderness under Moses. This was a rejection of Catholic doctrine, which made a strict distinction between clergy and laity.[3]

Christianity had gained prominence in the ancient world by promising liberation to slaves, but became a pillar of power in the fourth century, when it was installed as the state religion, with bishops in government pay. The Church of Rome still recognized the imitation of Jesus' communalism as the holy life, but this was made the "privilege" of monks and nuns, and denied to society, at least until the Second Coming, widely expected to happen in the year 1000. When that year came and went, and Jesus didn't appear on schedule, many people went through a period of shock.[4]

The working people were mostly serfs by then, no longer slaves as in the ancient Roman world, but tied to a master and a plot of land for life. In most areas there were also "free" but poverty-stricken and oppressed small farming peasantries. Among the serfs and peasants, "heresies" began to sprout and grow.[5]

Almost all the heretics believed that true Christianity had been destroyed; they attempted to return to Apostolic Christianity, refusing to accept their proscribed lots in life. All the heresies were met with violence from state and church, and most groups organized resistance, some leading extensive armed revolutionary struggles. When these failed, many of the survivors went off to form separatist communal groups. Thus it was with the Albigneses in 11th century Southern France, renewed by the Waldenses in the 12th century, and then the Moravian (Czech) Brethren, founded on the ashes of the Bohemian peasant revolution of 1414. The Brethren assimilated the Waldenses, hiding from persecution in mountain colonies for over 200 years.[6]

Later, the Reformation loosed Anabaptism in opposition both to Rome and to Luther. From the defeat of the German peasantry in the revolutionary war of 1515 arose the Mennonites, Hutterites, Schwenkfelders and Anabaptist Dunkards. A couple of decades later, the Dukbors arose in Russia, also meeting with persecution. All of these communal groups followed the Pilgrims and the Puritans to America.[7]

CITY ON A HILL

In 1630, a decade after the Mayflower, the first ship carrying settlers of the Massachusetts Bay Company left for America. The colony was chartered as a self-governing trading group with rights to a plot of land. En route, Governor John Winthrop gave a sermon that became their mission statement, and was later put forward by others as the mission of America: "We shall be as a City upon a Hill, the eyes of all people are upon us." Winthrop urged them to become a model society, hoping to touch off a social movement in England and elsewhere based on the emulation of their example. He urged the settlers to be closely united:

> wee must entertaine each other in brotherly Affeccion, wee must be willing to abridge our selves of our superfluities, for the supply of others necessities, wee must uphold a familiar Commerce together in all meekenes, gentlenes, patience and liberallity, wee must delight in eache other, make others Condicions our owne, rejoyce together, mourne together, labour, and suffer together, allwayes haveing before our eyes our Commission and Community in the worke, our Community as members of the same body.[8]

The English Puritan sect had begun in secret in the 1500s and practiced economic mutual aid among members; the Puritans met with bloody repression by the Crown, but their beliefs took deep root and spread. While the separationist Pilgrims and Puritans chose to immigrate and set up a "commonwealth" in America, the vast majority of Puritans chose to stay in Britain and try to set up their commonwealth right there. Revolutionary sentiment and anger were everywhere among the working population in 17th-century England, where hundreds of minor offenses were punishable by death. The British rulers opened up America to the sects as a safety valve against revolution. It didn't work.[9]

Just as the monarchical church-state was an integrated religious, economic and political organization, the British workers' organizations combined religion, economics, and politics, and became cells of organized resistance. The Puritan "nonconformist" sects were based on an ideology of struggle for liberty and equality, with an end of making life on earth as it is in heaven, which they saw as sharing and cooperating in the form of a "commonwealth" and not an autocracy. They were millenarian and looked forward to an imminent Second Coming, when the money-changers would be driven from the temple for good, the meek would inherit the earth, and the first would be last. They saw the actual Coming only as the final act of the victory over the forces of evil; in the meantime, the faithful should model their lives and society on the future "kingdom" as much as possible, even though this meant conflict with the established order.[10]

In 1642, twenty-two years after the Pilgrims sailed and twelve years after Winthrop's sermon, English Puritan sects organized a revolutionary army. In 1649, they overthrew and abolished the monarchy and the House of Lords, and declared the Commonwealth of Britain. But there was an internal struggle in the revolutionary movement. The Levelers, fighting for a fair redistribution of the land, were crushed by the merchant-capitalist Cromwellians; Cromwell's version of a commonwealth turned out to be rule by a religious-military-capitalist oligarchy.[11] It lasted only a decade; then the new money-rich merchants and the old land-rich nobles intermarried and joined fists to bring back the monarchy and the House of Lords.[12]

Thus, the early main Western tradition of social revolution was Anabaptist, and the strategy vacillated between separatism and social revolution. But the failures of the movement, especially of the Puritans during their decade of power in Britain, drove large segments of the people to distrust political movements in religious clothes. Revolution next flared in France and America as a secular movement based on concepts of the natural rights of all people and no longer on the Anabaptist millennium. The Puritan communal land system in America, and its destruction by land speculators, is discussed in an earlier chapter. The Puritan Congregationalist church was not disestablished in Massachusetts until 1833, four decades after separation of church and state was written into the US Constitution.

QUAKERS

Meanwhile, the restored British monarchy opened America to other "nonconformist" sects. In 1663, Dutch Mennonites formed Plockhoy's Commonwealth, a colony on the Delaware River. The Labadists, a commune of Protestant separatists, arrived from Holland in 1683, and set themselves up at Bohemia Manor in New York, where about one hundred of them lived for fifteen years.[13]

In 1683, the Crown put Pennsylvania in the hands of Quakers. The Quakers, too, had begun in secret, practicing mutual aid among members, who were mostly from the working classes. As in the other sects, merchants tended to acquire power in their organizations. The Quakers were adamantly antislavery and later played an important role in the Abolitionist movement.[14]

The Quakers invited all the various German Anabaptist communalists to immigrate. German Mennonites (which include the Amish) started coming to the US in 1684, followed by the Moravian Brethren and the Schwenkfelders. A group of millennial Pietists from Southern Germany formed the Women in the Wilderness Community in 1694, followed by several other Pietist communities. Two groups of Anabaptists united in America to form the Dunkards. Later, a group broke away to found the Ephrata colony. Soon, there were religious communalists throughout the colonies, involving a sizable portion of the population.[15]

A millennial spirit blazed through the New Light Baptist "Great Awakening" that overtook America's frontier communities between 1730 and 1740. Recognizing no authority between an individual or congregation and the Deity, the Awakening was a major force leading to the American Revolution. Many "independent" ministers were agitators for liberty, equality and independence.[16]

After the United States won independence, offshoots of Quakerism renewed the religious communal movement, now among the American-born. First came Jerusalem Community, organized after a vision of the Quaker Jemima Williamson, begun in 1788 in upper New York State. A decade later, it had 250 members and lasted over 30 years.[17]

In the mid-nineteenth century, there were at least 50 religious communal groups in the United States, averaging about 200 members.[18] Besides being attempts to gain a constructive sense of community by separating from the capitalist wage system and leading a spiritual life, all were expressions of a widespread dissatisfaction with the bounds and constraints, both economic and social, that accompanied the isolated nuclear family. In capitalist-dominated communities, each family was pitted against each other for survival. In reaction, communalism attempted to restructure society as a cooperating family. Oneida's group marriage, the Mormons' polygamy and the Shakers' celibacy were all attempts to create improved internal structures in these new extended families.[19]

SHAKERS

In 1793, the first Shaker commune was formed by the New Light followers of Ann Lee, an immigrant English factory worker and a Quaker.[20] At their height fifty years later, eighteen Shaker communes with around 8,000 members dotted the Northeast and Midwest. The United Society of Believers in Christ's Second Appearing, as they called themselves, attained almost complete self-sufficiency and practiced decision-making equality between the genders. Its members were primarily gathered from local converts in each area, and land was obtained either through pooled resources or by acquiring a farm already owned by a recruit. While most Anabaptist groups based themselves in the biological family, the Shakers were celibate and had to constantly take in new members, which was a factor in their eventual decline.

The Union of the Spirit (Hymn 35)

We love to dance, we love to sing,
We love to taste the living spring,
We love to feel our union flow,
Which round, and round, and round we go.[21]
...
Whoever wants to be the highest
Must first come down to be the lowest;
And then ascend to be the highest
By keeping down to be the lowest.[22]

Frederick William Evans, probably the most important Shaker leader and historian at Mount Lebanon community at its height, was the younger brother of George Henry Evans, fearless newspaper publisher, vocal supporter of Owenite communalism, the Working-men's Party, Abolitionism, and justly called the father of the Home-stead Act. The Evans brothers demonstrate the kinship of spiritual and secular communalism.[23]

MORMONS

The Mormons (members of the Church of Latter-Day Saints) were first organized in 1831 in upper New York State. They lived communally at first as a United Order, but this system was aban-doned after less than two years in favor of separate cooperative households practicing what they called plural marriage.[24]

After migrating to Utah in 1847, the church organized some of the first American mutual irrigation cooperatives in 1850. They set up a chain of cooperative stores between 1864 and 1882, ex-tending to almost every Mormon community, with 146 branches in 126 towns at its peak. But the wholesale, like the Church, was or-ganized theocratically and the stores were set up under a stock sys-tem with votes not limited to one per person, so eventually control shifted to an ever-smaller number of members. This cooperative distribution system continued until 1882, when the church hierar-chy decided to abandon that goal and opened the area to capitalist stores for the first time.[25]

Some Mormons made a new attempt in 1874 to create a Unit-ed Order on a larger scale than the first. Twenty-five families joined together, founding Orderville, which soon had a population of over five hundred. All members drew necessities from a common fund; all surpluses and debts were canceled once a year. Several other semi-communal settlements were organized within the next decade. But the patriarchal theocratic Church, by then committed to capitalism, disclaimed them, leading to great internal strife and to the eventual dissolving of the communes and division of property in 1899 after twenty-five years.[26]

Meanwhile, officially disavowing plural marriage, Utah joined the US as a state in 1896.

ONEIDA PERFECTIONISTS

The Perfectionists established their first commune in Vermont in 1846. Led by John Humphrey Noyes, they believed that the Sec-ond Coming had already taken place in the year 70, permitting them to form Christ's millennial kingdom themselves, free of sin and perfect in this world. Unlike any other recorded 19th-century community, they practiced what they called complex marriage, a form of structured group relationship in which all were heterosexually married to all others in the group.[27] They practiced birth control by male continence. In 1848, this extraordinary group moved to Oneida, New York, then branched out into Connecticut and New Jersey. Starting with 87 members in 1848, Oneida had over 300 at its height. Women and men had equal rights and voice in governance. Child-care nurseries permitted all parents to work. They sought to resolve conflicts through "mutual criticism" sessions. The community was self-supporting through agriculture and the industries of silk thread production, animal traps, silverware, palm frond hats, garden furniture, and leather travel bags. Menial tasks were rotated. In its later years, the community took on local employees.[28]

Oneida Perfectionist hymn (c. 1855)

We have built us a dome
On our beautiful plantation,
And now we all have one home,
And one family relation...[29]

Oneida finally crumbled on personality clashes. The Vermont and New Jersey branches closed in 1854; the Connecticut group disbanded after a tornado hit them in 1878. They abandoned complex marriage in 1879, and dissolved as a community in 1881. The Oneida New York group wound up as a capitalist silverware corporation.[30]

GERMAN SEPARATISTS

The German separatists kept coming. The Rappites founded Harmonie, Pennsylvania, in 1805, moved to Indiana in 1814, then ten years later back to Pennsylvania. Separatists from Wurttemberg founded the village of Zoar, Ohio, in 1817. Each set up a colony or colonies mostly scattered across the Northern states. In the early 1840s, a communal colony of German Catholics, St. Naziaz Community, was founded in Wisconsin; German Protestant True Inspirationists formed Amana in upper New York in 1842, later moving to six connected villages in Iowa; Bethel was started in Missouri in 1844, and Aurora in Oregon also in 1844; Bishop's Hill was organized by Swedish Anabaptists in Illinois in 1846. The Hutterites came in waves between 1874-79, settling in Dakota Territory.[31] Even though they all generally kept to themselves and made no attempt to recruit new members from outside, they still had tremendous influence on the areas in which they lived. Most eventually dispersed or gave up communalism, becoming cooperative; the Amana Inspirationists and the Hutterites are still flourishing today. Some depended on charismatic leaders, such as Father Rapp, who tended to run their groups autocratically; others, like the Hutterites, were semidemocratic. There are about fifty Hutterite communal colonies in the US today, mostly in South Dakota and Montana, organized on a patriarchal consensus system.[32]

CHRISTIAN SOCIALIST COMMUNALISM

With the development of the Christian Socialist movement, religious and secular communalism dovetailed. Christian Socialists, preaching the so-called social Gospel, formed a number of colonies in America after 1840, usually after periods of social upheaval. Hopedale was the first Christian Socialist colony, begun in 1841 in Massachusetts as an expression of the belief that the struggle for social justice was the true means of salvation. Hopedale lasted 15 years, with 235 members at its height.[33]

The social strife in the last decade of the 19th century brought about a new wave of Christian Socialist communalism. The Society of Christian Socialists was started in Boston in 1891 by a group of clergymen, to help bring about a cooperative commonwealth in America; many had been members of Nationalist Clubs. At first, the Society did educational and support activities, working with the Populists and other insurgent groups, including the strikers at both Homestead and Pullman. But class struggle in "the bloody 90s" was being played for keeps, and as the workers were met with increasingly violent defeats, at least one group of Christian Socialists drew back and went separationist. In 1898, the Christian Commonwealth Colony on a former slave plantation near Columbus, Georgia, was opened to any and all as a cell in "the visible Kingdom of God on earth."[34] In harsh and hostile conditions of mostly hill and swamp, 150 struggled to survive until their crops failed in the middle of their fourth year, and the community was hit with a terrible malaria epidemic.[35]

At about the same time, another group of Midwestern Dunkards migrated to the Pacific Northwest to form the Christian

Cooperative Colony in Sunnyside, Washington, where they practiced mutual aid.[36]

Altruria was formed by a group of San Francisco Bay Area Christian Socialists inspired by the W. D. Howells novel *A Traveler from Altruria* (1894). A network of clubs in Berkeley, Oakland, and San Francisco, also involved with consumer co-ops, bought 185 acres in Sonoma County, California in the fall of 1894. Seven families and a handful of single men moved there with great enthusiasm, but after a few months dissolved into economic chaos and, in the summer of 1895, disbanded into several smaller groups. They planned to reorganize into a chain of cooperating colonies, but that never materialized.[37]

THEOSOPHISTS

Spiritual communalism sprouted in the Theosophist movement, which looked to Eastern spirituality. Theosophists ran three communal schools in California between 1897 and the mid-1930s. Helena Blavatsky, cofounder, had belonged for a while to a Bellamyite Nationalist Club. Two of the communal schools were organized theocratically, but the third, Halcyon, was run on democratic principles; there were clashes among them. Theosophists were active in the later EPIC movement.[38]

TWENTIETH CENTURY

The Come-Outers, a Christian congregation, separated from the rest of society and moved onto Lopez Island in Puget Sound in 1912 as a communal sect of 175 members. They disbanded in 1920.[39] Pisgah Grande was an evangelical Pentecostal commune of almost 300 between 1914-21, north of Simi Valley, California. Among its many undertakings was an early "free store."[40]

Sunrise Community, organized by a Jewish group in 1933 in Michigan, grew quickly to over three hundred but collapsed over ideological struggles after three years.[41]

The Catholic Worker Movement organized numerous collective and communal projects beginning in the 1930s. Leaders Dorothy Day and Peter Maurin established rural communes in Illinois, Ohio, Pennsylvania, Michigan, Massachusetts, and ten other states. Many of these were in pre-existing Catholic farm communities. Some of the communes were interracial. With the mottos "eat what you raise and raise what you eat" and "prayer and work," they based their movement on cooperative living, open admission, rejection of mechanized farming, and Church doctrine. Many of the communalists were city people who initially knew little about farming; as in all such situations, there was some alienation between the communes and the surrounding rural communities. Tivoli, a collective farm in upper New York, continued to the end of the century.[42]

The Nation of Islam, founded in 1930, ran hundreds of community enterprises throughout the United States, including bakeries, restaurants, hair-care shops, and a 1,500-acre farm in Georgia. Its program, written in 1965, includes a colonization plan with the goal of becoming a separate territory or state.[43]

Koinonia Farm, begun in 1942 not far from Plains, Georgia, practiced partnership cooperative farming on communal land with surplus income from each member's crops going into a communal fund. When the farm took in its first black members in 1957, members were met with physical and economic violence, but dug in and held on. They were about sixty strong in 1980.[44]

The Vale was founded in 1946 in Yellow Springs, Ohio by a group of fifteen mostly Quaker families committed to cooperation on common land. It became a land trust in 1980. The community is still thriving today with eleven homes, twenty-two adults and eighteen children.[45]

The Bruderhof, a group in the Hutterite tradition, formed in 1920 in Germany, fled Hitler and immigrated to the United States in 1954. Members expanded into large communes in upper New York, Pennsylvania and Connecticut. Unlike most of the earlier immigrant Anabaptist groups, they took in outsiders, and by 1980 were made up of people from a wide variety of backgrounds.[46]

Reba Place Fellowship was founded in 1957 by a group of Mennonites. In 1980, Reba Place was a community of about 250 living as an extended family neighborhood in Evanston, Illinois.[47] In 2007, the Fellowship celebrated its fiftieth anniversary with "a weekend of sharing, memories, stories, music, and dance," attended by a hundred people from the Fellowship's past and present. In 2008, Reba Place still has over sixty members and appears to be thriving.[48]

THE SIXTIES

The communalist movement of the 1960s included many spiritual and religious communities embracing every Western and Eastern practice, created by many of the same forces that produced the secular communes of the era. Besides newly organized groups, numerous spiritual or religious communities formed in earlier decades gained new life in the '60s.

Some of the earliest intentional spiritual communities of the era were Lama in New Mexico, The Farm in Tennessee, and Brotherhood of the Spirit/Renaissance in Massachusetts. All of these were organized in a democratic spirit, albeit with limited democracy. Many of the early secular communes and communities of the 60s were also spiritual places, but not in a formal way.[49]

Numerous communal groups following Eastern religious practices formed in the 1960s and 1970s, including: Kripalu Yoga Ashram (Hindu) in Pennsylvania; Karme-Choling Meditation Center (Buddhist) in Vermont; and Abode of the Message (Sufi) in upstate New York.[50]

• • •

Overall, many religious and spiritual communities have had longer lifespans than secular ones. With some notable exceptions, however, most disbanded in the end and new ones formed. Just as generations of secular communalists never completed the far-reaching social revolution that they hoped for, generations of religious communalists never ignited the permanent deep spiritual revolution in the larger society that they hoped for. Nonetheless, spiritual communalism, like its secular counterpart, will surely continue to resurface time and again as a transforming force in American society.

Conclusion

COOPERATIVES TODAY AND THEIR POTENTIAL AS A STRATEGY OF SOCIAL CHANGE

The tapestry of US history is woven with the day-to-day struggles of hundreds of millions of ordinary people for better lives. Mutual-aid organizations such as cooperatives and unions have always been near the heart of those struggles. Those struggles embody the "the pursuit of happiness" that the Declaration of Independence boldly asserts is our inalienable right. America proudly proclaims that our society aspires to offer a fair and equal opportunity to all in that promised pursuit. Yet, after all these years and all these generations, have we really succeeded in structuring our society to offer a fair and equal opportunity to all?

LOOKING BACKWARD AND FORWARD

Throughout US history, urban wageworkers and small rural farmers have waged parallel struggles. The two groups have shared common roots, and often worked closely in coalition towards common goals. Both workers and farmers have organized cooperatives to try to solve their economic problems; when the economic system has stymied them, both have formed political organizations to try to change the rules of the system. Farmers and urban workers, the two parallel tracks of the American working people, have been bridged by their cooperatives. Recurrent uprisings of both workers and farmers have risen in response to economic inequities, and their trajectories have followed the country's economic cycles.

The differences between the rural and urban populations have always been more apparent than deep. Most of the families in the farm communities of the Midwest and West were formerly urban people from the East, drawn there by the offer of almost-free land. Cooperatives and mutual aid organizations bridged the gulf between farmers and urban workers. The Grange and the Farmers' Alliance worked in close coalition with the Knights of Labor in the Greenback-Labor Party and then the Populist Party. Grangers helped the railroad strikers in 1877; co-op stores joined arms with the unions in the Seattle General Strike of 1919; the self-help UXA aided the San Francisco General Strike of 1934; striking farmers of the American Agriculture Movement brought truckloads of food to striking coal miners in 1978.

Both farmers and urban workers have a long history of cooperatives. While farmers could be very individualistic, farm communities were usually very cooperative. It was not unusual for individualistic farmers to each belong to a half dozen different cooperatives. This was the case because cooperatives do not ask that members submerge individualism into a collectivity but, on the contrary, come together to enhance their lives. The Grange, Farmers' Alliance, and other farmer organizations had visions of a radically restructured system based on cooperation. The labor movement had similar visions. The cooperative unionism of early workers was abandoned by the American labor movement primarily because it was defeated. After the demise of the Knights of Labor at the end of the 19th century, most union workers believed that they could no longer win practical improvements through worker cooperatives in the face of brutal government and corporate opposition. So most of those still stuck in oppressive jobs moved on to simple trade unionism. Some still looked to new radical forms, such as the syndicalist model of a new society based on industrial unions, the anarchist vision of a stateless society, or the institution of a "workers' state." All of these radical movements painted pictures of a future society based on principles of equality and cooperation, which would arise after the oppressive structures were swept away.

Cooperative movements in America have always risen and fallen with the turns of the economic cycle. When money is scarce in hardening economic times, cooperatives have experienced a surge in membership, but the hardest of times have also killed them. Worker cooperatives have also often been formed during economic upturns, when workers can gather enough resources to try to make a go of it. Yet, during periods of general prosperity, people have also tended to explore more individualistic options, and have abandoned cooperation and social movements. The self-seeking tendencies in human nature have been magnified by the American glorification of the individual and neglect of community.

Nonetheless, in times of crisis the American people have repeatedly returned to mutual aid, and have called on government for support. The New Deal's promotion and support of cooperatives was the fruit of generations of struggle. From the earliest times, cooperators realized that they needed the backing of the powers of government to achieve their larger goals. Although the New Deal's programs were limited and bureaucratic, although some of their policies actually hurt some cooperatives, and although they backed off under assault from the financial-corporate oligarchy, the New Deal remains a beacon, and demonstrates what a partnership between progressives and government might accomplish.

DOES IT HAVE TO BE THIS WAY?

The beginning of this study asked why there are so few worker cooperatives. Hopefully, this history has shed some light on the answer.

Worker cooperatives have been marginalized and planned out of our economy. The "free market" is a fiction: all markets and economies are regulated and shaped. The tax laws and the money system offer businesses and corporations—particularly large corporations—numerous economic advantages that they do not offer to worker cooperatives. Worker cooperatives almost always begin small and undercapitalized, and involve people with underdeveloped business skills. Laws posing numerous obstacles to unionization have shaped the American labor market. A majority of nonunion workplaces has resulted in a weakened and struggling working population with few resources available to start businesses, even after pooling their resources to launch a cooperative. The economic life of society today is primarily organized on the capitalist wage system. Unemployment is structured into the system. In addition, a large number of jobless people are not counted in unemployment statistics, which include by definition only those actively seeking employment. There is also an underground economy whose members are also not included in statistics. The unemployed, the marginally employed, the not-working, as well as dissatisfied employees, all might find jobs in worker cooperatives, if that were an available option. Struggling communities and populations could be rejuvenated and elevated if the economic system facilitated and encouraged the organization of cooperatives, and if it made economic resources available to people wanting to organize them.

Many Americans have never known any work outside the wage system, and some even have difficulty conceiving of another way of structuring work, yet the wage system is neither a necessary fact of life nor a fundamental tenet of this country's history. Wage labor was introduced onto this continent as a form of bonded labor along with indentured servitude for whites and slavery for blacks. Cooperative and communal work were typical of Native America and of the early settlers. Although most Americans have little experience in cooperative work today, about 40 percent of the population has experience as a member of a cooperative such as a credit union, an electric cooperative, or a parent play group. That may seem like a small thing, but for many people it is their first adult experience with a democratic organization or an alternative system.

IS AMERICA DIFFERENT?

Many Americans still like to think that this country is different from the rest of the world, and since the 1830s have talked about "American exceptionalism." The United States—with its vast natural resources and experience of genocide, slavery, human exploitation, and environmental degradation—has certainly had a unique history. But with globalization, the American people are also learning that we are in the same leaking boat as the rest of the world's peoples. We are being forced to learn humility, and to work respectfully with other peoples to make a successful and sustainable world to leave to our descendants.

America is billed as a great experiment in democracy "of the people, by the people, and for the people," the land of equal opportunity. Business pundits loudly tout our economic system as the source of America's wealth and prosperity, making the US the richest, most powerful country in the world. They promote the capitalist wage system as if it were a beacon of freedom, proudly displaying it for the world to admire and copy. But the hard truth is that America's economy is not structured to give everyone a fair and equal opportunity, but to assure that a small elite always wins. Under its rule, advanced technology enriches primarily those in control. Whatever prosperity working people have is due not to the American capitalist system, but to America's position at the top of the world's food chain, reaping the wealth of the planet, just as ancient Rome's prosperity once came from plundering the then-known world. This wealth is increasingly consolidated by a small corporate elite, and less and less of it is shared with the middle and working classes. The individualistic consumerist lifestyle sponsored by corporate America is today's version of Rome's "bread and circuses." While promoting a xenophobic nationalism for the people, the giant corporations themselves have become increasingly multinational, with decreasing responsibility to the people of any country.

In the US and elsewhere, this triumph of corporations has been achieved through their control of the political and economic systems. US laws and international trade agreements favor and subsidize corporations over people, and corporate interests wrote the laws making that possible. But this is new only in its global extent. Capitalism has never been democratic, and when unchecked, it has always become monopoly. The very existence of cooperatives challenges corporations and capitalism; corporations have therefore always worked hard to weaken, discredit, and destroy them through waging price wars, enacting legislation that undercuts their viability, labeling them in the media as subversive and a failure, and using numerous other stratagems.

On the other side, the American working people have always taken inspiration from the proclamation of equality and the faith in social revolution expressed in the Declaration of Independence. To American workers in the early period, that meant the possibility of liberation from the wage system through self-employment, cooperation, public education, and democratic legislation. When bitter experience convinced some generations that the system was not reformable, some explored the option of revolution.

THE COOPERATIVE SECTOR

Economies are usually considered to have three sectors: (1) the business or private sector, which is privately owned and profit motivated; (2) the public sector which is owned by the government; and (3) the social enterprise sector—often called the *social economy*—which consists of voluntary, community, and not-for-profit activities organized around shared interests and purposes, distinct from government, family, and for-profit business. This sector is considered part of "civil society." The social economy is the home of most cooperatives, as their intrinsic characteristics set them apart from private businesses and corporations. A fourth economic sector is sometimes is included: "the informal sector," or "the informal economy." This includes all economic activity "under the radar," "underground," not monitored, taxed, or regulated by any government, including marginal survival activities and informal exchanges among friends and family members.[1] Cooperatives can also be found in this informal economy. They flourish in activities performed without any financial exchange and outside of the dominant economic system. Groups of this type include numerous voluntary organizations and associations formed for any purpose, such as musicians' gatherings, childcare exchanges, neighborhood watches, and small community associations.

Social enterprises besides cooperatives include community-owned enterprises and businesses operated by nonprofit organizations with primarily social objectives, whose surpluses are primarily reinvested for that purpose. Social enterprises today are a vital and growing sector worldwide. Nonprofits have been increasingly advancing their missions through entrepreneurial strategies, trading in goods or services, and helping to organize and support worker and community cooperatives.

The informal sector is part of every economic system, and in many "developing" countries, the informal economy involves a large part of the labor force—up to 60 percent according to some estimates. The International Cooperative Alliance, affiliated with the UN, today urges governments to promote cooperatives to transform their informal economies "into legally protected work, fully integrated into mainstream economic life."[2]

The growth of worker cooperatives worldwide has followed economic globalization, with their number and extent increasing significantly in both industrialized and developing countries. This is a reaction of mutual aid of the world's peoples in face of a deteriorating situation. While not long ago worker cooperatives were viewed internationally as a marginal phenomenon, today they are taken increasingly seriously as an important economic force in the world.[3]

WHY HAVE MANY WORKER COOPERATIVES FAILED?

Numerous worker cooperatives have been organized over the last 200 years, and most have ultimately failed. Are there flaws inherent in the concept or structure that make them unworkable? This historical study has tried to answer that question. Individual cooperatives, like any human organization, ultimately fail. In this, they are no different from any individual business. The majority of all new businesses fail in their first year. Standard advice to startups is to not expect a profit for the first two years. Since the beginning of the industrial revolution, most work has been increasingly dominated by costly technology, and most cooperatives have almost always begun under-capitalized.

Cooperatives, like any human organization, have a life span during which they usually have to change and develop, as the situation around them changes. Cooperatives are a response to a situation, and the situation is always in flux. Individual cooperatives don't last forever, since they are formed by people, who also don't last forever. The cooperatives of each new generation take on new and creative forms, as they are formed to meet new situations and new variations of situations, while consistently facing a heavy opposition from corporate interests and the politicians that serve them. So the lack of eternal longevity of any particular cooperative or any social structure is not an adequate way to judge its value. Cooperatives have sprung up anew in every generation, so the question should not be why individual cooperatives fail, but why American society has failed to structure cooperatives into the system.

People who are looking for a structural panacea for all the world's problems are barking up an empty tree. Social structures by themselves do not solve social issues. Societies don't freeze at some ideal moment. All societies have hard times. But there are also always moments when a people can come together and achieve something great. Each new generation creates structures to solve its needs, not mimicking some ideal form, but always in an intensely practical relation to the actual situation on the ground. The US has always been a land of enormous potential, and the American people have many times tried to rise up and achieve our potential. Right now our socio-economic system appears to me to be driving at breakneck speed toward a dead end. To prevent that crash, many people realize that we have to make a tidal shift in our priorities. That requires an alternative, an understanding that a better society is in fact possible.

Worker cooperation has always been close to the heart of America. It has been our common past, our heritage, and can become our common future.

CAN WORKER COOPERATIVES SUCCEED?

If the preservation of America's communities were really a national value, then the development of community worker cooperatives would be a national policy. Cooperatives are all about a balance between individual and community interest. But in America, we get a hollow freedom in exchange for a loss of community. The backroom government of America, consisting of all the biggest financiers, plans the economy with the aim of maximizing corporate profits, and they plan worker cooperatives out of it. There are few fields where many independent worker-run businesses can easily survive, so there are a very limited number of worker cooperatives, leaving the vast majority of people with little choice but to seek employment from a boss or corporation, which is often still wage slavery. Meanwhile, unionization has shrunk from over 35 percent 60 years ago to under 14 percent in 2005.

Today, the powers of government promote the system of corporate rule, prosperity for an elite, and increasing marginalization for working people and the middle classes. But instead of giving away the world's natural resources to corporate profiteers, society could use that wealth to promote full employment, prosperous communities, and the empowerment of people at work. The economic system could be changed to one that values the well-being of all people.

A proper role of government is to work to create a level playing field providing fair opportunities in an economic context in which society can prosper. But what is a level playing field in a world of vast economic inequality?

Beneath all the window dressing, the system has failed dismally to provide a decent life for vast numbers of Americans or to provide basic services or jobs for people. A social crisis of enormous proportions is deepening. For many, the system is still wage slavery. The corporations still fear worker cooperatives, for the same reasons they have used their power to put them down throughout American history. Yet if America is ever to fulfill its promise, the government must ensure that no one is forced into wage slavery, that everyone has a choice. This would signal that wage slavery would be finally abolished. The goal of promoting worker cooperatives on a national scale should be a core government policy.

Economic regulations do not have to favor corporations. The economic system could make loans available to groups of unemployed and underemployed to start worker-owned cooperative businesses in every field. Neighborhood and community co-ops could be empowered to do public work and services that benefit their local areas. The nation could promote a bottom-up participatory democracy in the workplace and in communities. Society, through the powers of government, could use our common resources to promote communities and neighborhoods working together and producing for our common social good, through a system of worker cooperatives and other social enterprises whose purpose would be to promote prosperity in the entire population, to improve the quality of life of all people, to empower people to exercise their inalienable right of the pursuit of happiness, and to realize their creative potentials. Some small steps have been taken in the direction of a mass movement for social and economic justice with worker cooperation at its heart, but a long uphill road awaits us.

Although capitalism, competition, and wage slavery run rampant on the surface of our country today, history may someday show that the working population was quietly gathering strength beneath the surface for its next challenge. And it may be that old-fashioned traditional American worker cooperation, with its promise of real freedom, may still prove stronger and deeper here than capitalism, and will be the force to ultimately abolish its unique system of wage bondage.

• • •

In what does real power consist? The answer is plain and short—in property... A general and tolerably equal distribution of landed property is the whole basis of national freedom... An equality of property, with a necessity of alienation constantly operating to destroy combinations of powerful families, is the very soul of a republic. While this continues, the people will inevitably possess both power and freedom; when this is lost, power departs, liberty expires, and a commonwealth will inevitably assume some other form.[4]
— Noah Webster, 1787

I hope we shall crush in its birth the aristocracy of our moneyed corporations, which dare already to challenge our government to a trial of strength and bid defiance to the laws of our country.[5]
— Thomas Jefferson, 1816

The strongest bond of human sympathy, outside of the family relation, should be one uniting all working people of all nations, tongues and kindreds.[6]

— Abraham Lincoln, 1864

If you and I must fight each other to exist, we will not love each other very hard.[7]

— Eugene Debs, 1908

Appendix 1.
Listing of Some Unique Cooperatives Today

This collection provides a broad glimpse into the extent of cooperatives in 2008. Numerous others, equally unique and successful, can be found throughout the US.

INDUSTRIAL

At the SUSTAINABLE WOODS COOOPERATIVES, in Lone Rock, Wisconsin, 150 members own and maintain over 20,000 acres of sustainable forestland, and run a 4.5-acre sort yard and a large solar kiln to process timber products. They provide land stewardship education, development of certified sustainable forest management plans, and harvesting, processing, and marketing services.[1]

FREEDOM QUILTING BEE, a handicraft co-op in Alberta, Alabama, was established in 1966 to provide sharecropping families with a more stable income. The women began selling quilts after many of their families lost their farms in retaliation for their civil-rights activities. In 1968, the co-op bought land and set up a sewing plant and homes for evicted families. By 1992, FQB had more workers than any other enterprise in the town.[2]

INKWORKS in Berkeley, California, has provided full-service high quality union offset printing at affordable prices since 1974, using recycled papers and vegetable oil-based inks, and offering discounts for peace and social justice organizations. Design Action Collective, a spin-off from Inkworks, specializes in design and communications.[3]

ISTHMUS ENGINEERING AND MANUFACTURING CO-OP, in Madison, began as a small collective in 1980, and retained its integrity as a worker co-op as it grew into a world-class builder of custom automated manufacturing machinery and equipment.[4]

BIG TIMBERWORKS, in Gallatin Gateway, Montana, builds custom timber-frame homes and other structures. Formed in 1999—when the business was sold to the employees—the co-op currently has 40 workers, 14 of whom are owner-members.[5]

SERVICES

SOLIDARITY SPONSORING COMMITTEE EMPLOYMENT AGENCY, a worker-owned temporary employment agency in Baltimore, places workers in jobs while training members to be owners and managers of the company. SCC trained 260 people in 2000. It is sponsored by AFSCME and BUILD, and was instrumental in the passage of the nation's first living-wage ordinance.[6]

CHILDSPACE MANAGEMENT GROUP provides childcare in three economically and ethnically diverse areas of Philadelphia. The co-op offers comparatively high pay for childcare specialists who are usually among the lowest paid workers in the job market.[7]

COOPERATIVE ECONOMICS FOR WOMEN, located outside Boston, organizes low-income women to generate income, and for community development. It has spun off successful sewing, house cleaning, catering, and childcare co-ops.[8]

ENTERPRISING STAFFING SERVICES provides temporary staffing service jobs for residents from an economically depressed section of Washington D.C. This employee-owned co-op has placed over 150 individuals in hospitality, office, healthcare, and construction jobs.[9]

COOPERATIVE HOME CARE ASSOCIATES, an employee-owned co-operative in New York City, provides quality jobs to more than 500 African-American and Latina women as homecare paraprofessionals, many of whom were previously dependent on public assistance.[10]

WAGES (Women's Action to Gain Economic Security), an Oakland house-cleaning co-op, promotes the social and economic empowerment of low-income women through cooperative business ownership. It develops eco-friendly house-cleaning companies that provide stable, safe and dignified work for its worker-owners while protecting the environment. It includes three associated co-ops: Emma's (Peninsula), Eco-Care (South Bay), and Natural Home Cleaning (East Bay).[11]

BELUGA SOFTWARE is a worker-owned technology cooperative established in 1999. Based in Olympia, Washington, Beluga writes and customizes software for use on the Internet, Unix, Linux, and Windows.[12]

LAND

Northern California Land Trust, founded in 1973 in Berkeley/Oakland, is the leading organization in the Western United States specializing in permanently affordable housing for people with no access to market rate housing. The community land trust ensures that the homes it builds or rehabilitates remain accessibly priced beyond the first homeowners. NCLT retains the rights to the land upon which the home stands. When a homeowner wishes to sell a house, NCLT ensures the selling price is affordable, regardless of current market prices.[13]

AGRICULTURAL

Big Tree Organic Farms, a nineteen-member grower-owned marketing cooperative, is the second largest supplier of organic almonds in the United States.[14]

Connecticut Agricultural Plastics Recycling Cooperative is a thirty-member co-op serving farmers, greenhouse growers, and nursery owners. In association with the Connecticut Green Industry Association, and state and federal Departments of Agriculture, the cooperative was formed to process films and drip tape from nurseries, greenhouses, and tobacco growers and to save money, protect the environment, and reduce landfills.[15]

Federation of Southern Cooperatives/Land Assistance Fund is a rural network of farm, marketing and housing co-ops, credit unions, and state associations. In its thirty-five-year history, the Federation has mobilized $50 million in resources for support of member co-ops, facilitated $75 million in sales through cooperative marketing and helped retain $87.5 million worth of land in African-American ownership. Its network of 16 community development credit unions had combined assets of $27.4 million with 14,633 members in 2001.[16]

Tres Rios Agricultural Cooperative, located in three river basins in Southern Colorado and Northern New Mexico, was started by nine farmers in 2001 to expand market opportunities for their organic vegetables, fruits, meats, eggs, grains, flours, baked goods, and seeds. The cooperative currently has thirteen member farms. With a refrigerated truck, the farmers are able to reach profitable markets in more populated areas of the states; products are sold through buying clubs and farmers' markets, and to restaurants and food services.[17]

FOOD

PEOPLE'S FOOD CO-OP, a natural food store in Portland, Oregon, is dedicated to serving the community since 1970. "We focus our energy on building a community consciousness, vitalizing our local economy, and promoting our interconnections to our bioregion and the earth. We realize these goals through conscious product selection, mindful business practices, and the fulfillment of cooperatives principles."[18]

RAINBOW GROCERY, an organic supermarket in San Francisco, is run by a worker cooperative of over 200 people. Rainbow provides natural, organic, vegetarian food and environmentally and health conscious products at affordable prices, and puts the ideals of sustainable living into practice through its successful business model. Rainbow was started in the early 1970s as a bulk-food-buying program, and became one of the members of a network of small community food stores in the People's Food System, using food distribution as a form of community organizing. Rainbow survived the collapse of the People's Warehouse and Food System to become the successful store it is today.[19]

MERCADO CENTRAL, a member-owned market in Minneapolis, offers food and other products primarily to the area's growing Latino population. Formed in partnership with Minneapolis' Neighborhood Development Center, the co-op has been widely credited with revitalizing the retail corridor in which it operates.[20]

ARIZMENDI, a group of bakery restaurants in San Francisco, Oakland, Emeryville, and Berkeley, specializes in pizza, morning pastries, and artisan bread. The first Arizmendi began in 2000 as a spin-off from the Cheeseboard collective, which was instrumental in helping all of these worker co-ops to organize and fly.[21]

PEOPLE'S GROCERY, building a local food system and local economy in West Oakland, is organized as a community-run nonprofit. It grows most of its produce in community gardens, and promotes youth enterprises, sustainable agriculture, and grassroots organizing. People's Grocery helps the community control its own food supply and become more self-reliant, using the basic human right to food as an organizing tool for health and social justice.[22]

NATIVE AMERICAN

INTERTRIBAL BISON COOPERATIVE, founded in 1990-91 by a group of Native people from nineteen tribes, ITBC coordinates and assists tribes in restoring bison herds "in a manner that is compatible with their spiritual and cultural beliefs and practices...We recognize the bison is a symbol of our strength and unity, and that as we bring our herds back to health, we will also bring our people back to health." Today, ITBC has a membership of fifty-one tribes and a collective herd of over eight thousand bison.[23]

DINEH COOPERATIVES was begun in 1971 as the community-owned Piñon Co-op in a remote part of the Navajo Nation, to bypass the exploitive practices of the local Anglo trading post. Its success soon led members to establish Dinah Cooperatives, Inc. (DCI) to help other Navajo communities. In the next two years, DCI helped set up over twenty cooperatives, and became a community development corporation. In 1981, members opened the Tseyi Shopping Center in Chinle, the first full-service shopping center in the Navajo Nation as a joint project between the tribe, the federal government, and a private enterprise. DCI went on to complete Chinle Hospital, Chinle Community Fire Department, and Tooh Dineh Industries, today the largest electronics manufacturer in Northern Arizona with a work force of over one hundred. In 2005, DCI was completing a fifty-bed Navaho Youth Corrections Center in Chinle, where incarcerated Navaho youth could be transferred for culturally appropriate rehabilitation.[24]

ROSEBUD SIOUX WIND DEVELOPMENT INITIATIVE, the first Native American-owned wind farm in the country with a 750-kw wind turbine, was completed in 2003 on the Rosebud reservation in South Dakota, as part of the tribe's program of sustainable economic development. The tribal enterprise was sponsored by several US agencies, NativeEnergy, and Co-op America. The Intertribal Council on Utility Policy (ICOUP), a confederation of twenty-three tribes primarily in the Great Plains, is sponsoring new tribal initiatives in wind on many reservations, including Pine Ridge, Saginaw Chippewa, Cheyenne River, Lower Brule, and White Earth.[25]

TRADE

EQUAL EXCHANGE offers fair trade gourmet coffee directly from small-scale farmer co-ops in Latin America, Africa, and Asia. It is now the largest fair trade certified coffee company in North America, with seventeen trading partners in ten countries in Latin America, Africa, and Asia. Founded in 1986 in West Bridgewater, Massachusetts, EE's goals are "to build long-term trade partnerships that are economically just and environmentally sound, to foster mutually beneficial relations between farmers and consumers, and to demonstrate through our success the viability of worker-owned cooperatives and fair trade."[26]

OKANOGAN FAMILY FAIRE is an example of the rebirth of a traditional barter fair that Eastern Washington, Northern Idaho, and other parts of the inland Pacific Northwest saw in the early 1970s. More than country swap meets, barter fairs combine trade with community gathering. They welcome handcrafts and discourage professional merchants. Some trace the tradition back to the potlatch of the Pacific Coast tribes. Barter fairs are usually held in back-country locations where participants camp for several days. Of the many annual barter fairs in the region, the largest and best known is the Okanogan Family Faire in Tonasket, Washington, connected with the Okanogan River Natural Foods Co-op.[27]

ENERGY

COMMUNITY ENERGY CO-OP is a nonprofit membership organization helping consumers and communities in the Chicago area control energy costs, including a car-sharing service.[28]

LAST MILE ELECTRIC CO-OP, formed by fifteen rural electric cooperatives, municipal utilities and other members from Washington, Oregon, Nevada, and California, researches and develops renewable energy projects such as wind farms to provide affordable, reliable, renewable cost-based electricity. Last Mile estimated having several hundred megawatts of wind-generated power on line by 2006.[29]

FINANCIAL

LATINO COMMUNITY CREDIT UNION offers fully bilingual financial services in the Raleigh-Durham area.[30]

ITHACA HOURS, a local currency in a small city, keeps work and money recycling in the community. Since 1991, the group has issued over $100,000 in local paper money to thousands of residents. Over 300 businesses accept them. The idea goes back to Robert Owen and Josiah Warren in the 1820s. The Ithaca Hour, worth $10, the average wage in the county, can buy plumbing, carpentry, electrical work, roofing, nursing, chiropractic, child care, car and bike repair, food, eyeglasses, and firewood. Many restaurants, movie theaters, bowling alleys, grocery stores, farmers' markets, garage sales, and the local hospital take them. The local credit union accepts them for mortgage and loan fees; some landlords accept them for rent. The Ithaca Health Alliance, founded in 1997, is a nonprofit, member-owned health security system spin-off from Hours that focuses on the needs of the uninsured, and has a mission of facilitating universal access to health care, including "alternative" medicines. Anyone in New York State can become a member, and receive services anywhere. The Health Alliance takes Hours as partial payment of its annual membership fee. In 2005, the Health Alliance opened a free health clinic in downtown Ithaca. The related Ithaca Health Fund provides financial assistance to members seeking preventative and emergency medical and dental care. The success of the Health Alliance has already led to the formation of the Philadelphia Health Co-op modeled on Ithaca.[31]

Appendix 2.
International Documents on Cooperatives

The United Nations and its affiliated organizations have resolved that cooperatives should be planned into the world economy. Below are excerpts from some of the key documents of the UN General Assembly, the International Cooperative Alliance (ICA), the International Organization of Industrial, Artisanal and Service Producers' Cooperatives (CICOPA), and the International Labour Organization (ILA).

CONTENTS

---

1. STATEMENT ON THE COOPERATIVE IDENTITY
Adopted by The General Assembly of The International Cooperative Alliance, 1995

• • •

A co-operative is an autonomous association of persons united voluntarily to meet their common economic, social, and cultural needs and aspirations through a jointly-owned and democratically-controlled enterprise.

• • •

Co-op Principles The cooperative principles are guidelines by which cooperatives put their values into practice.

1: Voluntary and Open Membership. Cooperatives are voluntary organizations, open to all persons able to use their services and willing to accept the responsibilities of membership, without gender, social, racial, political or religious discrimination.

2: Democratic Member Control. Cooperatives are democratic organizations controlled by their members, who actively participate in setting their policies and making decisions. Men and women serving as elected representatives are accountable to the membership. In primary cooperatives members have equal voting rights (one member, one vote) and cooperatives at other levels are also organized in a democratic manner.

3: Member Economic Participation. Members contribute equitably to, and democratically control, the capital of their cooperative. At least part of that capital is usually the common property of the cooperative. Members usually receive limited compensation, if any, on capital subscribed as a condition of membership. Members allocate surpluses for any or all of the following purposes: developing their cooperative, possibly by setting up reserves, part of which at least would be indivisible; benefiting members in proportion to their transactions with the cooperative; and supporting other activities approved by the membership.

4: Autonomy and Independence. Cooperatives are autonomous, self-help organizations controlled by their members. If they enter to agreements with other organizations, including governments, or raise capital from external sources, they do so on terms that ensure democratic control by their members and maintain their cooperative autonomy.

5: Education, Training and Information. Cooperatives provide education and training for their members, elected representatives, managers, and employees so they can contribute effectively to the development of their cooperatives. They inform the general public—particularly young people and opinion leaders—about the nature and benefits of cooperation.

6: Cooperation among Cooperatives. Cooperatives serve their members most effectively and strengthen the cooperative movement by working together through local, national, regional and international structures.

7: Concern for Community. Cooperatives work for the sustainable development of their communities through policies approved by their members.

---

2. COOPERATIVES IN SOCIAL DEVELOPMENT

United Nations Resolution A/RES/56/114, Adopted 18 January 2002

The General Assembly,

...Recognizing that cooperatives, in their various forms, promote the fullest possible participation in the economic and social development of all people, including women, youth, older persons and people with disabilities, and are becoming a major factor of economic and social development...

1. Takes note of the report of the Secretary-General;

2. Draws the attention of Member States to the draft guidelines aimed at creating a supportive environment for the development of cooperatives, to be considered by them in developing or revising their national policies on cooperatives;

3. Encourages Governments to keep under review, ...with a view to ensuring a supportive environment for them and to protecting and advancing the potential of cooperatives to help them to achieve their goals;

4. Urges Governments, relevant international organizations and specialized agencies, in collaboration with national and international cooperative organizations, to give due consideration to the role and contribution of cooperatives... by, inter alia: (a) Utilizing and developing fully the potential and contribution of cooperatives for the attainment of social development goals, in particular the eradication of poverty, the generation of full and productive employment and the enhancement of social integration; (b) Encouraging and facilitating the establishment and development of cooperatives, including taking measures aimed at enabling people living in poverty or belonging to vulnerable groups to engage on a voluntary basis in the creation and development of cooperatives; (c) Taking appropriate measures aimed at creating a supportive and enabling environment for the development of cooperatives by, inter alia, developing an effective partnership between Governments and the cooperative movement;

5. Invites Governments, in collaboration with the cooperative movement, to develop programmes to promote and strengthen the education of members, the elected leadership and professional cooperative management, where appropriate, and to create or improve statistical databases on the development of cooperatives and on their contribution to national economies;

6. Invites Governments, relevant international organizations, specialized agencies and local, national and international cooperative organizations to continue to observe the International Day of Cooperatives annually, on the first Saturday of July, as proclaimed by the General Assembly in its resolution 47/90;

7. Requests the Secretary-General, in cooperation with the relevant United Nations and other international organizations and national, regional and international cooperative organizations, to render support to Member States, as appropriate, in their efforts to create a supportive environment for the development of cooperatives and to promote an exchange of experience and best practices, through, inter alia, conferences, workshops and seminars at the national and regional levels...

---

3. WORLD DECLARATION ON WORKER COOPERATIVES
Adopted by CICOPA 2003 and International Cooperative Alliance 2005

General Considerations
1. Humankind permanently seeks a qualitative improvement of the forms of organizing work, and endeavors to achieve ever better, fairer and more dignifying labour relations.

2. At present, human beings carry out their occupational activities under three basic modalities: a) independently as self-employed, being then defined by one's own capacities and self-regulation; b) as wage earners, under the continuous subordination to an employer who provides a compensation resulting exclusively from individual or collective negotiations; or c) under a third form, called worker ownership, in which work and management are carried out jointly, without the typical limitations of individual work, nor exclusively under the rules of conventional wage-based labour.

3. Among the modalities of worker ownership, the one being organized through worker cooperatives has attained the highest

level of development and importance at present in the world, and is structured on the basis of the universal cooperative principles, values and operational methods enshrined in the Statement on the Cooperative Identity (Manchester, 1995), agreed upon within the framework of the International Cooperative Alliance (ICA), and incorporated in the ILO Recommendation 193/2002 on the Promotion of Cooperatives.

4. Worker cooperatives are committed to being governed by the above-mentioned Statement on the Cooperative Identity. Moreover, it has become necessary to define at world level some basic characters and internal operational rules that are exclusive to this type of cooperatives, which have specific goals and purposes that differ from cooperatives belonging to other categories. This definition will enhance the coherence and universal identity of cooperative worker ownership, stimulate its development, and produce recognition at world level of its social and economic function in creating decent and sustainable jobs, while also preventing deviations or abuses.

5. A world declaration is also needed in order to focus on the importance of cooperative worker ownership, the promotion of worker cooperatives, and their relations with cooperatives belonging to other categories, as well as with the State, international organizations, the entrepreneurial world and the trade unions. This is necessary to guarantee the development and promotion of worker cooperatives, as well as the full recognition of their role as actors in the solution of the problems of unemployment and social exclusion, and as proponents of one of the most advanced, fair and dignifying modalities of labour relations, generation and distribution of wealth, and democratization of ownership and of the economy.

6. Although CICOPA also affiliates cooperatives of individual artisans and other forms of cooperative management that are based on the central concepts of work and production, the present declaration is aimed specifically at worker cooperatives. This does not preclude that it could be, in so far as possible, used by and applied to users' cooperatives that also grant membership and ownership to their workers as a differentiated part from the other members in such a way that their interests are represented adequately, as well as to all the forms of management that grant special recognition to human work and to those who carry it out, such as workers' limited societies (sociedades anonimas laborales – SALs) that apply benefits of cooperative nature to their workers, and in general all those

enterprises of community character that provide special labour relations to their members besides offering them welfare services.

On the basis of the above above-mentioned considerations, CICOPA unanimously approves the following World Declaration on Worker Cooperatives.

I. Basic Characters

On the basis of the definition, values and principles enshrined in the Statement on the Cooperative Identity (Manchester, 1995), and incorporated in ILO Recommendation 193/2002 on the Promotion of Cooperatives, worker cooperatives contain the following basic characters:

1. They have the objective of creating and maintaining sustainable jobs and generating wealth, in order to improve the quality of life of the worker-members, dignify human work, allow workers' democratic self-management and promote community and local development.

2. The free and voluntary membership of their members, in order to contribute with their personal work and economic resources, is conditioned by the existence of workplaces.

3. As a general rule, work shall be carried out by the members. This implies that the majority of the workers in a given worker cooperative enterprise are members and vice versa.

4. The worker-members' relation with their cooperative shall be considered as different to that of conventional wage-based labour and to that of autonomous individual work.

5. Their internal regulation is formally defined by regimes that are democratically agreed upon and accepted by the worker-members.

6. They shall be autonomous and independent, before the State and third parties, in their labour relations and management, and in the usage and management of the means of production.

II. Internal Functioning Rules

In their internal operations, worker cooperatives must take into account the following rules. They shall:

1. Compensate the work of their members equitably, taking in consideration the function, the responsibility, the complexity and the specificity requested by their positions, their productivity and the economic capacity of the enterprise, trying to reduce the difference between the highest and the lowest compensations.

2. Contribute to the capital increase and the appropriate growth of indivisible reserves and funds.

3. Provide the workplaces with physical and technical facilities aimed at achieving an appropriate functioning and a good organizational climate.

4. Protect the worker-members with appropriate systems of welfare, social security and occupational health, and abide by the standards of protection in force in the areas of maternity, childcare and minors of age at work.

5. Practice democracy in the decisive instances of the organization and in all the stages of the management process.

6. Ensure permanent education and training for capacity building of members and information to the latter, in order to guarantee professional knowledge and the development of the worker cooperative model, and to stimulate innovation and good management.

7. Contribute to the improvement of the living conditions of the family nucleus and the sustainable development of the community.

8. Combat their being instruments aimed at making the labour conditions of wage-earning workers more flexible or precarious, and from acting as conventional intermediaries for jobs.

III. Relations within the Cooperative Movement
A strong invitation is made to the cooperative movement in general:

1. To make the promotion of worker cooperatives one of the main priorities within the world cooperative movement, and to effectively contribute to the creation of new enterprises of this type.

2. To establish strategic alliances that foster the development of worker cooperatives and to make their entrepreneurial projects possible, including the access to appropriate financing, and the promotion of the services that they offer and of the products that they produce.

3. To establish capital formation mechanisms in worker cooperatives, including the contribution to the latter of risk capital from cooperatives of other categories, with an economic compensation covering the opportunity cost and an appropriate participation in management, without endangering their autonomy and independence.

4. To promote the representative organizations of worker cooperatives at local, national, regional and international level, and the cooperation among them, and to support the creation of second-degree entities, entrepreneurial groups and consortia and common socio-economic agreements among cooperatives, in order to provide efficient entrepreneurial services, reinforce the cooperative movement, and strive for a model of society characterized by social inclusion and solidarity.

5. To promote initiatives that ensure that the State, in its different branches, create and improve the instruments for the development of this type of cooperatives, including relevant and appropriate legislation. This also implies furthering petitions to parliamentarians, in order to make such legislation possible.

6. To promote, in so far as possible, the integration of the wage-earning workers of the cooperatives as worker-members.

IV. Relation Relations with the State and with Regional and Intergovernmental Institutions

1. Governments should understand the importance of the promotion and development of worker cooperatives as effective actors of job creation and inclusion to working life of unemployed social groups. For this reason, governments should not discriminate against worker cooperatives, and should include the promotion and development of this type of enterprises in their policies and programs, in order to fight some of the major problems which the world suffers from, generated as a consequence of exclusionary globalization and development, such as unemployment and inequality.

2. In order to make cooperative worker ownership a real option, the States should establish national and regional regulatory schemes that recognize the specific legal nature of this type of cooperatives, allow them to generate goods or services under optimal conditions and to develop all their entrepreneurial creativity and potential in the interest of their worker-members and the community as a whole.

3. In particular, the States should:

• Recognize in their legislation that cooperative worker ownership is conditioned by labour and industrial relations that are distinct from wage-based labour and self-employment or independent work, and accept that worker cooperatives apply corresponding norms and regulations.

• Ensure the application of the general labour legislation to non-member workers of worker cooperatives, with whom conventional wage-based relations are established.

• Apply to worker cooperatives the ILO concept of Decent Work and clear, precise and coherent provisions regulating social protection in the fields of health, pensions, unemployment insurance, occupational health and labour safety, taking into consideration their specific labour relations.

• Define specific legal provisions regulating the fiscal regime and the self-managed organization of worker cooperatives that can enable and promote their development.

In order to receive an appropriate treatment from the State, cooperatives should be registered and/or audited.

4. Governments should ensure access to appropriate financing conditions for entrepreneurial projects launched by worker cooperatives by creating specific public funds, or loan guarantees or covenants for the access to financial resources and promoting economic alliances with the cooperative movement.

5. The States and the regional and inter-governmental organizations should promote projects based on exchanges of successful experiences, on information about, and development of structures of entrepreneurial and institutional support for worker cooperatives, within the framework of international and regional cooperation, for job creation, sustainable entrepreneurial initiatives, gender equality, and the fight against poverty and marginalization.

6. Cooperative worker ownership should be promoted as an option and an entrepreneurial model as much in processes of entrepreneurial change and restructuring, start-ups, privatizations, conversion of enterprises in crisis, and transmission of enterprises without heirs, as in the concession of public services and public procurement, in which the State should define conditioning clauses that stimulate local development through worker cooperative enterprises.

7. In the context of the relations with the State, it is important to highlight the guideline of ILO Recommendation 193 concerning the necessity to endeavor towards the consolidation of a distinctive area of the economy, which includes the cooperatives. It is an area in which profit is not the first motivation, and which is characterized by solidarity, participation and economic democracy.

V. Relations with Employers' Organizations

Employers' organizations can promote the development of cooperative worker ownership as an entrepreneurial form whose first objective is the creation of sustainable and decent jobs with an entrepreneurial added value, and as an appropriate exit strategy for the recovery of companies in crisis or in the process of liquidation, while respecting their autonomy, allowing their free entrepreneurial development and without abusing of this associative labour modality to violate the workers' labour rights.

VI. Relations with Workers' Organizations

The cooperative movement should maintain a permanent dialogue with the trade unions, as the representatives of the workers, in order to make sure that they understand the nature and essence of cooperative worker ownership as a distinctive modality of labour relations and ownership, overcoming the typical conflicts of wage-based labour, and that they support it in view of its importance and the prospects that it offers to human society.

This declaration is in correspondence with ILO Recommendation 193 approved by governments, employers' and workers' organizations worldwide ions worldwide. Therefore, we hope that the latter consider it seriously, in order to contribute to the solution of the grave world problem of unemployment that affects humanity and endangers world peace and human rights.

---

4. PROMOTION OF COOPERATIVES RECOMMENDATION
International Labour Organization, R193, 2002

The General Conference of the International Labour Organization...

Recognizing the importance of cooperatives in job creation, mobilizing resources, generating investment and their contribution to the economy, and

Recognizing that cooperatives in their various forms promote the fullest participation in the economic and social development of all people, and

Recognizing that globalization has created new and different pressures, problems, challenges and opportunities for cooperatives, and that stronger forms of human solidarity at national and international levels are required to facilitate a more equitable distribution of the benefits of globalization...

Recalling the principle embodied in the Declaration of Philadelphia that "labour is not a commodity", and

Recalling that the realization of decent work for workers everywhere is a primary objective of the International Labour Organization...

I. Scope, Definition and Objectives

1. It is recognized that cooperatives operate in all sectors of the economy. This Recommendation applies to all types and forms of cooperatives.

2. ...the term "cooperative" means an autonomous association of persons united voluntarily to meet their common economic, social and cultural needs and aspirations through a jointly owned and democratically controlled enterprise.

3. The promotion and strengthening of the identity of cooperatives should be encouraged on the basis of:

(a) cooperative values of self-help, self-responsibility, democracy, equality, equity and solidarity; as well as ethical values of honesty, openness, social responsibility and caring for others; and

(b) cooperative principles as developed by the international cooperative movement.. These principles are: voluntary and open membership; democratic member control; member economic participation; autonomy and independence; education, training and information; cooperation among cooperatives; and concern for community.

4. Measures should be adopted to promote the potential of cooperatives in all countries, irrespective of their level of development, in order to assist them and their membership to:

(a) create and develop income-generating activities and sustainable decent employment; (b) develop human resource capacities and knowledge of the values, advantages and benefits of the cooperative movement through education and training; (c) develop their business potential, including entrepreneurial and managerial capacities; (d) strengthen their competitiveness as well as gain access to markets and to institutional finance; (e) increase savings and investment; (f) improve social and economic well-being, taking into account the need to eliminate all forms of discrimination; (g) contribute to sustainable human development; and (h) establish and expand a viable and dynamic distinctive sector of the economy, which includes cooperatives, that responds to the social and economic needs of the community.

5. The adoption of special measures should be encouraged to enable cooperatives, as enterprises and organizations inspired

by solidarity, to respond to their members' needs and the needs of society, including those of disadvantaged groups in order to achieve their social inclusion.

II. Policy Framework and Role of Governments

6. A balanced society necessitates the existence of strong public and private sectors, as well as a strong cooperative, mutual and the other social and non-governmental sector. It is in this context that Governments should provide a supportive policy and legal framework consistent with the nature and function of cooperatives and guided by the cooperative values and principles...

7. (1) The promotion of cooperatives guided by the values and principles set out in Paragraph 3 should be considered as one of the pillars of national and international economic and social development...

8. (1) National policies should notably: ...(f) promote education and training in cooperative principles and practices, at all appropriate levels of the national education and training systems, and in the wider society... (i) facilitate access of cooperatives to credit; (j) facilitate access of cooperatives to markets; (k) promote the dissemination of information on cooperatives...

9. Governments should promote the important role of cooperatives in transforming what are often marginal survival activities (sometimes referred to as the "informal economy") into legally protected work, fully integrated into mainstream economic life.

III. Implementation of Public Policies for the Promotion of Cooperatives

10. (1) Member States should adopt specific legislation and regulations on cooperatives, which are guided by the cooperative values and principles...

11. (1) Governments should facilitate access of cooperatives to support services in order to strengthen them, their business viability and their capacity to create employment and income...

12. Governments should, where appropriate, adopt measures to facilitate the access of cooperatives to investment finance and credit...

13. For the promotion of the cooperative movement, governments should encourage conditions favoring the development of technical, commercial and financial linkages among all forms of cooperatives so as to facilitate an exchange of experience and the sharing of risks and benefits.

IV. Role of Employers' and Workers' Organizations and Cooperative Organizations, and Relationships Between Them

• • •

16. Workers' organizations should be encouraged to: (a) advise and assist workers in cooperatives to join workers' organizations; (b) assist their members to establish cooperatives, including with the aim of facilitating access to basic goods and services...

• • •

V. International Cooperation

18. International cooperation should be facilitated through: (a) exchanging information on policies and programmes that have proved to be effective in employment creation and income generation for members of cooperatives; (b) encouraging and promoting relationships between national and international bodies and institutions involved in the development of cooperatives...

• • •

Bibliographic Essay

GENERAL AMERICAN HISTORIES

A compass to the saga of the American working people, Howard Zinn's *A People's History of the United States* (1980) remains unsurpassed in scholarship, scope, and perspective. *Harvey Wasserman's History of the United States* (1972) vividly outlines the key struggles beginning after the Civil War. The history of the American economy is delineated with broad strokes in Seavoy's *An Economic History of the United States From 1607 to the Present* (2006), although he mischaracterizes the Knights of Labor.

Seavoy, Ronald E. *An Economic History of the United States From 1607 to the Present*. New York: Routledge, 2006.

Wasserman, Harvey. *Harvey Wasserman's History of the United States*. New York: Harper & Row, 1972.

Zinn, Howard. *A People's History of the United States*. New York: Harper & Row, 1980.

GENERAL COOPERATIVE HISTORIES

The earliest history of American cooperatives was also the first general history of American labor by a scholar. Richard T. Ely's *The Labor Movement in America* (1886) was as much about the cooperative movement and communalism as about the labor movement. Completed just after the Haymarket disaster (but before the trial), Ely writes about the cooperative movement as he saw it at its 19th century peak. It remains a fascinating study and a good read. Two years later an extensive, detailed historical survey of American cooperatives in every section of the country was published, the *History of Coöperation in the United States* (1888), written by a team of scholars under Herbert Baxter Adams, with an introduction by Ely. This tome offers an exhaustive snapshot of the 19th-century movement.

In 1918, the first volume of a landmark work appeared, *History of Labour in the United States* (1918-35), edited by John R. Commons, a protégé of Ely, and written by another team of scholars. The first two volumes are replete with histories of early working-class cooperatives. Commons has been a watershed for all histories of American labor written since. It remains a consistently reliable standard, with the caution that it leans toward defending the "pure and simple" unionism of the AFL and overly focuses on organizations. Together Commons' and Adams' histories remain the most important sources of information about the early movements. Another work crucial to the study of early cooperative history is Du Bois' *Economic Co-operation Among Negro Americans* (1907).

More recent historians of cooperatives have usually devoted inadequate attention to communalism, and the preponderance of histories and studies of communalism (or communitarianism) scarcely consider it in the context of the larger cooperative movement. Spann's *Brotherly Tomorrows* (1989), Fogarty's *All Things New* (1990), and Schehr's *Dynamic Utopia* (1997), are all valuable studies of cooperative communities, yet Spann contains only two sentences about the Knights of Labor worker cooperatives, Fogarty and Schehr discuss only the KOL colonies, and none of these books even mentions the Farmers' Alliance. I don't mean to fault these works for having parameters; I do believe, however, that setting that particular boundary obscures the historical picture that they are trying to elucidate. Case and Taylor's *Co-ops, Communes & Collectives* (1979) avoids that limitation and advantageously studies the full range of 1960s and 1970s countercultural institutions. I know of no scholarly history that adequately covers the entire broad range of worker-farmer-consumer cooperatives, and communalism. My own brief *History of Work Cooperation in America* (1980) can be seen as a preliminary outline of the present work.

Adams, Herbert Baxter. *History of Coöperation in the United States.* John Hopkins University Studies in Historical and Political Science, Sixth Series. Baltimore: John Hopkins Press, 1888.

Commons, John R., et. al. *History of Labour in the United States.* 4 vols. New York: Macmillan, 1918-35.

Du Bois, W. E. B. *Economic Co-operation among Negro Americans.* Atlanta, GA: Atlanta University Press, 1907.

EARLY PERIOD

A key account of Indian culture and collectivity, written by a leader of the Six Nations Confederacy, is *Basic Call to Consciousness* (1978), primarily the work of John Mohawk (Sotisisowah). Another authentic classic is Neihardt's *Black Elk Speaks* (1932), supplemented by *The Sixth Grandfather: Black Elk's Teachings* (1984) (ed. DeMaille). All of Jack D. Forbes' books offer invaluable knowledge about Indian history and culture, including *Native Americans of California and Nevada* (1969). An extraordinary anthology of early Native voices is Brotherson's *Image of the New World* (1979). Central to early anthropological studies, and still of great value, is Morgan's celebrated *Ancient Society* (1877). Margaret Mead's excellent *Cooperation and Competition Among Primitive Peoples* (1937) sets the standard for modern anthropology focused on Indigenous cooperation. Farb's *Man's Rise to Civilization: The Cultural Ascent of the Indians of North America* (1968) goes into cooperation extensively. The contributions of Native America are analyzed in detail in Weatherford's *Indian Givers* (1988). Bruce Johansen's *Forgotten Founders* (1982) follows the democratic traditions of the Native people that inspired colonial radicals. An excellent one-volume comprehensive Indian history is Josephy's *The Indian Heritage of America* (1968).

Brotherson, Gordon, *Image of the New World: The American Continent Portrayed in Native Texts*. London: Thames and Hudson, 1979.

DeMallie, Raymond J. *The Sixth Grandfather: Black Elk's Teachings*. Lincoln, Nebraska: University of Nebraska Press, 1985.

Farb, Peter, *Man's Rise to Civilization: The Cultural Ascent of the Indians of North America*. New York: Dutton, 1968.

Forbes, Jack D., *Native Americans of California and Nevada*. Healdsburg, CA: Naturegraph, 1969.

Johansen, Bruce E., *Forgotten Founders: How the American Indian Helped Shape Democracy*. Boston: Harvard Common Press, 1982.

Josephy, Alvin M., Jr. *The Indian Heritage of America*. New York: Knopf, 1968.

Mead, Margaret, ed. *Cooperation and Competition Among Primitive Peoples*. New York: McGraw-Hill, 1937. Reprinted. New York: Beacon, 1961.

Mohawk, John, ed. *Basic Call to Consciousness*. Rooseveltown, NY: Akwesasne Notes, 1978.

Morgan, Lewis Henry. *Ancient Society*. New York: Henry Holt, 1877. Reprinted. Tucson: University of Arizona Press, 1985.

Neihardt, John G. *Black Elk Speaks*. New York, William Morrow, 1932. Reprinted. New York: Washington Square Press, 1959.

Weatherford, Jack. *Indian Givers: How the Indians of the Americas Transformed the World.* New York: Crown, 1988.

Doyle's *English Colonies in America* (1889), and Usher's *The Pilgrims and their History* (1918) still provide a readable narratives, in spite of the prejudices of their times. Bradford's *Of Plymouth Plantation* (1647), has the great immediacy of a firsthand account. Powell's *Puritan Village* (1965) goes into that area in depth. Cronon's *Changes in the Land* (1983) attempts a ground-breaking ecological and Native American perspective. Trewartha's article "Types of Rural Settlement in Colonial America" (1946) provides an excellent outline.

Bradford, William. *Of Plymouth Plantation 1620-1647* New York: Random House, 1981.

Cronon, William. *Changes in the Land: Indians, Colonists, and the Ecology of New England.* New York: Hill and Wang, 1983.

Doyle, J. A., *English Colonies in America.* Vol. 2, *The Puritan Colonies.* New York: Holt, 1889.

Powell, Sumner Chilton. *Puritan Village.* New York: Doubleday, 1965.

Trewartha, Glenn T. "Types of Rural Settlement in Colonial America." *Geographical Review* 36, no. 4 (1946): 568-96.

Usher, Roland G. *The Pilgrims and Their History.* New York: MacMillon, 1918.

A clear narrative of the legacy of the Spanish colonies in the territorial US is Prago's *Strangers in Their Own Land* (1973). Griswold Del Castillo's *The Treaty of Guadalupe Hidalgo* (1990) digs profitably into important details.

Griswold Del Castillo, Richard. *The Treaty of Guadalupe Hidalgo: A Legacy of Conflict.* Norman: University of Oklahoma Press, 1990.

Prago, Albert. *Strangers in Their Own Land: A History of Maxican-Americans.* New York: Four Winds Press, 1973.

The forces transforming American society and its working classes between 1800 and 1860 are delineated in Commons and the other labor histories listed below, and in the following:

Laurie, Bruce. *Artisans into Workers.* New York: Noonday, 1989.

Montgomery, David L. *Workers' Control in America.* New York: Cambridge University Press, 1979.

Morris, Richard B. *Government and Labor in Early America*. New York: Columbia University Press, 1946.

Steinfeld, Robert J. *The Invention of Free Labor: The Employment Relation in English and American Law and Culture, 1350-1870*. Chapel Hill, NC: University of North Carolina Press, 1991.

Turner, Frederick J. *The Frontier in American History*. New York: Henry Holt, 1921.

WORKER COOPERATIVES

I know of no comprehensive study focused solely on the history of the worker cooperative movement in American history. There are a number of important works that cover different time periods, however, a few of which are mentioned below.

Movements after the Civil War are detailed in Horner's classic but unpublished dissertation, "Producers' Co-operatives in the United States, 1865-1890" (1978). Leikin's *The Practical Utopians: American Workers and the Cooperative Movement in the Gilded Age* (2005) closely examines the cooperatives of both the National Labor Union and the Knights of Labor, and brings to life the history of that critical time. Grob's *Workers and Utopia* (1961) offers a concise discussion of the post–Civil War era. Jackall and Levin's *Worker Cooperatives in America* (1984) offers glimpses into the earlier history while focusing mainly on the 1970s and 1980s. The National Labor Union is analyzed in Grossman's *William Sylvis, Pioneer of American Labor* (1945). An early history of the Knights of Labor, and still an important one, is Ware's *The Labor Movement in the United States 1860-1895* (1929), although he undervalues their cooperative movement. Any study must include Powderly's *Thirty Years of Labor* (1890) and *The Path I Trod* (1940), and his biography, Phelan's *Grand Master Workman* (2000). Several excellent studies of different aspects of the Knights are Fink's *Workingmen's Democracy* (1983), Voss' *The Making of American Exceptionalism* (1993), and Weir's *Beyond Labor's Veil* (1996) and *Knights Unhorsed* (2000). For bibliographic information about other organizations, see the endnotes.

Fink, Leon. *Workingmen's Democracy, The Knights of Labor and American Politics*. Urbana and Chicago: University of Illinois Press, 1983.

Grob, Jonathan P. *Workers and Utopia: A Study of the Ideological Conflict in the American Labor Movement 1865-1900*. Evanston: Northwestern University Press,1961. Reprinted. Chicago: Quadrangle Books, 1969.

Grossman, Gerald. *William Sylvis, Pioneer of American Labor.* New York: Columbia University Press, 1945. Reprinted. Evanston: the Sylvis Society, 1986.

Horner, Clare. "Producers' Co-operatives in the United States, 1865-1890." PhD diss., University of Pittsburg, 1978.

Jackall, Robert and Henry M Levin, eds. *Worker Cooperatives in America.* Berkeley: University of California Press, 1984.

Leikin, Steve. *The Practical Utopians: American Workers and the Cooperative Movement in the Gilded Age.* Detroit: Wayne State University Press, 2005.

Phelan, Craig. *Grand Master Workman.* Westport: Greenwood Press, 2000.

Powderly, Terence V. *Thirty Years of Labor, 1859 to 1889.* Columbus, OK: Excelsior Publishing, 1890.

_____. *The Path I Trod.* New York: Columbia University Press, 1940.

Voss, Kim. *The Making of American Exceptionalism, The Knights of Labor and Class Formation in the Nineteenth Century.* Ithaca: Cornell University Press, 1993.

Ware, Norman J. *The Labor Movement in the United States 1860-1895, A Study in Democracy.* New York: Appelton and Co., 1929.

Weir, Robert E. *Beyond Labor's Veil.* University Park: Pennsylvania State University Press, 1996.

_____. *Knights Unhorsed.* Detroit: Wayne State University Press, 2000.

FARMER COOPERATIVES & POPULISM

The histories of farmer cooperatives and the populist movement are inseparable. A thorough survey focused primarily on farmer (and consumer) cooperatives is Knapp's two-volume *The Rise of American Cooperative Enterprise 1620-1920* (1969) and *The Advance of American Cooperative Enterprise 1920-1945* (1973). However Knapp stresses "pure and simple" cooperativism, and somewhat neglects cooperatives as part of social justice movements. The classic history of the early Grangers is Buck's *The Granger Movement.* (1913). The groundbreaking history of the Farmers' Alliance was Hicks' *The Populist Revolt* (1931). Pollack's *The Populist Response to Industrial America* (1962) showed Populism as a class movement. Goodwyn's *The Populist Moment* (1978) goes deeply and lucidly into the core connection between the Farmers' Alliance cooperative movement and the Populist Party. That dynamic is further clarified by Schwartz in *Radical Protest and Social Structure* (1976). Of great value is Tindall's *A Populist Reader* (1966). The Colored Farmers' Alliance history is from Dunning's *Farmers' Alliance History and Agricultural Digest,* Holmes' "Demise of the Colored Farmers' Alliance," Miller's "Black Protest and White Leadership: A Note on the Colored Farmers' Alliance," and Spriggs' "The Virginia Colored Farmers' Alliance." The early history of the National Farmers Union is well told by its second president, Charles Barrett, in *The Mission, History and Times of the Farmers' Union*. A synopsis of the early history can also be found in Knapp, *Rise of American Cooperative Enterprise*. The middle years can be found in Tucker, "Populism Up-To-Date" (1947). The struggles during the Cold War are found in Field, *Harvest of Dissent* (1998). The domination by agribusiness and the Farm Bureau is delineated in Krebs' *The Corporate Reapers: The Book of Agribusiness* (1992).

Barrett, Charles Simon. *The Mission, History and Times of the Farmers' Union*. Nashville, TN: Marshall & Bruce, 1909.

Buck, Solon Justice. *The Granger Movement*. Cambridge: Harvard University Press, 1913. Reprinted. Lincoln: University of Nebraska Press, 1963.

Dunning, N.A. ed. *Farmers' Alliance History and Agricultural Digest*. Washington, D.C.: Alliance Publishing, 1891.

Field, Bruce E. *Harvest of Dissent: The National Farmers Union and the Early Cold War*. Lawrence, KS: University of Kansas Press, 1998.

Goodwyn, Lawrence. *The Populist Moment*. London: Oxford University Press, 1978.

Hicks, J. D. *The Populist Revolt*. Minneapolis: University of Minnesota Press, 1931. Reprinted. Lincoln: University of Nebraska Press, 1961.

Holmes, William F. "Demise of the Colored Farmers' Alliance," *The Journal of Southern History* 41, no. 2 (1975).

Knapp, Joseph. *The Rise of American Cooperative Enterprise 1620-1920*. Danville: Interstate, 1969.

_____. *The Advance of American Cooperative Enterprise 1920-1945*. Danville: Interstate, 1973.

Krebs, A.V. *The Corporate Reapers: The Book of Agribusiness*. Wash., DC: Essential Books, 1992.

Miller, Floyd J. "Black Protest and White Leadership: A Note on the Colored Farmers' Alliance," *Phylon* 33, no. 2 (1972).

Pollack, Norman. *The Populist Response to Industrial America*. Cambridge: Harvard University Press, 1962.

Schwartz, Michael. *Radical Protest and Social Structure: The Southern Farmers' Alliance and Cotton Tenancy, 1880-1890*. Chicago: University of Chicago Press, 1976.

Spriggs, William E. "The Virginia Colored Farmers' Alliance," *The Journal of Negro History* 64, no. 3 (1979).

Tindall, George P., ed. *A Populist Reader*. New York: Harper, 1966.

Tucker, Wm. B. "Populism Up-To-Date: The Story of the Farmers Union," *Agricultural History* 21, no. 4 (1947).

CONSUMER COOPERATIVES

The classic early survey is Sonnichsen's *Consumers' Coopera-tion* (1920). The history is well catalogued in Parker's *The First 125 Years* (1956). Furlough and Strikwerda's *Consumers Against Capitalism* (1999), offers a valuable world perspective today, not limited to only consumer cooperatives.

Furlough, Ellen, and Carl Strikwerda, eds. *Consumers Against Capitalism? Consumer Cooperation in Europe, North America, and Japan, 1840-1990.* Lanham: Rowman & Littlefield Publishers, 1999.

Parker, Florence E. *The First 125 Years: A History of Distributive and Service Cooperation in the United States, 1829-1954.* Superior: Cooperative League, 1956.

Sonnichsen, Albert. *Consumers' Coöperation.* New York: Macmillan, 1920.

GENERAL LABOR HISTORIES

Ely's 1886 book, noted above, was the standard labor history for over two decades. Beginning with Commons, labor historians both left and right largely ignore cooperatives after the Knights of Labor, and portray them as an early dead end of the labor movement. While Ely's book was written for a general audience, Commons' was a comprehensive and scholarly compilation journeying far beyond the general reader's tolerance. Philip S. Foner's *A History of the Labor Movement in the United States* (1947-94), in ten volumes, stands alongside Commons as a monumental work of scholarship. Its Marxist orientation, with a focus on class struggle and strikes, has all the strengths and blind sides of that perspective. Perlman's *History of Trade Unionism in the United States* (1926) is an excellent, one-volume version of Commons' by a member of his team. Jeremy Brecher's *Strike!* (1972) offers an in-depth panorama of that side of the labor movement. Boyer and Morais paint vivid vignettes in *Labor's Untold Story* (1955). Two standard "college-text" histories aiming at "balanced" overviews are Raybeck's *A History of American Labor* (1959) and Dulles and Dubofsky's *Labor in America* (1966). Two clear and concise outlines of the big picture can be found in Le Blanc's *A Short History of the U.S. Working Class* (1964), and Buhle and Dawley's *Working for Democracy* (1985). Arneson's *Encyclopedia of US Labor and Working-Class History* (2006) is a great resource.

Arneson, Eric, ed. *Encyclopedia of US Labor and Working-Class History.* New York: Taylor & Francis, 2006.

Boyer, Richard O. and Herbert M. Morais. *Labor's Untold Story*. New York: United Electrical Workers of America, 1955.

Brecher, Jeremy. *Strike!* San Francisco: Straight Arrow Books, 1972. Reprinted, with a new introduction. Boston: South End Press, 1977.

Buhle, Paul and Alan Dawley. *Working for Democracy, American Workers from the Revolution to the Present.* Urbana, IL: University of Illinois Press, 1985.

Commons, John R. *History of Labour in the United States.* 4 vols. New York: Macmillan, 1918-35.

Dulles, Foster Rhea and Melvin Dubofsky. *Labor in America, A History.* Arlington Heights, IL: Harlan Davidson. 1984. Revised 4th ed. 1993.

Ely, Richard T. *The Labor Movement in America.* New York: Thomas Y. Crowell & Co., 1886.

Foner, Philip. *A History of the Labor Movement in the United States.* 4 vols. New York: International Publishers, 1947-65.

Le Blanc, Paul. *A Short History of the U.S. Working Class.* New York: Humanity Books, 1999.

Perlman, Selig. *History of Trade Unionism in the United States.* New York: Macmillan, 1926.

Rayback, Joseph G. *A History of American Labor.* New York: Macmillan, 1959. Reprinted. New York: Free Press, 1966.

PICTORIAL WORKING-CLASS HISTORIES

Historical images of working people's lives and struggles rarely appear in mainstream media, so illustrated histories are particularly important. Before Commons' team of scholars wrote *History of Labour in the United States*, they compiled the massive *A Documentary History of American Industrial Society* (1910-11), in eleven volumes. It remains a unique and essential reference tool for all historians. Several valuable one-volume collections geared toward the general reader appeared in the 1970s: Cahn (1972), Schnapper (1975) and Morris (1977).

Cahn, William. *A Pictorial History of American Labor.* New York: Crown Publishers, 1972.

Commons, John R. *A Documentary History of American Industrial Society.* 11 vols. Glendale: Arthur H. Clark Company, 1910-11.

Morris, Richard B. *The U.S. Department of Labor History of The American Worker.* Washington, 1977.

Schnapper, M. B. *American Labor.* Washington: Public Affairs Press, 1975.

COMMUNALISM

Historians invariably trace some of the socialist movement's roots back to communalism, and socialist historians often provide insightful accounts of the communalist movement. Hillquit's *History of Socialism in the United States* (1903) offers a fascinating survey of communalism from the perspective of a leader of the Socialist Party in its salad days. Large parts of Egbert's *Socialism and American Life* (1952), a monumental work by a group of scholars, is about communalism. Fried's *Socialism in America* (1970) follows the same path. All of these important books have the same limitation in that none casts more than a glance at cooperatives. Egbert states, "these cooperative groups are considered to be socialistic only if they condemn the existing political and social order as a whole, and advocate a new social order to be accomplished by remolding human nature, human institutions, or both"(10). Using this definition he includes the IWW, but excludes the KOL without explanation. This attitude reflects the attempt by Marx to draw a clear and strong line between "utopian" and "scientific" socialism, while the cooperative movement crosses back and forth over that line. Social anarchism traditionally embraces cooperatives and cooperative communities, yet I know of no adequate history of that movement in America.

The best introduction to anarchist thought and history is Daniel Guérin's *Anarchism: From Theory to Practice*, with an introductory essay by Noam Chomsky. Its focus is on the European movement. Guérin's extensive anthology of anarchist writings, *No Gods No Masters: An Anthology of Anarchism* is essential reading. Woodcock's *Anarchism, A History of Libertarian Ideas and Movements* (1962) stresses individualist anarchism and mutualism, and is mostly devoted to the European movement. Woodcock has an odd view of the IWW, which he considers "at most a parallel movement to anarchism... and its central idea of the One Big Union was fundamentally opposed to the anarchists' passionately held ideals of localism and decentralization"(446).

For classical survey histories, no library should be without Noyes' *History of American Socialisms* (1870), Nordhoff's *The Communistic Societies of the United States* (1875), and Hinds' *American Communities and Co-operative Colonies* (1878). A later assessment by a New Llano resident is Wooster's *Communities of the Past and Present* (1924). Holloway's *Heavens on Earth* (1951) contains an excellent appraisal, and various gaps are filled in by Kagan's *New World Utopias* (1975).

For the Owenite Socialist movement, Bestor's *Backwoods Utopias* offers an insightful account. Two important niches are Hine's *California's Utopian Colonies* and LeWarne's *Utopias in Puget Sound.* African-American communalism is delineated in Rease's *Black Utopia.* Rexroth's *Communalism* is a strong read by an prominent poet. Conkin's *Tomorrow a New World* (1959) describes how the US government briefly played a significant role in the communalist movement. As mentioned earlier, Spann's *Brotherly Tomorrows* (1989), Fogarty's *All Things New* (1990), and Schehr's *Dynamic Utopia* (1997) are all important studies.

There is an abundance of valuable firsthand accounts. Two that deserve to be more widely read are Henson's *The Life of Josiah Henson, Formerly a Slave* (1848), and Codman's *Brook Farm* (1894). My own firsthand account, *Memories of Drop City* (2007), follows the movement of the 1960s.

Bestor, Arthur E. *Backwoods Utopias, The Sectarian Origins and the Owenite Phase of Communitarian Socialism in America, 1663-1829.* Washington, DC: American Historical Society, 1950. Reprinted. Philadelphia: University of Philadelphia Press, 1970.

Case, J. and R. Taylor, eds. *Co-ops, Communes & Collectives, Experiments in Social Change in the 1960s and 1970s.* New York: Pantheon Books, 1979.

Codman, John Thomas. *Brook Farm, Historic and Personal Memoirs.* Boston: Arena Publishing Co., 1894.

Conkin, Paul K. *Tomorrow A New World: The New Deal Community Program.* Ithaca, NY: Cornell University Press, 1959.

Curl, John. *History of Work Cooperation in America: Cooperatives, Cooperative Movements, Collectivity and Communalism from Early America to the Present.* Berkeley: Homeward Press, 1980.

_____. *Memories of Drop City, the First Hippie Commune of the 1960s and the Summer of Love.* New York: iuniverse, 2007.

Egbert, Donald Drew, Stow Persons, and T. D. Seymour Bassett, eds. *Socialism and American Life.* 2 vols. Princeton, NJ. Princeton University Press: 1952.

Fogarty, Robert S. *All Things New, American Communes and Utopian Movements 1860-1914.* Chicago: University of Chicago Press, 1990.

Guérin, Daniel. *Anarchism: From Theory to Practice.* Translated by Mary Klopper. New York: Monthly Review Press, 1970.

_____. *No Gods No Masters: An Anthology of Anarchism.* Oakland: AK Press, 2005.

Henson, Josiah. *The Life of Josiah Henson, Formerly a Slave.* Boston: Arthur D. Phelps, 1849. Reprinted, with a new introduction by Robin W. Winks. New York: Dover, 2003.

Hillquit, Morris. *History of Socialism in the United States.* New York: Funk & Wagnalls, 1903. 4th ed. 1910. Reprinted. New York: Dover, 1971.

Hinds, William A. *American Communities.* Oneida, NY: Office of the American Socialist, 1878. Reprinted. New York: Corinth Books, 1961.

Hine, R.V. *California's Utopian Colonies.* Pasadena: H.E. Huntington Library & Art Gallery, 1953. Reprinted. New Haven: Yale University Press, 1966.

Holloway, Mark. *Heavens on Earth.* London: Turnstile Press, 1951. Reprinted. New York: Dover, 1966.

Kagan, Paul. *New World Utopias.* New York: Penguin, 1975.

LeWarne, Charles P. *Utopias in Puget Sound. 1885-1915.* Seattle: University of Washington Press, 1975.

Nordhoff, Charles. *The Communistic Societies of the United States.* New York: Harper & Brothers, 1875. Reprinted. New York: Dover, 1966.

Noyes, John Humphry. *History of American Socialisms.* Philadelphia: J. B. Lippencott, 1870. Reprinted. New York, Dover, 1966.

Pease, William H., and Jane Pease. *Black Utopia.* Madison: State Historical Society of Wisconsin, 1963.

Rexroth, Kenneth. *Communalism.* New York: Seabury Press, 1974.

Schehr, Robert C. *Dynamic Utopia: Establishing Intentional Communities as a New Social Movement.* Westport, CT: Bergin & Garvey, 1997.

Spann, Edward K. *Brotherly Tomorrows, Movements for a Cooperative Society in America, 1820-1920.* New York: Columbia University Press, 1989.

Woodcock, George. *Anarchism.* New York: New American Library, 1962.

Wooster, Ernest S. *Communities of the Past and Present.* Newllano, LA: Llano Colonist, 1924. Reprinted. New York, AMS Press: 1974.

Notes

Introduction

1. Richard O. Boyer and Herbert M. Morais, *Labor's Untold Story* (New York: United Electrical Workers of America, 1955), 144-45.

2. Terence V. Powderly, *Thirty Years of Labor, 1859 to 1889* (Columbus, OK: Excelsior Publishing, 1890), 464-65.

3. National Cooperative Business Association, "About Cooperatives: Co-op Statistics," http://www.ncba.coop/abcoop_stats.cfm.

4. Bruce Laurie, *Artisans into Workers* (New York: Noonday, 1989), 15-16.

5. Benjamin Franklin, "The Internal State of America," *The Works of Benjamin Franklin* (London: printed for G. G. J. and J. Robinson, 1793), 247.

6. Reliable early labor statistics are hard to come by: the earliest U.S. censuses, between 1790 and 1870, only gathered data about "gainful workers," without distinguishing among self-employed, employee, and employer. See John J. Macionis, "Economy and Work" chap. 16 in *Sociology*, 11th ed. (Upper Saddle River, NJ: Pearson/Prentice Hall, 2007), 430; US Census Bureau, "Historical Statistics of the United States, Colonial Times to 1970," http://www.census.gov/compendia/statab/hist_stats.html.

7. Laurie, 87.

8. International Cooperative Alliance, "Statistical Information," http://www.ica.coop/coop/statistics.html.

9. See National Cooperative Business Association, "About Cooperatives," http://www.ncba.coop/abcoop.cfm.

10. John R. Commons, *History of Labour in the United States*, vol. 1 (New York: Macmillan, 1918), 278, 435-36, 569-71.

11. Clare Horner, "Producer Co-operatives in the United States" (Ph.D. diss., University of Pittsburg, 1978), 228-42.

12. Michael Schwartz, *Radical Protest and Social Structure: The Southern Farmers' Alliance and Cotton Tenancy, 1880-1890* (Chicago: University of Chicago Press, 1976), 217-34.

13. Ibid., 217.

14. Leon Fink, *Workingmen's Democracy: The Knights of Labor and American Politics* (Urbana and Chicago: University of Illinois Press, 1983), 18-35.

15. Howard Zinn, *A People's History of the United States* (New York: Harper & Row, 1980), 247-89.

16. Joseph Knapp, *The Rise of American Cooperative Enterprise 1620-1920* (Danville: Interstate, 1969), 38, 49; Steve Leikin, *The Practical Utopians, The Practical Utopians: American Workers and the Cooperative Movement in the Gilded Age* (Detroit: Wayne State University Press, 2005), 128-29; Selig Perlman, *A History of Trade Unionism in the United States* (New York: Macmillan, 1926), 166; Ellen Furlough and Carl Strikwerda, eds., *Consumers Against Capitalism? Consumer Cooperation in Europe, North America, and Japan, 1840-1990* (Lanham: Rowman & Littlefield Publishers, 1999), 132; Florence E. Parker, *The First 125 Years: A History of Distributive and Service Cooperation in the United States, 1829-1954* (Superior: Cooperative League, 1956), 59.

17. Parker, 55-58.

18. See Chapter 15.

19. UN, "Resolution, Cooperatives in Social Development," adopted January 18, 2002, http://www.copac.coop/unpubs.html. The UN reaffirmed the resolution in December, 2007.

20. ICA, "Statement on the Cooperative Identity," adopted by the ICA General Assembly, 1995, http://www.ica.coop/coop/principles.html.

21. The term *commune* also refers to a municipality in various European countries, as in the Paris Commune.

22. Robert Jackall and Henry M. Levin, eds., *Worker Cooperatives in America* (Berkeley: University of California Press, 1984), 257-73.

23. Horner, 137-59.

24. Ibid., 152-55; P. J. Honigsberg, B. Kamoroff and J. Beatty, *We Own It: Starting and Managing Coops, Collectives and Employee Owned Ventures* (Laytonville, CA: Bell Springs Publishing, 1982), 54.

25. Jackall and Levin, 38; Horner, 152.

26. For legal cooperative structures today, see Van P. Baldwin, *Legal Sourcebook for California Cooperatives*, 3rd edition (Davis, CA: Center for Cooperatives: 2004); Also see Honigsberg et al.

1. Early Cooperation in America

1. Indigenous and anthropological literature concur that economic cooperation and communalism are outstanding characteristics of Indian civilization, in distinction from Euro-American culture. See John Mohawk, ed., *Basic Call to Consciousness* (Rooseveltown, NY: Akwesasne Notes, 1978), 16, 71, 96-98. For an extensive anthropological study, see Margaret Mead, ed., *Cooperation and Competition Among Primitive Peoples* (New York: McGraw-

Hill, 1937. Reprinted. New York: Beacon, 1961), page references to the 1961 edition, 8, 87, 180, 240-64, 277, 313-20, 382-93, 427, 458-511. The term primitive is best taken to mean primal or close to the source. See also Frank Waters, *Book of the Hopi* (New York: Viking Press, 1963; New York: Ballantine, 1969), 120-122. Page references are to the 1969 edition; Kenneth Rexroth, *Communalism* (New York: Seabury Press, 1974), 8.

2. Peter Farb, *Man's Rise to Civilization: The Cultural Ascent of the Indians of North America* (New York: Dutton, 1968), 10, 30-32, 45, 73-75.

3. Alvin M. Josephy Jr., *The Indian Heritage of America* (New York: Knopf, 1968), 23-26.

4. Farb, 30-32.

5. Mead, 383.

6. John G. Neihardt, *Black Elk Speaks* (New York: Simon & Schuster: 1932; New York: Washington Square Press, 1972), 46-47. Page references are to the 1972 edition; Mead, 383-84; Farb, 110-12.

7. Fred Eggan, *Social Organization of the Western Pueblos* (Chicago: University of Chicago Press, 1950), 34-36, 189, 194.

8. Farb, 126-44.

9. Mohawk, 96-98; Jack Weatherford, *Indian Givers: How the Indians of the Americas Transformed the World* (New York: Crown, 1988), 142.

10. Raymond Friday Locke, *The Book of the Navajo* (Los Angeles: Mankind House Publishing, 1976), 16-20.

11. See contemporary Native American cooperatives in chapter 11.

12. Joseph M. Marshall III, *The Lakota Way* (New York: Viking Compass, 2001), 192.

13. See J. A Doyle, *English Colonies in America, vol. 2, The Puritan Colonies* (New York: Holt, 1889); Roland G. Usher, *The Pilgrims and their History* (New York: MacMillon 1918); William Cronon, *Changes in the Land: Indians, Colonists, and the Ecology of New England* (New York: Hill and Wang, 1983). Sumner Chilton Powell, *Puritan Village* (New York: Doubleday, 1965); and Glenn T. Trewartha, "Types of Rural Settlement in Colonial America," *Geographical Review* 36, no. 4 (1946): 568-96.

14. Frederick J. Turner, *The Frontier in American History* (New York: Henry Holt, 1921), 343.

15. Daniel J. Boorstin, *The Americans: The National Experience* (New York: Vintage, 1967), 51-57, as quoted by Knapp, *The Rise of American Cooperative Enterprise*, 443.

16. See Griswold Del Castillo, U.S. General Accounting Office, *Treaty of Guadalupe Hidalgo*, September 2001, GAO-01-951, 1-19; June 2004, GAO-04-59.

17. See Albert Prago, *Strangers in Their Own Land: A History of Mexican-Americans* (New York: Four Winds Press, 1973), and Richard Griswold Del Castillo, *The Treaty of Guadalupe Hidalgo: A Legacy of Conflict* (Norman: University of Oklahoma Press, 1990).

18. John A. Crow, *The Epic of Latin America*, 4th ed. (Berkeley: University of California Press, 1992), 54.

19. Ibid., 54-55.

20. U.S. General Accounting Office, September, 2001, 6.

21. Armando Navarro, *The Raza Unida Party* (Philadelphia: Temple University Press, 2000), 173.

22. U.S. General Accounting Office, September, 2001, 6-8.

23. Del Castillo Griswold, 72.

24. John Womack, Jr., *Zapata and the Mexican Revolution* (New York: Random House, 1969; New York: Vintage, 1970), 393-411. References are to the 1970 edition.

25. Ibid., 371-72.

26. U.S. General Accounting Office, June 2004, 2.

27. Doyle, 55-58; Knapp, *The Rise of American Cooperative Enterprise*, 5-7.

28. George E. McNeill, "Cooperation in Massachusetts," *Eighth Annual Report of the Massachusetts Bureau of Labour* (1877), quoted in Knapp, *The Rise of American Cooperative Enterprise*, 443.

29. Corporations, chartered by the various Crowns of Europe, played a major role in all the early colonies. All international trade in Spanish America went through the Casa de Contración, a corporation in Seville chartered in 1503. The Virginia Company founded Jamestown in 1607; the Dutch West Indies Company founded New Amsterdam and Albany in 1614; the Massachusetts Bay Company founded its colony in 1630; the New France Company founded Montréal in 1642. The Boston "tea party" was against the trade monopoly of the British East India Company. See Joseph S. Davis, "Corporations in the American Colonies," *Essays in the Earlier History of American Corporations* (Cambridge: Harvard University Press, 1917).

30. William Bradford, *Of Plymouth Plantation 1620-1647* (New York: Random House, 1981), 42.

31. Ibid., 42-43.

32. Sumner Chilton Powell, *Puritan Village* (New York: Doubleday, 1965), 4-12; Roland G. Usher, *The Pilgrims and their History* (New York: MacMillon, 1918), 5-17.

33. Doyle, 42.

34. Bradford, 83-84. The Virginia House of Burgesses, established in 1619 (the year before the Pilgrims landed), is credited as the first elected legislative assembly, but the franchise was limited to landholding males, the House met only once a year, and its acts could be vetoed without recourse by the governor, by the governor's council, and by the corporation in London.

35. Bradford, 112.

36. Ibid., 132.; Doyle, 61-62. That their early absolute communism

had been imposed on them is the context of the famous passage in which Bradford disparages their early "common course and condition" as "found to breed much confusion and discontent, and retard much employment that would have been to their benefit and comfort." (133).

37. Doyle, 71.

38. George D. Langdon, Jr., "The Franchise and Political Democracy in Plymouth Colony," *The William and Mary Quarterly* 20, no. 4 (1963): 514, 523, 525.

39. Slavery in the North, "Slavery in Massachusetts," http://www. slavenorth.com/massachusetts.htm.

40. William Cronon, *Changes in the Land: Indians, Colonists, and the Ecology of New England* (New York: Hill and Wang, 1983), 72-73; Glenn T. Trewartha, "Types of Rural Settlement in Colonial America," *Geographical Review* 36, no. 4 (1946): 568-96.

41. Powell, *Puritan Village*, 6-9.

42. Norman Macdonald, "English Land Tenure on the North American Continent: A Summary," *Contributions to Canadian Economics* 7 (1934): 21, 24-25; Trewartha, 579-80.

43. Knapp, *The Rise of American Cooperative Enterprise*, 5.

44. Ronald E. Seavoy, *An Economic History of the United States From 1607 to the Present* (New York: Routledge, 2006), 25, 50, 53.

45. Usher, *The Pilgrims and their History*, 63.

46. Wilbur Henry Siebert, *The Underground Railroad from Slavery to Freedom* (New York: The Macmillan Company, 1898), 118-19, 131, 166-68.

47. Zinn, 42-44; Richard B. Morris, *Government and Labor in Early America* (New York: Octagon Books, 1965), 310-16; Calvin B. Coulter, Jr., "The Import Trade of Colonial Virginia," *The William and Mary Quarterly* 2, no. 3 (1945): 306.

48. Usher, 212.

49. Morris, 35-39; Slavery in the North, "Introduction," http:// www.slavenorth.com/slavenorth.htm.

50. Slavery in New England was primarily urban, since plantations could not flourish in the climate. In 1710 there were probably about a thousand blacks in all of New England, but several times that in New York, New Jersey and Pennsylvania. New England ships went on to conduct much of the colonial slave trade, and the region grew rich off it. Captive local Indians, who could not be successfully enslaved on their ancestral lands, were shipped to the Caribbean in exchange for second-generation African slaves. The first US census in 1790 counted 2,805 slaves in New England (primarily in Connecticut), as well as 13,975 free blacks. The same census reported 36,323 slaves and 13,059 free blacks in the Mid-Atlantic colonies, and 655,079 slaves and 32,162 free blacks in the South. Slavery in the North, http://www.slavenorth.com/slavenorth.htm.

51. Herbert Aptheker, *Negro Slave Revolts in the United States, 1526-*

1860 (New York: International Publishers, 1939), 15-20, 71-72; Zinn, 36.

52. Herbert Aptheker, "Maroons Within the Present Limits of the United States," *The Journal of Negro History* 24, no. 2 (1939): 167-84; Henry Louis Gates and Anthony Appiah, *Africana: The Encyclopedia of the African and African American Experience* (New York: Basic Civitas Books, 1999), 1253.

53. Zinn, 32-38; Cheryl Janifer LaRoche, "On The Edge Of Freedom: Free Black Communities, Archaeology, and the Underground Railroad" (PhD diss., University of Maryland, 2004), 105-11.

54. Encyclopedia of Chicago Online, "Mutual Benefit Societies" http://www.encyclopedia.chicagohistory.org/pages/866.html (accessed March 15, 2008); Commons, *History of Labour in the United States*, 1: 85.

55. Encarta Encyclopedia, "Benjamin Franklin," http://encarta. msn.com/encyclopedia_761576775/franklin_benjamin.html (accessed March 15, 2008).

56. Knapp, *The Rise of American Cooperative Enterprise*, 7-8.

57. Ibid., 8.

58. Ibid.

59. Ibid., 9.

60. Ibid., 7-9.

61. Nina Mjagkij, *Organizing Black America: An Encyclopedia of African American Associations* (New York: Taylor & Francis, 2001), 234-36.

62. Ibid., 235.

63. Du Bois, W. E. B, *Economic Co-operation among Negro Americans* (Atlanta, GA: Atlanta University Press, 1907), 92-108.

64. John Bradbury, *Travels in the Interior of America* (London: Sherwood, Neely, and Jones, 1817), 293-94.

65. Alexis de Tocqueville, *Democracy in America*, trans. Henry Reeves (Paris: C. Gosselin, 1835), http://xroads.virginia.edu/~HYPER/DETOC/1_ch12.htm.

66. Ibid., http://xroads.virginia.edu/~Hyper/DETOC/ch2_05.htm.

67. Commons, *History of Labour in the United States*, 1: 85-86.

68. Ibid., 87,

69. Ibid., 85-87; Morris, 200-07.

2. The Revolutionary Movements Begin

1. Joseph G. Reybeck, *A History of American Labor* (New York: Macmillan, 1959; New York: Free Press, 1966), 6, 7-23; Foster Rhea Dulles and Melvin Dubofsky, *Labor in America, A History* (Arlington Heights, IL: Harlan Davidson. 1984. Revised 4th ed. 1993), 1-15; Philip Foner, *A History of the Labor Movement in the United States* (New York: International Publishers, 1947) 1:19-24; Zinn, 42-47; Morris, 35, 301-04.; Laurie, 15-18.; Robert J. Steinfeld, *The Invention of Free Labor: The Employment Relation in English and American Law and Culture, 1350-1870* (Chapel Hill, N.C.: University of North Carolina Press, 1991), 3-14. See also Herbert G. Gutman, "Work,

Culture, and Society in Industrializing America, 1815-1919," *The American Historical Review* 78, no. 3 (1973): 531-88. For the period between 1800 and the Civil War, I have relied on Commons, Laurie, Morris, Steinfeld, and others referenced below. See Bibliography for more.

2. Zinn, 46-47; Raybeck, 11; Steinfeld, 10-11.

3. Commons, *History of Labour in the United States*, 1: 4-5; Dulles and Dubofsky, 2-3.

4. Foner, *A History of the Labor Movement in the United States*, 1: 33-36; Raybeck, 25-27.

5. Foner, *A History of the Labor Movement in the United States*, 1: 34-43.

6. Weatherford, 135-36; Bruce E. Johansen, *Forgotten Founders: How the American Indian Helped Shape Democracy* (Boston: Harvard Common Press, 1982), 54, 60, 76.

7. Ibid., 125; Johansen, 119.

8. Thomas Paine, *The American Crisis*, no. 2 (1777), Thomas Paine National Historical Association, http://www.thomaspaine.org/Archives/Crisis-2.html.

9. Foner, *A History of the Labor Movement in the United States*, 1:65, 82-83; Zinn, 90-93.

10. Foner, *A History of the Labor Movement in the United States*, 1: 84-87; Zinn, 90-92.

11. Thomas Paine, *Agrarian Justice* (1797) in *Common Sense and Other Writings* (New York: Barnes and Noble: 2005).

12. Zinn, 92-94.

13. Ibid., 90-97.

14. Encarta Encyclopedia, "Immigration from 1775 to 1840," http://encarta.msn.com/encyclopedia_761566973_2/Immigration.html (accessed March 15, 2008); David A. Wilson, *United Irishmen, United States: Immigrant Radicals in the Early Republic* (Ithaca: Cornell University Press, 1998), 2-8, 58-60.

15. Foner, *A History of the Labor Movement in the United States*, 1: 85-87.

16. Ibid., 87; Philip S. Foner, ed., *Thomas Jefferson: Selections from His Writings* (New York: International Publishers, 1943), 24.

17. "[A]s a result of the democratic measures adopted during the years when Jefferson was in power, the movement to extend the franchise, the curbing of arbitrary power of the judiciary, the abolition of undemocratic and aristocratic practices in government, and the opening of opportunities for the masses to obtain cheap land in the west through the Louisiana Purchase—the basis of American democracy was considerably broadened." Foner, *Thomas Jefferson*, 28.

18. Foner, *A History of the Labor Movement in the United States*, 1: 82-89; Foner, *Thomas Jefferson*, 28.

19. Thomas Jefferson to James Madison, 1785. ME 19:17. Thomas Jefferson on Politics & Government, "Quotations/50: Property Rights,"

http://etext.lib.virginia.edu/jefferson/quotations/.

20. Thomas Jefferson, *Autobiography* (1821), http://avalon.law.yale.edu/19th_century/jeffauto.asp.

21. Foner, *Thomas Jefferson*, 56-57.

22. Thomas Jefferson to John Taylor, 1816. ME 15:18. Thomas Jefferson Randolph, ed., *Memoirs, Correspondence, and Private Papers of Thomas Jefferson*, 4 vol. (London: Henry Colburn and Richard Bentley, 1829), 4: 285-288; Thomas Jefferson on Politics & Government, "Quotations/36. Money," http://etext.lib.virginia.edu/jefferson/quotations.

23. Ibid.

24. Laurie, 38-40; Raybeck, 49-53.

25. Seavoy, 77, 118-68; Raybeck, 98-99; Foner, *A History of the Labor Movement in the United States*, 1: 82-86.

26. Laurie, 15-18; Commons, *History of Labour in the United States*, 1: 25-30.

27. Dulles, 25-26.

28. Foner, *A History of the Labor Movement in the United States*, 1: 22-24.

29. Laurie, 35-37, 44-45.

30. Commons, *History of Labour in the United States*, 1: 83.

31. Rayback, 17.

32. Morris, 196.

33. William Haber, *Industrial Relations in the Building Industry* (Cambridge: Harvard University Press, 1930), 275; Commons, *History of Labour in the United States*, 1: 158, 186-87; Laurie, 64.

34. Commons, *History of Labour in the United States*, 1: 97; 127-28.

35. Ibid., 108-09; Raybeck, 54.

36. Rayback, 49.

37. Charles G.Steffen, *The Mechanics of Baltimore: Workers and Politics in the Age of Revolution 1763-1812* (Urbana: University of Illinois Press, 1984), 114.

38. Ibid., 115-16.

39. Commons, *History of Labour in the United States*, 1: 128-30.

40. Ibid., 127-29.

41. Ibid., 175-76; Zinn, 90; Foner, *A History of the Labor Movement in the United States*, 1: 82.

42. Commons, *History of Labour in the United States*, 1: 124.

43. Rayback, *A History of American Labor*, 56-57. Another six conspiracy trials in the 1820s implicitly recognized the right of association to raise wages, though at the same time they also outlawed picketing, sympathetic strikes, and the distribution of scab lists.

44. Commons, *History of Labour in the United States*, 1: 97.

45. Ibid., 98.

46. Ibid., 92-95.

47. Ibid., 92, 98.

48. Ibid., 95.

49. Ibid., 98.

50. Ibid., 97-99.

51. Ibid., 98.

52. However, the general boom period was blotched by a severe downturn in the Eastern industrial sector beginning in 1816, long before the panic of 1819.

53. Samuel Rezneck, "The Depression of 1819-1822, A Social History," *The American Historical Review* 39, no. 1 (1933): 28-47; Dulles, 31-32.

54. Albert Fried, *Socialism in America, From the Shakers to the Third International* (Garden City, NY: Anchor, 1970), 85-93.

55. Arthur E. Bestor, *Backwoods Utopias, The Sectarian Origins and the Owenite Phase of Communitarian Socialism in America, 1663-1829* (Washington, DC: American Historical Association, 1950; Philadelphia: University of Philadelphia Press, 1970), 160-201. Citations are to the 1970 edition.

56. Fried, 117-23.

57. Ibid., 118-19.

58. Joseph L Blau, ed., *Social Theories of Jacksonian Democracy* (New York: Liberal Arts Press, 1954; Indianapolis: Hackett, 2003), xxvii, 342-46.

59. Laurie, 18.

60. Robert Owen, *Report to the County of Lanark* (Glasgow: Wardlaw & Cunninghame, 1821), 1-2.

61. Harrison, 165; Bestor, 185-86.

62. Mark Holloway, *Heavens on Earth* (London: Turnstile Press, 1951; New York: Dover, 1966), 119. Citations are to the Dover edition.

63. Ibid., 119-20.

64. Knapp, *The Rise of American Cooperative Enterprise*, 18; Commons, *History of Labour in the United States*, 1: 95-96, 99, 511.

65. Knapp, *The Rise of American Cooperative Enterprise*, 18.

66. Commons, *History of Labour in the United States*, 1: 95.

67. Ibid., 96.

68. Knapp, *The Rise of American Cooperative Enterprise*, 18; Commons, *History of Labour in the United States*, 1: 96-97.

69. Parker, 3.

70. George Jacob Holyoake, *History of Co-operation* (Philadelphia: Lippincott, 1879) 2: 320.

71. Parker, 3.

72. Commons, *History of Labour in the United States*, 1: 169-72.

73. Ibid., 125-27, 136, 156-58, 376-78.

74. Dulles, 68; Commons, *History of Labour in the United States*, 1: 466.

75. Commons, *History of Labour in the United States*, 1: 378, 436.

76. Laurie, 89-90, Commons, *History of Labour in the United States*, 1:

466-69.

77. Commons, *History of Labour in the United States*, 1: 302-25; 438-53.

78. Ibid., 306-18.

79. Ibid., 302.

80. Ibid., 302-15.

81. Ibid., 235-41; Dulles, 58; Raybeck, 77.

82. Ibid., 158, 186.

83. Ibid., 303-05.

84. Ibid., 302.

85. Ibid., 307.

86. Parker, 3; Perlman, 33.

87. Foner, *A History of the Labor Movement in the United States*, 1: 106.

88. Ibid., 105; Commons, *History of Labour in the United States*, 1: 418; Rosalyn Fraad Baxandall, et. al., *America's Working Women: A Documentary History, 1600 to the Present* (New York: Random House: 1976), 58.

89. Baxandall, et al., 58-62; Commons, *History of Labour in the United States*, 1: 318-19.

90. Commons, *History of Labour in the United States*, 1: 311-12.

91. Ibid., 318.

92. Ibid., 379.

93. Ibid., 379-80.

94. Ibid., 315.

95. Ibid., 335.

96. Raybeck, 76-80; Foner, *A History of the Labor Movement in the United States*, 1: 122-14.

97. Commons, 1: 425-34.

98. Ibid., 435-36.

99. Ibid., 467.

100. Ibid., 378, 466-69.

101. Ibid., 435-36.

102. John R. Commons, *A Documentary History of American Industrial Society*, 6 vol., *Labor Movement 1820-1840* (Glendale: A.H. Clark, 1910), 2: 299.

103. Commons, *History of Labour in the United States*, 1: 467-68.

104. Ibid., 467.

105. Ibid., 348-350; 454-455.

106. Foner, *A History of the Labor Movement in the United States*, 1: 121-42.

107. Raybeck, 68-74.

108. Foner, *A History of the Labor Movement in the United States*, 1: 133.

109. Ibid., 122-24; Donald Drew Egbert, Stow Persons, and T. D. Seymour Bassett eds., *Socialism and American Life* (Princeton, NJ: Princeton University Press: 1952), 1: 230.

110. Dulles, 79-80.

111. Fried, 124-32.

112. Commons, *History of Labour in the United States*, 1: 236-37.

113. Raybeck, 69-70.

114. Commons, *History of Labour in the United States*, 1: 235-38.

115. Dulles, 37.

116. Raybeck, 73-74

117. William MacDonald, *Jacksonian Democracy, 1829-1837* (New York: Harper, 1906), 185.

118. Raybeck, 72-73.

119. Foner, *A History of the Labor Movement in the United States*, 1: 141-42.

120. Dulles, 60-61; Foner, *A History of the Labor Movement in the United States*, 1: 115-17.

121. Foner, *A History of the Labor Movement in the United States*, 1: 118.

122. Raybeck, 81, 92-97.

3. The Movements Renewed & the Corporations Rise

1. Commons, *History of Labour in the United States*, 1: 458-59, 491.

2. Carl J. Mayer, "Personalizing the Impersonal: Corporations and the Bill of Rights," *Hastings Law Journal* 41, no. 3 (1990), http://www.reclaimdemocracy.org/personhood/mayer_personalizing.html.; Richard L. Grossman and Frank I. Adams, "Taking Care Of Business:_Citizenship And The Charter Of Incorporation," *The Nancho Archives, An Arsenal of Incendiary Ideas*, http://www.nancho.net/bigbody/chrtink1.html.

3. Seavoy, 106-09; see also vii-ix, 80-82, 96-101, 121-22. Seavoy documents how government policies promoted the growth of corporations, particularly in the industrialized North, through the first half of the 19th century, and how huge government contracts during the Civil War led to their empowerment throughout the country after 1865. For early history, see also Joseph S. Davis, "Corporations in the American Colonies," in Joseph Stancliffe Davis, ed., *Essays in the Earlier History of American Corporations* (Cambridge: Harvard University Press, 1917; Clark, N.J.: Lawbook Exchange, 2006).

4. Commons, *History of Labour in the United States*, 1: 106-07; Foner, *A History of the Labor Movement in the United States*, 1: 55-56.

5. Foner, *A History of the Labor Movement in the United States*, 1: 67-68; Raybeck, 49.

6. Dulles, 73.

7. Ibid., 74; Raybeck, 50.

8. Commons, *History of Labour in the United States*, 1: 91-92, 101-04; Raybeck, 49-50.

9. Dorothy Ross, *Origins of American Social Science* (New York: Cambridge University Press, 1991), 26-29.

10. Seavoy, 165-66; Raybeck, 50.

11. Seavoy, 106-07.

12. Commons, *History of Labour in the United States*, 1: 491.

13. Dulles, 63.

14. Commons, *History of Labour in the United States*, 1: 507-08, 565-73.

15. Ibid., 506-08.

16. Ibid., 487-510.

17. Ibid., 565.

18. Ibid.

19. Herbert Aptheker, *And Why Not Every Man* (Berlin: Seven Seas, 1961), 16, 23; Commons, *History of Labour in the United States*, 1: 565.

20. Commons, *History of Labour in the United States*, 1: 567.

21. Ibid., 566.

22. Ibid., 569-70; Perlman, 32; Foner, *A History of the Labor Movement in the United States*, 1: 180-81; Raybeck, 97.

23. Foner, *A History of the Labor Movement in the United States*, 1: 180-81.

24. Commons, *History of Labour in the United States*, 1: 506-07.

25. Ibid., 507.

26. Ibid., 498-510.

27. Ibid., 500-01.

28. Ibid., 507.

29. Ibid., 508.

30. Ibid., 507.

31. Ibid., 569-70.

32. Foner, *A History of the Labor Movement in the United States*, 1: 224-25; Dulles, 74-75.

33. US Census Bureau, "Historical Statistics of the United States," http://www.census.gov.

34. Foner, A History of the Labor Movement in the United States, 1: 179; Donald Cope McKay, The National Workshops: A Study in the French Revolution of 1848 (Cambridge: Harvard University Press, 1965).

35. Commons, History of Labour in the United States, 1: 567.

36. Ibid., 568.

37. Foner, *A History of the Labor Movement in the United States*, 1: 229.

38. Commons, History of Labour in the United States, 1: 568; Morris Hillquit, History of Socialism in the United States (New York: Funk & Wagnalls, 1903; New York: Dover, 1971), 144-50; Egbert, Persons and Basset, 1: 159, 231. See also Carl Wittke, The Utopian Communist: A Biography of Wilhelm Weitling, Nineteenth-Century Reformer (Baton Rouge: Louisiana State University Press, 1950).

39. Commons, *History of Labour in the United States*, 1: 571.

40. Ibid., 571, footnote 15.

41. Ibid, 571.

42. Ibid, 506-07.

43. Knapp, *The Rise of American Cooperative Enterprise*, 18-19; Commons, *History of Labour in the United States*, 1: 496-505

44. Knapp, The Rise of American Cooperative Enterprise, 11.

45. Ibid.

46. Ibid.

47. Ibid., 12-14.

48. Ibid., 21-24.; See Edwin Charles Rozwenc, *Cooperatives Come to America: The Protective Store Movement 1845-1867* (Philadelphia: Porcupine Press, 1975).

49. Parker, 4.

50. Ibid.

51. Herbert Baxter Adams, *History of Coöperation in the United States*, John Hopkins University Studies in Historical and Political Science, Sixth Series (Baltimore: John Hopkins Press, 1888), 19-32; Parker, 4-8; Commons, *History of Labour in the United States*, 1: 509, 571-73.

52. Adams, 20.

53. Knapp, *The Rise of American Cooperative Enterprise*, 22.

54. Parker, 4.

55. Knapp, *The Rise of American Cooperative Enterprise*, 21.

56. Ibid., 22.

57. Ibid., 23.

58. Adams, 21; Commons, *History of Labour in the United States*, 1: 573.

59. Knapp., 24.

60. Parker, 5-6; Knapp 25.

61. Parker, 7; Adams, 24.

62. Adams., 26-29.

63. Ibid., 24-25.

64. Knapp, *The Rise of American Cooperative Enterprise*, 22-23.

65. Commons, *History of Labour in the United States*, 1: 509.

66. The primary source for the early history of Rochdale is George J. Holyoake, *Self-Help By the People*, 10th ed. (London: 1857; New York: Scribners, 1907) and Holyoake, *The History of Co-operation in England*, 2 vol. (London: Trubner & Co., 1875). An excellent contribution is David J. Thompson, *Weavers of Dreams* (Davis, CA: Center for Cooperatives, 1994). See also Albert Sonnichsen, *Consumers' Coöperation* (New York: Macmillan, 1920), 23-29; Ellen Furlough and Carl Strikwerda, eds. *Consumers Against Capitalism? Consumer Cooperation in Europe, North America, and Japan, 1840-1990* (Lanham: Rowman & Littlefield Publishers, 1999), 8-10.

67. Holyoake, *Self-Help By the People*, 1: 11.

68. Knapp, *The Rise of American Cooperative Enterprise*, 42.

69. Sonnichsen, 43-46.

70. Ibid., 22-39.

71. Ibid., 28.

72. Ibid., 35.

73. Ibid., 40-54.

74. The history of the UCA is told in Adams, 141-42; Commons, *History of Labour in the United State*s, 2: 39-41; Parker 25; Knapp 1: 30-31. An extensive discussion can be found in Leikin, *The Practical Utopians*, 1-17.

75. Knapp, *The Rise of American Cooperative Enterprise*, 30.

76. Leikin, *The Practical Utopians*, 14.

77. Ibid., 9-12.

78. Ibid.,18-20.

79. Knapp, *The Rise of American Cooperative Enterprise*, 31; Commons, *History of Labour in the United States*, 2: 40-41.

80. Commons, *History of Labour in the United States*, 2: 41.

81. Leikin, *The Practical Utopians*, 7, note 165.

82. Ibid., 16.

83. Commons, *History of Labour in the United States*, 2: 41.

84. Steven Leikin, "The Citizen Producer: The Rise and Fall of Working-Class Cooperatives in the United States," in Furlough and Strikweda, eds., *Consumers against Capitalism*, 97.

85. Leikin, *The Practical Utopians*, 17-22.

86. Anna Rochester, *The Populist Movement in the United States* (New York: International, 1943), 10.

87. Commons, *History of Labour in the United States*, 1: 4.

88. Aptheker, *And Why Not Everyman*, 39.

89. Zinn, 176-85.

90. Seavoy, 167-69.

91. Aptheker, *And Why Not Everyman*, 16-20.

92. Zinn, 170-73; Herbert Aptheker, *Negro Slave Revolts in the United States, 1526-1860* (New York: International Publishers, 1939), 48-52; Herbert Aptheker, *Nat Turner's Slave Rebellion* (New York: Grove Press, 1966).

93. Foner, *A History of the Labor Movement in the United States*, 1: 294.

94. Ibid., 266-77.

95. Aptheker, *And Why Not Everyman*, 13; Leikin, *The Practical Utopians*, 9, 12; see Douglass' work in the Colored National Labor Union in Chapter 4.

96. Merle Eugene Curti, *The Growth of American Thought* (New Brunswick, Transaction Publishers: 1982), 511.

97. Holyoake, 1: iii.

98. Perlman, 33; Newspapers of Oneida County, NY, http://oneida.nygenweb.net/news.htm; Commons, *History of Labour in the United States*, 1: 302-15.

99. Foner, *A History of the Labor Movement in the United States*, 1: 267.

100. Zinn, 121.

101. Jean H. Baker, *James Buchanan* (New York: Macmillan, 2004), 117.

102. Wasserman, 63.

103. Zinn, 184; Richard O. Boyer, and Herbert M. Morais, *Labor's Untold Story* (New York: United Electrical Workers of America, 1955), 14.

104. Boyer and Morais, 18.

105. Zinn, 184-87.

106. Seavoy, 188-90.

4. The Aftermath of the Civil War

1. Abraham Lincoln, Letter to Col. William F. Elkins, November 21, 1864, quoted by Scott G. McNall, *The Road to Rebellion* (Chicago: University of Chicago Press, 1988), 36.

2. Zinn, 235-46.

3. Foner, *A History of the Labor Movement in the United States*, 1: 389-93; Zinn, 193-95.

4. Wasserman, 64.

5. Foner, *A History of the Labor Movement in the United States*, 1: 418.

6. Commons, *History of Labour in the United States*, 2: 111.

7. Richard T. Ely, *The Labor Movement in America* (New York: Thomas Y. Crowell & Co., 1886), 162.

8. Seavoy, 185-201; Boyer and Morais, 21-22; Commons, *History of Labour in the United States*, 2: 42-44.

9. Commons, *History of Labour in the United States*, 2: 54; Foner, *A History of the Labor Movement in the United States*, 1: 419.

10. Jonathan P Grossman, William Sylvis, *Pioneer of American Labor* (New York: Columbia University Press, 1945; Cincinnati: The Sylvis Society, 1986), 191-92. See Commons, *History of Labour in the United States*, 2: 53-55, 85-155, especially 110-112. See Horner, 41, 72-85; Leikin, *The Practical Utopians*, 26-30; Montgomery, 114-28; Foner, *A History of the Labor Movement in the United States*, 1: 373, 417-20.

11. Raybeck, 118; Foner, *A History of the Labor Movement in the United States*, 1: 371, 376-77. Sylvis claimed 600,000 members, but that figure was almost surely exaggerated.

12. Commons, *History of Labour in the United States*, 2: 96-102; Raybeck, 116-17.

13. Grossman, 232.

14. Ibid., 228; Commons, *History of Labour in the United States*, 2: 127-28.

15. Commons, *History of Labour in the United States*, 2: 123; Dulles, 104-05.

16. Knapp, 31.

17. Boyer and Morais, 35.

18. Ely, 347.

19. Foner, *A History of the Labor Movement in the United States*, 1: 417; Commons, *History of Labour in the United States*, 2: 53; Grossman, 189-92.

20. Ely, 183.

21. Commons, History of Labour in the United States, 2: 112-14.

22. Ibid., 53.

23. Ibid., 53-55.

24. Grossman, 210-19.

25. Commons, History of Labour in the United States, 2: 53-57.

26. Grossman, 201.

27. Commons, History of Labour in the United States, 2: 54.

28. Ibid.

29. Ibid., 137.

30. The New York State Public Employees Federation, "Kate Mullaney: A True Labor Pioneer," http://www.pef.org/katemullaney.htm.

31. Philip S. Foner, *Women and the American Labor Movement from Colonial Times to the Eve of World War 1* (New York: The Free Press, 1979), 155-56; Carole Turbin, *Working Women of Collar City: Gender, Class, and Community in Troy, New York, 1864-1886* (Urbana and Chicago: University of Illinois Press, 1978), 121-24.

32. Foner, *A History of the Labor Movement in the United States*, 1: 399.

33. Commons, *History of Labour in the United States*, 2: 137-38; Raybeck, 123; Foner, *A History of the Labor Movement in the United States*, 1: 403-07.

34. Du Bois, 152.

35. Bettye C. Thomas, "A Nineteenth Century Black Operated Shipyard, 1866-1884: Reflections Upon Its Inception and Ownership," *The Journal of Negro History* 59, no. 1 (1974): 1-12.

36. Du Bois, 152-54; Laurie, 159; Leikin, *The Practical Utopians*, 34; Maryland Online Encyclopedia, "Isaac Myers," http://www.mdoe.org/myersisaac.html (accessed October 9, 2008).

37. Commons, *History of Labour in the United States*, 2: 119-24; Raybeck, 123-26.

38. Grossman 210-12.

39. Ibid., 247-54.

40. Boyer and Morais, 35.

41. Grossman, 247-54.

42. Commons, *History of Labour in the United States*, 2: 120-23; 128-29. Boyer and Morais, 35.

43. Boyer and Morais, 36.

44. Commons, History of Labour in the United States, 2: 131-32.

45. Grossman, 195-96.

46. Ibid.

47. Sonnichsen, 35.

48. Albert S. Lindeman, *A History of European Socialism* (New Ha-

ven: Yale University Press, 1983), 69-70; Furlough and Strikweda, 11-12; Grossman, 196.

49. Commons, *History of Labour in the United States*, 2: 131-32.

50. Ibid., 2: 205; Julius Braunthal, *History of the International*, 2 vol. (New York: Praeger, 1967), 1: 85-91.

51. Timothy Messer-Kruse, *The Yankee International* (Chapel Hill: The University of North Carolina Press, 1998), 135.

52. Hillquit, 173.

53. Commons, *History of Labour in the United States*, 2: 131-32.

54. Ibid., 2: 153-56; Foner, *A History of the Labor Movement in the United States*, 1: 423-29.

55. Raybeck, 128.

56. Commons, *History of Labour in the United States*, 2: 153; Raybeck, 128.

57. Commons, *History of Labour in the United States*, 2: 154-55.

58. Ibid., 155.

59. Dulles, 95-96.

60. Commons, *History of Labour in the United States*, 2: 151, 195.

61. Foner, *A History of the Labor Movement in the United States*, 1: 439-42.

62. Adams, 156-58; Commons, *History of Labour in the United States*, 2: 53-55.

63. Adams, 158-60.

64. Leikin, *The Practical Utopians*, 151.

65. Horner, 139-41.

66. Grossman, 215.

67. Horner, 228-42.

68. Commons, *History of Labour in the United States*, 2: 162-63.

69. Ibid., 157-67; Raybeck, 129.

70. Horner, 58.

71. Ibid, 55-58.

72. Don D. Lescohier, *The Knights of St. Crispin*, (New York: Arno, 1969) 5-11; Commons, *History of Labour in the United States*, 2: 76-79, 140-41; 152-53; Ira B.Cross, *History of the Labor Movement in California* (Berkeley: University of California Press, 1935) 57, 308-09.

73. Lescohier, 49.

74. Ibid., 51.

75. Ibid., 51-52

76. Horner, 53.

77. Adams, 493.

78. Lescohier, 49-55; Commons, *History of Labour in the United States*, 2: 79.

79. Horner, 68.

80. Kimberly A. Zeuli and Robert Cropp, *Cooperatives: Principles and*

Practices in the 21st Century (Madison: University of Wisconsin Center for Cooperatives, 2004), 15.

81. Knapp, T*he Rise of American Cooperative Enterprise*, 12.

82. Ibid.

83. Ibid., 11-13; 19-21.

84. Commons, *History of Labour in the United States*, 1: 563.

85. Ibid., 522, 563; Seavoy, 175.

86. Seavoy, 172-75; Wasserman, 61-65; Hicks, *The Populist Revolt* (Minneapolis: University of Minnesota Press, 1931; Lincoln: University of Nebraska Press, 1961), 8-11. Citations are to the 1961 edition; Rochester, 10-13.

87. Seavoy, 201-04; Wasserman, 63-66.

88. Knapp, *The Rise of American Cooperative Enterprise*, 47.

89. Buck, Solon Justice, *The Granger Movement* (Cambridge: Harvard University Press, 1913; Lincoln: University of Nebraska Press, 1963), 3-39. Citations are to the 1963 edition. The history of the National Grange co-operatives can be found in Adams, 33-36; Buck, 239-79; Knapp, *The Rise of American Cooperative Enterprise*, 46-57; Parker 10-12; Wasserman, 66-69.

90. Knapp, The Rise of American Cooperative Enterprise, 46.

91. Buck, 40-44; Knapp, *The Rise of American Cooperative Enterprise*, 46-47.

92. Buck, 52.

93. Knapp, *The Rise of American Cooperative Enterprise*, 47.

94. Buck, 240-41; Knapp, *The Rise of American Cooperative Enterprise*, 48.

95. Wasserman, 66; Buck, 51.

96. Buck, 271; Parker, 11.

97. Buck, 270-74.

98. Knapp, *The Rise of American Cooperative Enterprise*, 50.

99. Buck, 267-70; Knapp, *The Rise of American Cooperative Enterprise*, 49-50.

100. Buck, 260-66; Knapp, *The Rise of American Cooperative Enterprise*, 51-52.

101. Buck, 10; A.V. Krebs, *The Corporate Reapers: The Book of Agribusiness* (Washington, DC: Essential Books, 1992), 149.

102. Wasserman, 65-66; Buck, 9-15.

103. Wasserman, 68.

104. Ibid.; Buck, 276.

105. Wasserman, 69.

106. Buck, 80-101; Commons, *History of Labour in the United States*, 1: 248-51.

107. Buck, 58-59.

108. Ibid., 53.

109. Wasserman, 69; Buck, 308; Commons, *History of Labour in the*

United States, 2: 250-51.

110. Foner, *A History of the Labor Movement in the United States,* 1: 486; Boyer and Morais, 63; Rochester, 32.

111. *The Oxford Companion to United States History*, "Greenback Labor Party," http://www.encyclopedia.com/doc/1O119-GreenbackLaborParty. html (accessed October 12, 2008).

112. Wasserman, 87.

113. Buck, 194-205, 231-35.

114. Wasserman, 69.

115. Ibid., 69-72; Knapp, *The Rise of American Cooperative Enterprise*, 55.

116. Zinn, 277-88.

117. Commons, *History of Labour in the United States*, 2: 172.

118. History of the Sovereigns can be found in Adams, 37-52; Knapp, *The Rise of American Cooperative Enterprise*, 32-35; Parker, 18-21; Commons, *History of Labour in the United States*, 2: 171-75.

119. Knapp, *The Rise of American Cooperative Enterprise*, 33.

120. Leikin, *The Practical Utopians*, 20.

121. Adams, 39-40; Commons, *History of Labour in the United States*, 2: 172

122. Leikin, *The Practical Utopians*, 20.

123. Knapp, *The Rise of American Cooperative Enterprise*, 33.

124. Parker, 19.

125. Commons, *History of Labour in the United States*, 2: 174.

126. Ibid.

127. Parker 20; Knapp, *The Rise of American Cooperative Enterprise*, 34.

128. Knapp, *The Rise of American Cooperative Enterprise*, 35.

129. Adams, 40-46; Commons, *History of Labour in the United States*, 2: 175; Knapp 35.

130. Adams, 53-57.

131. The history of the IWA is told in Braunthal, 1: 85-194; Commons, *History of Labour in the United States*, 2: 203-34; Messer-Kruse, 45-71; George Woodcock, *Anarchism* (New York: New American Library, 1962), 165-70, 178-81.

132. Braunthal, 1: 88-91.

133. Commons, *History of Labour in the United States*, 2: 204-05; Braunthal, 1: 85-94.

134. Braunthal, 1: 121-41.

135. Commons, *History of Labour in the United States*, 2: 205-07; Braunthal, 1: 95-100.

136. Braunthal, 1: 131; Marx, "Inaugural Address of the IWA," and "Instructions for the Delegates of the Provisional General Council," in *Selected Works* (Moscow: Progress 1969), 2: 17-16, 81-82.

137. Marx, *Selected Works*, 2: 81-82.

138. Braunthal, 1: 123-25.

139. Marx, *Selected Works*, 2:16-17; Marx, "The Civil War in France," *Selected Works*, 2: 223-224.

140. Ibid.

141. Woodcock, 165-71.

142. Commons, *History of Labour in the United States*, 2: 413-17; Messer-Kruse, 6-7; 58-59.

143. Frederick Engels, Introduction to *The Civil War in France*, by Karl Marx, *Selected Works*, 2: 223.

144. Marx, *Selected Works*, 2: 81; See the classic eyewitness account: Prosper Olivier Lissagaray, *History of the Paris Commune of 1871*, trans. Eleanor Marx Aveling (Brussels: H. Kistemaeckers, 1876; London: Reeves and Turner, 1886; London: New Park Publications, 1976).

145. Braunthal, 1: 181-82.

146. Commons, *History of Labour in the United States*, 2: 209-11; Messer-Kruse, 157-61; Egbert, Persons and Basset, 1: 235. The American section of the IWA became very active when the organization moved to New York, organizing large mass meetings and demonstrations of the unemployed in that and other cities. Victoria Woodhull was a prominent leader in New York. But the American section was split between those looking to the unions as centers of struggle and those looking to electoral politics. A group that included Woodhull left the New York Section to found the Equal Rights Party, fielding the Woodhull–Frederick Douglass ticket in the presidential election of 1872, while "scientific" socialists centered on F. A. Sorge assumed leadership in the America-based IWA. Messer-Kruse, 119, 123-27, 200-201; Fried, 183-87.

147. V. I. Lenin, "The Paris Commune and the Tasks of the Democratic Dictatorship," in *Collected Works* (Moscow: Progress, 1972), 9: 141.

148. Commons, *History of Labour in the United States*, 2: 269-71.

149. Philip Foner, *The Workingmen's Party of the United States* (Minneapolis: MEP Publications, 1984), 34-35.

150. Commons, *History of Labour in the United States*, 2: 271.

5. The Knights of Labor & "The Great Upheaval"

1. Dulles, 108-08, 116; Jeremy Brecher, *Strike!* (San Francisco: Straight Arrow Books, 1972), xxiii-xxv.

2. Commons, *History of Labour in the United States*, 2: 186-91; Brecher, 1-22; Boyer and Morais, 58-64.

3. Boyer and Morais, 61-63.

4. Nell Irvin Painter, *Standing at Armageddon: The United States 1877-1919* (New York: Norton, 1987), 16; Commons, *History of Labour in the United States*, 2: 187-91; Brecher, 11-13; Boyer and Morais, 63; Dulles, 115.

5. Rutherford B. Hayes Presidential Center, "The Disputed Elec-

tion of 1877," http://www.rbhayes.org/hayes/president/display.asp?id=511&subj=president.

6. Zinn, 200-02.

7. Center for Politics & Public Affairs, "The Compromise of 1877," http://www.fandm.edu/x2335.xml; Boyer and Morais, 58-59.

8. Zinn, 200-02.

9. Walter Lindner, "The Pittsburgh Rebellion of 1877," *Marxist-Leninist Quarterly* 2, no. 2 (1965): 54-84, http://www.plp.org/labhist/wl-pittsb1877.pdf.

10. Christopher Waldrep and Michael A. Bellesiles, *Documenting American Violence: A Sourcebook* (New York: Oxford University Press US, 2006), 353.

11. Commons, *History of Labour in the United States*, 2: 191; Brecher, 8-9.

12. Commons, History of Labour in the United States, 2: 334.

13. Powderly, *Thirty Years of Labor*, 117-20; William Cahn, *A Pictorial History of American Labor* (New York: Crown Publishers, 1972), 118.

14. Powderly, *Thirty Years of Labor*, 453.

15. Ibid, 118.

16. David Montgomery, *Labor in the Industrial Era*, http://www.dol.gov/oasam/programs/history/chapter3.htm.

17. Brecher, 28; Ely, 76.

18. Brecher, 30.

19. Commons, *History of Labour in the United States*, 2: 196-98; 430-31.

20. Robert E. Weir, *Beyond Labor's Veil* (University Park: Pennsylvania State University Press, 1996), 46-56.

21. Ibid, 104.

22. Commons, *History of Labour in the United States*, 2: 332-34; Norman J. Ware, *The Labor Movement in the United States 1860-1895, A Study in Democracy* (New York: Appelton and Co., 1929), 38, 76; Ely, 79.

23. Commons, *History of Labour in the United States*, 2: 332-34; Raybeck, 144.

24. Powderly, *Thirty Years of Labor*, 248; Eleanor Marx and Edward Aveling, *The Working Class Movement in America* (London: Swan Sonnenschein and Company: 1888. New York: Humanity Books, 2000), 142.

25. Commons, *History of Labour in the United States*, 2: 347.

26. Ibid.; Raybeck, 146; Weir, *Beyond Labor's Veil*, 10.

27. Commons, *History of Labour in the United States*, 2: 248-49.

28. Raybeck, 137-39.

29. Leikin, *The Practical Utopians*, 25-28.

30. Foner, *A History of the Labor Movement in the United States*, 2: 14-15.

31. Ibid., 2: 13; Commons, *History of Labour in the United States*, 2: 357-60.

32. Wasserman, 113; Perlman, 85; Zinn, 259; Foner, *A History of the*

Labor Movement in the United States, 2: 16.

33. Perlman, 84-85.

34. Commons, *History of Labour in the United States*, 2: 431.

35. Ibid., 2: 437; Leikin, *The Practical Utopians*, 66-69.

36. Leikin, *The Practical Utopians*, 67-68, 71.

37. Commons, *History of Labour in the United States*, 2: 435.

38. Powderly, *Thirty Years of Labor*, 465.

39. Commons, *History of Labour in the United States*, 2: 432; Powderly, *Thirty Years of Labor*, 464-65.

40. Horner, 228-42.

41. Leikin, *The Practical Utopians*, 73-81; Commons, *History of Labour in the United States*, 2: 435.

42. Ely, 185.

43. Perlman, 433.

44. Commons, *History of Labour in the United States*, 2: 437; Leikin, The Practical Utopians, 83-85; Robert E. Weir, *Knights Unhorsed* (Detroit: Wayne State University Press, 2000), 125.

45. Raybeck, 113-14; Commons, *History of Labour in the United States*, 2: 414-15.

46. Weir, *Knights Unhorsed*, 26; Commons, *History of Labour in the United States*, 2: 433; Leikin, *The Practical Utopians*, 24.

47. Weir, *Knights Unhorsed*, 23-46.

48. Commons, *History of Labour in the United States*, 2: 433; Weir, *Knights Unhorsed*, 26-27.

49. Leikin, *The Practical Utopians*, 81-83.

50. Victor Drury, *The Polity of the Labor Movement* (Philadelphia: Frederick Turner, 1885), 61-62

51. Adams, 162-67.

52. Ibid., 164.

53. Ibid., 162-65.

54. Leikin, *The Practical Utopians*, 117-22.

55. Adams, 207; Leikin, *The Practical Utopians*, 117-53.

56. Leikin, *The Practical Utopians*, 121.

57. Adams, 201; Leikin, *The Practical Utopians*, 120; Commons, *History of Labour in the United States*, 2: 76

58. Adams, 204-05; Leikin, *The Practical Utopians*, 118.

59. Leikin, *The Practical Utopians*, 117; Adams, 199.

60. Adams, 200, 205.

61. Adams, 201; Leikin, *The Practical Utopians*, 117.

62. Adams, 207.

63. Ibid., 208-10; Leikin, *The Practical Utopians*, 126.

64. Adams, 208-13; Leikin, *The Practical Utopians*, 126.

65. Leikin, *The Practical Utopians*, 126.

66. Adams, 217; Leikin, *The Practical Utopians*, 123.

67. Adams, 215; Leikin, *The Practical Utopians*, 123.

68. Leikin, *The Practical Utopians*, 123-26.

69. Adams, 215-16.

70. Leikin, *The Practical Utopians*, 128-29.

71. Ibid., 123, 151.

72. Ibid., 144-45.

73. Ibid., 147. 150.

74. Ibid., 149.

75. Adams, 69, 86-91.

76. Ibid., 494-95.

77. Horner, 239.

78. Adams, 108-25; 168-80; 523-33. Other businesses offering profit sharing included New England Granite Works, in Westerly, Rhode Island; New Haven Wire; George H. Kingman shoes in Brokton; the Boston Herald; Springfield Foundry, in Massachusetts; Rumford Chemical Works, in Providence; Sperry carriage hardware in Ansonia, Connecticut; Rogers, Peet & Company clothing in New York City; Haines, Jones & Cadbury plumbing supplies in Philadelphia; Hoffman and Billings foundry in Milwaukee.

79. Leikin, *The Practical Utopians*, 81.

80. Weir, *Knights Unhorsed*, 141-59.

81. Ibid., 143.

82. Commons, *History of Labour in the United States*, 2: 361; Perlman 85; Krebs, 150-51; Rochester, 17-18.

83. Commons, *History of Labour in the United States*, 2: 362.

84. Ibid., 2: 356-59.

85. Dulles, 133; Raybeck, 162; Foner, *A History of the Labor Movement in the United States*, 2: 52.

86. Commons, *History of Labour in the United States*, 2: 367-75.

87. Fried, *Socialism in America*, 184-86; Egbert, Persons and Basset, 1: 236.

88. Commons, *History of Labour in the United States*, 2: 292; Fried, 186.

89. Fried, 186-87; Commons, *History of Labour in the United States*, 2: 291-93.

90. Fried, 187.

91. Raybeck, 253-54.

92. Fried, 208-12.

93. Commons, *History of Labour in the United States*, 2: 291.

94. Ibid., 2: 297-99; Egbert, Persons and Basset, 1: 237-38.

95. Commons, *History of Labour in the United States*, 2: 298-99.

96. Ibid., 2: 396, note 2; Jonathan P. Grob, *Workers and Utopia: A Study of the Ideological Conflict in the American Labor Movement 1865-1900* (Evanston: Northwest University Press, 1961. Chicago: Quadrangle Books, 1969), 112. Some historians estimate the FOLTU membership in 1884 to be as low as 25,000, with another 200,000 trade unionists unaffiliated (Raybeck, 158).

See also Foner, *A History of the Labor Movement in the United States*, 2: 95.

97. Grob, 99-119; Dulles, 142-45; Commons, *History of Labour in the United States*, 2: 430-38.

98. Raybeck, 157-60.

99. Commons, *History of Labour in the United States*, 2: 396-99.

100. Ibid., 140.

101. Ibid., 375-78; Raybeck, 155-119; Friedrich Sorge, *Labor Movement in the United States* (Westport, CN: Greenwood press, 1977), 135.

102. Commons, *History of Labour in the United States*, 2: 377-78.

103. Ibid., 379-80; Paul Avrich, *The Haymarket Tragedy* (Princeton, NJ: Princeton University Press, 1984), 181-84.

104. Commons, *History of Labour in the United States*, 2: 383.

105. Henry David, *The History of the Haymarket Affair* (New York: Russell & Russell, 1936. New York: Collier, 1963), 156; Brecher, 45.

106. Boyer and Morais, 92-93

107. Avrich, 197-240; David, 171-200; Brecher, 46-47.

108. Brecher, 46-48; Boyer and Morais, 97; Commons, *History of Labour in the United States*, 2: 392-93.

109. Commons, *History of Labour in the United States*, 2: 394.

110. Raybeck, 174.

111. Ibid.

112. Weir, *Beyond Labor's Veil*, 252-54.

113. Weir, *Knights Unhorsed*, 125.

114. Grob, 188-89.

115. Commons, *History of Labour in the United States*, 2: 437-38.

116. Weir, Beyond Labor's Veil, 327.

117. Commons, *History of Labour in the United States*, 2: 482.

118. Raybeck, 178.

119. The last Minneapolis cooperative barrel shop closed in 1931 (Horner, 114).

120. Avrich, 415-27.

121. Raybeck, 180; Boyer and Morais, 108.

122. The Fair Labor Standards Act of 1938 (29 U.S. Code Chapter 8) made the eight-hour day the legal day's work throughout the nation.

123. Knapp, *The Rise of American Cooperative Enterprise*, 38; Horner, 219-28.

124. Kim Voss, *The Making of American Exceptionalism: The Knights of Labor and Class Formation in the Nineteenth Century* (Ithaca: Cornell University Press, 1993), 232.

125. Bob Feinberg, "The Great Cowboy Strike of '83," *San Francisco Chronicle*, April 19, 1983, 3.

126. Adams, 478-81.

127. David Armstrong, "Baseball—very good to whom?" *Berkeley Daily Californian*, June 6, 1981, 5.

6. "The Bloody Nineties"

1. Knapp, 59.

2. See Michael Schwartz, *Radical Protest and Social Structure: The Southern Farmers' Alliance and Cotton Tenancy, 1880-1890* (Chicago: University of Chicago Press, 1976); J.D.Hicks, *The Populist Revolt; and Lawrence Goodwyn, The Populist Moment* (London: Oxford University Press, 1978); Knapp, 57-60; Commons, *History of Labour in the United States*, 2: 489-92; Wasserman, 69-75; Zinn, 277-88.

3. Lawrence Goodwyn, *The Populist Moment* (London: Oxford University Press, 1978.), 120-21.

4. Schwartz, 9-12, 98-102.

5. William F. Holmes, "The Demise of the Colored Farmers' Alliance," *The Journal of Southern History* 41, no. 2 (1975): 190.

6. Floyd J. Miller, "Black Protest and White Leadership: A Note on the Colored Farmers' Alliance," *Phylon* 33, no. 2 (1972): 169-74.

7. Richard Wormser, *The Rise and Fall of Jim Crow* (New York: Macmillan, 2003), 73; Goodwyn, 118-23, 190; Zinn, 283-86.

8. Wormser, 73.

9. Ibid., 20-23, 72-76.

10. Knapp, 59; Zinn, 277-81.

11. Knapp, 61.

12. Hicks, *The Populist Revolt*, 134-44; Knapp, 59.

13. Knapp, 65.

14. Ibid., 65-67,

15. Wasserman, 71.

16. Ibid., 72.

17. Zinn, 287.

18. Hicks, *The Populist Revolt*, 103, 115: Commons, *History of Labour in the United States*, 2: 491.

19. Zinn, 281-82; Schwartz, 144-45.

20. Wasserman, 72-74.

21. Hicks, *The Populist Revolt*, 186-89; Zinn 282-83.

22. Goodwyn, 39, 41.

23. *The Handbook of Texas Online*, "Lamb, William Robert," http://www.tshaonline.org/handbook/online/articles/LL/fla62.html (accessed October 12, 2008).

24. Hicks, *The Populist Revolt*, 229-36; Goodwyn, 86-87; Zinn, 283; Commons, *History of Labour in the United States*, 2: 494.

25. Hillquit, 291.

26. Boyer and Morais, 112; Hicks, *The Populist Revolt*, 438-45.

27. Wasserman, 77.

28. Zinn, 285; Boyer and Morais, 110.

29. Zinn, 286; Rochester, 16.

30. Hicks, *The Populist Revolt*, 263.

31. Ibid., 321-23.

32. Ibid., 365-66; Wasserman, 94-96, 104.

33. Goodwyn, 270-85; Pollack, 123-27; Boyer and Morais, 135-36.

34. Knapp, *The Rise of American Cooperative Enterprise*, 66-67; Wasserman, 105.

35. Wasserman, 106.

36. Zinn, 255.

37. Wasserman, 107-08; Zinn, 254-55.

38. Knapp, *The Rise of American Cooperative Enterprise*, 194-200.

39. Zinn, 286; Donald L. Grant, *The Way It Was In The South: The Black Experience in Georgia* (Athens, GA: University of Georgia Press, 1993), 176-78.

40. *MSN Encarta Encyclopedia*, "Segregation in the United States," http://encarta.msn.com/encyclopedia_761580651/segregation_in_the_united_states.html (accessed October 12, 2008).

41. Ibid.

42. Hicks, *The Populist Revolt*, 251-54, 334, 410; Zinn, 283-86.

43. Zinn, 285.

44. Seavoy, 240-41.

45. Zinn, 247-49.

46. Wasserman, 30-33.

47. Donald A. Frederick, "Antitrust Status of Farmer Cooperatives: The Story of the Capper-Volstead Act," U.S. Department of Agriculture Cooperative Information Report 59 (September 2002), 22-25, http://www.rurdev.usda.gov/RBS/pub/cir59.pdf; Zinn, 253-54.

48. Frederick, 25-27.

49. Wasserman, 29.

50. Ibid., 39-42.

51. Brecher, 66-69.

52. Commons, *History of Labour in the United States*, 2: 496-49; Brecher, 53-63.

53. Brecher, 64-65.

54. Ibid, 63-64.

55. Raybeck, 198.

56. Dulles, 164-65.

57. Raybeck, 200-01, 232-37.

58. Pollack, 52-56.

59. Hillquit, 259; Raybeck, 227; Brecher, 86.

60. Boyer and Morais, 123-31.

61. Raybeck, 227.

62. Fried, 192-95; Foner, *A History of the Labor Movement in the United States*, 2: 294-96; 400-01.

63. Raybeck, 226-29; Fried, 194; Commons, *History of Labour in the*

United States, 2: 519; Egbert, Persons and Basset, 1: 244-52.

64. Foner, *A History of the Labor Movement in the United States*, 2: 167.

65. Commons, *History of Labour in the United States*, 2: 519; Weir, *Knights Unhorsed*, 177.

66. Commons, 2: 482-84.; Raybeck, 178-81.

67. Hillquit, 278.

68. Ibid., 276-78.

69. Perlman, 283-84.

70. Foner, *A History of the Labor Movement in the United States*, 2: 398-401.

71. Ibid., 400-01.

72. Perlman, 211.

73. Fred Thompson and Patrick Murfin, *The IWW: Its First Seventy Years, 1905-1975* (Chicago: Industrial Workers of the World, 1976), 21.

74. Foner, *A History of the Labor Movement in the United States*, 2: 401-03; Fried, 377-90.

75. Parker, 23.

76. Ibid, 427.

77. Ibid., 23-24; Knapp, *The Rise of American Cooperative Enterprise*, 43-44.

78. Parker, 22.

79. Ibid.

80. Ibid., 22-23.

7. "The Progressive Era"

1. Fried, 378-90.

2. Boyer and Morais, *Labor's Untold Story*, 144-45.

3. Wasserman, 137.

4. Parker, 39.

5. Ibid., 43.

6. Raybeck, 232.

7. Boyer and Morais, 141.

8. Fried, 447-48.

9. Industrial Workers of the World, "The Founding Convention of the IWW," http://www.iww.org/culture/articles/zinn13.shtml.

10. IWW, "Industrial Union Manifesto, Issued by Conference of Industrial Unionists at Chicago, January 2, 3 and 4, 1905," http://www.iww.org/cic/history/manifesto.html.

11. Fried., 449; Joyce L. Kornbluh, ed., *Rebel Voices, An I.W.W. Anthology* (Ann Arbor: The University of Michegan Press, 1968), 1-2; Thompson and Murfin, 21.

12. Zinn, 330.

13. Fried, 450.

14. Ibid., 451; Kornbluh, 4.

15. Kornbluh, 4-5; Fried, 451.

16. Kornbluh, 4-5.

17. Thompson and Murfin, 26.

18. Kornbluh, 51.

19. Fried, 451.

20. Kornbluh, 3.

21. Fried, 451; Kornbluh, 49-50; Wasserman, 152.

22. Kornbluh, 6.

23. Foner, *A History of the Labor Movement in the United States*, 4: 14.

24. Fried, 452; Wasserman, 155.

25. Kornbluh, 67.

26. Ibid.

27. Raybeck, 282; Thompson and Murfin, 111, 126.

28. Kornbluh, 27

29. Kornbluh, 17.

30. Fried, 382; Zinn, 346.

31. Raybeck, 240; Berger obituary, "Burgher Berger," *Time*, August 19, 1929. http://www.time.com/time/magazine/article/0,9171,737669,00.html.

32. Raybeck, 240; Loren Baritz, ed., *The American Left: Radical Political Thought in the Twentieth Century* (New York: Basic Books,1971), xi.

33. Raybeck, 240; S. M. Lipset, *Agrarian Socialism* (Berkeley: University of California Press, 1950. California Paperback Edition, 1971), 27. Citations are to the 1971 edition.

34. Lipset, 27-28.

35. Zinn, 333; Wasserman, 138.

36. Joseph R. Knapp, *The Advance of American Cooperative Enterprise 1920-1945* (Danville: Interstate, 1973), 99-100, 103-05.

37. US Department of Agriculture, Carolyn Dimitri, Anne Effland, and Neilson Conklin, "The 20th Century Transformation of U.S. Agriculture and Farm Policy," *Electronic Information Bulletin* no. 3 (June 2005), http://www.ers.usda.gov/publications/eib3/eib3.htm.

38. Knapp, *The Advance of American Cooperative Enterprise*, 99-109; Wasserman, 109.

39. Frederick, 59-60.

40. Knapp, *The Rise of American Cooperative Enterprise*, 432; J.W. Mather, K.C. DeVille, A.L. Gessner and C.C. Adams, "Cooperative Historical Statistics," Revised 1998 U.S. Department of Agriculture, *Cooperative Information Report* 1, Section 26, http://www.rurdev.usda.gov/rbs/pub/cir1s26.pdf.

41. Frederick, 73-75; Dimitri, Effland, and Conklin, http://www.ers.usda.gov/publications/eib3/eib3.htm.

42. Knapp, *The Advance of American Cooperative Enterprise*, 68.

43. Ibid., 69.

44. Knapp, *The Rise of American Cooperative Enterprise*, 261; Knapp, *The Advance of American Cooperative Enterprise*, 25.

45. Knapp, *The Advance of American Cooperative Enterprise*, 5-7.

46. Ibid. 25-26.

47. Ibid. 6-7.

48. Knapp, *The Rise of American Cooperative Enterprise*, 176-77.

49. Orville Merton Kile, *The Farm Bureau Through Three Decades* (Baltimore, MD: Waverly Press, 1948), 18, quoted by Elisabeth S. Clemens, *The Peoples Lobby: Organizational Innovations and the Rise of Interest Group Politics in the United States, 1890-1925* (Chicago: University of Chicago Press, 1997), 149.

50. For the early history of the Farmers Union, see Charles Simon Barrett, *The Mission, History and Times of the Farmers' Union* (Nashville, TN: Marshall & Bruce, 1909), and Knapp, *Rise of American Cooperative Enterprise*, 176-82. For the middle years see Wm. B. Tucker, "Populism Up-To-Date: The Story of the Farmers' Union, *Agricultural History* 21, no. 4 (1947), 198-208. For their struggles during the Cold War, see Bruce E, Field, *Harvest of Dissent: The National Farmers Union and the Early Cold War* (Lawrence, KS: University of Kansas Press, 1998).

51. Tucker, 199.

52. Knapp, *The Rise of American Cooperative Enterprise*, 177.

53. Tucker, 201.

54. Knapp, *The Rise of American Cooperative Enterprise*, 180; Tucker, 202.

55. Knapp, *The Rise of American Cooperative Enterprise*, 179-81.

56. Tucker, 202.

57. Robert Minor, "A Yankee Convention," *The Liberator*, April, 1920, 28-34, www2.cddc.vt.edu/marxists/history/usa/culture/pubs/liberator/1920/04/index.htm.

58. Tucker, 203-04.

59. The history of Equity is primarily from Knapp, *The Rise of American Cooperative Enterprise*, 182-93.

60. Knapp, *The Rise of American Cooperative Enterprise*, 183.

61. Ibid., 183-84.

62. Ibid., 184.

63. Ibid.

64. Ibid., 188.

65. Ibid.

66. Ibid., 185.

67. Ibid., 190-91.

68. Ibid., 191-92.

69. Ibid., 190.

70. Ibid., 191.

71. Ibid.

72. Ibid., 192.

73. Ibid., 191-92.

74. Ibid., 189.

75. Ibid., 189-90.

76. Parker, 66.

77. Ibid.

78. Robert Loren Morlan, *Political Prairie Fire: The Nonpartisan League, 1915-1922* (St. Paul: Minnesota Historical Society Press, 1955), 21.

79. Ibid., 25.

80. The history of the NPL can be found in Morlan and Lipset.

81. Lipset, 29; Morlan, 75-79.

82. Lipset, 29.

83. Ibid., 30-31.

84. Morlan, 336.

85. Ibid., 256-61; 340, 347.

86. Lipset, 154-55.

87. Knapp, *The Rise of American Cooperative Enterprise*, 201-03; Krebs, 275-78.

88. Ibid., 107.

89. Ibid., 107-08.

90. Ibid., 202-03.

91. Krebs, 277.

92. Knapp, *The Rise of American Cooperative Enterprise*, 205-06.

93. Ibid., 205-06.

94. Ibid., 202.

95. Ibid., 204.

96. Ibid.

97. Ibid., 205.

98. Knapp, *The Advance of American Cooperative Enterprise*, 14.

99. Ibid., 35, 39.

100. Ibid., 41.

101. Ibid., 48-49.

102. Krebs, 276.

103. Ibid., 278-80.

104. Lowell K. Dyson, *Red Harvest, The Communist Party and American Farmers* (Lincoln: University of Nebraska, 1982), 54-57.

105. Knapp, T*he Advance of American Cooperative Enterprise*, 179-81.

106. Dyson, 35.

107. Ibid.

108. Ibid., 38-40.

109. Ibid. 41, See also Lowell K. Dyson, "Red Peasant International in America," *The Journal of American History* 58, no. 4 (1972): 958-73.

110. Knapp, *The Advance of American Cooperative Enterprise*, 120.

111. Ibid., 121.

112. Ibid., 124-25.

113. Ibid., 122.

114. Ibid., 124-29; 137.

115. Ibid., 136-40.

116. Ibid., 135-41.

117. Parker, 325.

118. Ibid., 325-26

119. Ibid., 39-41.

120. Ibid., 77.

121. Sonichsen, 157.

122. Ibid., 156-57; Knapp, *The Rise of American Cooperative Enterprise*, 400.

123. Parker, 71; Knapp, *The Rise of American Cooperative Enterprise*, 401.

124. Parker, 70-73.

125. Sonnichsen, 157.

126. Parker, 326.

127. Ibid., 327.

128. Ibid.

129. Colston E.Warne, "The Co-Operative Chain Stores of the Illinois Miners," *The University Journal of Business* 2, no. 3 (1924): 310-27; *The University Journal of Business* 2, no. 4 (1924): 432-54.

130. Parker, 328.

131. Knapp, *The Rise of American Cooperative Enterprise*, 397; Parker, 49-55.

132. Knapp, *The Rise of American Cooperative Enterprise*, 397.

133. Ibid., 398; Parker, 49.

134. Parker, 49-50.

135. Knapp, *The Rise of American Cooperative Enterprise*, 400.

136. Parker, 53-54.

137. Knapp, *The Rise of American Cooperative Enterprise*, 407.

138. Ira B. Cross, *The Cooperative Store in the United States*, Twelfth Biennial Report of the Wisconsin Bureau of Labor and Industrial Statistics 1905-06, 33.

139. Knapp, *The Rise of American Cooperative Enterprise*, 408-09.

140. Parker, 45.

141. Knapp, *The Advance of American Cooperative Enterprise*, 170-71.

142. Parker, 41-42.

143. James P. Warbasse, *Three Voyages* (Superior, WS: Cooperative League of the U.S.A., 1956), 113-14.

144. Parker, 43.

145. Ibid., 41-42.

146. Ibid., 55-56.

147. Ibid.

148. Warbasse, *Three Voyages*, 65.

149. John P. McGovern Historical Collections and Research Center, "James P. Warbasse," http://mcgovern.library.tmc.edu/data/www/html/people/warbasse/Contents.htm.

150. Theodore M. Brown, "James Peter Warbasse," *American Journal of Public Health* 86, no. 1 (1996): 109-110, http://www.ajph.org/cgi/reprint/86/1/109.pdf.

151. James P. Warbasse, *Cooperative Democracy* (New York: Harper & Brothers, 1936), 61.

152. Parker, 56; Warbasse, *Three Voyages*, 116-17.

153. Parker, 378-89.

154. Ibid., 369.

8. World War I and the Conservative Reaction

1. Zinn, 350-56.

2. Fried, 508.

3. Ibid., 506-07; Zinn, 355.

4. Kornbluh, 316.

5. Ibid., 117.

6. Dulles, 212-14.

7. Fried, 506-08, 521-26

8. See Lenin, "On Cooperation," *Collected Works*, 2nd ed. (Moscow: Progress Publishers, 1965), 467-75.

9. Zinn, 356-57.

10. Ibid., 361; Fried, 509.

11. Zinn, 361; Fried 511.

12. *Encyclopedia of Oklahoma History and Culture*, "The Green Corn Rebellion," Oklahoma Historical Society, http://digital.library.okstate.edu/encyclopedia/entries/G/GR022.html (accessed July 17, 2008).

13. Fried, 509-10.

14. Zinn, 356-59.

15. Braunthal, 2: 166-68, 171-73.

16. Fried, 512-14.

17. Ibid., 514-19.

18. Bartiz, 135; Fried 515; Raybeck, 284-85.

19. Raybeck, 285-86; Brecher, 104.

20. Fried, 516; Baritz, 137.

21. Fried., 515-16; Baritz, 137-39.

22. Baritz, 145, 150.

23. Fried, 517.

24. Ibid.

25. Robert Vincent Daniels, *The Rise and Fall of Communism in Russia: reflections on the Soviet experience* (New Haven: Yale University Press, 2007), 74-75.

26. Hiroaki Kuromiya, *Stalin's Industrial Revolution: Politics and Workers, 1928-1932* (London: Cambridge University Press, 1988), 256-61; Edwin L. James, "Lenin Takes Hold Of Co-Operatives," *New York Times*. February 7, 1920, http://query.nytimes.com/mem/archive-free/pdf?_r=1&res=9C02E3D7133BEE32A25754C0A9649C946195D6CF; W.L., "Consumer Co-operatives in Russia," *American Journal of Economics and Sociology* 10, no. 1 (1950): 70; G. Maximoff, "Syndicalists in the Russian Revolution" Direct Action Pamphlet no. 11 (London: South London DAM-IWA, Black Flag Collective and Volya, 1985).

27. Brecher, 101.

28. Dulles, 221.

29. Brecher, 115, 134; Dulles, 228.

30. Dulles, 230.

31. Brecher, 123; Dulles, 225.

32. History Committee of the General Strike Committee, *The Seattle General Strike of 1919*, http://flag.blackened.net/revolt/hist_texts/seattle1919_p2.html; Dana Frank, *Purchasing Power, Consumer Organizing, Gender, and the Seattle Labor Movement, 1919-1929* (New York: Cambridge University Press, 1994); Brecher, 104-14; Harvey O'Connor, *Revolution in Seattle* (New York: Monthly Review Press, 1964), 128; Robert L. Friedheim, *The Seattle General Strike* (Seattle: University of Washington Press, 1964), 77.

33. Frank, 41-42.

34. Ibid.

35. Ibid.

36. Brecher, 107-08.

37. Frank, 45.

38. Ibid., 42-46; O'Connor, 128; Minor, 33.

39. Brecher, 110.

40. Ibid., 112-13.

41. Frank, 33. 95; Zinn, 370.

42. Frank, 46, 145.

43. Ibid., 42.

44. Ibid., 42, 56.

45. Ibid., 46-47.

46. Ibid.

47. Ibid., 43.

48. Parker, 77-78.

49. Frank, 147.

50. Ibid., 146.

51. Ibid., 145-47.

52. Minor, 34.

53. Ibid., 33-34.

54. Ibid., 34; Brecher, 127.

55. Parker, 96-97; J.P. Warbasse, ed., "Co-operative Bread And

Strikes," *Co-Operation* 9, no. 4 (1923): 66, http://fax.libs.uga.edu/ HD2951xC776/co23/; Co-op bakery contributes to strikers, "Co-operative Plant Has $350,000 Trade," *New York Times*, May 7, 1922, http:// query.nytimes.com/mem/archive-free/pdf?_r=1&res=9E04E1DE1439E F3ABC4F53DFB3668389639EDE&oref=slogin.

56. Perlman, 237-38.

57. Ibid, 253-57; See Glenn E. Plumb, and William G. Roylance, *Industrial Democracy: A Plan for Its Achievement* (New York: B. W. Huebsch, 1923).

58. Perlman, 251.

59. Dulles, 219-29.

60. Perlman, 253-54.

61. Raybeck, 280-81.

62. Ibid., 291.

63. Brecher, 101ff.

64. Zinn, 356-60.

65. Wisconsin Historical Society "Victor Berger," http://www.wisconsinhistory.org/topics/vberger/index.asp

66. *American Law Encyclopedia Online*, vol. 5 "John Edgar Hoover," http://law.jrank.org/pages/7411/Hoover-John-Edgar.html (accessed October 18, 2008); Foner, 8: 25; Federal Bureau of Investigation, "The Palmer Raids," http://www.fbi.gov/page2/dec07/palmerraids122807.html.

67. Boyer and Morais, 212.

68. Ibid.

69. Ibid., 213.

70. Eugene V. Debs Internet Archive, http://www.marxists.org/archive/debs/index.htm.

71. Kornbluh, 351-57.

72. Parker, 57.

73. Ibid., 106-10.

74. Furlough and Strikwerda, 121.

75. Ibid.

76. Ibid.

77. Warbasse, *Cooperative Democracy*, 214-18.

78. Ibid.

79. Parker, 58.

80. Ibid., 68-71.

81. Warbasse, *Three Voyages*, 31.

82. Ibid., 66-69.

83. Ibid., 77.

84. Ibid., 46, 66, 69.; Knapp, *The Rise of American Cooperative Enterprise*, 410; Sonnichsen, 150-51.

85. Knapp, *The Rise of American Cooperative Enterprise*, 410-11.

86. Parker, 83.

87. Knapp, The Rise of American Cooperative Enterprise, 416.

88. Knapp, *The Advance of American Cooperative Enterprise*, 170-71;

89. Warbasse, "Pacific Co-operative League in Receiver's Hands," Co-operation 8, no. 7 (1922): 66-657.

90. Knapp, *The Rise of American Cooperative Enterprise*, 416.

91. Ibid., 416-17.

92. Parker, 93-97.

93. Ibid., 111-16.

94. Ibid., 107.

95. Ibid.

96. Ibid.

97. Knapp, 177-78.

98. Parker, 107.

99. Knapp, 573.

100. Parker, 117-19.

101. Ibid., 118-19; Knapp, *The Advance of American Cooperative Enterprise*, 180.

102. Parker, 118.

103. Knapp, *The Advance of American Cooperative Enterprise*, 179-82.

104. Parker, 119; Knapp, *The Advance of American Cooperative Enterprise*, 183.

105. Parker, 121.

106. Knapp, *The Advance of American Cooperative Enterprise*, 183-85.

107. Parker, 97-99.

108. Knapp, *The Advance of American Cooperative Enterprise*, 221.

109. Ibid., 221-22.

110. Raybeck, 299-300; Dulles, 246-47.

111. Fried, 518; See K. C. MacKay, *The Progressive Movement of 1924* (New York: Columbia University Press, 1947).

112. Fried, 518.

113. See Richard J. Altenbaugh, *Education for Struggle: The American Labor Colleges of the 1920s and the 1930s* (Philadelphia: Temple University Press, 1990).

114. Ibid., 61, 63.

115. Ibid., 64-65. See also Sheldon Aubut's Duluth History Historical Photos, "Work Peoples' College," http://www.cityhistory.us/duluth/photos/photos05.htm.

116. Altenbaugh, 66-67.

117. Richard J. Altenbaugh, "Workers' Education As Counter Hegemony: The Educational Process At Work People's College, 1907-1941," Syracuse University Kellogg Project, http://www-distance.syr.edu/altenbaugh.html.

118. Ibid.

119. Altenbaugh, *Education for Struggle*, 60-70, 245-47.

120. Charlie Chaplin Official Web Site, "Charlie Chaplin Biography," http://www.charliechaplin.com/en/categories/5-Biography/articles/21-Biography; Tino Balio, *United Artists: The Company Built by the Stars* (Madison: University of Wisconsin Press, 1976).

121. Chaplin Official Web Site; Stuart Miller, "The Ripple Effect," *Variety*, October 16, 2005, http://www.variety.com/index.asp?layout=variety100&content=jump&jump=general&articleID=VR1117930598.

122. Chaplin Official Web Site, "Charlie Chaplin Biography;" Balio, *United Artists*.

123. Knapp, *The Rise of American Cooperative Enterprise*, 138-40. Desjardins adapted elements of the Schultze-Delitzsch and the Raiffeisen systems.

124. Ibid., 140.

125. Ibid., 141; Also see Dictionary of Canadian Biography Online, "Desjardains, Alphonse," http://www.biographi.ca/EN/ShowBio.asp?BioId=41452 (accessed July 13, 2008); Parker, 280-82.

126. Knapp, *The Rise of American Cooperative Enterprise*, 198.

127. Ibid., 449-51.

128. National Association of Housing Cooperatives, *Cooperative Housing Bulletin*, Richard Siegler and Herbert J. Levy, "Brief History Of Cooperative Housing," www.coophousing.org/HistoryofCo-ops.pdf; Commons, *History of Labour in the United States*, 1: 519-21; Parker, 214-21.

129. Parker, 214; Siegler and Levy, 2.

130. Parker, 214; Siegler and Levy, 2. Parker says it was begun in 1916, Siegler, 1918.

131. Hudson View Gardens, "HVG History," http://hudsonview-gardens.com/hvghistory.aspx.

132. Siegler and Levy, 2; Parker, 217; Knapp, *The Advance of American Cooperative Enterprise*, 182.

133. Richard Plunz, *A History of Housing in New York City: Dwelling Type and Social Change in the American Metropolis* (New York: Columbia University Press, 1992), 151-60.

134. Siegler and Levy, 3.

135. Parker, 215, 218; Plunz, 161-63.

9. The Great Depression & the Conservative Advance

1. *MSN Encarta Encyclopedia*, "The Great Depression in the United States," http://encarta.msn.com/encyclopedia_761584403/great_depression _in_ the_united_states.html (accessed October 18, 2008).

2. Knapp, *The Advance of American Cooperative Enterprise*, 206-24; Parker, 97-99, 125-31; California Emergency Relief Administration, *Handbook of Consumer Coops in California* (Sacramento: State of California, 1935), 135.

3. Knapp, *The Advance of American Cooperative Enterprise*, 289; Jackall and Levin, 56-58.

4. Clark Kerr and A. Harris, *Self-Help Cooperatives in California* (Berkeley: Bureau of Public Administration, University of California, 1939); California Emergency Relief Administration, 135-38. In *Self Help Cooperatives*, Kerr and Harris define a self-help production cooperative as "a democratic association of the unemployed and underemployed who have organized to obtain the necessities of life through their own production of goods" (1).

5. Knapp, *The Advance of American Cooperative Enterprise*, 290; Parker, 130.

6. California Emergency Relief Administration, *Handbook*; Knapp, *The Advance of American Cooperative Enterprise*, 289-91; Parker, 128-31; Jackall and Levin, 37-55, 57-84.

7. Arthur Hillman, *The Unemployed Citizens League of Seattle* (Seattle: University of Washington, 1934).

8. Knapp, *The Advance of American Cooperative Enterprise*, 289; Hillman, *The Unemployed Citizens League*; T. H. Watkins, *The Hungry Years: A Narrative History of the Great Depression in America* (New York: Macmillan, 2000), 96-97.

9. Brecher, 147; Ronald Edsforth, *The New Deal: America's Response to the Great Depression* (New York: Blackwell Publishing, 2000), 96-97.

10. Paul S. Taylor and Clark Kerr, "Whither Self-Help?" *Survey Graphic* (July 1934), 328-31, 348; Clark Kerr, *Self Help: The Cooperative Barter Movement in California 1932-33* (Berkeley: University of California, 1939).

11. Taylor and Kerr, "Whither Self-Help?" 329.

12. Ibid; Watkins, 97-99.

13. Taylor and Kerr, "Whither Self-Help?" 329.

14. California Emergency Relief Administration, *Handbook*, 135.

15. Ibid.

16. Taylor and Kerr, "Whither Self-Help?" 329; Watkins, 98; Constantine Maria Panunzio, *Self-help Coöperatives in Los Angeles* (Berkeley: University of California Press, 1939), 9.

17. Taylor and Kerr, "Whither Self-Help?" 330.

18. Ibid., 329; Hjalmar Rutzebeck, *Hell's Paradise* (Boston: Bruce Humphries, Inc., 1946), 44.

19. Taylor and Kerr, "Whither Self-Help?"330.

20. Ibid., 331.

21. Ibid.

22. Ibid.

23. Ibid., 330.

24. Ibid.

25. Ibid.; California Emergency Relief Administration, *Handbook*.

26. "Lady Reporter Visits Berkeley Self-Help Co-operative," *Voice of the Unemployed*, December 15, 1934; "Co-operative Mattress Factory if Operation: News from the Berkeley Self-Help Co-operative," *Voice of the*

Unemployed, November 10, 1934.

27. "Lady Reporter," *Voice of the Unemployed*, December 15, 1934.

28. California Emergency Relief Administration, *Research Project on Self-Help Co-operatives in California, Final report, "A Brief History of the UXA"* (Sacramento: State of California, 1935), 216-23.

29. "Pacific Co-operative League," *Voice of the Unemployed*, December 15, 1934.

30. Ibid.; Kerr and Harris, *Self Help*.

31. California Emergency Relief Administration, *Research Project*, 231-34.

32. Kerr, *Whither Self-Help*, 331.

33. This historical sketch of the UXA is based on California State Emergency Relief Administration's report in *Research Project on Self-Help Co-operatives in California* (1935); five articles in the *San Francisco Chronicle* by Gene Bowles, Jan 15-19, 1933; three articles in the *San Francisco Post-Enquirer* by Harver C. Scott, January 25-27, 1933; "Rutzebeck Explains Ideals of U.X.A." and "A Glimpse of UXA Activities," *Voice of the Self-Employed* 1, no. 1 (1933) and 1, no. 2 (1933), respectively; "The Story of the UXA, A Speech in Congress by Albert E. Carter," *The Llano Colonist*, November 10, 1934, 14. The sketch is fleshed out by UXA member Rutzebeck's novelistic memoir, *Hell's Paradise*; and informed by Upton Sinclair's novel about the UXA, *Co-op*.

34. Albert E. Carter, "The Story of the U.X.A.," *The Voice of the Self-Employed*, no. 4 (April, 1934), 8.

35. California Emergency Relief Administration, *Handbook*.

36. Fried, 518.

37. U.S. Presidential Elections, Online source for U.S. presidential elections, "1932," http://uspresidentialelections.webs.com/19201960.htm#100665736.

38. Boyer and Morais, 274-75; Dulles, 255-56.

39. Knapp, *The Advance of American Cooperative Enterprise*, 230-34.

40. Ibid., 231-32.

41. Krebs, 278; Keith J. Volanto, "Leaving the Land: Tenant and Sharecropper Displacement in Texas during the New Deal," *Social Science History* 20, no. 4 (1996): 533-51.

42. Knapp, *The Advance of American Cooperative Enterprise*, 243-44.

43. Ibid, 347.

44. Ibid., 348.

45. Ibid., 373; Parker, 135.

46. Parker, 136; Knapp, *The Advance of American Cooperative Enterprise*, 317-20.

47. Parker, 136; Knapp, *The Advance of American Cooperative Enterprise*, 329-39.

48. Knapp, *The Advance of American Cooperative Enterprise*, 305.

49. Parker, 137; Knapp, *The Advance of American Cooperative Enterprise*, 309-15.

50. Paul K. Conkin, Tomorrow a New World: The New Deal Community Program, (Ithaca, NY: Cornell University Press, 1959), 222.

51. Ibid.

52. Parker, 137.

53. Ibid.; Knapp, *The Advance of American Cooperative Enterprise*, 304-07.

54. Parker, 132.

55. Arthur Schlesinger, *The Coming of the New Deal, 1933-1935* (New York: Houghton Mifflin, 1958), 128.

56. Knapp, *The Advance of American Cooperative Enterprise*, 378.

57. Parker, 132-32; Knapp, *The Advance of American Cooperative Enterprise*, 377-78.

58. Knapp, *The Advance of American Cooperative Enterprise*, 289; Conkin, 203.

59. Rutzebeck, 88.

60. Ibid., 89-92.

61. Conkin, 131-45; California Emergency Relief Administration, *Handbook*.

62. California Emergency Relief Administration, *Handbook*.

63. California Emergency Relief Administration, *Research Project*.

64. Taylor and Kerr, "Whither Self-Help?" 348; California Emergency Relief Administration, *Research Project*, 219-20; 233-34.

65. Taylor and Kerr, "Whither Self-Help?" 330.

66. Ibid.

67. California Emergency Relief Administration, *Research Project*, 233.

68. Bruce E. Field, *Harvest of Dissent: The National Farmers Union and the Early Cold War* (Lawrence, KS: University of Kansas Press, 1998), 24.

69. Ibid., 23-24,

70. Ibid., 24-27, 54.

71. Lowell K. Dyson, "Radical Farm Organizations and Periodicals in America, 1920-1960," *Agricultural History* 45, no. 2 (1971): 111-20.

72. Ibid, 113.

73. Ibid.

74. Ibid.

75. Ibid.; Dyson, *Red Harvest*.

76. Boyer and Morais, 283.

77. Ibid., 282-89.

78. Brecher, 156.

79. Ibid, 155-56; Boyer and Morais, 287.

80. "News from the Berkeley Self-help Cooperative," *Voice of the Self-Employed*, November 10, 1934, 11; Sinclair, *Co-op, A Novel of Living Together*

(New York: Farrar & Rinehart, 1936), 317-19.

81. Brecher, 157.

82. Boyer and Morais, 286-87.

83. Ibid., 287-88.

84. Ibid., 290-328.

85. Raybeck, 346.

86. Ibid., 347-48.

87. Brecher, 150-61.

88. Dulles, 264-67.

89. Raybeck, 350.

90. Ibid.

91. Greg Mitchell, "Summer of '34: Upton Sinclair's EPIC Campaign," *Working Papers* 9 no. 6 (1982): 28-36, and 10 no. 1 (1983): 17-27.

92. Upton Sinclair, *I, Governor of California, and How I Ended Poverty* (Los Angeles: End Poverty League, 1934).

93. Upton Sinclair, *EPIC Answers* (Los Angeles: End Poverty League, 1934).

94. Upton Sinclair, *The Autobiography of Upton Sinclair* (New York: Harcourt Brace, 1962), 271.

95. Mitchell, "Summer of '34," *Working Papers* 10, no. 1: 24.

96. *Epic News*, August 6, 1934.

97. Mitchell, "Summer of '34," *Working Papers* 10, no. 1: 19.

98. Mitchell, "Summer of '34," *Working Papers* 9, no. 6: 36.

99. Mitchell, "Summer of '34," *Working Papers* 10, no. 1: 23

100. Sinclair, *Autobiography*, 274.

101. Mitchell, "Summer of '34," *Working Papers* 10, no. 1: 24.

102. Ibid., 25.

103. Mitchell, "Summer of '34," *Working Papers* 9, no. 6: 30.

104. Sinclair, *Co-op*, 309-13.

105. Clark Kerr, "Self-Help Cooperatives in California," *1939 Legislative Problems*, no. 9 (Berkeley: Bureau of Public Administration, University of California, 1939), 4; Sinclair, *Co-op*, 405.

106. Rutzebeck, 115-23; Jonathan Rowe, "Entrepreneurs of Co-operation," *Yes Magazine*, Summer, 2006 http://www.yesmagazine.org/article.asp?ID=1464.

107. Sinclair, *Co-op*, 404-05, 420- 24; Rutzebeck, 188-96.

108. Parker, 129-30.

109. Jackall and Levin, 67-69.

110. Parker, 129-30; Panunzio, 108-09; Kerr, *Self-help*, 4.

111. Parker, 130.

112. Jackall and Levin, 67.

113. California Emergency Relief Administration, *Handbook*, 135-38.

114. Parker, 153-54.

115. Knapp, *The Advance of American Cooperative Enterprise*, 374-75.

116. Ibid., 375-76.

117. Ibid.

118. Ibid., 377.

119. Ibid., 382.

120. Ibid., 398-99; *Cooperation* 20, no. 11 (1934): 175-77; and 20, no. 12 (1934): 184.

121. Parker, 160-63.

122. Dyson, *Red Harvest*, 152; Donald H. Grubbs, *Cry From the Cotton: The Southern Tenants Farmers Union and the New Deal* (Chapel Hill, NC: University of North Carolina Press, 1971); *The Encyclopedia of Arkansas History and Culture*, "Southern Tenant Farmers' Union," http://encyclopediaofarkansas.net/encyclopedia/entry-detail.aspx?entryID=35 (accessed October 18, 2008).

123. Dyson, *Red Harvest*, 151.

124. Grubbs, 63-64, 121, 131-33.

125. Dyson, Red Harvest, 153-57; Grubbs, 44-47.

126. Grubbs, 89; Dyson, *Red Harvest*, 155.

127. Dyson, *Red Harvest*, 162; *The Encyclopedia of Arkansas History and Culture*, "Southern Tenant Farmers."

128. Dyson, *Red Harvest*, 163-65.

129. Ted Nace, "Breadbasket of Democracy," *Orion Magazine* (May-June, 2006), http://www.orionmagazine.org/index.php/articles/article/171.

130. "Mandan Historical Society, William 'Wild Bill' Langer," http://www.mandanhistory.org/biographieslz/williamlanger.html.

131. Ibid.; Dyson, *Red Harvest*, 116-31; Lipset, 154-55.

132. Community Environmental Defense Fund, "Anti-Corporate Farming Laws in the Heartland," http://www.celdf.org/AntiCorporate-FarmingLawsinHeartland/tabid/130/Default.aspx; Caroline Tauxe, "Family cohesion vs. capitalist hegemony: Cultural accommodation on the north Dakota farm," *Dialectical Anthropology* 17, no. 3 (1992), 291-317.

133. Lipset, 154-56.

134. Ibid., 103.

135. Ibid., 290-92.

136. *The Canadian Encyclopedia*, "Co-operative Commonwealth Federation," http://www.thecanadianencyclopedia.com/index.cfm?PgNm=TCE&Params=A1ARTA0001902 (accessed October 18, 2008).

137. Knapp, *The Advance of American Cooperative Enterprise*, 252-54, 286-87.

138. Ibid, 403-04.

139. US Dept. of Agriculture, "Farm Marketing, Supply and Service Cooperative Historical Statistics" (2004), 1-2, 127.

140. California State Emergency Relief Administration, *Handbook*,

48-49.

141. Robert Neptune, *California's Uncommon Markets: The Story of the Consumer Cooperatives, 1935-1976* (Berkeley: Associated Cooperatives, 1971, 1977), 12.

142. Parker, 127-28.

143. Neptune, 12.

144. Boyer and Morais, 332-34.

145. Ibid., 329-33; Zinn, 398-403.

146. Parker, 166-70.

147. Brecher, 227-28.

148. Ibid., 228.

149. Ibid., 230.

150. Ibid., 228.

151. Boyer and Morais, 344-46; Brecher, 228-29.

152. Brecher, 228-29.

153. Boyer and Morais, 347; Dulles, 344-48; Raybeck, 398-400.

154. Geoffrey R. Stone, *Perilous Times: Free Speech in Wartime from the Sedition Act of 1798 to the War on Terrorism* (New York: W. W. Norton & Company, 2004), 334-35; Spartacus Educational, "Internal Security Act," http://www.spartacus.schoolnet.co.uk/USAinternal.htm.

155. Boyer and Morais, 346-54, 360.

156. Parker, 371; Knapp, *The Advance of American Cooperative Enterprise*, 531.

157. Parker, 172-74.

158. Ibid., 346, 371.

159. Knapp, *The Advance of American Cooperative Enterprise*, 471-75.

160. Field, 161.

161. Ibid., 162-64.

162. Parker, 176.

10. The Berkeley Co-op

1. *Co-op News*, 1 April 1987, 13 May 1987, 8 July 1987, 26 August 1987.

2. See Paul Rauber, "Co-op's New Structure," *Co-op News*, July 1, 1987; "Support for Hybrid Option," *Co-op News*, July 15, 1987; Laurie Goodstein, "Hybrid Plan Moves Ahead," *Co-op News*, March 8, 1988; Leta Mach, "Consumers Cooperative of Berkeley to Try New Organization Concept," *NCBA Cooperative Business Journal* 1, no. 7 (1987): 1.

3. For Neptune and Fullerton, see bibliography.

4. *Co-op News*, April 1, 1962.

5. Ibid., July 17, 1967.

6. Ibid., June 12, 1967.

7. Ibid., July 3, 1967.

8. Ibid. February 12, 1968.

9. Ibid, June 19, 1967.

10. Ibid., December 20, 1965.

11. Ibid., March 2, 1970.

12. Robert Schildgen, "Failure From Neglect of Co-op Principles," in Michael Fullerton, ed., *What Happened to the Berkeley Co-op?* (Davis, CA: The Center For Cooperatives, 1992), 45.

13. *Co-op News,* January 4, 1971.

14. Ibid., January 12, 1976.

15. Neptune, 191.

16. *Cooperative Grocer,* "Second Annual Human Resources Survey," May-June 2002, http://www.cooperativegrocer.coop/articles/index.php?id=393. In this survey conducted in 2002, 86 percent of small stores, 63 percent of medium-sized, and 45 percent of large stores had member work programs. A median of 32 members worked 86 hours per week.

17. *Co-op News,* June 12, 1974.

18. Ibid., November 17, 1976.

19. Ibid., December 8, 1986.

20. Ibid., July 15, 1987.

21. Fullerton, 96.

11. Cooperatives & Counterculture

1. Most of the material in this section is well documented from many sources available to research historians.

2. Peter Matthiessen, *Sal Si Puedes: Cesar Chavez and the New American Revolution* (New York: Random House, 1969), 22-23.

3. Ray Marshall and Lamond Godwin, *Cooperatives and Rural Poverty in the South* (Baltimore: John Hopkins 206ress, 1971), 70-72.

4. Ibid., 43-51.

5. Peter Nabokov, *Tijerina and the Courthouse Raid* (Albuquerque: University of New Mexico, 1969); Reies Lopez Tijerina, *The Spanish Land Grant Question Examined* (Albuquerque: Alianza Federal de Pueblos Libres, 1966).

6. "A Program For Survival," *The Black Panther,* July 7, 1975, 27; Charles Earl Jones, *The Black Panther Party (reconsidered): Reflections and Scholarship* (Baltimore, MD: Black Classic Press, 1998), 29-31; Bobby Seale, *Seize the Time: The Story of the Black Panther Party* (Baltimore, MD: Black Classic Press, 1991), 456-62.

7. Art Goldberg, "Bobby and Erika, Free At Last (until next time)," *Ramparts Magazine,* August 1971, 46.

8. "We are forming the structure of the new society within the shell of the old" is originally from the preamble to the IWW Constitution (1908). Many writers have used that phrase to describe the 60s movement and point out the continuity, including Straughton Lynd, "The Movement: A New Beginning," *Liberation* 14, no. 2 (May 1969).

9. See Emmett Grogan et al., eds., *The Digger Papers* (San Francisco:

The Diggers, 1968), http://www.diggers.org/digger_papers.htm.

10. The Collective Directory Group, eds., *The Directory of Collectives* (San Francisco: Collective Directory Group & InterCollective, 1977-85).

11. Jackall and Levin, 88.

12. See *Directory of Collectives*.

13. John Curl, *History of Collectivity in the San Francisco Bay Area* (Berkeley: Homeward Press, 1982), 52.

14. John Case and Rosemary C.R. Taylor, *Co-ops, Communes and Collectives: Experiments in Social Change in the 1960s and 1970s* (New York: Pantheon, 1979), 90.

15. See *Turnover, Newsletter of the Peoples Food System in the San Francisco Bay Area*, no. 12 (May-June, 1976), 3-6; no. 13 (July-August, 1976), 21; no. 15 (October, 1976), 21-23; *Berkeley Barb*, November 23, December 7 and 21, 1978, January 4, 1979; *Grassroots*, July 1 and 15, 1981; Morris Older, "The Peoples Food System," in John Curl, ed., *History of Collectivity in the San Francisco Bay Area* (Berkeley: Homeward Press, 1982), 38-51.

16. See *Common Ground 2* (Oakland: Free Spirit Press, 1976).

17. Livermore Action Group, *Livermore Weapons Lab Blockade/Demonstration Handbook* (Berkeley: Livermore Action Group, 1982).

18. Ibid.; UC Nuclear Free, "A Peoples' History of UC Weapons Lab Management," http://www.ucnuclearfree.org/blog/history4.htm.

19. UC Nuclear Free, "A Peoples' History."

12. Bay Warehouse Collective & Heartwood Cooperative Woodshop

1. These are personal firsthand accounts, based on my recollections and the materials in my archives.

2. From a grant proposal to the Associated Students of UC Berkeley. I have the original in my archives. Page 2.

3. *New Morning* article. I have the original manuscript in my archives, but not the published version. Pages 1, 2, 6.

4. Grant proposal to the Associated Students of UC Berkeley, 1.

5. Ibid.

6. Ibid., 3.

7. Ibid. 4.

8. *New Morning* manuscript.

9. We call the shop manager the *dungaloz*, which, according to Rick, means in Armenian something like, "stupid little darling." The title *dungaloz* was created when Rick decided he hated the name shop manager.

13. Cooperatives in the Mainstream

1. Jackall and Levin, 53-54; Parker, 525-39; Daniel Zwerdling, *Democracy At Work* (Wash., DC: Association for Self-Management, 1978), 165-

80, David Montgomery, *Workers' Control in America* (New York: Cambridge University Press, 1979), 174-75; David Ellerman, "The Legitimate Opposition At Work: The Union's Role in Large Democratic Firms," *Economic and Industrial Democracy* 9 (1988): 437-53.

2. Zwerdling, 41-52; "Sabotage at Lordstown?" *Time*, February 7, 1972; Daniel Nelson, *Farm and Factory: Workers in the Midwest, 1880-1990* (Bloomington: Indiana University Press, 1995), 183-84.

3. Zwerdling, 17-30.

4. Ibid., 91-100; Jackall and Levin, 171-213.

5. Thad Williamson, David Imbroscio, Gar Alperovitz, *Making a Place for Community: Local Democracy in a Global Era* (New York: Routledge, 2003), 192.

6. The ESOP Association, "ESOP Statistics," http://www.esopassociation.org/media/media_statistics.asp.

7. The ESOP Association, "What is an ESOP?" http://www.esopassociation.org/about/about_whatis.asp; Jackall and Levin, 245-49.

8. Steel Heritage, "Fort Pitt Steel Castings," http://www.skymagik.net/tubecityonline/steel/fortpitt.html.

9. Zwerdling, 53-76.

10. Marc Bendick, Jr. and Mary Lou Egan, "Worker Ownership and Participation Enhances Economic Development in Low-Opportunity Communities," *Journal of Community Practice* 2, no. 1 (1995): 61–85.

11. Hank Johnston and Bert Klandermans, eds., *Social Movements And Culture* (New York: Routledge, 1995), 97-104; Mahoning Valley History, "Remembering Black Monday," http://mahoninghistory.blogspot.com/2007/09/remembering-black-monday.html.

12. Jackall and Levin, 251; Christopher Meek and Warner Woodworth, "Employee Ownership and Industrial Relations: The Rath Case," *National Productivity Review* 1 no. 2 (2006): 151-63; Craig Cox, "Workers: Buying In, Taking Over," *Co-op Magazine*, January, 1981, 14-16.

13. Jeannine Kenney, "Old Tax Law May Launch New Worker Co-ops," *Cooperative Business Journal*, March 2003, http://ncba.coop/pdf/WorkerCo-ops1042.pdf.

14. The ICA Group, "About ICA," http://www.ica-group.org/1st%20Row/about_ica.html.

15. The ICA Group, "FAQs about Worker Cooperatives," http://www.ica-group.org/2nd%20Row/FAQs2.html.

16. Anne L. Gessner, "Statistics of farmer cooperatives 1955-56: Marketing, Farm Supply and Related Services," Farmer Cooperative Service, U.S. Dept. of Agriculture (1958).

17. Knapp, *The Advance of American Cooperative Enterprise*, 25-26, 212.

18. ICA Group Annual Reports, 2001, 2002, 2006, 2007. http://www.ica-group.org/2nd%20Row/icapublications.html.

19. Ralph D. Christy, "The Role of Farmer Cooperatives in a

Changing Agricultural Economy," *Southern Journal Of Agricultural Economics* 19, no. 1 (1987): 21.

20. Zwerdlin, 101-12.

21. Jason Manning, "The Midwest Farm Crisis of the 1980s," http://eightiesclub.tripod.com/id395.htm; Donn A. Reimund, *The U.S. Farm Sector in the Mid-1980's*. Agricultural Economic Report Number 548, Superintendent of Documents, U.S. Government Printing Office; Donald G. Kaufman and Cecilia M. Franz, *Biosphere 2000: Protecting Our Global Environment* (Dubuque, Iowa Kendall Hunt, 2000), 321.

22. Callie Rogers, Jordan Holmes, and Ashley Bunch, "Losing the Family Farm," Aggie Horticulture, Texas A & M AgriLife Extension, aggie-horticulture.tamu.edu/syllabi/201h/projects/hortfamfarm.pps; Manning, "The Midwest Farm Crisis of the 1980s."

23. Charles Walters Jr., *Holding Action* (New York & Kansas City: Halcyon House, 1968); National Farmers Organization, "History," http://www.nfo.org/history.htm.

24. The National Grange of the Order of Patrons of Husbandry, "History," http://www.nationalgrange.org/about/history.html.

25. Krebs, 280-86.

26. "Nixon: The Odds on Survival Shorten," *Time*, August 12, 1974; Robert Cohen, "Tricky Dick's Quick Milk Fix," *Tamara, Journal of Postmodern Organization Science* 1 no. 2, (2001): 25-33, http://www.zianet.com/boje/tamara/issues/volume_1/issue_1_2/2Cohen_Corp_Predators.htm.

27. American Agriculture Movement, "History of the American Agriculture Movement," http://www.aaminc.org/history.htm.

28. John A. Ackermann, "The Impact of the Coal Strike of 1977-1978," *Industrial and Labor Relations Review* 32, no. 2, (1979): 175-88.

29. "Farmers' Caravan Takes Food To Striking Miners," *New York Times*, March 6, 1978.

30. Reginald Stuart, "Striking Farmers, at Rally, Back Miners With Speeches and Food; Symbolic Significance Two Hours of Speches," *New York Times*, March 7, 1978.

31. Ackermann, 175-77.

32. Ryan J. Stockwell, "Growing A Modern Agrarian Myth: The American Agriculture Movement, Identity, And The Call To Save The Family Farm" (masters thesis, Miami University, Ohio, 2003); Nebraska Studies, "Farmers Call For A Strike," http://www.nebraskastudies.org/1000/frameset.html.

33. "US Co-operatives: 1976," *Co-op News*, October 6, 1976.

34. Ibid.; "A Turnaround Year for Consumer Co-ops—But Still A Long Way To Go," Cooperatives: Partners for Progress, Special Section, *Co-op News*, 1973.

35. Bob Schildgen, "Co-ops co-ops co-ops: we're but on small part of the co-op world," *Co-op News*, October 18, 1982.

36. Ibid.; Roger Glasgow, "The Small Co-op Movement in California," *Co-op News*, September 14, 1979.

37. CUNA, "United States Credit Union Statistics," http://advice. cuna.org/download/longrun/us_totals.pdf; The Credit Union Association of Oregon, "Credit Union History," http://www.cuao.org/posted_docs/ unsecure/documents/About/The_Credit_Union_History.pdf.

38. ILWU, "The ILWU Story: Health, Pensions and Housing," http://www.ilwu19.com/history/the_ilwu_story/health.htm; Grif Fariello, "The Life and Times of Harry Bridges (1901-1990)," http://unionsong.com/reviews/bridges.

39. Bob Klein, "Red Citadel in the Bronx," *In These Times*, June 15, 1997, 18; Ross Whitsett, "Urban Mass: A Look at Co-op City," *The Cooperator*, http://cooperator.com/articles/1354/1/Urban-Mass/Page1.html; Alan Feuer, "Haven for Workers in Bronx Evolves for Their Retirement," *New York Times*, August 5, 2002.

40. Richard Siegler and Herbert J. Levy, "Brief History of Cooperative Housing," National Association of Housing Cooperatives, http:// www.coophousing.org/HistoryofCo-ops.pdf.

41. Johnston Birchall, "Rediscovering the Cooperative Advantage: Poverty Reduction Through Self-Help" (Geneva: Cooperative Branch, International Labour Organization, 2003), 31-32.·

42. Ronald Lawson, *The Tenant Movement in New York City, 1904-1984* (New Brunswick, N.J.: Rutgers University Press: 1986), http://tenant.net/ Community/history/hist05a.html; Neil F. Carlson, "Thirty Years of Self-Help Housing in New York City: UHAB Comes of Age," http://www. uhab.org/index.cfm?fuseaction=Page.viewPage&pageId=483&parentID =474&nodeID=1.

43. Lawson, http://tenant.net/Community/history/hist04a.html.

44. Ibid., http://tenant.net/Community/history/hist05a.html.

45. US House of Representatives Office of the Law Revision Counsel, "National Consumer Cooperative Bank Act (92 Stat. 499, 12 U.S.C.A. 3001), August 20, 1978," http://law2.house.gov/download/pls/12C31. txt.

46. *American Law Encyclopedia*, vol. 7, "National Cooperative Bank," http://law.jrank.org/pages/8716/National-Cooperative-Bank.html (accessed October 22, 2008); Jay Richter, *Where Credit Was Due: The Creation of the National Consumer Cooperative Bank* (Cooperative League of the USA, 1985).

47. *American Law Encyclopedia*, "National Cooperative Bank," http:// law.jrank.org/pages/8716/National-Cooperative-Bank.html (accessed December 11, 2008).

48. William B. Eddy, *Handbook of Organization Management* (New York: CRC Press, 1983), 471-72; "Co-op Bank Attacked From Inside," *Co-ops Today*, December, 1981, 24; "Bank Update: Reagan Threatening to Cut

Bank," *Co-op Magazine* 8, no. 1 (January, 1981), 19.

49. National Cooperative Business Association, "About NCBA," http://www.ncba.coop/about_hist.cfm; National Cooperative Business Association, "CLUSA: Our History," http://www.ncba.coop/clusa_history.cfm.

50. "Co-op, USA: Facts and Figures, 1979," Cooperative League of the USA, (1979).

51. Jackall and Levin, 88, 139.

14. Surviving

1. Dean Baker, *The United States Since 1980* (New York: Cambridge University Press, 2007), 71.

2. Treasury Direct, "Historical Debt Outstanding - Annual 1950 – 1999," http://www.treasurydirect.gov/govt/reports/pd/histdebt/histdebt_histo4.htm; Peter F. Galderisi, Roberta Q. Herzberg, and Peter McNamara, *Divided Government: Change, Uncertainty, and the Constitutional Order* (New York: Rowman & Littlefield, 1996), 68.

3. I have the archives of the InterCollective Minutes. The last minutes are dated April 2, 1986. One item states, "Why keep meeting? We discussed the fact of dwindling energy around the meetings. Energy seems to pick up for a time after every event we do. The next class series may pull in new energy." A series of weekly Community Classes at UC Berkeley were planned for that month. They were announced in the *Collective Networker Newsletter* no. 95 (April, 1986): Sustainable Farming and Cooperative Distribution; Communal Living in the Bay Area; How and Why to Start A Collective; Preventing and Healing Burnout. The next InterCollective meeting, scheduled for March 18, may have been the final meeting of the organization.

4. Cooperative Grocer, "Survey 1999," http://www.cooperativegrocer.coop/articles/index.php?id=306 ; Cooperative Grocer, "Survey 2000," http://www.cooperativegrocer.coop/articles/index.php?id=352; Cooperative Grocer, "Human Resources Survey 2001," http://www.cooperativegrocer.coop/articles/index.php?id=332; Cooperative Grocer, "Human Resources Survey 2002," http://www.cooperativegrocer.coop/articles/index.php?id=393.

5. US Federation of Worker Cooperatives, "Membership: Federation Partners," http://www.usworker.coop/about/memberlist; IndyBay, "NOBAWC History," http://www.indybay.org/newsitems/2002/06/29/1352121.php.

6. HPLinux, "History of Linux, by Ragib Hasan," http://netfiles.uiuc.edu/rhasan/linux; HPLinux, "History of Linux," http://www.xplinux.biz/support/history.htm; PC Update, "Linux: the big picture," http://liw.iki.fi/liw/texts/linux-the-big-picture.html.

7. University of Wisconsin Center for Cooperatives, "Alternative

Energy Technology Links," http://www.uwcc.wisc.edu/links/altenergylinks.html.

8. International Bicycle Fund, "Community Bicycle Programs," http://www.ibike.org/encouragement/freebike.htm.

9. John Hively, *The Rigged Game: Corporate America and a People Betrayed* (Montréal: Black Rose Books, 2006), 155.

10. University of Wisconsin Extension, "Toward a Sustainable Community: A Toolkit for Local Government," www4.uwm.edu/shwec/sustk; Gordon Leslie Clark, "Contested Terrain: Republican Rhetoric, Pension Funds and Community Development," Social Science Research Network, http://papers.ssrn.com/sol3/papers.cfm?abstract_id=141871.

11. Upside Down World, "Recuperated Enterprises In Argentina: Reversing The Logic Of Capitalism, by Marie Trigona," http://upsidedownworld.org/main/content/view/235/32.

12. WAGES, "Transforming Women's Lives," http://www.wagescooperatives.org.

13. "Cooperative Home Care Associates," http://www.chcany.org.

14. Jeannine Kenney, "Old Tax Law May Launch New Worker Co-ops," *Cooperative Business Journal* (March 2003), https://ncba.coop/pdf/WorkerCo-ops1042.

15. Ronald Lawson, *The Tenant Movement in New York City, 1904-1984* (New Brunswick, N.J.: Rutgers University Press: 1986), http://tenant.net/Community/history/hist05a.html.

16. Ibid.

17. Robert Neuwirth, "Squatters' Rites," *City Limits Magazine Online*, September/October 2002, http://www.citylimits.org/content/articles/articleView.cfm?articlenumber=860.

18. Birchall, 32.

19. UHAB "Programs Overview," http://www.uhab.org/index.cfm?fuseaction=Page.viewPage&pageId=473; UHAB, "Co-op Development", http://www.uhab.org/index.cfm?fuseaction=Page.viewPage&pageId=488&parentID=473&nodeID=1.

20. US Federation of Worker Cooperatives, "About," http://www.usworker.coop/about.

21. Eastern Conference for Workplace Democracy, http://east.usworker.coop/; Western Worker Cooperative Conference, http://www.west.usworker.coop.

22. NOBAWC, http://www.nobawc.org/article.php?list=type&type=6.

23. VAWC, http://wiki.valleyworker.org/index.php?title=Valley_Alliance_of_Worker_Cooperatives.

24. USFWC, "Members," http://www.usworker.coop/about/memberlist.

25. ICA, "About ICA," http://www.ica-group.org/1st%20Row/

about_ica.html.

26. University of Wisconsin Center for Cooperatives, http://www.uwcc.wisc.edu; Rural Cooperatives Center, University of California, Davis, http://cooperatives.ucdavis.edu/about/index.htm; Quentin Burdick Center for Cooperatives, http://www.ag.ndsu.nodak.edu/qbcc/MissionandGoals/miss.htm; Arthur Capper Cooperative Center, http://www.agecon.ksu.edu/accc/about_accc.htm; Cornell University Cooperative Enterprise Program, http://cooperatives.aem.cornell.edu/about.htm; Southern New Hampshire School of Community Economic Development, http://www.snhu.edu/388.asp.

27. NCBA, "About NCBA," http://www.ncba.coop/about.cfm.

28. Ibid.

29. Cooperative Grocers' Information Network, http://www.cgin.coop.

30. NCB, "About NCB: History," http://www.ncb.coop/default.aspx?id=714.

31. NCB, "National Cooperative Business Association Resources," https://www.ncba.org/resources.cfm?rcatid=6&atitle=Cooperative+Banks.

32. National Cooperative Bank, "About NCB," http://www.ncb.coop/default.aspx?id=552; CoBank, "Welcome," http://www.cobank.com/index.htm.

33. Ibid.

34. National Council of Farmer Cooperatives, "About ACFC," http://www.ncfc.org/about-ncfc.html.

35. Ohio Employee Ownership Center, "About," http://dept.kent.edu/oeoc; Vermont Employee Ownership Center, "About VEOC," http://www.veoc.org/aboutus.shtml; National Center for Employee Ownership, http://www.nceo.org.

36. NAHC, "About NAHC," http://www.coophousing.org/DisplayPage.aspx?id=62.

37. NASCO, "About Us," http://www.nasco.coop/node/17.

38. CICOPA, "What is CICOPA?" http://www.cicopa.coop/quees.php?lang=en.

39. International Cooperative Alliance, "Introduction," http://www.ica.coop/ica/index.html.

40. "Report of the United Nations Secretary-General on Cooperatives in Social Development," 2001, http://www.copac.coop/publications/unpublications.html

41. USDA, "Rural Business and Cooperative Services," http://www.rurdev.usda.gov/rbs; USDA, "Agribusiness and Cooperatives," http://www.csrees.usda.gov; USDA "Farm Credit Administration," http://www.fca.gov/index.html.

42. Cooperative College, Andrew Bibby and Linda Shaw, "Making

a Difference: Co-operative Solutions to Global Poverty," www.andrewbibby.com/pdf/making%20a%20difference.pdf.

43. World Social Forum, "About, WSF," http://www.wsf2008.net/eng/about.

44. Ibid.

15. Cooperatives & Communalism

1. From Congressional Record, 1941, vol. 87: I.

2. Clifford F. Thies, "The Success of American Communes," *Southern Economic Journal* (July 1, 2000).

3. See Timothy Miller, *The 60s Communes: Hippies and Beyond* (Syracuse, NY: Syracuse University Press, 1999), 249-56.

4. T. Jefferson to Cornelius Camden Blatchly, 1822. ME 15:399, Thomas Jefferson on Politics & Government, "Quotations/50. Property Rights," http://etext.lib.virginia.edu/jefferson/quotations.

5. Robert S Fogarty, *All Things New: American Communes and Utopian Movements 1860-1914* (Chicago: University of Chicago Press, 1990), 227-33.

6. Fried, 11.

7. Commons, *History of Labour in the United States*, 1: 493-94, 506-07; Bestor, 87-88.; Fried, 74-76.

16. The Early Communalist Movements

1. Fried, 64. Too many books on communalism pay slight regard to the social and economic conditions that made the movement attractive to so many Americans over so many generations. Many scholars and historians treat the communalism as if it was simply the result of the play of ideas, the power of charismatic leaders, or the lure of utopias, while the primary forces driving the movement were poverty, economic oppression, and the lack of opportunity. See also Egbert, Persons and Basset, 1: 155-62.

2. The depression in the industrial sector was triggered by the lifting of the embargo at the end of the Napoleonic Wars, permitting foreign traders to unload large amounts of their products on the American market. This resulted in a general economic recovery but devastation to industries (Perlman, 7).

3. Edward K. Spann, *Brotherly Tomorrows, Movements for a Cooperative Society in America, 1820-1920* (New York: Columbia University Press, 1989), 79-80; Fried, 64; Fogarty, 168, 206-07.

4. Bestor, 97-99; Fried, 64-66, 85-89; Egbert, Persons and Basset, 1: 161-72.

5. Harrison, 133.

6. Fried, 65-67; Harrison, 6, 151-53.

7. Harrison, 154-55.

8. Ibid., 12-13; Fried, 66-67.

9. Spahn, 22.

10. Fried, 68.

11. Ibid.

12. Ibid., 68-69.

13. Bestor, 99-101.

14. Fried, 69.

15. Ibid., 94-111

16. Holloway, 104-05; Bestor, 114-22; See Harlow Lindley, ed., *New Harmony as Seen by Participants and Travelers* (Philadelphia: Porcupine Press, 1975); Paul Brown, *Twelve Months in New Harmony* (Philadelphia: Porcupine Press, 1973).

17. Harrison, 101.

18. John Humphry Noyes, *History of American Socialisms* (Philadelphia: J. B. Lippencott, 1870. New York: Dover, 1966), 73-80.

19. Bestor, 202-07.

20. Harrison, 164-65; Bestor, 171-75.

21. Bestor, 176-79.

22. Fried, 72; Bestor, 205-07.

23. Fried, 72.

24. Holloway, 114-15.

25. Woodcock, 456-59.

26. Commons, *History of Labour in the United States*, 1: 499-506; Egbert, Persons and Basset, 1: 173-89.

27. Horace Greeley, *Recollections of a Busy Life* (New York: Ford and Co., 1868), 151-58.; Charles Fourier, *Design For Utopia: Selected Writings* (London: Sonnenschein, 1901. New York: Schocken, 1971), 120-23; See Carl J. Guarneri, *The Utopian Alternative: Fourierism in Nineteenth Century America* (Ithaca: Cornell University Press, 1991).

28. Fried, 76-79; Holloway, 134-35; Commons, *History of Labour in the United States*, 1: 496-500.

29. Commons, *History of Labour in the United States*, 1: 504-05; Fried, 78.

30. Brisbane, *A Concise Exposition of the Doctrine of Association* (New York: J.S. Redfield, 1843. New York: Shocken, 1971), 73-74.

31. Holloway, 141-42.

32. Ibid., 142-54; Fried, 79.

33. Fried, 80.

34. *The Harbinger* 4 (1847).

35. Holloway, 128-31; 152-54; Fried, 80-81.

36. Noyes, 233-37.

37. Commons, *History of Labour in the United States*, 1: 506-07.

38. Noyes, 587-89.

39. Ibid., 154-81; 97-101; See Marianne Orvis, *Letters From Brook Farm: 1841-1847* (Philadelphia: Porcupine Press, 1973).

40. Holloway, 198; Commons, *History of Labour in the United States*, 1: 513-15.

41. Carl Wittke, *The Utopian Communist* (Baton Rouge: Louisiana State University Press, 1950); Commons, *History of Labour in the United States*, 1: 513-15; Egbert, Persons and Basset, 1: 159.

42. Holloway, 198-211; See Albert Shaw, *Icaria: A Chapter in the History of Communism* (Philadelphia: Porcupine Press, 1973); Egbert, Persons and Basset, 1: 155-62, 189-90.

43. Fried, 82.

44. David W. Blight, *Passages to Freedom: The Underground Railroad in History and Memory* (New York: Harper Collins, 2001).

45. Thomas Jefferson to Frances Wright, 1825. ME 16:120, Thomas Jefferson on Politics & Government, "Quotations/32. Racial Policy," http://etext.lib.virginia.edu/jefferson/quotations.

46. Bestor, 223-26.

47. Northampton Community, "History," http://www.noho.com/sojourner/history.html.

48. See Alice F. McBee, *From Utopia to Florence: The Story of a Transcendentalist Community in Northampton* (Philadelphia: Porcupine Press, 1975); Northampton Community, http://www.noho.com/sojourner/history.html.

49. Josiah Henson, *The Life of Josiah Henson, Formerly a Slave* (Boston: Arthur D. Phelps, 1849. Reprinted with a new introduction by Robin W. Winks. New York: Dover, 2003), vii-xiii; 77-78, 91-92, 125-26; William H. Pease and Jane Pease, *Black Utopia* (Madison: State Historical Society of Wisconsin, 1963), 63-83.

50. Henson, xvii-xviii.

51. Uncle Tom's Cabin Historic Site, "History," http://www.uncle-tomscabin.org.

52. Cheryl Janifer LaRoche, "On The Edge Of Freedom: Free Black Communities, Archaeology, and the Underground Railroad" (PhD diss., University of Maryland, 2004), 110. See also Sundiata Keith Cha-Jua, *America's First Black Town* (Champaign: University of Illinois Press. 2000), ix.

53. Pease and Pease, 39-41.

54. Ibid. 41-44.

55. Ibid. 46-62.

56. Ibid., 92.

57. Ibid., 102.

58. Ibid., 87-108.

59. Ibid., 109-22.

60. Samuel A. Johnson, "The Emigrant Aid Company in Kansas,"

Kansas Historical Quarterly 1, no. 5 (1932): 429-41.

61. Pease and Pease, 124.

62. The Gullah, "About the Gullah," http://www.yale.edu/glc/gullah.

63. Pease and Pease, 126-29.

64. John R. Rachal, "Gideonites and Freedmen: Adult Literacy Education at Port Royal, 1862-1865," *The Journal of Negro Education* 55, no. 4 (1986): 45-56.

65. Pease and Pease, 123-141.

66. Clyde Woods, *Development Arrested: The Blues and Plantation Power in the. Mississippi Delta* (London and New York: Verso, 1998), 7.

67. Ibid., 62; Black Past Remembered, "Davis Bend, Mississippi," http://www.blackpast.org/?q=aah/davis-bend-mississippi-1865-1887.

68. William Sherman Savage, *Blacks in the West* (Westport, CN: Greenwood Press, 1977), 101-03. The "Five Civilized Tribes" were the Cherokee, Chickasaw, Choctaw, Muscogee (Creek), and Seminole. They were called that because they had adopted many of the settlers' customs and maintained comparatively good relations with them. Nonetheless they had been deported from the Southeast to Oklahoma in a series of land grabs in the 1830s. In the decades after the Civil War, most of their Oklahoma land base was broken up and taken away. Nonetheless, they maintained their communities and continue today.

69. Wasserman, 177.

70. Hannibal Johnson, *Acres of Aspiration: The All Black Towns in Oklahoma* (Austin, TX: Eakin Press, 2002).

71. African-American Resource Center, http://www.tulsalibrary.org/aarc/towns/towns.htm.

72. R.V. Hine, *California's Utopian Colonies* (Pasadena: H.E. Huntington Library & Art Gallery, 1953; New Haven: Yale University Press, 1966), 9.

73. Fogarty, *All Things New*, 57-59; William A. Hinds, *American Communities* (Oneida, NY: Office of the American Socialist, 1878; New York: Corinth Books, 1961), 156-57.

74. Charles LeWarne, *Utopias on Puget Sound 1885-1915* (Seattle: University of Washington Press, 1975), 5-8.

75. Leikin, *The Practical Utopians*, 73.

76. Fogarty, 145-46; Leikin, *The Practical Utopians*, 59.

77. Leikin, *The Practical Utopians*, 139.

78. Ibid, 59, 139.

79. Kagan, *New World Utopias*, 84.

80. Laurence Gronlund, "Socializing a State," *Social Democracy* no. 2 (March, 1898): 1, http://debs.indstate.edu/t531t5_1898.pdf; Howard H. Quint, *The Forging of American Socialism* (Indianapolis: Bobbs-Merrill, 1953), 317-18.

81. Hine, 78-100; Paul Kagan, *New World Utopias* (New York: Penguin, 1975), 84-100.

82. Hine, 78-100.

83. Kagan, 99.

84. Ibid., 95-99.

85. Ibid., 99-100

86. LeWarne, 13.

87. Ibid., 15-54.

88. Fogarty, 98-101.

89. Ibid, 156-60; Spann, 231-34; Hillquit, 330.

90. Parker, 427.

91. Fogarty, 160.

92. Ibid., 161; LeWarne, 55-56.

93. Spann 240-41; Fogarty, 162-64; Fried, 379.

94. Ibid.

95. LeWarne, 55-57.

96. Ibid., 168-71.

97. Ibid., 55-113.

98. Ibid., 111.

99. Ibid., 129-67.

100. Ibid., 114-28.

101. Ibid., 168-226.

102. Fogarty, 121-24; Ernest S. Wooster, *Communities of the Past and Present* (Newllano, LA: Llano Colonist, 1924; New York, AMS Press: 1974), 40-43.

103. Fogarty, 197.

104. Hine, 142-44.

105. Henry George, *Progress and Poverty* (New York: D. Appleton, 1879, 4th ed. 1881), 328.

106. Fried, 191.

107. Egbert, Persons and Basset, 1: 239-41; Fogarty, 169-72, 271.

108. Fogarty, 169-70.

109. Ibid., 171-72.

17. Communalism in the 20th Century

1. Fogarty, 212-13.

2. Hine, 114-31; Kagan, 118-37; Wooster, 117-32.

3. Kagan, 136.

4. Hine, 177.

5. David Sarasohn, "The Election of 1916: Realigning the Rockies," *The Western Historical Quarterly* 11, no. 3 (1980): 291.

6. Wooster, 70-74. Wilber S. Shepperson, *Retreat to Nevada: A Socialist Colony of World War I* (Reno: University of Nevada Press, 1966); James R. Green, *Grass-Roots Socialism: Radical Movements in the Southwest 1895-1943*

(Baton Rouge: Louisiana State University Press, 1980).

7. Conkin, 47-48.

8. Yamato Colony, "History," http://www.geocities.com/mrtaka-hashi2000/yamato_colony/Yamato_Colony.html#History; A History of Japanese Americans in California, "Historic Sites: Yamato Colony," http://www.nps.gov/history/history/online_books/5views/5views4h103.htm; Roy J. Smith, "The California State Land Settlements at Durham and Delhi," *The Journal of Land & Public Utility Economics* 20, no. 2 (1944): 170-171; Adon Poli, "What Has Happened to Durham and Delhi?" *The Journal of Land & Public Utility Economics* 22, no. 2 (1946): 182-90.

9. 2000 US Census, http://www.census.gov/main/www/cen 2000.html.

10. LeWarne, 229; Wooster, 138-39.

11. Robert G. Wesson, "The Soviet Communes," *Soviet Studies* 13, no. 4 (1962): 353; Sidney Webb and Beatrice Webb, *Soviet Communism, A New Civilization?* (London: Longmans, Green and Co. Ltd., 1935, New York: Charles Scribners' Sons, 1936), 1: 213-14.

12. LeWarne, 229. According to one account, members of both Kuzbas and Seyatel were reportedly victims during the Stalinist purges of 1934-38. "The founders of... Seyatel...simply 'vanished in the night'. So did many of the Americans... from the famous 1920s Kuzbas industrial colony." Michael Gelb, "Karelian Fever: The Finnish Immigrant Community during Stalin's Purges," *Europe-Asia Studies* 45, no. 6 (1993): 1102.

13. Conkin, 331; See also Knapp, *The Advance of American Cooperative Enterprise*, 288-316.

14. Conkin, 4-7; 26.

15. Ibid., 93-96.

16. Ibid., 131-34.

17. Ibid., 81; Subsistence Homesteads Division, http://www.novelguide.com/a/discover/egd_02/egd_02_00500.html.

18. Conkin, 237-55

19. Resettlement Administration, http://www.novelguide.com/a /discover/egd_02/egd_02_00449.html.

20. Conkin, 166-171.

21. Knapp, *The Advance of American Cooperative Enterprise*, 308.

22. R. G. Tugwell, "Review: Tomorrow a New World: The New Deal Community Program, by Paul K. Conkin," *Political Science Quarterly* 75, no. 2 (1960): 260-263.

23. Conkin, 229-33.

24. Ibid, 138.

25. Ibid., 137-138, 140; *The Encyclopedia of Arkansas History & Culture*, http://encyclopediaofarkansas.net/encyclopedia/entry-detail.aspx?entryID=2397 (accessed May 19, 2008).

26. Conkin, 294-304; Will Lissner, "Utopian Rural Pastor to Global

Missioner," *American Journal of Economics and Sociology* 36, no. 1 (1977): 17-18.

27. Conkin, 169, 210-11; Edward C. Banfield, *Government Project* (Glencoe, IL: The Free Press, 1951).

28. "Quits FSA, Likening Project To Soviet's," *New York Times*, January 3, 1939; "Casa Grande Property Up For Sale," *Prescott Evening Courier*, December 16, 1947.

29. Conkin, 256-276.

30. Murray Lundberg, "The Matanuska Colony: The New Deal in Alaska," http://explorenorth.com/library/yafeatures/bl-matanuska.htm.

31. Ibid.

32. Conkin, 199-202; Donald Holley, "The Negro in the New Deal Resettlement Program," *Agricultural History* 45, no. 3 (1971): 179-93.

33. Conkin, 199-202.

34. Ibid.

35. Ibid.

36. Ibid.

37. Knapp, *The Advance of American Cooperative Enterprise*, 325-28.

38. Ibid.; See George L. Hicks, *Experimental Americans: Celo and Utopian Community in the Nineteenth Century* (Urbana: University of Illinois Press, 2001).

39. Craig H. Long, "Bayard Lane: The Borsodi Experiment," Montebello History, http://www.villageofmontebello.com/History.html.

40. School of Living, "History," http://www.schoolofliving.org.

41. Robert Griffith, *The Politics of Fear: Joseph R. McCarthy and the Senate* (University of Massachusetts Press, 1970), 49.

42. Timothy Miller, *The 60s Communes: Hippies and Beyond* (Syracuse, NY: Syracuse University Press, 1999) xviii, 249-53; see Benjamin Zablocki, *Alienation and Charisma: A Study of Contemporary American Communes* (New York: The Free Press, 1980); see also Case and Taylor.

43. Gail Braccidiferro, "A Place for Rest, and Unrest, At a 57-Acre Camp in Voluntown," *New York Times*, August 29, 2004; J. George and L. Wilcox, *American Extremists* (New York: Prometheus, 1996), 233-34.

44. Case and Taylor, 285; Miller, xvii-xx.

45. Miller, 23-26, 64, 77-83, 89-90, 118-24. Sixteen groups were full members of the Federation of Egalitarian Communities (FEC) between 1976 and 2002. The FEC is presently comprised of six full member groups and seven organizing "communities-in-dialogue" (http://www.thefec.org/taxonomy/term/3).

46. Bobby, 403.

47. Ron Jacobs, *The Way the Wind Blew: A History of the Weather Underground* (New York: Verso, 1997) 38-41, 66-68.

48. *Prairie Fire* (Berkeley, 1974).

49. John Curl, *Memories of Drop City, the First Hippie Commune of the*

1960s and the Summer of Love (New York: iuniverse, 2007).

50. *Online Communities Directory*, "Intentional Communities," http: // directory.ic.org/ (accessed October 28, 2008).

18. Spiritual Communalism

1. Rexroth, 8.
2. Fried, 26-30; Egbert, Persons and Basset, 1: 119-21.
3. Holloway, *Heavens on Earth*, 26-30; Rexroth, 97-98.
4. Rexroth, 25-34.
5. Ibid., 39-40, 51-52.
6. Ibid., 35-36, 40-41, 83.
7. Ibid., 41, 62, 130-31,122, 177.
8. Doyle, 2: 97-99; John Winthrop, "City upon a Hill," 1630. Hanover Historical Texts Project, http://history.hanover.edu/texts/winth-mod.html.
9. See Virginia DeJohn Anderson, *New England's Generation: The Great Migration and the Formation of Society and Culture in the Seventeenth Century* (Cambridge University Press, 1991).
10. Rexroth, 134-36.
11. Ibid., 134, 143-47; *MSN Encarta Encyclopedia*, "Oliver Cromwell," http://encarta.msn.com/encyclopedia_761563187/Oliver_Cromwell. html (accessed October 28, 2008).
12. See Austin Woolrych, *Britain in Revolution 1625-1660* (Oxford University Press, 2002).
13. Fogarty, 23, 34.
14. Rexroth, 62, 134-37.
15. Holloway, 31-52.
16. Holloway, 81-84; Egbert, Persons and Basset, 1: 128-31.
17. Holloway, 59-63.
18. Charles Nordhoff, *The Communistic Societies of the United States* (New York: Harper & Brothers, 1875; New York: Dover, 1966), 285-86; Holloway, 18.
19. Fried, 30; See also Nordhoff, and Hinds.
20. Holloway, 53-79; Egbert, Persons and Basset, 1: 132-39.
21. Shakers, *Millennial Praises* (Hancock, Massachusetts: Shakers, 1813); Fried, 16.
22. Nordhoff, 172.
23. Rexroth, 204-05.
24. Daniel H. Ludlow, ed., *Encyclopedia of Mormonism* (New York: Macmillon, 1992), 1493-95.
25. Parker, 8-9.
26. Holloway, 216-17.
27. Ibid., 179-97; Noyes, 614-45.
28. Nordhoff, 259-60; Egbert, Persons and Basset, 1: 140-51.

29. Nordhoff, 299.

30. See Spencer Klaw, *Without Sin: The Life and Death of the Oneida Community* (New York: Allen Lane, 1993).

31. Holloway, 88, 162, 165, 171, 213; Rexroth, 183, 187, 193, 206.

32. Holloway 88-100; Rexroth, 191-208.

33. Fogarty, 168-69; Fried, 335-47; Egbert, Persons and Basset, 1: 119-21, 199.

34. Fried, 341.

35. Fried, 341-42, 359-61.

36. *The Online Encyclopedia of Washington State History*, "Sunnyside - Christian Cooperative Colony," http://historylink.org/essays/output.cfm?file_id=5316 (accessed July 21, 2008).

37. Fogarty, 141-42.

38. Kagan, 48-83.

39. LeWarne, 227-29.

40. Kagan, 138-57.

41. Michigan Jewish History, http://www.michjewishhistory.org/pdfs/vol42.pdf.

42. See Mark Zwick and Louise Zwick, *The Catholic Worker Movement: Intellectual and Spiritual Origins* (New York: Paulist Press, 2005); Jeffrey Marlett, *Saving the Heartland: Catholic Missionaries in Rural America, 1920-1960* (DeKalb: Northern Illinois University Press, 2002), 71-72.

43. Nation of Islam, "What the Muslims Want," http://www.seventhfam.com/temple/program/want.htm.

44. Intentional Communities, "Koinonia Farm," http://directory.ic.org/647/Koinonia_Farm (accessed July 22, 2008).

45. Ibid., "The Vale," http://directory.ic.org/1237/The_Vale.

46. See Benjamin David Zablocki, *The Joyful Community: An Account of the Bruderhof, a Communal Movement Now in its Third Generation* (Baltimore: Penguin Books, 1971).

47. Intentional Communities, "Reba Place Fellowship," http://directory.ic.org/975/Reba_Place_Fellowship. (accessed July 22, 2008).

48. Reba Place, http://www.rebaplacefellowship.org.

49. Lama Foundation, http://directory.ic.org/667/. Lama_Foundation; "The Farm," http://directory.ic.org/403/. The_Farm; "History of the Brotherhood of the Spirit/Renaissance Community," http://www.acornproductions.net/history.php.

50. Kripalu Yoga Ashram, http://www.kripalu.org/about/5; Karme-Choling Meditation Center, http://www.karmecholing.org; Abode of the Message, http://www.theabode.net.

Conclusion

1. Macionis, *Sociology*, 431.

2. World Declaration on Worker Cooperatives, approved by the ICA

General Assembly, 2005. See Appendix II, http://www.usworker.coop/public/documents/Oslo_Declaration.pdf.

3. The International Organisation of Industrial, Artisanal and Service Producers' Co-operative Alliance (CICOPA), "What Is CICOPA?" http://www.cicopa.coop/quees.php?lang=en.

4. Noah Webster [A Citizen of America], "An Examination into the Leading Principles of the Federal Constitution," in David Wooton, ed., *The Essential Federalist and Anti-Federalist Papers* (Indianapolis: Hackett Publishing, 2003), 132-35.

5. Thomas Jefferson, letter to George Logan. November 12, 1816. FE 10:68. Thomas Jefferson on Politics and Government, "Quotations/35. Commerce and Agriculture," http://etext.lib.virginia.edu/jefferson/quotations.

6. Abraham Lincoln, "Remarks on the Interest of Labor in Respecting Rights of Property," a reply to a committee from the Workingmen's Association of New York, March 21, 1864, in Marion Mills Miller, ed., *The Life and Works of Abraham Lincoln* (New York: The Current Literature Publishing Co, 1907) 5:185.

7. Eugene Debs and Bruce Rogers, eds., *Debs: His Life, Writings and Speeches* (Chicago: Charles H. Kerr & Co., 1908), 490.

Appendix 1

1. Sustainable Woods Cooperatives, http://sustainablewoods.net.

2. Freedom Quilting Bee, http://www.ruraldevelopment.org/FQB-history.html.

3. Inkworks, http://www.inkworkspress.org/article.php?list=type&type=21; http://www.designaction.org.

4. Isthmus Engineering and Manufacturing Co-op, http://www.isthmuseng.com/aboutus/company2/company.aspx.

5. Big Timberworks, http://www.bigtimberworks.com.

6. Solidarity Sponsoring Committee Employment Agency, http://www.buildiaf.org/services.htm.

7. Childspace Management Group, http://www.childspacecdi.org/about.cfm.

8. Cooperative Economics For Women, http://cooperativewomen.org.

9. Enterprising Staffing Services, http://www.ess-dc.com, http://www.leaffund.org/2a_staff_serv_co.html.

10. Cooperative Home Care Associates, http://www.chcany.org/index-2.html.

11. WAGES, http://www.wagescooperatives.org.

12. Beluga Software, http://www.belugasoftware.com/index_s.html.

13. Northern California Land Trust, http://www.nclt.org/index.

php?option=com_content&task=view&id=39&Itemid=45.

14. Big Tree Organic Farms, http://www.bigtreeorganic.com/ Home.html.

15. Connecticut Agricultural Plastics Recycling Cooperative, "Networks, 12/2004, 2", http://www.ncba.coop/pdf/Networks1104WEBv1. pdf; National Cooperative Business Association, "Success Stories," http:// www.ncba.coop/serv_cbd_cw_stories.cfm.

16. Federation Of Southern Cooperatives/Land Assistance Fund, http://www.federationsoutherncoop.com.

17. Tres Rios Agricultural Cooperative, http://www.tres-rioscoop.com/), http://www.organicvolunteers.com/farmfinder_frame. asp?FID=6264&opp_type=6&page=81.

18. People's Food Co-op, http://www.peoples.coop.

19. Rainbow Grocery, http://www.rainbowgrocery.org/aboutus/ index.html.

20. Mercado Central, http://www.mercadocentral.net.

21. Arizmendi, http://www.arizmendibakery.org/about.

22. People's Grocery, http://www.peoplesgrocery.org/mission.html.

23. Intertribal Bison Cooperative, http://www.itbcbison.com/ about.php.

24. Dineh Cooperatives, http://www.prattcenter.net/cdc-dci.php; http://www.ruralisc.org/dineh.htm.

25. Rosebud Sioux Wind Development Initiative, http://webapps01.un.org/dsd/caseStudy/public/displayDetailsAction.do;jsessioni d=D9C5EA583E68A4B1E0583F9B9B7C6FE9?code=243.

26. Equal Exchange, http://www.equalexchange.com.

27. Okanogan Family Faire, http://www.okanoganfamilyfaire.net.

28. Community Energy Co-op, www.energycooperative.org/; http://www.cntenergy.org.

29. Last Mile Electric Co-op, http://www.ourwind.org/windcoop.

30. Latino Community Credit Union, http://www.latinoccu.org / en/about.

31. Ithaca HOURS, http://www.ithacahours.org.

Illustration Credits

1A. Native American Cooperation

Fishing in Chesapeake Bay; Town Gardens in Virginia: Engraving by Theodore de Bry for Hariot, *A Briefe And True Report of the New Found Land of Virginia* (1590).

Copper mining, near Lake Superior: Library of Congress.

Buffalo hunt, Great Plains: Painting by George Catlin, c. 1832, Smithsonian Institution, National Museum of American Art.

1B. Early Settler Cooperation

Colonial industries: *Poor Richard's Almanac* (1765), Yale University Library.

Community harvest: New York Historical Society.

Fire fighting: Pennsylvania State Library.

2A. Workers' Emerging Struggles

Thomas Paine: New York Public Library.

Horace Greeley: Library of Congress.

Working Men's Ticket: New York Historical Society.

Transcript of the Trial of the Boot & Shoemakers: U.S. Dept. of Labor.

2B. Beginnings of Industrialization:

Mill workers: Smithsonian Institution.

Factory workers: McCormick Historical Library.

Anti-slavery poster: Connecticut Historical Society.

Union card: New York Public Library.

Worker protest: Library of Congress.

3. IWA & National Labor Union

Frederick Douglass: National Archives.

William Sylvis; Isaac Meyers: International Moulders and Allied Workers Union.

NLU Boot and Shoe Cooperative: *Leslie's Illustrated Weekly*, 1871.

Thomas Phillips; IWA card: State Historical Society of Wisconsin.
Victoria Woodhull: National Archives.

4. National Grange
Oliver Kelly; "Ceres" Adams; Grange Rally: State Historical Society of
    Wisconsin.
John Trimble: State Historical Society of Wisconsin.
Sovereigns and Grange publications: Commons, *A Documentary History of
    Industrial Society.*
Grange cartoon: Library of Congress.

5. Knights of Labor
Seal of the Knights: Pennsylvania State Library.
Uriah Stephens; Terence Powderly: Library of Congress.
Leonora Barry: Archives of the Catholic University of America.
Frank J. Ferrell: *Leslie's Illustrated Weekly*, 1886.
Victor Drury: Schlesinger Library, Radcliffe College.
Barrel label: *Journal of United Labor*, Haverhill, Mass., 1885.
Joseph Buchanan: *The Story of a Labor Agitator*, Joseph R. Buchanan, New
    York: The Outlook Co., 1903.

6A. Farmers Allliance & Populism
Alliance Flag and Parade: http://www.irwinator.com/126-5480.htm
    (Downloaded 12/28/08).
C. W. Macune: U.S. Dept. of Agriculture.
Tom Watson: http://projects.vassar.edu/1896/watson.html (Downloaded
    12/31/08).
Alliance Posters: http://www.nebraskastudies.org (Downloaded
    12/28/08).
H.S. Doyle: Ali, *Black Populism in the New South.*
Mary Elizabeth Lease: State Historical Society of Wisconsin.
Alliance Rally: *Review of Reviews*, September, 1896.

6B. Populism
The vote for Weaver: *The National Atlas of the United States*; Hicks, *The
    Populist Revolt.*
James Weaver: McNeill, *The Labor Problem of Today.*
Bryan on the stump: Nebraska Historical Society.

7A. Bloody '90s & Progressive Era
Debs poster: Chicago Historical Society.
Debs button: http://recollectionbooks.com (Downloaded 12/16/08).
Edward Bellamy: http://www.teoriagenerale.it (Downloaded 12/7/08).

Victor Berger: http://www.wpri.org/blog/wp-content/uploads/Berger-Campaign.jpg (Downloaded 1/3/09).

Farmer-Labor button: http://www.spartacus.schoolnet.co.uk/USAfarmerlabor.htm (Downloaded 12/20/08).

Non-Partisan League rally: State Historical Society of North Dakota.

7B. Industrial Unionism.

Mother Jones: Catholic University Library, Washington, D.C.

Eugene V. Debs: Library of Congress.

Bill Haywood: New York Public Library.

IWW poster: *Solidarity*, April, 1917.

Industrial Unionism Stickerette: IWW.

Daniel DeLeon: New York Public Library.

STLA Membership Certificate; Union Label: State Historical Society of Wisconsin.

8A. Self-Help in the Great Depression

Carl Rhodehamel: Rhodehamel family.

Upton Sinclair: Free Online Library, http://sinclair.thefreelibrary.com (Downloaded 12/18/08).

E.P.I.C. Plan Emblem: *How We Ended Poverty*, End Poverty League.

UXA: Photograph by Dorothea Lange: Bancroft Library, U. of California.

Unemployed Citizens League: woodcut by Blanding Sloan, 1935, Bancroft Library, U. of California.

8B. Cooperatives in the Depression

Farmers Coop Creamery: Yamhill County Historical Society, Lafayette, OR.

Southern Tenants Farmers Union: National Sharecroppers Fund.

Coop cannery: Coop quilting; Pacific Cooperative League: Bancroft Library, Berkeley.

9. Consumer Co-ops

James Warbasse; Albert Sonnichsen; Congress of the ICA: Cooperative League/National Cooperative Business Association.

Berkeley Co-op 1938; 1970: Associated Cooperatives.

Grange store; Dos Palos Rochdale: National Cooperative Business Assn. (Cooperative League).

10A. The Sixties and Seventies

Uprisings Bakery; Taxi Unlimited; Davis Food Co-op; Bound Together Books: *Directory of Collectives*, 1983, 1985.

El Tecolote Masthead; Bay Warehouse; Diggers: author's collection.

Jamaica Plains Food Co-op; Cambridge Bike Repair Collective,
    photographs by Shelly Rotner: *No Bosses Here.*
Panther free breakfast: BPP Photo Exhibit, http://www.itsabouttimebpp.
    com/Photo_Exhibits/louder_than_words.html (Downloaded 12/20/08)

10B. The Seventies and Eighties
Food System Newsletter; Collective Conference poster; *Women's Center
    Newsletter; Collective Networker*; Heartwood Cooperative Woodshop:
    author's collection.
Food System Workers, photograph by David Symonick: *Grassroots.*

11A. Communalists
A. J. Wayland: Tennessee State Library. http://www.tennessee.gov/tsla/
    exhibits/utopia/ruskin_images.htm (Downloaded 12/18/08).
Robert Owen: British Museum, London.
Albert Brisbane: Museum of the City of New York.
George Ripley: Library of Congress Prints and Photographs Division,
    Daguerreotype collection.
Job Harriman: Huntington Library.
Josiah Henson: *Autobiography of Josiah Henson,* 1858.
Frances Wright; Josiah Warren: International Typographers Union.
Burnette Haskell: Bancroft Library.
New Harmony: Indiana Historical Society.
Brook Farm: Massachusetts Historical Society.
Nashoba: Fanny Trollope, *Domestic Manners of the Americans,* 1832.
Communalist publications: Commons, *A Documentary History of American
    Industrial Society.*

11B. Communities
Kaweah: Bancroft Library, U of California.
Equality: University of Washington Library.
Llano del Rio. Photograph by Walter Millsap: Kagan Collection,
    California Historical Society Library.
Drop City: author's collection.

11C. New Deal Communities
Penn-Craft; Westmoreland Homesteads; Norvelt: *Norvelt and Penn-Craft,
    Pennsylvania: Subsistence-Homestead Communities of the 1930s* http://
    www.lib.iup.edu/depts/speccol/exhibits/norvelt.html (Downloaded
    1/4/09).
Arthurdale: *Arthurdale, West Virginia, a New Deal Community.* Photo by Ben Shahn,
    1937, Library of Congress. http://www.arthurdaleheritage.org/history/a-
    cooperative-community/mcca-furniture (Downloaded 1/4/09).

Index

"Passim" (literally "scattered") indicates intermittent discussion of a topic over a cluster of pages.

C

About the Author

JOHN CURL has been a member of Heartwood Cooperative Woodshop in Berkeley for over thirty years, and has belonged to numerous other cooperatives and collectives. He is a longtime boardmember of PEN, chair of West Berkeley Artisans and Industrial Companies, a social activist, and has served as a city planning commissioner. He is a professional woodworker, and resides in Berkeley, CA.

Other Works by John Curl

Memoir:
Memories of Drop City

Translation:
Ancient American Poets

History:
History of Work Cooperation in America
History of Collectivity in the San Francisco Bay Area

Poetry:
Scorched Birth
Columbus in the Bay of Pigs
Decade: the 1990s
Tidal News
Cosmic Athletics
Ride the Wind
Insurrection/Resurrection

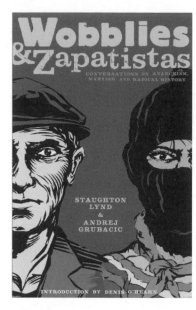

ALSO AVAILABLE FROM PM PRESS

Wobblies & Zapatistas:
Conversations on Anarchism,
Marxism, and Radical History
by Staughton Lynd &
Andrej Grubacic
ISBN: 978-1-60486-041-2
$20.00

Wobblies & Zapatistas offers the reader an encounter between two generations and two traditions. Andrej Grubacic is an anarchist from the Balkans. Staughton Lynd is a lifelong pacifist, influenced by Marxism. They meet in dialogue in an effort to bring together the anarchist and Marxist traditions, to discuss the writing of history by those who make it, and to remind us of the idea that "my country is the world." Encompassing a Left libertarian perspective and an emphatically activist standpoint, these conversations are meant to be read in the clubs and affinity groups of the new Movement.

The authors accompany us on a journey through modern revolutions, direct actions, anti-globalist counter summits, Freedom Schools, Zapatista cooperatives, Haymarket and Petrograd, Hanoi and Belgrade, 'intentional' communities, wildcat strikes, early Protestant communities, Native American democratic practices, the Workers' Solidarity Club of Youngstown, occupied factories, self-organized councils and soviets, the lives of forgotten revolutionaries, Quaker meetings, antiwar movements, and prison rebellions. The book invites the attention of readers who believe that a better world, on the other side of capitalism and state bureaucracy, may indeed be possible.

"Here we have the best of a non-dogmatic Marxism listening to a most creative and humane anarchism. But this book is never weighted down by unforgiving theory. Just the opposite: it is a series of conversations where the reader feels fully present."
  –Margaret Randall, author of *Sandino's Daughters*, *When I Look Into the Mirror and See You*, and *Narrative of Power*

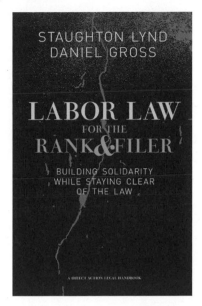

Have you ever felt your blood boil at work but lacked the tools to fight back and win? Or have you acted together with your co-workers, made progress, but wondered what to do next? If you are in a union, do you find that the union operates top-down just like the boss and ignores the will of its members?

Labor Law for the Rank and Filer: Building Solidarity While Staying Clear of the Law is a guerrilla legal handbook for workers in a precarious global economy. Blending cutting-edge legal strategies for winning justice at work with a theory of dramatic social change from below, Staughton Lynd and Daniel Gross deliver a practical guide for making work better while re-invigorating the labor movement.

Labor Law for the Rank and Filer demonstrates how a powerful model of organizing called "Solidarity Unionism" can help workers avoid the pitfalls of the legal system and utilize direct action to win. This new revised and expanded edition includes new cases governing fundamental labor rights as well as an added section on Practicing Solidarity Unionism. This new section includes chapters discussing the hard-hitting tactic of working to rule; organizing under the principle that no one is illegal, and building grassroots solidarity across borders to challenge neoliberalism, among several other new topics. Illustrative stories of workers' struggles make the legal principles come alive.

"Some things are too important to leave to so called "experts": our livelihoods, our dignity and our rights. In this book, Staughton Lynd and Daniel Gross have provided us with a very necessary, empowering, and accessible tool for protecting our own rights as workers."
–Nicole Schulman, co-editor *Wobblies! A Graphic History* and *World War 3 Illustrated*

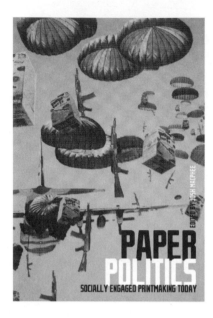

Paper Politics is a major collection of contemporary politically and socially engaged printmaking. This book showcases print art that uses themes of social justice and global equity to engage community members in political conversation. Based on an art exhibition which has traveled to a dozen cities in North America, *Paper Politics* features artwork by over 200 international artists; an eclectic collection of work by both activist and non-activist printmakers who have felt the need to respond to the monumental trends and events of our times.

Paper Politics presents a breathtaking tour of the many modalities of printing by hand: relief, intaglio, lithography, serigraph, collagraph, monotype, and photography. In addition to these techinques, included are more traditional media used to convey political thought, finely crafted stencils and silk-screens intended for wheat pasting in the street. Artists ranging from the well-established (Sue Coe, Swoon, Carlos Cortez) to the up-and-coming (Favianna Rodriguez, Chris Stain, Nicole Schulman), from street artists (BORF, You Are Beautiful, Sixten) to rock poster makers (EMEK, Seripop).

Become a Friend of

In the year since its founding – and on a mere shoestring – PM Press has risen to the formidable challenge of publishing and distributing knowledge and entertainment for the struggles ahead. With over 30 releases in 2008, we have published an impressive and stimulating array of literature, art, music, politics, and culture. Using every available medium, we've succeeded in connecting those hungry for ideas and information to those putting them into practice.

Friends of PM allows you to directly help impact, amplify, and revitalize the discourse and actions of radical writers, filmmakers, and artists. It provides us with a stable foundation from which we can build upon our early successes and provides a much-needed subsidy for the materials that can't necessarily pay their own way. You can help make that happen--and receive every new title automatically delivered to your door once a month--by joining as a Friend of PM Press. Here are your options:

- $25 a month: Get all books and pamphlets plus 50% discount on all webstore purchases
- $25 a month: Get all CDs and DVDs plus 50% discount on all webstore purchases
- $40 a month: Get all PM Press releases plus 50% discount on all webstore purchases
- $100 a month: Sustainer - Everything plus PM merchandise, free downloads, and 50% discount on all webstore purchases

Just go to **WWW.PMPRESS.ORG** to sign up. Your card will be billed once a month, until you tell us to stop. Or until our efforts succeed in bringing the revolution around. Or the financial meltdown of Capital makes plastic redundant. Whichever comes first.

PM PRESS was founded at the end of 2007 by a small collection of folks with decades of publishing, media, and organizing experience. PM co-founder Ramsey Kanaan started AK Press as a young teenager in Scotland almost 30 years ago and, together with his fellow PM Press coconspirators, has published and distributed hundreds of books, pamphlets, CDs, and DVDs. Members of PM have founded enduring book fairs, spearheaded victorious tenant organizing campaigns, and worked closely with bookstores, academic conferences, and even rock bands to deliver political and challenging ideas to all walks of life. We're old enough to know what we're doing and young enough to know what's at stake.

We seek to create radical and stimulating fiction and nonfiction books, pamphlets, t-shirts, visual and audio materials to entertain, educate and inspire you. We aim to distribute these through every available channel with every available technology - whether that means you are seeing anarchist classics at our bookfair stalls; reading our latest vegan cookbook at the café; downloading geeky fiction e-books; or digging new music and timely videos from our website.

PM PRESS is always on the lookout for talented and skilled volunteers, artists, activists and writers to work with. If you have a great idea for a project or can contribute in some way, please get in touch.

PM PRESS
PO Box 23912
Oakland CA 94623
510-658-3906
www.pmpress.org